REFLECTIONS OF A MUSIC LOVER

By the same author

FROM A MUSIC LOVER'S ARMCHAIR (1926)
THE APPEAL OF JAZZ (1927)
THE SOUL OF MUSIC (1950) (ILLUSTRATED),
WITH A FOREWORD BY ERNEST NEWMAN
THE DIVINE QUEST IN MUSIC (1957), WITH A
FOREWORD BY THE DEAN OF WINDSOR AND A
PREFACE BY SIR ADRIAN BOULT
ADVENTURE IN MUSIC (1964)
REVELATION IN SHAKESPEARE (1964)

Robert

R.W.S. MENDL M.A. Oxon

Reflections
of a Music Lover

LONDON

NEVILLE SPEARMAN

This edition first published in Great Britain
by Neville Spearman Ltd
112 Whitfield Street, London, W1

© R. W. S. Mendl, M.A. Oxon

Set in 10-pt Pilgrim 2-pt leaded and printed by
Northumberland Press Ltd, Gateshead and bound
by W. J. Rawlinson, 45 Calthorpe Street, London
W.C.1

To my wife and our son

CONTENTS

CONTENTS

PREFACE

I have summarised the main purposes of this book in Chapter 1, the Prologue. I would add here that, whilst my reflections on the various composers discussed are set within the framework of my own music-loving life, I have found it desirable, for the sake of continuity and completeness, to include in my autobiographical narrative some passages which in themselves have little or nothing to do with music at all. The background, I felt, had to some extent to be filled in, if the story was to be comprehensible and unified.

The composers are not dealt with in their proper order of dates, but, so to speak, in mine, as explained in the Prologue. I have, therefore, included a chronological list of them at the beginning of the book, for the convenience of readers.

The bibliography names those books which I have principally consulted. The index contains only the names of composers and of professional executive musicians, not amateurs, although some amateur musicians are mentioned here and there in the text.

I am grateful to the proprietors and editor of 'Musical Opinion' for their assent to my using in Chapters 7, 22 and 37 certain extracts, suitably adapted, from my article 'Opera, Drama, Music', which appeared in its issue of December, 1964, and to my friend Sidney Colwell for helping me to check the typescript.

I was born in July, 1892, and I expect this to be my last book about music. Whether certain other literary ambitions of mine will be fulfilled, will depend on the state of my health and the length of my life. 'Eheu, fugaces....'!

R.W.S.M.

ILLUSTRATIONS

Chronological List of the
Composers Mentioned in this Book

Stanford	1852-1924	Dunhill	1877-1946
Messager	1853-1929	Medtner	1880-1951
Moszkovsky	1854-1925	Bloch	1880-1959
Janáček	1854-1928	Bartók	1881-1945
Humperdinck	1854-1921	Kodály	1882-1967
Elgar	1857-1934	Stravinsky	1882-
Puccini	1858-1924	Webern	1883-1945
Wolf	1860-1903	Bax	1883-1953
Albeniz	1860-1909	Berg	1885-1935
Mahler	1860-1911	Prokofiev	1891-1953
Delius	1862-1934	Bliss	1891-
Debussy	1862-1918	Milhaud	1892-
E. German	1862-1936	Howells	1892-
Richard Strauss	1864-1949	Hindemith	1895-1963
Nielsen	1865-1931	Weinberger	1896-
Sibelius	1865-1957	Rubbra	1901-
Busoni	1866-1924	Walton	1902-
Granados	1867-1916	Tippett	1905-
Skriabin	1872-1915	Shostakovich	1906-
Vaughan-Williams	1872-1958	Messiaen	1908-
Rachmaninov	1873-1943	Britten	1913-
Holst	1874-1934	Boulez	1926-
Schoenberg	1874-1951	Stockhausen	1928-
Hahn, R.	1875-1947	Penderecki	1930-
Ravel	1875-1937	R. R. Bennett	1936-
Falla	1876-1946		

PART ONE

CHAPTER ONE

Prologue

In this volume I have attempted something quite different from my three other post-World War II books about music. *The Soul of Music* and its complementary *Adventure in Music* were sets of variations on the theme of the relationship between music and the world outside itself. *The Divine Quest in Music* was a study of the spiritual aspects of the art—its relationship to God.

The present work is frankly more autobiographical. I have voiced my reflections, as an old man, on what I feel to be the essential qualities of the art of many of the great composers, in some cases relating these to their personal characters, within the framework of my own experiences over a long life of hearing and loving music. The amount of space devoted to one composer should not be taken as an indication that I regard him as more important or more significant than another who is treated more briefly. Handel, for example, is, in my view, an even greater composer than such a brilliant genius as Berlioz; but the latter is a more extraordinary figure than the 'beloved Saxon' and requires more discussion in a book such as this: both of them are special favourites of mine. And when I reach modern times, I make no apology for saying that this or that composer whom his contemporaries have regarded as a great genius is, in my humble opinion, a smaller man or even of little worth, if this is how I feel about him. It is the business of a writer about any art to be frank and sincere, even if his views prove unpopular.

In the 19th century it was customary to look at the personal characters of great composers through rose-coloured spectacles: because a man created beautiful music, he must, it was apparently thought, have had a beautiful soul, though there was a confusion of thought in this attitude: for when we call music 'beautiful', we are using the word in its aesthetic sense, whereas its application to the soul is moral, not aesthetic; true, the greatest or most beautiful music is also the most exalted—which implies a spiritual

2

element. Nevertheless, it is important to keep the distinction between aesthetic and moral beauty clear in our minds.

After the 19th century, a reaction set in; but even so, musical biography has, for the most part, never gone to the lengths to which the 'debunking' of geniuses went at the hands of Lytton Strachey and others in the non-musical world.

Nowadays, not only is a book about a composer often divided into two distinct parts, 'the man' and 'the artist', but the tendency is to draw a sharp contrast between them, and to leave the matter there, in some cases as a puzzle unsolved or a divergence unreconciled.

In the pursuit of truth, the distinction must, indeed, be drawn. We must, so far as possible, ascertain, and face up to, the facts about a great composer's private life, and perhaps at first sight we may be baffled by an apparent inconsistency between the character of the man and the quality of his art; but if so, for a true judgment two things are necessary: (1) to make sure that we are viewing his personality as a whole and are not obsessed by a partial aspect of it, for it may be as fallacious to concentrate on his faults as it was for our ancestors to see only his virtues; and (2) to remember that an artistic creator often rises, in his art, above the lower side of his nature.

In discussing this subject, the word 'man' has two senses, and it is convenient to differentiate between them by printing either a large or a small 'm'. 'The man' is the individual in his personal capacity, his human relationships, apart from his musical creations. 'The Man', on the other hand, is the whole being, comprising not only 'the man' in the more limited sense just described, but the creative artist as well. Too much of the bewilderment about the complex problems presented by such composers as Beethoven and Wagner, for instance, is due to a tendency to overlook 'The Man' altogether. 'The man' and 'the artist' so often diverge, that the gulf may seem almost unbridgeable; yet it is only by ascertaining the nature of 'The Man'—the entire being—that we can see how the two can exist together, how the actions of his private life, his words, his letters, can be the product of the same mind that has produced his music.

Fundamentally, the distinction so often made between 'people' and 'things' is misleading, so far as 'things' made by men are concerned. Man-made things are products of the personality of the maker. This applies even in the case of mass-produced articles

3

such as motor-cars; they spring from the designs conceived by the mind of the inventor, however many intervening mentalities, hands, and machines may come between that and the finished product. And in the case of a work of art, the link is more immediate: the picture is the direct, authentic creation of the painter's mentality and imagination, and similarly with the other visual arts and with some forms of literature. Drama and music normally depend upon performers for their interpretation and their presentation to the recipients, but even in their case the work of art, when it has sprung from its creator's brain and has been put on paper, is a 'thing', yet is nevertheless part of his person. When we say about the Sonata Pathétique 'That is Beethoven', we are uttering a truth which is, perhaps, more significant than we realise without thinking out the meaning of our words. The sonata is a bit of the The Man Beethoven, however distinct it may be from the man in his private life.

In this book I do not deal with every composer whom professional critics, musical historians, or ordinary music lovers like myself, have considered great. For this is not a history, and my list of great composers is certainly not intended to be regarded as exhaustive. I have written here my own musical autobiography chronologically, and have discussed each composer more or less in the order in which he entered my life or assumed importance in it, but only in any detail at the stage at which I had sufficient experience of his work to make this appropriate. Thus, Tchaikovsky is treated to a separate little chapter early in the book; and so is Bizet, because Carmen predominates over his other works and was the first serious opera that I heard; Bach has his separate chapter just after the account of my Harrow days, because it was there that Percy Buck revealed his greatness to me; Beethoven, in any fulness, comes later, when I had acquired a fairly comprehensive knowledge of his art; and so on.

I have dealt with the personal characters of a few composers in some detail, in other cases to a slight extent, and in others not at all. This may, at first sight, seem haphazard, but it has been done deliberately, according to a plan. There are some composers who are, so to speak, completely integrated personalities: I have taken two examples of this—Bach and Elgar, one belonging to the first half of the 18th century, the other to the end of the 19th century and the early part of the 20th. I am not here saying that there are not others—Haydn, for instance, and Brahms and Bruck-

4

ner. By 'integrated personalities' I mean that there is complete—
or almost complete—harmony, or analogy, between the man and
the artist. Bach and Elgar are two supreme cases of this, and we
know enough about their personal characters to be able to analyse
these fairly fully, and to show how closely they are related to
their art-work.

On the other hand, there are certain 'problem boys'. Berlioz is
one instance, Chopin another:— Berlioz, because in addition to
being what I have called a 'controlled' romantic, he persistently
set religious, and even liturgical texts to music, with the utmost
sincerity and conviction, and yet professed himself to be an unbeliever; Chopin, because, according to some authorities, he was
in his private life more feminine than masculine, and the question
immediately arises, is this fact—if it is a fact—reflected in his
music? Even Franck, 'the divine musician' as Guy de Ropartz
called him, the composer of music which was either directly
religious or at any rate spiritual in character, evinces another
aspect too—a romantic, disturbed side which appears in some of
his music; and the question is, was it part also of his character as
a man? In other words, he is not such a straightforward case as
he is presented as being in Vincent d'Indy's book about him. Beethoven has long been a subject of controversy: his music is generally
agreed to be gloriously spiritual, whilst his character has sometimes been idealised, sometimes denigrated; I believe the truth
to lie somewhere between these two presentations of it, but even
so, the question arises how a man with great and heroic qualities
but also certain faults of character was a composer of almost
consistently noble music. Wagner is an exceedingly complex case;
there is only a little to be said in his favour as a man, yet in his
art he was capable of expressing goodness and splendour of
character and of motive by means of music which is aesthetically
'beautiful', as well as conveying evil and wickedness through music
that is characteristic, striking and appropriate.

I mention these special cases here—two as representing 'integrated personalities' and five who in their very divergent ways set
us problems in any attempt to 'reconcile' the man and the artist.

I have not thought it necessary to say so much about the personal characters of Gluck, Verdi, Mussorgsky or Hugo Wolf, for
instance. Of course, these men are most interesting in themselves
(even apart from the actual quality of their music), as their biographers have shown—particularly Ernest Newman and Alfred

Einstein as regards Gluck, Newman again and Frank Walker in the case of Wolf, Francis Toye and Frank Walker in their books about Verdi, and M. D. Calvocoressi on the subject of Mussorgsky. But it is possible, I believe, to have a complete understanding of the art of these composers without knowing much, or perhaps anything, about their personal natures. The reason for this is that they were mainly composers of operas, or, in Wolf's case, of *lieder*, in which no autobiographical elements appear. Gluck's art—all that matters to us—consists of his six greatest operas and his ballet music *Don Juan*, and so long as we know the libretto, or even the story, of the ballet, all we need to do is to surrender ourselves to the music—though of course his preface to *Alceste* is of great importance as a key to his artistic ideals and as a landmark in musical history. The same applies to Weber, who was primarily a composer of operas and one other important work, the Concertstück (and even this is based on a 'programme', a story unconnected with Weber's life or personal character); and also to Verdi, though he soaked himself in the texts of the Requiem and of his *Four Sacred Pieces* and composed one charming string quartet. Mussorgsky is at his greatest in his operas, and even his other works are songs or *Pictures from an Exhibition*, in which there is no ground for seeking traces of Mussorgsky the man. Wolf, apart from his *Italian Serenade* and string quartet, and his unduly neglected opera *Der Corregidor*, was wrapped up in composing *lieder*, conspicuous for being close, detailed, musical embodiments of the poetry of other men, to an extent not reached, or indeed sought after, by Schubert, Schumann and Brahms in their songs. We need to know nothing about Wolf's personality in order to understand his *lieder*. Wagner, apart from the *Siegfried Idyll*, was, of course, primarily a composer of operas, just as Gluck, Weber, Verdi and Mussorgsky were; yet these stage works of his are exceptional in that they contain strong autobiographical elements (as indeed the *Idyll* does, too), and also a great deal of symbolism.

It may well be asked, what has all this to do with my reminiscences of performances or the early musical influences in my life? The answer lies rather deeper than the question implies. This is essentially a book about my love of music and the composers who have meant most to me or simply have made appreciable contributions to my musical experience. And music can only appeal to me if I hear it—or have heard it. Performances which seem to me to touch the heart of the matter, or which first opened my mind to the greatness of the music, are therefore relevant to the subject of this book.

The greatest music is, for me, never merely 'entertainment'. On the other hand, I dislike the word 'edifying'; and 'moral' is too narrow and misleading a term to describe its effect. I can best define it as a spiritual enrichment of my life, and I believe that many music lovers feel the same about it. This is something wider than 'religious', though it of course includes music which is religious in the strict sense or, indeed, liturgical, in addition to other kinds. 'Enjoyment' is a better word here than 'entertainment'; for if—after several attempts—we cannot enjoy a work of art, we had better leave it alone.

This, then, is my musical testament: to pass on to other music lovers some record of what I believe to be the essential features of many of the great composers, in the light of my own experiences.

CHAPTER TWO

Early Childhood

I inherited a love of music both from my father's and my mother's side. My paternal grandmother (née Hyam, though her family changed their name to Halford after her marriage) was a pupil of Clara Schumann and only gave up playing the piano because of rheumatism. She adored listening to music, all her life, her special 'loves' being Beethoven, Wagner, Mozart and Schumann. Her husband was far less musical than she was. He was Ferdinand Mendl, born at Tabor in Bohemia (now part of Czechoslovakia), but his mother came from Trieste, which, though then included in the Austro-Hungarian empire, was largely Italian in population; so she brought up all her children to speak Italian, and though he migrated to London (where he met my grandmother, a London girl) in his youth and became a naturalised Englishman, he spoke English with an Italian accent to his dying day. An amusing and genial old gentleman, he liked only cheerful entertainments, and thus, though he did enjoy hearing music, his tastes were limited to predominantly happy or light-hearted compositions.

My maternal grandfather, Assur Henry Moses, who was born in London in 1830 and died there in March, 1918, was one of the 'Grand Old Men' of Anglo-Jewry, deeply religious and devoted to his family. (He had been a widower ever since my mother was seven). He was a great public benefactor of the deaf and dumb, having introduced the oral method of instructing deaf and dumb children of all denominations to this country through an acquaintance in Holland. He was honorary secretary of the Association for the Oral Instruction of the Deaf, in London, for 45 years. He was a lover of Mozart and the operas of Bellini, Donizetti and early and middle Verdi, and he enjoyed Beethoven, but found Wagner quite beyond him : he told me in my boyhood how much he disliked *Tristan und Isolde*. At that time, appreciation of Wagner in England was in its infancy, and my grandmother Mendl was something of a pioneer in being an ardent Wagnerian—as she was

8

in other ways. When motor cars were in their early days and she had travelled in one at, I suppose, 20 or 25 miles per hour at the most, she said to me 'You know, Bob, I do love travelling at the hell of a lick!' A delightful old woman, universally beloved.

My father, in addition to being very generous, hospitable, witty and highly intelligent (some would say, brilliant), was a very musical man; yet music did not occupy so large a part in his life as it has in mine. He was Sigismund Ferdinand Mendl (later, Sir S. F. Mendl, K.B.E., honoured for his services to H.M.G. in World War I); really, my grandmother, as a native Englishwoman, ought to have prevented her husband from giving such foreign names to their first-born child, born in London, and destined for education at an English public school and at University College, Oxford. However, this detail did not impede my father in his career at the Bar, in politics (he was Liberal M.P. for Plymouth at one time), in the City, and in public service. He was a great reader, quick and wide in his reading. But all these multifarious activities may have prevented him from acquiring so thorough a knowledge of music as he might have done; nevertheless, he greatly enjoyed it, and used to take full advantage of our geographical proximity to the Queen's Hall—which was to prove an inestimable blessing for me. He had a gift for playing by ear on the piano, and had a beautiful touch and an ability to reproduce harmonies; but oddly enough, his sense of rhythm was less acute than his melodic or harmonic sense. His ability to play by ear (which I inherited) prompted him not to trouble to play from the score; he even found difficulty in reading the bass clef!

My mother was far less musical, but nevertheless enjoyed the concerts and operas to which he took us, and nearly always accompanied him and me. A very pretty woman, with a lovely, sympathetic and modest character, she was not gifted artistically as her two sisters were, nor indeed so intellectual. Her eldest sister, Mrs Mary Raphael (who was one of my two godmothers and was widowed before I was born) was a painter by profession and became a writer of novels and travel books, when rheumatism made painting difficult; she was an interesting and fascinating woman, who also enjoyed music in her own way: more of this later. The youngest of the three sisters, Alice Moses, who devoted her life to living with and caring for her ageing father, until his death, to her religion, her relatives and friends, and to her art, was the really musical one of the trio. She had a good mezzo-

9

soprano voice, and was a pupil of Tosti. As he taught in Mande-ville Place, she called herself 'Alice Mandeville' for professional purposes. She was an extremely artistic musician, and regarded music as being somewhat truly divine, as is evident from her musical diary which came into my possession after her death in 1952. (I had already written most of my book *The Divine Quest in Music* before I read that diary; but after reading it, I realised that she and I to a large extent had shared a common outlook on music, without my having been fully conscious of this fact in my boyhood; but, probably, it partly accounts for her having exerted an important formative influence on my attitude towards music in those early days.) She had a gift for languages and was equally skilful in singing German *lieder*, French and Italian songs, in their original tongues, as well as English ones. I shall have more to say about Aunt Alice and Elgar later on. In my boyhood I heard her recitals in the Bechstein Hall (later to be called the Wigmore Hall), and she often sang after dinner, with a professional accompanist, at my parents' parties.

So did my Uncle Charles Mendl (later, Sir Charles, the well-known Press Attaché at the British Embassy in Paris and an immensely popular and charming host and friend to countless people). Charles paid fairly frequent visits to London in my boyhood and youth, and, though he was an amateur, his lovely, velvety-quality baritone voice and his taste for music had justified him in having lessons from Jean de Reszke in Paris. My early experience of many of the songs of Schubert, Schumann, Brahms, Richard Strauss, Rey-naldo Hahn and others, was largely due to hearing him sing them with so much feeling at my parents' house, 14 Devonshire Street, London, W. (where I was born on July 28th, 1892).

These people were the principal ones among my relatives who influenced and who consciously or unconsciously encouraged my love of music in my early childhood. I loved my father's only surviving sister, Mrs Frederick Elkin (my Aunt Ida) very dearly, but she did not exert a *musical* influence upon me. My Uncle Louis Mendl was much less musical than my father (than whom he was 13 years younger), but came occasionally to concerts with us. He was great fun, had many friends in the theatrical and musical worlds (Francis Toye and Geoffrey Toye among them) and was a most sympathetic uncle; somehow, he first had the opportunity of going to the Gilbert and Sullivan operas after his Army Service in World War I, and became a great 'G and S.'

enthusiast; but this was short-lived, for—alas!—he died from a tumour on the brain in 1924. My mother's brother, my Uncle Harry Moses, was not musical at all. He was a doctor, an exceptionally brave man who won a very fine M.C. and Bar in the R.A.M.C. in France during World War I, and was very keen on 'objets d'art' and literature, but his concern for music practically confined itself to an interest in the professional career of his sister Alice, to whom he was devoted. My (elder and only) brother Tom was far less a lover of music than I have always been, though he was not quite so 'low-brow' as he made out! I remember entering his house in the late 1940's and finding him listening-in to Mozart's so-called *Jupiter* Symphony, which he described as 'a lovely thing'; his enjoyment of 'old Beethoven'—'old' being, of course, a term of endearment; and how he simply loved Elgar's violin concerto, with Yehudi Menuhin as soloist, at a concert in the Royal Albert Hall in the company of a friend soon after World War II. The truth is, he liked serious music in small doses, but nothing more recent than Elgar.

At the Devonshire Street house, my parents had a 'drawing-room grand' Bechstein piano, and an 'upright grand' (from the same makers) in my mother's boudoir. It was on this latter instrument that I had my first piano lessons from Beatrice Fry, sister of C. B. Fry, the famous cricketer; she taught me to practise Mozart's infantile, charming little minuets; and after her, the process was continued by her successor, Olive Baly, who was a great Mozart enthusiast. So I was to some extent brought up on Mozart from my early childhood, long before I knew Haydn in any form except the Emperor's Hymn. Mozart's finest symphonies, a few of his pianoforte concertos, the overtures to his best-known operas, and some of the arias, were performed at Henry Wood's Sunday afternoon concerts at Queen's Hall, to which my parents used to take me even as a small boy.

At Fretherne House School, London, I sang treble in Dr McNaught's tonic-solfa class: the items which I chiefly remember to this day from that experience are *The Silver Swan* by Orlando Gibbons (my first acquaintance with any composition of the so-called 'Golden Age' of English music) and *O who will o'er the downs so free?*

Carlotta de Feo, an Italian lady who lived in London (and who included Oda Slobodskaya among her many pupils) was a well-known teacher of singing and a great friend of my Aunt Alice and, through her, of my family. I knew her from my early boy-hood, and many were the occasions in my life when I went to concerts with her and she dined with my parents. She was a delightful and most amusing companion, a warm-hearted woman, and one of the most intensely musical human beings whom I have ever met. She and I remained close friends until her death at the age of 80 in Genoa after World War II.

Reverting to my childhood—it was at this period that Wood was introducing Tchaikovsky's orchestral works to London audiences; my father, and, in her own way, my mother too, were caught up in the wave of enthusiasm which swept through the British music-loving public and produced here a love of this composer's compositions that has persisted through subsequent generations in most parts of the world. The 4th, 5th and 6th Symphonies, the Concertos No. 1 in B flat minor for pianoforte and in D for violin, the Variations on a Rococo theme for 'cello and orchestra, the overtures and symphonic poems, the *Casse Noisette* (*Nutcracker*) Suite, the *Chant sans paroles* and the Theme and Variations from the Suite in G, were, in consequence, my staple diet in my fairly early boyhood. I believe that I heard Tchaikovsky's Fifth Symphony six times before I ever heard the Fifth of Beethoven! I remember 'escorting' my Aunt Mollie Raphael to a concert at which Wood was conducting this work of the Russian master, and that at the end of it she emerged with an exclamatory 'Oh!' as from an ecstatic dream. On another occasion, at the dramatic pause in the latter part of the Finale, after a loud chord *on the dominant,* and in spite of the fact that Wood held up his arms horizontally, 'Grandpa Mendl' murmured 'splen-did' and started to clap! He was 'hushed' peremptorily by indignant neighbours, and afterwards gently reprimanded by his far more musical wife.

At that time, my knowledge of Tchaikovsky's personal character was confined to the few biographical notes contained in the analyti-cal programmes, but as his orchestral works then occupied so large a part of my music-loving life, I propose to devote my next chap-ter to a brief, present-day, reflection on Tchaikovsky as man and artist.

CHAPTER THREE

Interlude on Tchaikovsky

By blood, Tchaikovsky was only three-quarters Russian. His maternal grandfather was a Frenchman. It is possible that this admixture may have accounted for certain French traits in his character—his reserve, almost amounting to shyness, and his polished manners—as well as his preference for the music of Bizet and Délibes over that of his two greater, German, contemporaries, Wagner and Brahms; and the fact that his music was more cosmopolitan in idiom than that of the other Russian composers of his day. As a child, he was terribly sensitive. As an adult, he became a secret drinker and a neurotic, and though he once fell in love with a woman, Désirée Artôt (who married another man before Tchaikovsky could make up his mind to do so), he was so homosexually inclined that in 1877 he actually married a nymphomaniac with whom he was not in love, in the hope that he would thereby conquer his abnormality. Of course the marriage crashed in ruins, and quickly too. Thenceforward, Tchaikovsky's friendships, his affection for certain close members of his family, and his art, were his consolations for his morbidity and pessimism. There is little or no evidence of his having regularly 'practised' homosexuality, though he wrote to his sister Alexandra Davidov in the autumn of 1876: 'I am so confirmed in my habits and tastes that it is impossible to cast them off like an old glove. Besides I am far from possessing an iron will and since writing to you I have already given way three times to my natural inclinations.' All his life he battled against his abnormality. He seems to have been outwardly charming, and this may account for the charm which is a marked characteristic of much of his music. His most remarkable friendship was with Madame Nadejda von Meck, the widow who admired his music so much that she gave him generous financial help for many years, but whom he avoided meeting, to prevent mutual embarrassment, though they constantly corresponded. That friendship ended sadly, for in 1890 she discontinued her annuity to him, believing herself to be on the verge of bankruptcy; actually, her belief was illusory, and was due to a nervous disease which caused her death less than three months after his; but he thought that she had invented her financial difficulties as an excuse for stopping the annuity, and was deeply wounded; it was tragic that he never learnt the truth, for his unawareness of it overturned his faith in 'the best of mankind', as he told his friend Jurgenson.

Tchaikovsky believed in God and prayed to Him, as we know from his correspondence with Madame von Meck and with Balakirev and his diary; but he wrote very little church music.

His musical successes and the honours bestowed on him by the French Academy and Cambridge University did something to console him in the last year or two of his life, and there is nothing to support the idea that he committed suicide: he felt ill, defiantly drank a glass of unboiled water at lunch, refused to see a doctor, and died of cholera at the age of 53, shortly after the first performance of the *Pathétique* Symphony.

Tchaikovsky's personal melancholy, amounting at times to morbidity and self-pity, and the sadness of his life, arouse our compassion, and are reflected in some parts of his music—the Trio for pianoforte, violin and 'cello in memory of his dear friend Nicholas Rubinstein, the Finale of the *Pathétique*, and even the aptitude which he showed for portraying so vividly the tragedies of fictitious characters such as Romeo and Juliet, Hamlet, Manfred, Eugen Onegin and Tatiana, or of Paolo and Francesca, who though historical, were depicted by him in Hell according to the poetic vision of Dante. But it is quite untrue to say—as has so often been said—that Tchaikovsky's music is predominantly pessimistic. The two piano concertos, the violin concerto, the Fourth and Fifth Symphonies, the Suite in G, all end in happy or triumphant mood. And he was a great master both of humour and of delicacy in music. Think of the delicious drolleries of the wood-wind in the trio section of the Scherzo from the Fourth Symphony, the wit of the Chinese Dance in the *Nutcracker* and of its miniature overture, the 'meowing' of Puss-in-Boots in *The Sleeping Beauty*, or the light-hearted frolics in the Finale of the violin concerto.

Tchaikovsky's music retains its immense popularity for three main reasons: his wonderful gift of pouring out simple, expressive and beautiful melodies; his ability to portray a rich variety of human emotions, ranging from hopeless grief to triumph or gaiety; and his brilliant mastery of colourful and delicate orchestration.

14

His ballets—particularly *The Sleeping Beauty* and *Swan Lake* and the best numbers in *Nutcracker*—are as important for assessing his genius as are his concert works or his two finest operas, *Eugen Onegin* and *The Queen of Spades*. The two first-named are among the most perfect ballet scores ever composed, full of grace, humour, drama, and fairyland, and in perfect harmony with their subjects. Moreover, the *charm* of Tchaikovsky's music appears over and over again—in the ballets, in the Second Symphony, in the violin concerto, in the pizzicato Scherzo of the Fourth Symphony and the Waltz movement of the Fifth, in the 5/4 Allegretto of the *Pathétique*, and in the serenade for strings. And even the Finale of the *Pathétique*, which can sound morbid if its rhythms are distorted and if its sorrowful tones are excessively underlined, becomes an expression of noble grief when it is played under a great conductor who understands Tchaikovsky and does not exaggerate the intense sadness.

Tchaikovsky is a great composer; but even in the course of my boyhood I was to discover that he is not among the few supreme ones; and the chief reason for this is that his music lacks the exaltation of spirit which is to be found in the art of Beethoven, Bach and Handel. But if ever there was a case of a creative musician rising, in his art, above the morbidities of his own temperament and the pathetic facts of his own life, Tchaikovsky is that composer.

CHAPTER FOUR

Discovering Beethoven and others

It was my paternal grandmother, Jeannette, who, realising that I was being 'fed' so much on Tchaikovsky, whetted my appetite to hear Beethoven's Fifth Symphony. 'I love "the C minor"', she used to say, and she took me to hear it, under Wood's direction, for the first time. Its effect upon me was instantaneous and tremendous. This was the first major event in my musical experience. It was, indeed, more than that: it was a turning point in my whole existence. From that afternoon, I became an ardent devotee of Beethoven: I had previously been taught to play a few of the easier movements of his sonatas on the piano, but from this time my great musical object was to hear more and more of his works. By the time I went from Fretherne House School, in London, to Harrow at the age of 13, I had heard all the 'odd number' symphonies except the First, several of the overtures, the last three pianoforte concertos and the one for violin, and a good many of the piano sonatas played by professional artists chiefly in the Bechstein Hall (as the Wigmore Hall was then called)—and some of these works several times.

My grandmother did not restrict her concert-going to orchestral occasions. She also loved piano recitals, and in her enthusiastic company I heard many of the piano works of Beethoven, Mozart, Schumann and Chopin. My father was by no means behindhand in his love of the music of the three first-named of these composers and others created for orchestra, and my mother and he and I heard at the Queen's Hall not only many of Beethoven's orchestral masterpieces, but the greatest of Mozart's symphonies, those of Schumann, and several of Mendelssohn's orchestral works. I enjoyed the *Scotch* Symphony so much at my first experience of it, and it went by so quickly for me, that after it was all over, Wood having only made momentary pauses between the movements, I fondly imagined that the end of the Symphony was the end of the first movement only, and was quite disappointed when

16

my father explained to me that there were no more movements to follow! At that stage, of course, I knew nothing about sonata or symphonic 'form'.

Meanwhile, I was gradually becoming familiar with some, at least, of the great German *lieder* and a few of the finest French songs, through hearing them sung either by my Aunt Alice at her occasional recitals in the Bechstein Hall, or by her and my Uncle Charles after dinner at our house when my parents had guests.

My father was, on the whole, less attracted to chamber music than to orchestral music, and the world of the string quartet seemed to be uncharted territory for him; in fact it was I who was to introduce him to some of the great Beethoven and Mozart quartets later on in our lives. But at the period of which I am speaking, he loved Beethoven's *Archduke* Trio in B flat (op. 97) for piano, violin and 'cello, and Schubert's in the same key, and took me to hear them.

There were some great gaps in my musical upbringing at this time. Neither my father nor his mother had any great liking for sacred choral music; and in consequence, in those days I never heard the oratorios of Handel, Haydn or Mendelssohn (except an occasional aria from them included in a mainly orchestral concert). My father professed no great liking for Handel, though years afterwards, when some friends took my mother and him to a performance of *Messiah* at the Royal Albert Hall, they came back enthusiastic! My father used to say that he didn't like Haydn; but I think this was partly nonsense, due perhaps to his having on some occasion not been interested in one of Haydn's symphonies; in his old age, I caught him out, by turning on a Haydn work on the radio just after it had started, so that he didn't know the name of the composer: at the end, I asked him whether he had enjoyed it—to which he replied 'Yes, very much'—and who he thought was the author of it: he looked at me quizzically and enquired whether it was by his beloved Mozart; but he characteristically saw the joke against himself when I revealed the truth to him!

On one of Charles's visits to London, he came with my parents and me to one of Wood's Sunday concerts, and my father and he were amazed that a composer who lived so long ago as J. S. Bach could have written works which made such a great appeal to them as the Third Brandenburg Concerto and the Suite No. 2 in B minor for flute and strings (Albert Fransella was the admirable soloist)! This sounds rather strange to us today, but most music lovers in England in those days do not seem to have gone back earlier than Bach and Handel. My knowledge of Bach at that stage was almost confined to a few of the instrumental works, and of Handel to some of the Concerti Grossi, which I also loved.

One of the greatest events in my life was my first hearing of Beethoven's Ninth Symphony. We had been spending a summer holiday at Harrogate, and travelled home in time to go to a charity concert at Queen's Hall in the evening. My parents did not realise that it was going to last about three hours! I do not remember now what any of the other items were, except Bach's great motet *Sing ye to the Lord*, superbly sung by the Sheffield Choir under Dr Henry Coward. The Ninth Symphony came last: of course I was too tired (and too young) to appreciate it properly, but I was nevertheless swept off my feet, both by the glorious work itself and by Artur Nikisch's conducting of it. I always remember those slight jerky movements which electrified whatever orchestra played under him, and the overwhelming effect he produced, apparently by the simplest and most unobtrusive means.

But I have gone too far ahead in my narrative, chronologically. For at the tender age of six, I was taken by my father (who never let the grass grow under his feet) and my mother, with my brother, to my first theatre, and this was not a pantomime or a children's play, but a matinee of *The Sorcerer*! I was a very sensitive, tender-hearted child, I suppose, for at the end of the first Act, when the stage was darkened and John Wellington Wells, the sorcerer, put everybody there to sleep, I thought that they would never wake up again and burst into tears! Even when the curtain fell on that Act and the lights in the auditorium were turned on, I was still inconsolable. There was nothing for it. My father had to take me home in a hansom!

As a boy, also, I was taken to *Patience*, *The Mikado* and *Iolanthe*, all of which I enjoyed immensely; I revelled in the lilt of the tunes, the colourful costumes and the amusing librettos (so far as I could really understand them at that time of my life). In those days, Rosina Brandram (the contralto) and Rutland Barrington (who was Pooh-Bah) were in the original parts which they played in the D'Oyly Carte Company; I saw Walter Passmore as Koko, Bunthorne, and the Lord Chancellor, and afterwards C. H. Workman—both of whom were excellent. Henry Lytton was, for instance, Archibald Grosvenor in *Patience*, and it was only at a

18

later date that he took over the role of the leading comedian in all the operas. This is, however, not the point at which to dilate either on Gilbert and Sullivan or on my life-long affection for their light operas: more of that anon.

But this reference to my earliest experiences of opera, albeit in its lighter form, leads me to speak of my first acquaintance with opera in its more serious aspect. The first 'grand' opera to which I was taken, was *Carmen*, at Covent Garden. The name-part was performed by an Italian singer called Giachetti, whom neither my parents nor my brother nor I greatly liked, as she had a tendency towards a vocal wobble. But Don José was played by Caruso. I was told that this was not really one of his best parts. I can only say that to my inexperienced ears and eyes he was magnificent. Never had I heard a tenor voice like that, or one so superbly produced. Above all, his singing was so full of feeling that he brought tears to everyone's eyes, and his acting was exceptionally good for an operatic singer of those days. Looking back now, it seems almost appropriate that the Don José of that performance overshadowed the Carmen. For much more recently I have come to realise that Don José, rather than Carmen, is the protagonist of that wonderful opera.

Puccini was entering the London operatic scene at that time, and my father was not the only one among my relatives to fall under his spell. I had the good fortune to hear *La Bohème* on a Melba-Caruso night. She had a voice of most lovely quality, beautifully produced, but she left me (and some others of my acquaintance) quite unmoved; it seemed to me almost expressionless singing, especially when compared with Caruso's. I do not now remember the rest of the cast, though I recall that Mancinelli conducted, and that the limpid melodies played on the strings as well as being sung, and the beautiful writing for the harps, particularly impressed me. I retain my affection for *La Bohème* to this day, and none of the other operatic tragedies by Puccini that I heard could vie with it. About this period, I was taken to *Madame Butterfly* and *Tosca*. I have enjoyed the melodies and orchestration of both; but *Tosca* is too much of a 'shocker' or 'melodrama' in its subject, to appeal to me, and the music (I have always felt) is suited to this and does not rise above it. *Butterfly* is, of course, pathetic in the extreme, but a central feature of the libretto has always left an unpleasant taste in my mouth: Pinkerton sings a beautiful duet with Butterfly in the first Act and appears to be utterly sincere

19

in his love for her; yet the whole essence of the story is that after that he leaves her, and when he comes back, he brings with him an American wife; Butterfly, who with her baby has been faithfully waiting for his return, dies of a broken heart. How false, in retrospect, was Pinkerton's musical protestation of love for her in Act I! What a heartless rotter he turns out to be! The evening, for me, at that first hearing was only saved by the supreme artistry of Emmy Destinn (who later reverted to her original name, Destinnova). I have heard this opera several times, but I never can overcome that fundamental distaste for the personality of Pinkerton and the consequences of his despicable behaviour! And if this feeling of mine is justified, does it not mean that Puccini, in writing seemingly genuine love music for him to sing in Act I, had really composed 'out of character'? Pinkerton never meant to remain permanently loyal to Butterfly, and Puccini should somehow have indicated his falseness from the start. Many years later (between the Wars), I heard *Turandot*, which I admired but did not much enjoy: the subject and most of the music are too hard and cruel for my liking. But *Gianni Schicchi*, which I did not hear until after World War II, is great fun and charming; I can honestly say that this and *La Bohème* are the only Puccini operas that I have greatly cared for.

I do not remember whether I heard *Aida* and *Cav.* and *Pag.* during these early years or in my Harrow days during the holidays. But whenever it was, I enjoyed *Aida* greatly: the name part in this opera, too, was sung by Destinn, and Radames by Zenatello— both magnificently: I have admired and loved *Aida* ever since —more than most of the Verdi operas. I was not, and never have been specially attracted either to Mascagni's *Cavalleria Rusticana* or even to Leoncavallo's *Pagliacci* (in spite of Caruso's great singing in the part of Canio), though from the first I was more struck by it than by *Cavalleria*.

One Whitsun weekend, in my Fretherne House School days, my parents and I went to Sonning-on-Thames. It rained incessantly. So my father, characteristically, suggested that we should cut short the little holiday by returning to London on the Monday morning, and go to *Die Meistersinger* at Covent Garden. 'You can always get into the Opera at short notice', he declared. Whether he was correct about this at that period, I cannot say, but on this occasion he proved right. I have heard that there are three versions of this great work of Wagner's: his complete one, which

20

is *immensely* long and has a third Act lasting about two hours, and two shorter versions, one briefer than the other. As this performance started at 7, and (without a long dinner interval such as Covent Garden used to have in the *Ring* operas) ended, so far as I can remember, about 11 p.m., it must have been one of the shorter ones. At any rate, it was conducted by Hans Richter, and the part of Hans Sachs was played by Van Rooy, the great Dutch artist whom I have never found equalled in this role by any other. I revelled in the whole opera. I had, of course, heard Wagner excerpts in the concert room, and used to enjoy chiefly the Prelude to the *Meistersinger*, and the usual concert selection from its third Act, and the overture to *Tannhauser*. But this was my first experience of a Wagner opera in the theatre. I shall come to my early experiences of his others in due course in this narrative.

Meanwhile I was able to go on widening my acquaintance of concert masterpieces in the Queen's Hall until I went to Harrow. I adored Schubert's *Unfinished* Symphony almost as much as those of Beethoven, and the piano concerto of Schumann was one of my special favourites.

But now I am going to return to Bizet. He was most certainly not a 'single masterpiece' composer. Yet *Carmen* does tower above all his other works to such an extent that, though it was some time before I heard any of them except the *first L'Arlésienne* Suite, I feel justified in interrupting my autobiographical narrative at this point, in order to consider briefly the personality and art of Bizet, in juxtaposition with one another, as I view them today.

CHAPTER FIVE

Bizet and 'Carmen' [1]

Georges Bizet was an only child. His father was a man of humble origin, who became a teacher of singing and a composer in a modest way. The mother was slightly higher in the social scale, very intelligent, a gifted pianist, a warm-hearted soul with strong maternal instincts. Georges was a devoted son, who, dying at 36¾, was survived by his father; but he lost his mother when he was barely 23. From his boyhood he was extremely industrious, a sincere, impetuous youth, who loved the society of his fellow human beings, and also loved natural beauty, and Rome, where he spent three happy years after winning the *Prix de Rome*. He was frank and loyal, but quick-tempered, though he lost no time in retracting an unfair comment or an unduly harsh remark. He was intolerant only of deceit or intrigue. Unlike some composers, he was deeply interested in literature and the other arts besides music, and when he went from Rome, on a tour in Italy in 1859, the association of various places with Cicero, Homer and Ulysses, Fra Diavolo, Scribe, Tiberius and Nero, fascinated him; 'but' (he he wrote), 'Virgil and Horace will console me for the tyrants.'

In spite of his precocity and the subsequent emergence of his genius, there was always a certain lack of self-confidence latent in him. He was a Christian in the broad sense—though he once described himself as 'more pagan than Christian'—but he had no use for organised religion. He was not particularly ambitious for money, but longed for the world's applause and was resentful when he did not get it. Although he had a hot temper, he was witty and charming. He once said that he was too much of an egoist to be a good teacher, but in fact he turned out to be a conscientious and modest one.

The character of Carmen in his greatest opera was not pure

---

[1] In writing the biographical part of this chapter, I am indebted to Winton Dean's admirable book *Georges Bizet* (1965 edition) which can now be regarded as the definitive English work on Bizet as man and artist.

fiction, so far as Bizet was concerned; for there was, so to speak, a recurrent 'Carmen influence' in his own life before he married. He kept a mistress in Rome, and had a strong appetite for prostitutes. In 1861 he had two 'affairs' simultaneously; one of them was with his parents' maid, Marie Reiter, and resulted in the birth of an illegitimate son in 1862. The 'Carmen complex' is revealed by the relationship of Myrra and Yorick in *La coupe du roi de Thulé*, years before the opera *Carmen* was written; and it is more likely that 'Céleste Mogador', the stage name of Madame la Comtesse de Moreton de Chabrillan), that colourful character who had been, in turn, prostitute, actress, circus rider, novelist, dramatist, authoress of a book of memoirs, and wife and widow of a member of an old aristocratic family, had an 'affair', starting in 1865, with Bizet, who was then her neighbour at his cottage at Le Vésinet.

But in 1867 he fell deeply in love with Geneviève Halévy, a daughter of his old teacher, and from then onwards his character changed. At first her family would not hear of the marriage. Then in 1868 he had severe attacks of the quinzy, of which he had been intermittently a victim from the age of 14 and which was ultimately to be one of the contributory causes of his death. He went through 'some kind of spiritual crisis'.[2] He recorded that he was changing his skin, as artist and as man—'purifying' himself and 'becoming better'. He developed an interest in philosophy, and reached a dilemma in which on the one hand he conceived that 'religion' would ultimately yield to 'reason', yet on the other hand he recognised that 'the societies most deeply tainted with superstition have been the greatest promoters of art.... Art decays in proportion as reason advances.... The imagination lives on chimeras, on visions. You suppress the chimeras, and goodbye imagination!' Yet he 'remained critical, detached, half idealist, half sceptic'. Winton Dean[3], whilst recording this, thinks that it accounts for the fact that 'for the remaining years of his life Bizet composed music that showed a remarkable power to enter into and interpret, as it were from within and without at once, the emotional and psychological states of all manners of persons'. It was the period when he was working on his ill-fated opera *La coupe du roi de Thulé*, of which, alas!, only a few fragments survive—thanks to the scandalous way in which the competition was conducted. On March 3rd, 1869, he entered on his difficult marriage to Gene-

---

[2] Winton Dean, ibid., p. 75.
[3] Winton Dean, ibid., p. 77.

viève, with the eventual assent of her family. Her father had died when she was thirteen, and two years later her sister Esther died suddenly at the age of twenty. Geneviéve inherited nervous instability both from her father and especially from her mother Léonie, who, though 'a good companion' socially and a talented amateur sculptress, was chronically extravagant and subject to fits of insanity which necessitated her confinement. She crazily accused Geneviève of having caused Esther's death. No wonder that Geneviève was ill-balanced and a constant victim of fear, and unable afterwards to live with Léonie.

Such were the mother and daughter with whom poor Bizet found himself encumbered. Nevertheless, his own character had become balanced and sympathetic, and this fact, for the short period of his unhappy marriage, whilst it helped the two women, itself weakened his own powers of resistance to his ill-health and the disappointments of his artistic career. As Mina Curtiss says, 'he lacked the instinct for self-preservation'.[4] The *Carmen* complex of his own pre-marital life had disappeared, except in the general sense that his soul was in torment during his marriage to Geneviève. The evidence is all against any idea that he had a love affair with Galli-Marié, who created the part of Carmen, and all in favour of his having been a loyal and compassionate husband, though the marriage was not happy and he and Geneviève parted company for a while in 1874.

Eventually, his illness, the psychological strains of his marriage, and the virtual failure of his greatest masterpiece at its first production in Paris, proved too much for him. A severe onslaught of rheumatism, fever, great pain and depression, and two heart attacks, caused his sudden death in June, 1875. His own tendency towards irony was surpassed by the irony of fate whereby after his death, *Carmen* swept through the world in triumph and has continued to be one of the best loved operas in musical history.

It is not surprising that this sensitive, sympathetic observer of human nature, with his brilliant musical gifts, his colourful personality, and his vivid imagination, should have been able to produce the wonderful opera by which he is best known and which towers over all his other works. What is, in its own way, equally remarkable, is that at the age of seventeen he should have composed that delightful little masterpiece, the Symphony in C—

---

[4] See Winton Dean, ibid., p. 83. Mina Curtiss: *Bizet and his world.*

brimful of the happiness of youth. Here are no heart-searchings, no conflicts.

> 'The year's at the spring,
> And day's at the morn',

as Pippa sings in Browning's drama. The only exception to the gaiety is the *Adagio*, with its remote, almost oriental, character, and the languorous atmosphere of its chromatic effects on the woodwind and pizzicato strings. How extraordinary that this fresh and fragrant work remained unknown until 1933 when Reynaldo Hahn, to whom Geneviève had given it, deposited it at the Paris Conservatoire, Chantavoine described it in an article in a magazine, and Mr D. C. Parker (who wrote the first English biography of Bizet) brought it to the notice of Weingartner, who first conducted it at Basle in February, 1935. Since then, it has delighted audiences throughout the world; and Balanchine had the insight to invent an enchanting ballet without a story, to fit its enchanting strains. Normally, Bizet's music required to be inspired by ideas external to music. The Symphony in C was the one *brilliant* exception. He even told Saint-Saëns in later years that he could do nothing without the theatre, and that he was not made for the symphony. And the one outstanding work which he wrote for the piano (on which he was himself a superb executant) was not 'absolute' music, but a suite of twelve witty and charming little pieces, each of which aptly represented a child's game or playing —*Jeux d'enfants*, composed for piano duet in 1871. Bizet afterwards orchestrated five of these with his usual mastery, under the title of *Petite suite d'orchestre*.

Apart from these works, it is true that Bizet's genius lay in the direction of the theatre. His early opera *Les Pêcheurs des perles* (1863) foreshadows the much greater *Carmen*, with its warm sympathy for the three principal characters in their predicament, its wealth of melody, and its romantic and, at times, delicate, orchestration. It contains at least two really beautiful melodies—the 'friendship' duet between Nadir and Zurga (the tune of which recurs several times), and Nadir's love-song. In his one-act opera *Djamileh* (1872) Bizet reached his operatic maturity. The libretto is nothing much, but it afforded him an opportunity to give vent to his instinctive taste for exotic music, to voice convincingly the emotions of the characters, and to bring most of them, anyhow, to life most vividly, particularly Djamileh herself—the girl who, having become the mistress of the voluptuous Haroun, falls deeply in love with him and eventually by her devotion wins him to give up his former practice of changing one mistress for another every month and to reciprocate her love. The music for *L'Arlé-sienne* (his next stage work) suffers from the disadvantage of being only incidental music for a play, but intrinsically it is splendid —dramatic, subtle, passionate, enchanting, and tragic, according to the needs of the story. There have been very few opportunities this century to see and hear Daudet's play in a theatre—none in my experience—and most of us have had to be content with concert performances of the two orchestral suites embodying the various musical numbers, the first of which was arranged by Bizet himself, the second after his death by his friend Guiraud, the composer.

Carmen is one of the greatest tragic music dramas of all time. It was, indeed, Bizet's achievement to introduce into French opera a dramatic quality which was blended, in perfect balance, with lyrical beauty. And, ironically, he did this in a musical *tragedy* not only designed for the Paris *Opéra Comique*, but framed in the structure of the *opéra comique* genre which prevailed in that theatre and contained spoken dialogue between the musical numbers. The recitatives so often still used in *Carmen* were composed by Guiraud, not by Bizet, and ought to have been scrapped everywhere, decades ago. There is no more case for them than there would be for someone—Heaven forbid!—to invent recitatives to replace the spoken dialogue in *Fidelio*. The latter, in spite of its victorious conclusion, is obviously not a 'comic opera' in any English sense of the term, and just because *Carmen* has a tragic ending, this is no reason to introduce a device which was, before Bizet, associated at that particular theatre with operas which ended happily.

Carmen not only ends in tragedy, but is intensely dramatic throughout. It combines brilliant character drawing, both in music and in the libretto, with a strongly dramatic plot; beautiful melodies with a vivid expression of profound human emotions; and a typically French clarity of thought with a use of Spanish rhythms which are essentially heard and felt, as it were, through the ears and brain of a Frenchman and yet evoke the atmosphere of Spain, though composed by a man who had never set foot in that country.

The principal character is not Carmen, but Don José, who is shown first as a decent, soldierly man, in love with the sweet,

26

innocent Micaela, and devoted to his mother. As the drama proceeds, we see—and hear—him degenerating under the bad influence of Carmen, caught in her spell, and ultimately dragging her with himself to catastrophe. Carmen's character, on the other hand, remains the same throughout: she is passionate, bewitching, and unfaithful, though gay and extremely courageous. Pity and terror (Aristotle's essential ingredients for tragedy), jealousy, revenge, 'nemesis', and the struggle between sacred and profane love, are all linked in this masterly opera with lyrical beauty, instrumental delicacy, and charm. And the greatest tragedy of all, left in our minds as we leave the theatre, is that Bizet died just after *Carmen* had been produced, not only before he could know how widely it was to be acclaimed after its initial failure, but before he could enrich the world with a succession of other operas of the same calibre.

One could hardly call so tormented a soul as Bizet's an 'integrated personality', even in the rather special sense in which I am using that expression in this book; but it would, I think, be true to say that, whatever conflicts there were in his personal life, there was no conflict, no inconsistency, between the man and the artist. Indeed, in his greatest completed opera, though Don José is not in any sense a portrait of Bizet himself, there is an element of autobiography: Carmen is an artistic embodiment of a feminine influence which had, before his marriage, entered into his own life; and above all, his personal experiences enabled him, with his genius and his vivid, intense imagination and his human sympathy, to penetrate into the very souls of the two principal characters of his masterpiece and so to produce a tragic music drama which has won the hearts of music lovers everywhere for about a century already and shows every sign of continuing to do so as the years go by.

CHAPTER SIX

1905 to 1910

Some men profess, at any rate, to regard their school days as having been the happiest period of their lives. I think there is a certain element of 'rose-coloured spectacles' in this attitude. In my experience, what most boys enjoyed chiefly at that stage was the holidays: during the term, they longed for them; and towards the ends of the 'hols' they did not look forward to returning to school, though they usually became acclimatized again, even at a boarding school, within a few days. In spite of the kindness and fairness of many masters, there were often the sternness of discipline, the irksomeness of work, the dread of examinations, and for *some* boys—the lack of aptitude for games which appeal to the majority but were, in my day at least, unduly idolised at public schools. Moreover, some boys can be very cruel to one another—like adults, though possibly in ways different from adult cruelty, and though most of them probably outgrow this characteristic afterwards.

However, I am indebted to Harrow School for several things:—

1. my further education in music at the hands of Dr Buck,[5] and particularly his revelation to me of the greatness of Bach;
2. my development of a love for the Greek and Latin poets and some of the dialogues of Plato, which culminated in a two-year period in the 'Twelve' (a higher division of the Classical Sixth Form), a few prizes, and a leaving scholarship to Oxford—though I was largely specialised in classics rather too early from the standpoint of my general education;
3. a few lasting friendships, curtailed in one or two cases alas! —like my even more numerous Oxford ones—by the appalling slaughter of the youth of Britain in World War I;
4. the excellent tuition which my housemaster and first tutor,

[5] Afterwards, Sir Percy Buck.

George Townsend Warner, gave me in essay-writing;
5. opportunities to foster a life-long devotion to the works of Shakespeare and also Browning.

These 'debts' are not here set out in any order of importance; in any case, the first-named is the one chiefly relevant to the subject of this book.

I entered what is now known (again) as 'Bradbys' house in September, 1905. And my father personally initiated me into my music lessons with Percy Buck, that splendid musician and organist, who was immensely popular with all the boys in the school, whether they were pupils of his or not. He had, of course, the advantages of being a dear, delightful man, extremely handsome, and an old Oxford Rugger Blue. He was usually gentle and tolerant, but capable of righteous, though very rare, indignation and disciplinary action if recalcitrant choristers started talking or making fools of themselves during rehearsals of the School Choral Class in Speech Room. At the Music Schools he taught me the piano and elementary harmony, and in due course I managed to win the second prize for music—largely on the strength of my interest in musical history, which he encouraged; I had not—and never have had—enough 'agility of finger'[6] to become a good amateur pianist. Buck used to give short weekly organ recitals on Sunday afternoons in Speech Room, and it was in this way that I, like many other boys, acquired a listener's knowledge of the great Bach organ works especially. He loved Bach above all composers—even Beethoven—and it was thanks to him that I first became acquainted with the *St. Matthew Passion*. Together we went through many passages from it on a piano. He obtained permission for a small party of us boys to go up to London in term-time under the charge of E. C. Mercer, the Assistant Music Master, to hear the annual Holy Week (abbreviated) performance of it in St Paul's Cathedral. And on another occasion, when it fell in the Easter holidays and when I was a little older, Dr Joseph Wood, the Headmaster, who was a Prebendary of the Cathedral, gave me two 'prebendal stalls', and I took the opportunity of initiat-

[6] I owe this expression to Donald Somervell (afterwards, Lord Somervell, P.C.), also a pupil of 'P.C.B.' and a somewhat older contemporary of mine at Harrow, who applied it to himself in conversation with my wife and me many, many years afterwards when we met at the Royal Festival Hall, not long before his death.

ing my father into the glories of Bach's inspiration. This love of Bach, which began in earnest for me under Buck's guidance, was the chief musical 'discovery' of my Harrow days, though it in no way detracted from my increasing adoration of Beethoven. The *St. Matthew Passion* led me on to hearing, in the holidays and afterwards, performances of the *St. John Passion*, the *Mass in B minor*, and other works. Percy Buck, in introducing me to the *St. Matthew*, was, I think, anxious not to be responsible for disturbing in any way the faith in which I had been brought up, and thus also for doing anything which my parents (particularly my mother) would not like. So he told me to regard the words as 'simply the most pathetic story in the world'. Be that as it may, I have always thought, in after years, that this great devotional masterpiece was one early, contributory cause, of which I was wholly unconscious at the time of my first acquaintance with it, but which, after a very long period of mere 'Theism', helped to bring me eventually to the Christian religion.

In the Choral Class we sang Bach's *Christians, grave ye this glad day*, excerpts from Handel's *Messiah*, from Mendelssohn's *Elijah*, and from Brahm's *German Requiem*, and also Stanford's ballad *Phaudrig Crohoore*. There were occasional concerts for the whole school by professional performers in Speech Room; and William Ackroyd, who taught boys the violin, formed locally a small professional chamber music organisation, which gave concerts in a little hall on the Hill; this enabled me to develop a knowledge of a few of the trios, quartets and quintets by the great composers in my boyhood, which was to be greatly extended later on at Oxford.

Then there were the School songs, which were not only sung at a Speech Room Concert at the end of certain terms, but above all (from the standpoint of frequency) at House Singing, which took place in the various houses once a fortnight, with either Buck or Mercer presiding at the piano. On these latter occasions, selections from the copious quantity of excellent Harrow School songs were supplemented by traditional national songs—English, Scottish, Welsh and Irish. It was customary for boys to be 'put on' by their fellow-members of the House to sing solos. The boys used to like to 'put' me 'on' especially to one called *Fairies*, though whether this was because it was one of the best songs in the Harrow book or because I had a most unfairylike appearance, I was never quite sure! They also had a trick of 'putting on' my brother and me (during our 'overlapping' period at Harrow) and the two Aveling brothers to sing *Awa'*, *Whigs*, *awa'*, because we were the only four boys in the House who were Liberals—or rather, had fathers who were Liberals.

Another of my activities, too, was that I was a member of the Bradby's Singing 'Eight', which one year won the Inter-House competition.

Mercer was a good singer. He used to delight the School especially by his renderings of two of Stanford's 'Songs of the Sea' (*Drake's Drum* and *The Old Superb*), set to Henry Newbolt's words, in Speech Room concerts. And I remember his telling us boys in Bradbys, at House Singing, that if we wanted the best model for good diction in singing, we had better get our parents to take us to hear Henry Lytton of the D'Oyly Carte Opera Company in Gilbert and Sullivan. How right he was!

An 'epoch-making' musical experience which nearly ended in fiasco, was an expedition—also under Mercer's leadership to London one Saturday afternoon, principally to hear Beethoven's Ninth Symphony, to be played at Queen's Hall under Henry Wood. E. H. W. Meyerstein (in after life well known as a writer of prose and verse), being the senior boy of the little party and a Monitor, was entrusted with the task of booking the tickets. He duly rang up the Box Office and asked them to reserve the seats, but evidently did not realise that it was necessary to send the money in advance! Of course, when we presented ourselves at Queen's Hall, our tickets had been sold, and there were no others available. Amid our desolation, I suggested that we had better console ourselves by going to the Zoo! We accordingly started up Portland Place, but had not got far, before I suddenly had the idea that, just possibly, a few members of the audience might be obliged to leave at the interval, before the Symphony, and that in that event the Box Office would be only too pleased to sell to us over again the requisite number of cheap seats in the Balcony, to enable us to hear that one work. And so it turned out! Poor Mercer had missed hearing Debussy's *The Blessed Damozel*, to which he was very much looking forward, but we all heard the mighty 'Ninth', from scattered positions in the Balcony. There have, no doubt, been at least equally great performances of it in my experience, but none has left a more indelible impression on my mind than that one, so nearly missed, yet retrieved by so narrow a margin!

31

So much for music in term-time. But meanwhile, there were all sorts of musical excitements to be had in the holidays.

My closest friend at Bradbys was Harry Atheling Russell Bousted, a boy of golden character—loyal, fearless, straight and charming—who was also to be one of my 'set' of special friends at University College, Oxford, afterwards, and whose heroic death in the Royal Flying Corps in World War I on the Western Front was one of the greatest personal tragedies in my experience: England, indeed the world, could ill afford to lose such a man. He and I had complete unity of outlook on the basic things of life. Yet we had no 'tastes' in common at all. He had, for instance, no interest either in serious music or in poetry, not even Shakespeare. He had, however, a very musical father. Atheling kindly invited me to a most enjoyable dance at his parents' house at Wimbledon during the holidays, and they put me up for the night after it. He had told me that his father was a keen amateur organist and had installed at home an organ of vast dimensions, the pipes of which extended to various parts of the house. Nevertheless, I was taken by surprise at being woken up in bed by the loud note of a deep diapason the next morning! Mr Boustead had a habit of practising on his beloved instrument before breakfast.

With one exception, to be mentioned later, my *special* musical experiences in the holidays during my Harrow period, all took place in London. In spite of having heard many of the Beethoven orchestral works, I had never yet had a chance of hearing the Pastoral Symphony. It had always been performed either in term-time or when we were away. Eventually I summoned up courage and wrote to Henry Wood. He replied in characteristic fashion: he would conduct the work at Queen's Hall in September before we all went back to school; and, of course, he was as good as his word. I have, naturally, associated this adorable symphony with him ever since. No wonder that all music lovers loved him!

It was at some time during my Harrow days that in the holidays I heard *Tristan und Isolde* for the first time, at Covent Garden, with my parents. And the conductor was—Nikisch! It made a tremendous impact upon me, but I cannot now remember how that performance compared with subsequent ones, such as Bruno Walter's, for example. I recall that the Tristan was no more than adequate and not of the same calibre at Litvinne, who *sang* Isolde gloriously; the only snag about her interpretation was that her appearance was note quite suited to Wagner's conception of the slim, youthful princess, for she had a figure like a beer-barrel! My Mendl grandparents took me to my second hearing of *Die Meistersinger*, again with the great Van Rooy as Hans Sachs, and I enjoyed it as much as the first. It was the one Wagner opera that 'Grandpa Mendl' liked, because it is a happy opera with a joyful ending: he could not tolerate tragedies.

My grandmother took me to *The Ring* in two instalments; this was the only way to arrange it, owing to school terms, but was perfectly feasible, because one cycle was performed at the Royal Opera House towards the end of the Easter holidays—when we went to *Das Rheingold* and *Die Walküre*—and the second came in the closing days of the summer opera season, about the end of July. So I got home from Harrow just in time for *Siegfried* and *Götterdämmerung*. Grannie's enthusiasm knew no bounds, and they were indeed very fine performances, again under Richter. Yet I had my youthful misgivings: I found *The Ring* too sinister, and the more I thought about it afterwards the more averse to it I became. Later still, this anti-Wagnerian reaction was to spread to his other works as well, even to *Die Meistersinger*; but I was too grateful to my dear grandmother to betray my feelings at the time, and it was only as the years went by that I had to let her know that I just *disliked* Wagner! I am always sorry that it was not until after her death (January, 1923) that I (in 1928) became a convert; by an irony of circumstance, during my enthusiasm for Wagner, my father, in his old age, turned against him—but that was in the course of the Nazi régime: my father professed to hear anticipations of the Nazi spirit in Wagner's music, especially in *The Ring*. I shall have more to say about this subject in a later chapter.

In August, 1908, when I was sixteen, my parents and brother and I went to Montana, in Switzerland, for a holiday; (this was our third trip to that lovely country). At the next table to ours in the dining room two striking young people were seated, who, as we subsequently learned, had been married only six months before and were now on what was virtually their honeymoon. The young woman, who was beautiful to look at, leaned forward and said to my mother 'Excuse me, but there is a grasshopper climbing up your dress! May I remove it for you?' For a few days after that, she was known as 'The grasshopper lady', but we soon discovered that they were Arthur Rhys-Roberts and

33

his wife Dilys. He was a solicitor, and a partner of David Lloyd-George, and (at a later stage than the time which I am now describing) was appointed Official Solicitor to the Supreme Court. His wife was already, in 1908, well known as a contralto singer, using still her maiden name, Dilys Jones, for professional purposes. From that time dates a long and close friendship with my family, only disturbed by the sad event of Arthur's premature death. In August, 1908, at the Montana hotel, someone initiated the idea of getting up a concert in aid of a charity, to be performed by any hotel visitors who had any pretensions to executive musical ability. Of course, Dilys was asked whether she would consent to sing, and, of course, she said 'yes'. There was a slight obstacle over the question of an accompanist, but eventually it was agreed that Dilys would sing a few songs, the piano part of which either my father (by ear) or even I could play. Dilys's glorious, rich quality voice and artistry were in any case sufficient to swamp the shortcomings of the more youthful of her two collaborators! After we all returned to London, she and Arthur were often guests at my parents' house. In those old days she was very kind in frequently singing *lieder* and Welsh folk-songs (in Welsh) to the delight of ourselves, our near relatives and other guests after dinner. It is convenient to refer at this point to my experience of Dilys as an artist generally. Though she appeared as Lady Mortimer, with her Welsh song and speeches, in Herbert Beerbohm Tree's production of *Henry IV, Part I,* and in small parts in *The Ring* under Richter at Covent Garden, she was chiefly known as one of the leading contraltos of her day at concerts and in oratorio, and especially for her outstanding performances of Bach, for whose music she felt herself to be particularly suited. A deeply religious woman, she dedicated her art to the interpretation of his liturgical masterpieces as few in her generation were able to do. I never forget her singing of the great alto arias in the *St. Matthew Passion,* and a certain memorable performance of the Mass in B minor at Westminster Abbey by the Bach Choir under Sir Hugh Allen, in which the soloists were Agnes Nicholls, Dilys, Gervase Elwes and Campbell McInnes—as fine a quartet for Bach as one could get anywhere. Dilys remained a dear friend of my wife's and mine throughout her long widowhood, until her death on Michaelmas Day, 1967. It was during my Harrow days, in the holidays, that my Aunt Mollie Raphael took me to Gluck's *Orfeo,* with Marie Brema as Orpheus and producer. It was put on for a short run at

34

the Savoy Theatre, and I remember not only Marie Brema's beautiful performance but the very artistic production, and particularly the dancers in the Elysian Fields who were silhouetted against the back cloth like the figures on a Greek vase. This was my first Gluck opera, and many years were to elapse before I had an opportunity of hearing others; for a long time now Gluck has been one of my specially favourite composers.

These were great days for Elgar. Aunt Alice introduced me to *The Dream of Gerontius*, with Gervase Elwes in the name part. I heard the *Enigma Variations*, and—in company with Harry Strauss (subsequently, Lord Conesford), who had been at Fretherne House with me—the First Symphony, by which we were greatly impressed, at one of its early performances.

When I left Harrow in July 1910, Dr Wood kindly offered to read all Virgil's work with me, if my parents could stay a few weeks of that summer within access of Woodbridge, Suffolk, where he was to be. Naturally I availed myself of so great a privilege and opportunity, most gratefully; my parents and Tom and I stayed at Aldeburgh—associated half a century later with Benjamin Britten and an annual musical festival—and so I used to make way between the two places on an inspiring poetical pilgrimage. That autumn I kept my classics fresh in London with the help of a private tutor, F. W. Pearson, who visited our house daily (67 Gloucester Place, then), and who proved to be a congenial companion in Latin and Greek, until I sat (successfully) for the open classical scholarship examination at Oxford early in December, held jointly by University College and two other colleges. One evening, Mr Pearson came with my parents and me to to a concert at Queen's Hall, conducted by Richter. It was one of the only two occasions on which I heard him conduct Beethoven, or indeed anything other than Wagner at Covent Garden. This time, the chief work was the Second Symphony; at the other concert (I do not recall when) he performed the Fourth. I well remember how impressed I was by the breadth, nobility and delicacy of his renderings.

I was present at the first performance of Elgar's violin concerto, with Kreisler (to whom it was dedicated), as soloist, and Wood with the Queen's Hall Orchestra, and have loved it deeply ever since.

I had gone to Harrow at 13, a tremendous Beethoven enthusiast; I left it, at 18, as a great Bach enthusiast too, thanks in no small

35

measure to the ways in which Percy Buck had—if I may be pardoned the expression!—'opened my ears' to the wonders of Bach, and to the fact that in 1907 my paternal grandparents had given me the '48' as a birthday present. From my Harrow days onward Beethoven and Bach have consistently been, in my eyes, the two supreme composers who tower above all others and whose music, moreover, stands—jointly—first in my affections.

Because of the advent of Bach into my life about this time, as a major influence, I have chosen this point in my narrative to say something in the next chapter about the personality and art of that mighty genius.

A recent photograph of the author

Born March 21st 1685. — Died July 28th 1750.

J. S. Bach

CHAPTER SEVEN

The Majesty of Bach

J. S. Bach came of a clan of musicians such as the world has never seen. In C. S. Terry's article on the Bachs in Grove's Dictionary of Music and Musicians (5th edition) there are 38 of them extending from the 16th to the 19th century, with J. S. Bach (1685-1750) marking the central climax and towering above the rest of his kinsmen even more mightily than Mont Blanc does over its Alpine chain. Concerning the Bachs before Johann Sebastian, his most distinguished son, C.P.E., wrote:— 'The Bachs not only displayed a happy contentedness, indispensable for the cheery enjoyment of life, but exhibited a clannish attachment to each other'. They were a race of cantors, organists and town musicians. There were annual family reunions, with a hymn followed by an 'extempore' chorus based on amusing popular songs, and the music ending with hearty laughter. Into this jovial picture, one side of the character of J. S. Bach, with his generosity and geniality and devotion to his family—the counterpart of the jolly tunes of some of the Allegros in his instrumental works—seems to fit quite naturally.

But the death of his father in his boyhood brought him away from Eisenach, his birthplace, to the household of his elder brother, Johann Christoph, at Ohrdruf, where he had constant access to his brother's organ and where he went to a strictly orthodox school. In that theological atmosphere it is not surprising that the musical tendency of his immediate forebears to the secular side should have given way to an ecclesiastical influence, which drew him into the service of the Lutheran Church. With the exception of the six years (1717-23) at Cöthen, where he was 'Kapellmeister' and Director of Chamber Music at the court of Prince Leopold of Anhalt-Cöthen, and where he composed his concertos, suites and sonatas for various instruments, Bach's whole adult life (after apprenticeship at the Michaeliskirche at Lüneberg) was spent as organist and/or choirmaster or cantor in a church or church-school at one German town after another—Arnstadt, Mühlhausen,

Weimar and Leipzig. But this does not mean that his career was entirely serene. He frequently had to face opposition from the Church Authorities—whether due to their conservative objections to his desire for improvements or partly to his own determination and its obverse side, his irritability, especially when convinced that he was in the right. He was immensely industrious, independent to the extent of standing up against authority, and confident in planning the way he intended to follow.

An incident at Arnstadt when he was twenty showed that as a youth he was not to be trifled with. A bassoon player who was a pupil at the Gymnasium, accompanied by five others, threatened him with a cane and called for an apology for his having reflected on the pupil's competence as a performer. Bach denied the charge, the bassoonist shouted abuse at him and started to beat him up, whereupon Bach drew his sword, and his assailant had to be rescued by his companions. Bach in due course had to appear before the Consistorium and admitted that he called the young man a 'Zippelfagottist'.

He was a vigorous fighter when provoked, but as he matured, the pugnacity shown on that youthful occasion was transformed from a physical to an oral mode of expression. In all those disputes with Church or Church-School Authorities throughout most of his life he was sometimes—perhaps usually—in the right, though his independence and persistence occasionally turned into bad temper. These were, however, after all, only minor blemishes. Bach would not have been human if he had had no faults. His principal traits were his determination, his devotion to his religion, his love for each of his two wives in succession and for his numerous children, his generosity and hospitality, and the warmth and sweetness of his nature: this is revealed, for example, in the charm of his dedicatory poem to the infant Prince Emanuel Ludwig, Crown Prince of Anhalt, first-born son of Prince Leopold (written after his appointment to Leipzig). He was, moreover, basically modest: when asked at Weimar for the secret of his mastery of the organ, he replied 'There is nothing wonderful about it. You merely strike the right note and the organ does the rest'.

Though ill-suited for being a schoolmaster, he was a marvellous teacher of individuals. His sons (his most eminent pupils) told Forkel that he had submitted himself to the discipline of self-instruction, and so could meet and overcome the difficulties of others. His teaching was methodical, carefully planned, clear and definite—whether in the playing of the clavier or in composition.

Though his supreme greatness as a composer was never realised in his lifetime—not even, apparently, by himself—he became greatly respected in Germany as an organist and practical musician, as the years went on.

C. S. Terry[7] describes his noble and devout end, working at his Chorale Preludes in spite of failing eyesight, which became total blindness as a result of a paralytic disorder, and showing firm courage and serenity in facing death.

Such was the man who produced religious music (in the strict sense of the term) which in its majesty and riches has hitherto been approached only by Handel's *Messiah* and *Dettingen Te Deum* and equalled only by Beethoven in his *Missa Solemnis.* There is no conflict between Bach as a man and Bach as an artist. True, his little human failings find no place in his music; but even men whose personal character was less exalted than Bach's rise above themselves in their creative work, and in Bach's case his transcendent genius undoubtedly towers over his personal character, good though that was.

Bach dedicated his art to God. Even his instrumental compositions other than the works for the organ are 'sacred' in the wider sense of the term, though they are unconnected with any liturgical purpose. There is no trace in them of any meretricious element, any false emotion, any fierceness, or anything sordid. They express joy, meditation, sorrow, exaltation, gaiety of the purest and most unsullied kind.

For Bach there was no *fundamental* distinction between 'sacred' and 'secular' music. The opening chorus of the *Christmas Oratorio, Jauchzet, frohlocket* ('Stand up, be joyful') was originally written for the birthday ode of the Queen of Saxony: the drums and trumpets which begin the Oratorio may not fit in with the ordinary Christian conception or the story of the nativity of Jesus, but they are intrinsically an appropriate expression of mankind's triumphant joy at the 'good news' of the birth of the Divine Saviour. Even so divine an inspiration as *Schlafe, mein Liebster* ('Slumber, Beloved'), the Cradle Song (No. 19) in the *Christmas Oratorio*, reflecting on the infant Jesus in his cot, was taken from the secular cantata *Der Wahl des Hercules* ('The Choice of Hercules'): the innocent, sleeping child is perfectly suited by the same music,

---

[7] *Johann Sebastian Bach: A Biography* (2nd edition), pp. 263-4.

whether it be Hercules or Jesus. As I have often stressed elsewhere,[8] music does not individualise, but universalises—deals with emotions and thoughts in generalised terms and does not really paint detailed portraits of *individuals*, as pictures do or as a writer can do, but is simply 'appropriate' to them in general, musical language. Even though *Die Wahl des Hercules* was composed for the birthday of the electoral Prince Friedrich, Bach struck down to the roots of the conception of tenderness in contemplation of the innocent slumber of the infant.

The music of eight arias and the last chorus (*Wir sitzen uns mit Thränen nieder*) from the *St. Matthew Passion* were used for Bach's work in memory of Prince Leopold of Cöthen, who had died while Bach was composing his great Passion music. Bach had no time to write fresh music for the funeral ceremonies while he was at work on his mighty masterpiece, 'so he asked Picander to write the text for the mourning ode in such a way that it could be adapted to the movements already written of the Passion'.[9] The Prince was a very great friend of Bach (as well as having been his employer) and Bach's music expressing his and our grief at the events leading up to the Crucifixion of Jesus was perfectly appropriate also for conveying his personal sorrow at the passing of his dear friend. Serene sorrow, combined with faith in God, is the refrain of the glorious closing chorus in the *St. Matthew Passion*; it was also the religious emotion which filled Bach's soul on the occasion of the Prince's death.

There is nothing to the detriment either of Bach's personal character or of his integrity as an artist, in such instances as these. He reproduced some music from his secular cantatas in the B minor Mass. He wrote the words 'In Nomine Jesu' in the Little Clavier Book, which was composed for his eldest son as a boy and was entirely non-liturgical. In his rules of accompaniment for his pupils he wrote 'Like all music, the figured bass should have no other end and aim than the glory of God and the recreation of the soul'— though the figured bass itself is, after all, a technical device.

He was a supreme craftsman, yet the fugues, as well as the preludes, in the '48' are not mere exercises, but vehicles of various moods and emotions, and to hear *The Art of Fugue*, that marvel of ingenuity, is a deeply spiritual experience. His organ works, not

[8] In *The Soul of Music* and *The Divine Quest in Music*.
[9] Albert Schweitzer: *J. S. Bach*, translated by Ernest Newman, Vol. II, p. 208.

only the chorales based on old hymns or the *St. Anne* fugue, but those which have no titles other than 'prelude', 'fugue', 'toccata' or 'sonata', correspond to great ecclesiastical architecture, because of their intrinsically exalted character, and not simply because of the historical association between the organ and church worship.

I am not alone in finding in the music of Bach a deep and unending spiritual significance, which Beethoven's art alone equals in the musical world. And nowhere is this more conspicuous than in the *St. Matthew Passion*, with which I have 'lived', on and off, throughout my life ever since Percy Buck introduced me to it at Harrow. I have heard it in a wide variety of settings, in church or cathedral, in the concert hall, and even in a vast building called the 'Festhalle' at Frankfurt-on-Main in 1911, which somewhat resembled our London Olympia. No place have I found more satisfying than the lovely church of St Bartholomew-the-Great at Smithfield, where the London Bach Society have so often since World War II presented it in its original German and where the whole atmosphere and the performance have been as ideal as anything could be in this imperfect world. But a concert hall—though Bach himself never contemplated such a place for the performance either of this or of the *St. John Passion* or of the B minor Mass or any of his liturgical works—can be completely satisfying if the rendering is sufficiently fine, for Bach's music is so deeply religious and potent that it seems to transform the secular setting into a sacred one.

Opera implies a theatre. Wagner called his mature operas 'dramas', and his disciples gave them the title 'music dramas'. If, however, a musical work is written for performance in a theatre, there is no fundamental difference between an 'opera' and a 'music drama', even though Wagner radically reformed the species. But the term 'music drama' can fittingly be applied not only to operas, but to some non-theatrical compositions, and the greatest of all 'music dramas', in this sense, hitherto composed, in my view, are Bach's *Passions* according to St Matthew and St John, and Handel's *Messiah*. We cannot call any setting of the Mass 'dramatic' (though it may have its dramatic moments): thus the Mass in B minor is not a 'drama' in its structure or its conception. But Bach—like some of his predecessors—selected the story of the Passion of Christ, and treated it dramatically: there are unutterably beautiful or sublime reflective choruses, chorales, arias and concerted numbers, which might be said to correspond artistically to the choruses in the ancient Athenian tragedies or those of Shakespeare's *Henry V*;

41

but the Evangelist's eloquent narrative continually introduces dramatic solos and short choruses actually impersonating the characters of the great story or the people of Jerusalem in supremely convincing and expressive music.

These great liturgical masterpieces of Bach are profoundly religious, and Christian, in the strict sense of those terms. But they are so tremendous that they transcend the orthodox conception which they were intended to embody and attain to a universal significance. Hence their appeal even to non-Christians—and indeed to agnostics and atheists—who, if they are lovers of music, sense the grandeur and spiritual beauty of them—though they (and *Messiah* and Beethoven's *Missa Solemnis*) are, in my view, the most complete embodiment of Christianity in music that the world has yet known.

You will not find a great deal of the portrayal of evil in Bach's music. In the *St. Matthew Passion*, the cruelty in 'Let him be crucified' is vividly portrayed by chromaticism and uneven rhythm, the wickedness of Judas is very briefly conveyed in a few terse, simple utterances, and the advent of those who came with swords and staves to seize Jesus is described in harsh tones by the Evangelist. In the cantatas, the devil is represented by the serpent, who is depicted by a twisting motive; but this method is pictorial: there is no *intrinsic* expression of evil in the music. But Christian, profound compassion is the dominant note throughout, in both the settings of the 'Passion', as it is in the *Crucifixus* of the B minor Mass. There is also righteous anger ('Leave him! Leave him! Bind him not!'). We could hardly imagine Bach devoting long pages of his scores to the portrayal of evil as Wagner did in *Parsifal* with its pictures of the wicked Klingsor and of the sexual allurements of the Flower Maidens and Kundry in the second Act, the sinister figures of Telramund and Ortrud in *Lohengrin*, the profane lust typified by the Venusberg in *Tannhaüser*, the voluptuous strains of the Rhinemaidens in the first scene of *Das Rheingold*, or the embodiment of evil contained in Alberich and Hagen. It fitted in with Wagner's dramatic purposes to exhibit all these things in his operas, but it was easier for him to do so than it would have been for Bach, for there was a strongly unpleasant side to Wagner's own character, whereas Bach was predominantly a good and beneficent Christian, who, moreover, so far as we can judge, did not even encounter very *pronounced* evil in others in his private life.

His attitude to death is comforting, not depressing. In his cantatas, he looks forward to it as a release and welcomes it, sometimes with weariness but more often with serenity or gladness, or even with ecstasy. In each of the two 'Passions' the tragedy of the Crucifixion is followed by a final chorus of infinite tenderness, comfort and sublime resignation, though naturally Bach had in mind the Resurrection, to which he gave exultant expression, after the profound, noble grief of the *Crucifixus*, in the B minor Mass.

All this fits in perfectly well with Bach's fine personal character, but the latter is, of course, transcended by the unsurpassed glory of his art. This, however, applies to most great creative artists. We may be able to reconcile their personality with their artistic work, and in Bach's case there is no difficulty in doing so; but in scarcely any instance can it ever be said that the splendour and beauty of the music, the poetry, the pictures, or the sculpture, are fully matched by the character of the man: in his personal relationships he may, on the whole, be a good man, but he is seldom equal in grandeur to his stature as an artist. That would, surely, be expecting almost too much from human nature. If a man is a great and influential saintly or religious leader, we have hardly a right to look, as well, for outstanding gifts in him as an artistic creator. It is rare enough to find so wide a human benefactor as Leonardo da Vinci, who excelled in engineering and scientific invention as well as in painting, or so many-gifted an artist as Michelangelo, who was a great genius in the spheres of sculpture, painting, architecture, and poetry. Berlioz and Wagner were able to write librettos for their wonderful music. But in most cases, the real greatness of a composer of outstanding genius is to be found in his music, and not equally—if at all—in his private life. The composer rises above the man, even though, as in the cases of Bach and Elgar, the man himself had a fine character, quite consistent with the particular quality of his music.

CHAPTER EIGHT

Germany, 1911

In January, 1911, I heard that I had won the senior classical scholarship at University College, Oxford ('Univ.', where my father, my Uncle Louis, my cousin Frank Mendl, and my brother had been undergraduates), and as I had already passed Responsions (the University entrance examination) and was not due to go into residence until October, I had a carefree outlook when I set out for Frankfurt-on-Main. My father had arranged for me to become a 'pensionaire' for six months from a date in January with Frau Sophie Stern[10] at 28 Obermain-Anlage in order to learn some German and to continue my musical studies, and also, frankly, to relax and enjoy myself after my strenuous efforts at Harrow and afterwards. He accompanied me on the journey, particularly as I knew scarcely a word of the language, in order to instal me and to make the acquaintance of the people with whom I was to spend (as it turned out) six of the happiest months of my life. He himself put up at a hotel for two or three nights before returning to London, but on the evening of our arrival we both had supper in Frau Stern's flat. She was a charming, delightful, cultured widowed lady in her sixties, who spoke only a little English and talked the purest German of her native Hanover. The other persons present that evening were her niece by marriage, Hanna Stern, who lived with her invalid mother in the flat below, and a Hungarian boy of about my age called Paul Schanzer, who was studying in the Frankfurt Akademie and who talked fluent English, having been for two terms at a school at Hastings. Hanna also talked good English, though was possibly surpassed in this respect by her mother, Frau Doktor Stern (widow of a doctor of medicine), who, just because she had long been confined to an invalid's chair, had had time to become extremely well-read and was familiar with most of the works of Shakespeare and Dickens, for instance, in English. I did not meet 'Frau Doktor' until later; my father

[10] An acquaintance had given him the introduction.

did not have the opportunity of meeting her at all. (The two old ladies were the widows of two brothers). Paul, an extremely intelligent, cultured, amusing and charming fellow, was courteous enough to accompany my father and me back to the hotel after the evening was over, and then he and I returned to the flat, where he also was a 'paying guest'. Hanna, with whom both he and I became great friends, was 25—seven years older than myself; she was a devoted daughter, a professional artist in drawing, book plates, 'petits points' and other work, and was also just as cultured generally as the two older ladies, a great lover of music, and a very charming young woman. My father took a great fancy to all the three whom he met that evening, and—as I learnt afterwards—they (not surprisingly!) felt the same towards him. The next day, he and I had an interview with the Head of the musical Conservatorium, whose advice, however, was that, as I did not know any German, I should not handicap myself by becoming a student there and trying to learn the piano and harmony in a language with which I could not hope to become familiar for some weeks or months, but should take music lessons as a private pupil from one of their professors, who was English, but had lived in Frankfurt for sixteen years. This alternative worked out well in practice, and I myself arranged for my teacher to speak to me in German as soon as I was sufficiently acquainted with it. Before my father returned to London, he took me to a performance of Offenbach's *The Tales of Hoffman* at the municipal opera house, which we both enjoyed: I have always found this opera attractive on the several subsequent occasions that I have been to it. I practised the piano daily at Obermain-Anlage. Frau Stern used to teach me German, in my bed-sitter, for a period every morning, and together we read such things as the First Part of Goethe's *Faust*, his *Egmont* and various of his lyrics, and also Ibsen's *Doll's House* in a German version.

Another English boy (Loftus Benjamin) arrived as a 'p.g.' soon after I did, and we were naturally thrown together a good deal, as the others all had their different occupations in the afternoons. He and I often went for a swim in the indoor *Schwimmbad*, and afterwards to tea at the *Palmgarten*, where a small orchestra played mostly light music such as selections from Viennese operettas, but nearly all of it good in quality, and sometimes short works of a more serious kind, such as Beethoven's *Egmont* overture. Loftus was a pleasant boy, of excellent character, not nearly so keen

45

on music as I was, but nevertheless capable of enjoying a visit to the opera. The only disadvantage of our companionship was that it inevitably impeded our learning the German language. Even Paul had to be pulled up by me sometimes for talking English: he spoke his native language, and German, and English with equal facility, and it must have seemed unnatural to a Hungarian to address an Englishman in German.

There was also a French *pensionaire* at Frau Stern's, but he was somewhat younger than we three other boys were, and not very intelligent; he was at school daily, and we did not see much of him except at meals.

Paul, Loftus, and I used to assemble in Hanna's room pretty regularly after lunch for about an hour, when we talked about almost everything that interested us.

During my stay in Frankfurt, I took full advantage of the opportunities of hearing music. I always went in very cheap seats, and was thus able to go to about thirty concerts before the season ended in the spring, and about fifty operatic performances in the five months: the season at the opera house lasted until a month before I left in the summer, when it closed for the annual four weeks' holiday. I used to get a reserved ticket at the opera for 1 mark 60 pfennigs, or even for 1 mark in the gallery! I not only heard and saw operas which I had never witnessed before, but some which unfortunately I have had little or no opportunity to see since then, such as Weber's charming *Oberon* (as well as *Der Freischütz*), Humperdinck's *Königskinder,* and Johan Strauss's *Der Zigeunerbaron* (which I have always enjoyed just as much as, or even more than, *Die Fledermaus*—I suppose, because it is more romantic!). I was present at the first Frankfurt performance of Richard Strauss's *Der Rosenkavalier*, which at a first hearing I did not much like. My greatest operatic joys at Frankfurt were Beethoven's *Fidelio*, which I had never heard before and to which I went four times, and the only two Mozart operas that were available while I was in Germany—*Figaro* and *Die Zauberflöte* (*The Magic Flute*), each of which I also witnessed four times: one of these performances of *Die Zauberflöte* was in Munich and remained unsurpassed—in fact, I think, unequalled in my experience—to this day: the singing, orchestra and production were all superb, and there was the only consummate *Queen of the Night* that I have ever heard—a soprano named Bosetti, who treated the *coloratura* with the fury that Mozart intended, and not, as so many do, merely as an opportunity for pyrotechnics. Hanna, Paul, Loftus and I had all gone to Munich for the Whitsun weekend; we visited the great picture galleries, spent a day on one of the Bavarian lakes near the city, amid magnificent scenery, and frequented the little *Simplicissimus* cabaret, which was great fun; we also heard a Cherubini Mass in one of the churches, but I do not now remember much about it.

I had arrived in Germany an anti-Wagnerian, and I must say that Frau Stern and Hanna were very tolerant with me! In spite of my feelings, I went to two Wagner operas while I was in Frankfurt—*Tannhäuser*, which I had not yet heard and which I found boring (an opinion that I have long since reversed), and *Die Meistersinger*, because Hanna was anxious that I should give it a trial on German soil. I pointed out to her that the performances which I had heard in London had been under Richter, with first-rate singers and a first-rate orchestra; and actually the Frankfurt one was not up to that level. My antipathy to the works of that great genius continued for many years.

Mengelberg was conductor at the symphony concerts in those days, and of course Beethoven was my hero; but I was greatly attracted to the orchestral works of Bach, Handel (the *Concerti grossi*), Haydn, Mozart and Schubert, and interested in hearing Mahler's Fourth Symphony for the first time; and I very much enjoyed Schumann's *Paradies und die Peri*—a rarity which I have never met since.

The performance of the *St. Matthew Passion* in the enormous 'Festhalle', mentioned in the preceding chapter, was not ideal: the acoustics of the place were lamentable: the sound seemed to wander round the edge of the circle in which we all sat, until eventually it reached our ears!

But I must recall my greatest concert hall excitements in Germany. Eugene Ysaye and Raoul Pugno gave a violin and piano recital, at which they played the Franck sonata, one of Mozart's and Beethoven's *Kreutzer*. This was to be the first of several occasions on which I heard these two great artists perform together. I had three ever memorable experiences at Wiesbaden, which was only about forty minutes' train journey away from Frankfurt. Carl Schuricht was to conduct Beethoven's *Missa Solemnis* there—'im Grossen Saale des Kurhauses—prachtvoll!', as Frau Stern said—and she introduced me to a friend of hers who was a member of the choir; by this means, after I had attended both the *Hauptprobe* (final rehearsal) in the morning, and the evening performance of that sublime work—which I was hearing for the first time—I was invited to the supper given to all the performers afterwards. Carl Schuricht walked round and spoke to the guests, and when he came to me, I rose, clinked glasses with him, and toasted Beethoven in champagne! It was a great performance, and it is wonderful to think that he continued to conduct the *Missa Solemnis* as an octogenarian, after World War II!

The other two Wiesbaden occasions were concerts conducted by Nikisch. The first was all Tchaikovsky—*Romeo and Juliet*, the Theme and Variations from the Suite in G, and the Fifth Symphony. I have never heard these performances equalled, and even those blasé English critics who have been known to decry that Symphony, in terms with which I profoundly disagree, would, I believe, have been moved by Nikisch's interpretation. The other Nikisch concert was one of the greatest musical experiences of my life: it was devoted to Beethoven—the Eighth Symphony, the Third *Leonora* overture, and the *C minor*. Nikisch electrified the orchestra in the *Eighth*; as for the *Leonora*, I thought the roof would come off! It was tremendous in its effect. Then, after the interval, man's victorious tussle with Fate was blazed forth to us in all the glory of the Fifth Symphony. Nikisch performed every 'repeat', even the one in the Finale, which only Klemperer has also done in my experience. But the chief thing that impressed me about him was that he produced these glorious performances by means of the slightest gestures imaginable. My Frankfurt music teacher told me that he had played the viola under Nikisch with only one rehearsal, and that that great conductor's secret was that by sheer personality he literally magnetized the orchestra.

The last great Frankfurt excitement was the final concert of the season, when Mengelberg conducted a Beethoven programme consisting of the First and Ninth Symphonies. Again I went (alone) to the *Hauptprobe* in the morning and to the evening performance in company with Hanna and the other two boys. The morning session was the longer of the two, and I refreshed myself with a swim in the afternoon. The combination of these two works makes an excellent scheme (which I have heard on subsequent occasions), and of course I was swept off my feet by the sublimities of *The Ninth*, as I always am to this day.

Eventually my happy stay came to a close; this was, however, not to be 'goodbye' but only 'au revoir' to the Stern family and

48

Paul, for I received a charming invitation from the latter to spend a fortnight with his parents and brother in Hungary the next summer, and this also enabled me to see the three Stern ladies again on my way there and back.

Meanwhile, late in July 1911, before I left German soil to join my parents at Wengen, in Switzerland, where they were to have a summer holiday, I spent ten very pleasant days with Frau Stern at a lovely spot in the Black Forest.

There are two impressions of a general kind which have always remained with me from my sojourn in Germany in 1911. The first is that, though the enjoyment of serious music of course occupied a far larger place in the life of the people than it did in England in those days, it was a mistake to assume that they were *all* really musical—even the highly educated and cultured ones; and in this connection I was surprised to hear some members of the audience at concerts in the stalls talking while the music was being performed! I do not remember encountering this in our own country, and it occurred to me that though the love of music was far more widespread in Germany than here, the small minority in England who went to concerts at all were all ardent music lovers, indeed that there existed here an unsurpassedly *musical* proportion of our population, tiny though it then was.

My other general impression was unconnected with music. I told my parents when I rejoined them that I was convinced that Germany was heading towards war. The majority of the people were too docile: that was just the danger; they seemed to lack a political sense and to have no democratic instincts; they obeyed implicitly anyone in any kind of uniform, and seemed almost to be in awe even of tramway conductors and railway officials! I witnessed army officers pushing civilians (even old ladies) out of their way, as they swaggered along the pavement. The ruling classes, the military, were, in those days, distinctly aggressive. It all seemed to fit in with what I had read in our English Press about the writings of Treitschke and Bernhardi, and the German idea that 'ein guter, frischer Krieg' ('a good, fresh war') was a desirable thing—not to mention the Agadir incident, which occurred while I was in Germany and which caused my father to write to me 'All the same, I do not propose to recall my Ambassador from Frankfurt!'

One of the first things that I did when I went up to 'Univ.' was to join the Oxford University Officers Training Corps.

CHAPTER NINE

Oxford, from 1911 until World War I

I went up to 'Univ.' in October, 1911, and started reading Honour Classical Moderations, with the brilliant and kindly Dr A. B. Poynton as my tutor. From the start, I revelled in the opportunity to read the whole of Homer's *Iliad* and *Odyssey*, and Virgil again, to study Greek Drama and at any rate a few more of the great Athenian tragedies and Aristotle's 'Poetics' but became sorry that Poynton persuaded me to take Theocritus rather than a selection of the plays of Aristophanes. I put up with having to do translations into Greek and Latin prose and verse, and regretted having to read so many speeches of Cicero and even Demosthenes.

There were 140 graduates at the College, and about 3,600 in the whole University. Oxford was a small, peaceful 'city' in those days, with horse-drawn trams in the High Street and very few motor cars to disturb one's enjoyment of its tranquillity and the beauty of its buildings. At 'Univ.' it was usual for men to form themselves by a quite natural and spontaneous process into 'sets' of about a dozen friends of their own 'year', though they often had also, as I had, individual friends outside their particular 'set'; moreover, all the scholars and exhibitioners of the college dined together at a special table in Hall, and this automatically brought me into contact with some individuals senior or junior to myself. I made some of the best friends of my life at 'Univ.', but, alas!, a high proportion of them were killed in World War I, and many, too, have pre-deceased me since then. Alfred Foster, a charming and handsome fellow, and an immediate contemporary of mine, was a good amateur pianist, with a special 'penchant' for Chopin, whose works he used often to play on the hired piano which I installed in my room. (He was to be one of the war victims). Otherwise, the only *really* musical man among my close friends

50

in the college was Guy Garrod, who was a year senior to me. He was, I think, the most versatile man I have ever known. Having been head boy at Bradfield, he was a classical scholar of 'Univ.', acted leading parts in the Oxford University Dramatic Society, rowed in the college 'Eight' at a time when 'Univ.' rowing was at its height (the college went to head of the river in the 'Eights' in the summer term of 1914), shot for the 'Varsity, was a half-blue in the cross-country running, and played the violin, in addition to the piano. He performed in a string quartet at the Oxford University Musical Union, which in those days was only a performing society and which I did not join; the Oxford University Musical Club was a separate institution, giving weekly chamber music concerts or piano recitals performed by professionals; Guy and I were both members of the latter, and we remained close friends until his death in January, 1965. He became a regular R.A.F. officer after World War I, and rose to great eminence in it, ending up as Air Chief Marshal, with honours thick upon him. He remained his gallant, charming, modest self always; and everywhere he went on service, he took his violin with him and kept up his playing. After World War II, he and I had several delightful concert and operatic experiences together.

Frederick Beechman (nicknamed 'Beechers' and elder brother of N. A. Beechman, who was at Balliol and who later in life attained some distinction in politics) was a cultured, highly intelligent, amusing and popular member of my little 'set'. He was a Modern History scholar. He, too, had a taste for serious music, and a pleasant singing voice. I used to do my best at accompanying him on my hired piano in some of the less difficult songs of Schumann. He survived the war, in which he became a major in the Machine Gun Corps and won the M.C., but died in the great influenza epidemic soon afterwards.

By the way, that piano had a surprising adventure one night! Someone was having a 21st birthday in the college, and a bunch of guests in their hilarity thought it would be rather a joke to remove my piano from my first-floor room across the Quadrangle to 'a certain place'. It so happened that I was extraordinarily tired that night, and went on sleeping in my adjoining little bedroom in complete unconsciousness of the disturbance going on next door! When I emerged from my slumber next morning and went into the sitting room I was astonished to find that the piano was missing from its place. I asked the 'scout' (college servant) whether he knew where it was. 'Well, Sir', he replied with some hesitation, 'it's in the lavatory, Sir!' So, immediately after breakfast, I made my way to the college lavatories, which in those days consisted of two rows of W.C's facing one another, with a space between, in the southern precincts of the college, and there, sure enough, was the (upright grand) piano, upon which, without more ado, I played Chopin's Funeral March, standing up. I am glad to say that the instrument had suffered no more damage than a few scratches.

Noel G. Salvesen (known as 'Sonny' to his friends) and his cousin, Max Salvesen (a son of Lord Salvesen, the Scottish judge) were, both of them, Gilbert and Sullivan enthusiasts; and as I had the piano-vocal scores of most of the 'G. & S.' operas, 'Sonny' used to delight in singing many of the solo songs from them to my amateurish accompaniment in my room: it didn't matter for what pitch of voice they were written; he was 'game' for singing soprano, contralto, tenor or bass songs in his firm, baritone voice with equal zest. And there were frequently other members of our little 'coterie' there, ready to join in any choruses. The Salvesens were two of many former members of Edinburgh Academy who came up to Univ. 'Sonny' was a classical scholar of my year, with rooms on the same staircase as mine, and a fine athlete. He was in the college Rugger XV the year we won the inter-college cup, and only narrowly missed getting his 'Blue'. He was a delightful, exceedingly popular man. Max was a very good-looking, charming, attractive fellow, and beautifully dressed when the occasion demanded it. He and Atheling Boustead and George Robinson (another Old Harrovian) were very close friends of one another. Max and Atheling were among those who laid down their lives in World War I.

Both of the Salvesen cousins were my companions—as were others—at performances by the D'Oyly Carte Opera Company, which used to visit Oxford for two weeks including Eights Week, every summer term. Such was the demand by undergraduates for seats, that the college messenger would queue for tickets from about 3 a.m. until the Box Office at the New Theatre opened, on behalf of all the undergraduates who wanted them. I cannot pretend, in retrospect, that the orchestral playing was of a very high order or worthy of Sullivan's masterly and delicate scoring, but those were the days of Henry Lytton as leading comedian, Fred Billington in the parts 'created' by Rutland Barrington such as Pooh-Bah and others, and Olive Turner who charmed all of us in

University College, Oxford—from an old print in the author's possession

Dorothy, in 1925, shortly before her marriage to the author

the chief soprano rôles.

In all these ways, I became familiar, in the course of those three years, with all the Gilbert and Sullivan operas (except *Ruddigore* which was not revived until 1921) from *Trial by Jury* to *The Gondoliers* inclusive, and have never ceased to love them.

H. M. D. Parker ('Michael') was at Hertford College, but often came to Univ. to see 'Sonny', who had been at Edinburgh Academy with him and who was secretly engaged to, and subsequently married, Michael's youngest sister. Thereby I became very friendly with the Parker family; Michael himself was a music lover, and another of his sisters, Denne, was a professional mezzo-soprano and a fine artist. My wife and I have kept up with them since. Denne, as a widowed lady (Mrs Gilkes), has become a well-known and popular person at Stratford-upon-Avon, where she has taught elocution by means of singing lessons to successive members of the Royal Shakespeare Company.

> In a frivolous demeanour
> We had tea at the Cadena;
> We would see and hear Miss Dando
> In her famous 'rallentando',
> With her finely pointed chin
> Pressed against her violin,
> Swaying coyly to and fro
> To the rhythm of her bow—
> Tea-time music by Moskovsky,
> Grieg and—what is more—Tchaikovsky;
> Yes, we certainly got pleasure
> In the moments of our leisure,
> As we ate our toasted scone,
> Dainty cakes with icing on;
> Sipping tea, with nought to fret,
> While we smoked a cigarette.
> Listen to the little band, oh!
> What a joy was our Miss Dando!
> (I should whisper, at this stage,
> She was of uncertain age).

There were three 'venues' for hearing serious music in my Oxford experience. At the Musical Club, in its premises in the High Street, I got to know many of the great works of chamber music—quartets

53

by Haydn, quartets and quintets of Mozart, all the Beethoven quartets and a large assortment of the chamber music of Schubert, Schumann, Dvořák, and Brahms. We had visits from the English and the London String Quartets, and as members of the club were asked to show hospitality to them I had the pleasure and privilege of entertaining Ivor James and Felix Salmond, the respective cellists of those two bodies, at dinner in the Univ. Hall, before the concerts. Donald Tovey several times gave piano recitals, invariably including a Beethoven sonata, and also participated in chamber music. I heard the Bach concertos for two and for three klaviers performed with only a few strings, in the chamber music fashion.

Then there were the Balliol Concerts on Sunday evenings, run by Dr Ernest Walker, who frequently officiated at the piano himself. My chief recollections of these are the performances by Myra Hess, then a stocky, handsome young woman, with a talent for the piano which even at that time almost amounted to genius; by Irene Scharrer, a pianist of a rather gentler, more restrained type; and by the sisters May and Beatrice Harrison, so gifted on the violin and the 'cello respectively. We thus enjoyed most of the standard sonatas for violin or 'cello and piano in the course of my time at Oxford.

At the Town Hall, there were occasional choral or orchestral concerts, and two great and famous pianists gave recitals there, Teresa Carreño, who was one of the finest all-round performers on the instrument that I have ever heard, and Paderewsky, who was magnificent in Chopin, but whom I was perhaps presumptuous at my age in thinking not at all outstanding in the works of other composers.

My only other musical activity that occurred at Oxford itself (apart from my own humble efforts on the piano when I was alone), was a small start in musical journalism. One of my Univ. friends, Edgar MacWilliam, began editing a magazine called *The Tripod*, and he invited me to write an article for it. I complied, with one on *The Jena Symphony* (a work attributed by some to Beethoven), and he was good enough to accept another from me later on, entitled *The Drum in Beethoven*. The only significance of these was that they were literally my first, elementary, modest publications about music. 'Mac' was a charming, artistic man, who shared an attractive sitting room in 'No. 90 High Street' (a building adjoining Univ., owned by the college, and used as an overflow), with Philip Shaw, a loyal friend of sterling character who had a steady-

54

ing influence on the vague, art-loving 'Mac'. They had been friends at Charterhouse previously. Philip was subsequently killed on the Western front: his younger brother, Patrick, was at Balliol and survived his war service; as a keen music-lover, he became a frequent companion of mine at concerts after World War I. 'Mac', after his service in that war, became a schoolmaster, joined the administrative staff of the R.A.F. in World War II and was killed in his middle age, being in an aeroplane which was shot down in the Channel after observing the Dieppe raid in the course of his duty.

The three annual terms at Oxford occupied only 24 weeks of the year. We were all expected to spend part of the vacations studying for our examinations. I used to take a quarter or third of the vacation time as a complete holiday, and allot a regular six hours a day to work during the rest of the time. There were, of course, ample opportunities for enlarging my musical experience in London. For example, Ysaye and Pugno performed all the Beethoven violin and piano sonatas in chronological order, at Queen's Hall, and I heard these in the company of my cousin Joan Elkin,[11] who was still only in her early or middle 'teens. These were lovely concerts, but there was a dash of amusement in them too, for Ysaye used sometimes to prod the white-bearded Pugno to walk a little faster on to the platform and generally seemed to enjoy gently 'ragging' him! I remember that I used to speak of them as 'I say and Pugnose'!

At various stages of my life, I have had what the Germans would, I suppose, call a *schwärm*, a kind of passion, for one particular composer, whose works I had not 'discovered' before. But the difference between my feeling and the typical *schwärm* is that in my case it has come to stay, to take its permanent place, as it were, beside my loves for the music of other great composers. It was during my Oxford period that my affections were first aroused in this form for the art of Brahms. Not only did I hear and enjoy a lot of his superb chamber music at the Musical Club, but the Third Symphony and in due course the three others and the concertos, in London, at this stage of my life. I remember the time when the Fourth Symphony was looked upon as a difficult and puzzling work, but I first heard it under Fritz Steinbach, who was a great advocate of the Brahms symphonies, and in con-

[11] Joan later married Alan Green, who attained distinction in the Indian Civil Service, and received a knighthood. He, too, was a keen music lover.

sequence I loved it from then onwards. I wrote to my grand-mother in the course of my first Brahms enthusiasm, that I felt as if a new world had opened up before me—only less wonderful than that revealed by the glorious Beethoven himself.

In order to continue or complete the narrative about my Frankfurt friends contained in the previous chapter, I must record here briefly that I travelled to Munich in the summer of 1912, changing 'en route' at Frankfurt, where Frau Stern met me for lunch and a chat in the station; Hanna was in Munich, in the company of the charming man whom she subsequently married, a fellow-artist named Mateo Cristiani; after a few days with them there, I went on to Vienna, where I missed my connection for Budapest and found time to drive round the city but not to enter any of the buildings; I had a delightful stay with Paul Schanzer and his parents at Budapest, and also at Trencsen, in the Southern Carpathians, with him and his elder brother and family; then, a few days at Frankfurt with Frau Stern, 'Frau Doktor', and Hanna : this was to be the last time I was to see them, though I kept up a correspondence with Hanna until World War I broke out, heard news of them during that war through her brother who was a doctor resident in Switzerland, and resumed occasional letters with Hanna between the wars. To complete this particular picture, 'Frau Doktor' died at 86 shortly before World War II; Mateo Cristiani was forbidden to exhibit his pictures anywhere in Germany during the Nazi régime because his wife, Hanna, was of Jewish blood (though he was not); and when I wrote to her after World War II to ask for news of them and of Frau Stern, I received a reply from him to say that Hanna had died of cancer during the war, and that he was living quietly and working at his art; he did not mention Frau Stern, whose death, at an advanced age, I presumed to have taken place. My only other meeting with Paul Schanzer was when he and his charming wife visited London after World War I for the British Empire Exhibition and dined with my parents and me at their flat. None of these matters relates (except by association) to music, but I mention them for the sake of continuity.

I travelled back from Frankfurt in 1912 direct to Perth—pausing in London at home only for an early morning bath—and went on the following day to Strathpeffer to join my parents and grandmother on their holiday in the Highlands.

In the spring of 1913 I succeeded in getting a First Class in 'Honour Mods' by the narrowest squeak possible. That seemed to indicate that on the one hand I had worked very hard (being not at all a brilliant person, I have always had to do this in order to achieve anything), but that on the other hand I had not done an hour too much!

For the 'Greats' Final examination ('Literae Humaniores') I had as tutor in Ancient History G. H. Stevenson, an attractive and amusing Scotsman who was also a music lover and a good amateur organist; and in philosophy, E. F. Carritt, a good-looking man, with a fine, penetrating mind, whose excellent book 'The Theory of Beauty' has helped to fill for me a gap which the 'Greats' curriculum left blank, on the subject of aesthetics: I have found it recurrently valuable in my humble literary efforts concerning music.

In the Long Vacation of that year, my mother and I sailed for Buenos Aires, in order to join my father and return with him. He had had to go there early in the year, to relieve his partner (my second cousin Frank Mendl) who had not had a holiday in England for a considerable time. We were able to go ashore 'en route' at Lisbon, Madeira, Rio de Janeiro, and Santos, for a few hours each—which we found most interesting and attractive. My brother was also working in the B.A. office of 'Mendl & Co.' I could do no work for 'Greats' on the voyage, but I had taken some books with me, and read Plato and Herodotus in my bedroom on the top floor of the hotel. There was nothing much else for me to do in the day-time anyhow, but I went three times to the Colon Opera House in the evening—with my mother to a very good performance of Massenet's *Manon*, and to a lavish production of Weber's *Oberon* which easily surpassed those at Frankfurt, and (by myself) to my first experience of *Parsifal*: the copyright ban on performances of this work outside Bayreuth did not apply in South America, and in spite of my continuing anti-Wagnerism I was glad to avail myself of the chance of hearing and seeing it: since then, I have done so many times at Covent Garden.

In the course of the first half of 1914, the family firm encountered certain commercial difficulties. My father had always brought me up from boyhood with the idea of becoming a barrister (I think in some ways he regretted having left the Bar himself). I had not enjoyed my efforts at speaking in the Harrow Debating Society, and I never attempted to participate in the Oxford Union debates. Though I had an open mind, I had some doubts about my suitability for advocacy. And when, now, my father suggested that it would be a good idea for me to try to get into the Civil Service on finishing at Oxford, as it might turn out that he and my mother would not be able to support me during the usual long wait for briefs to start coming in at the Bar, I must confess that I seized upon the alternative with alacrity. I was greatly attracted by the thought of serving the community—and also of not having to get up on my feet and speak in court!

Classical 'Mods' and 'Greats', though wide in their scope of philosophy, ancient Greek and Roman History, languages and literature, did not include quite enough subjects to cover the enormous field required for the Civil Service Examination. So I arranged to join a course in English Literature and Psychology at Oxford, due to start in the summer vacation of 1914.

When we happy young men at 'Univ.' wished one another a pleasant vacation in June of that year, little did we think that in many cases it was really goodbye for ever, so far as life on this earth is concerned.

I am, however, now going to present my readers with a violent antithesis. At Oxford I had come to know all that were then available of the most brilliant series of light operas that the world has ever known, my joy in which has lasted all my life. And by the end of this third academic year there, through becoming acquainted with so much of Beethoven's chamber works, in addition to my previous experiences of his other compositions, I had enjoyed the blessing of hearing at least the greater part of the music of that prodigious genius, which has influenced me so deeply throughout the years. Before, therefore, I speak, however briefly, about the terrible disaster which mankind brought upon itself that summer, I am going to devote the next two chapters, first to the subject of Sullivan and Gilbert and then to the personality and art of Beethoven. The pre-war period was over. A very different world presented itself to our agonized gaze from August, 1914, onward. Before I recall in any way the memories of it, let me fortify myself by some reflections on these two completely contrasted manifestations of the art of music.

CHAPTER TEN

Sullivan and Gilbert

Yes, in that order. Not that I regard Gilbert as less important for the final result than Sullivan, but simply because this book is mainly about music and musicians.

Light music is to be found in the works of many of the great masters. But there are certain composers who shone only in light music, and of these the greatest, in my opinion, and certainly the one that I personally love best, is Sullivan. Neither Johann Strauss the younger nor Offenbach, for all their charm and verve and fun, possess the fragrance of Sullivan, the limpidity of his melodies, or the delicacy and mastery of his orchestration. He was largely Irish in origin, but his mother had Italian blood in her veins; he was born and educated at first in London and later studied music in Germany. Be that as it may, there is something specifically British about his music. We are far away from the champagne and the continental night clubs and the 'naughtinesses' of so many of the European counterparts! But he equals them in his wit and charm, which is not the kind of superficial charm that some people can turn on and off at will, but is an outward manifestation of an inward grace.

Perhaps just because the deepest, grandest and most spiritual music of the masters means so much to me, I find an urgent need for the utmost relaxation in the finest light music—and for me this means the comic operas of Gilbert and Sullivan, which only Messager's *Véronique* and *Monsieur Beaucaire* (and not even Lehar's *The Merry Widow*) approach in my affections.

I have lived with 'Gilbert and Sullivan' virtually all my life, and have already referred to some of my early experiences of them. Since my Oxford days I have always kept up with 'G. & S.' performances, which are a never-failing joy to me if they are good and even when—as sometimes—they have only been fairly good. It is, of course, an 'ear-opener' when first-rate artists, such as Elsie Morison, Marjorie Thomas, John Cameron, Owen Brannigan,

Geraint Evans and Richard Lewis, sing isolated numbers of these operas, accompanied by the Royal Philharmonic Orchestra or the B.B.C. Symphony Orchestra, under Sir Malcolm Sargent or his successors, whether in a concert hall at the Proms. or on gramophone records broadcast by radio.

In my middle and old age, I have come to rate certain of the operas more highly than others. The greatest of them, I think, are *Patience* (among earlier ones), *Iolanthe, Princess Ida, The Yeoman of the Guard, The Mikado,* and *The Gondoliers. Trial by Jury, The Sorcerer, H.M.S. Pinafore,* and *The Pirates of Penzance* are delightful too, but both composer and librettist acquired greater subtlety, more originality and character, from *Patience* onwards. (I was glad when *Ruddigore* was revived in 1921). I used to put *The Mikado* at the top of the list, until I dethroned it in favour of *The Gondoliers.* When one is considering operas (whether light or serious), as opposed to instrumental works, one must regard the creation as a whole—both music and libretto; and if I do this from a personal, perhaps rather subjective, standpoint, I find that my enjoyment is slightly impaired by two factors affecting Gilbert's libretti. First, he had a tendency, manifested in several of the operas, to sneer at elderly, unattractive women—which leaves a nasty taste in one's mouth and unfortunately reached its zenith in the portrait of Katisha in *The Mikado.* Secondly, though this is not his fault, the 'book' of *The Mikado* is to a considerable extent taken up with threats of tortures, executions, and being buried alive: *of course* it is all a joke, and there was a time when I, like everyone else, used to think it very funny. In the 1880's when *The Mikado* was produced, Gilbert could regard such things as so remote and fantastic that one could laugh at them in a comic opera, and so did we all for many years; but in our time, both in the Far East and in Europe and elsewhere, millions of innocent people have been tortured and put to death and even—some of them—buried alive; and today, when I see *The Mikado,* I simply cannot enjoy jokes about such horrors which have been only too real in my generation. Its libretto remains as *brilliant* as ever, and its music as enchanting. But nowadays I personally get more unalloyed pleasure, as a whole, out of *Iolanthe, Princess Ida, The Yeomen of the Guard,* and, above all, *The Gondoliers,* than from *The Mikado.*

The little dig at the Fairy Queen in *Iolanthe* for being 'massive' doesn't matter a rap. But there is one important point of production in *The Yeomen*, on which I take, I know, an unorthodox view: Gilbert originally wrote, as a stage direction, that Jack Point at the end of the opera was to 'fall insensible' on the stage, and intended this to be merely a swoon; but it was, I think, George Grossmith (senior), the 'creator' of the part, who suggested to him that it would a more artistic finish to the opera if Point were to fall down dead, from a broken heart; Gilbert agreed, but he never caused the original stage direction to be altered in print. Point's death has become a tradition, and I believe it to be a mistake: *The Yeomen* is more serious than any of the others, but this almost turns it into a tragedy; it is, at most, a tragi-comedy; and the music at this point is pathetic, but not tragic. The right ending, I think, would be for Jack Point to fall in a swoon, but to be revived with burnt feathers by a pretty member of the chorus!

It has often been said that Gilbert's words and Sullivan's music fit one another perfectly. So they do in a sense, or sometimes, or even, perhaps, for the most part. But in a number of instances, this harmony is achieved either through the kindly Sullivan obligingly giving way to the brilliant ironic Gilbert, or by way of a contrast (whether deliberate or not on Sullivan's part) between particularly fine music and witty, caustic words. Examples of the first of these two methods are in some of the patter songs, where the words are paramount and the music keeps pace almost in the background: for instance, the song of the 'modern major-general' in *The Pirates*, and even the Duke of Plaza Toro's first solo 'In enterprise of martial kind' in *The Gondoliers*; or the duet between Bunthorne and Grosvenor in *Patience* where Sullivan's music jogs along with a merely amiable tune, which is all that is wanted to 'set off' Gilbert at his most scintillating ('Francesca da Rimini, mimini, pimini, "Je-ne-sais quoi" young man!', and so on). The second method—in which Sullivan does not give way to Gilbert but provides a strong, simultaneous contrast to him—is to be found in such illustrations as these:— in *Pinafore*, the amusing words

> 'But in spite of all temptations
> To belong to other nations
> He remains an Englishman'

are set by Sullivan to a sincerely stirring, patriotic melody. In *Iolanthe*, Gilbert's satirical words for the entrance and chorus of Peers are submerged in a superb piece of serious choral and orchestral composition by Sullivan[12]; the composer produces one of his loveliest melodies for the Fairy Queen while according to Gilbert she is humorously and allusively singing about the

> '... amorous dove,
> Type of Ovidius Naso!
> This heart of mine
> Is soft as thine,
> Although I dare not say so!'

—and asking whether the Brigade of Captain Shaw (then Head of the Fire Brigade) could

> 'with cold cascade
> Quench my great love, I wonder!'

In the same opera a melody comparable in fervent, patriotic glory and stately majesty to *Rule, Britannia* or *Heart of Oak* is contrasted with Gilbert's extremely funny satire:—

> 'in Good Queen Bess's glorious days,' we are told,
> 'The House of Peers made no pretence
> To intellectual eminence,
> Or scholarship sublime';

in the days of Napoleon and Wellington,

> 'The House of Peers, throughout the war,
> Did nothing in particular,
> And did it very well';
> 'And while the House of Peers withholds
> Its legislative hand,
> And noble statesmen do not itch
> To interfere in matters which
> They do not understand,
> As bright will shine Great Britain's rays
> As in King George's glorious days!'

---

[12] Eric Blom in 'Grove' (5th edition), called this 'a skit on all the grand operatic marches from *Norma, The Prophet* and *Rienzi* to *Aida*.' I disagree: it is no skit; it is a grand march in its own right. (Cf. Thos. F. Dunhill: 'Sullivan's Comic Operas', p. 101.)

Again, Sullivan opens Act II with a charming melody for Private Willis to sing to Gilbert's comic words.

On the other hand, the music is sometimes amusing on its own account: in *The Mikado* the orchestra has brilliantly witty effects in the trio describing the supposed 'execution' of Nankipooh; and in *Iolanthe*, Sullivan is musically ironical as the orchestra plays an exceedingly subtle refrain in a *minor* key at the first entrance of the Lord Chancellor, who proves to be one of Gilbert's most richly comic characters—before that noble lord has uttered a word.

Gilbert's unkindly streak on the subject of elderly spinsters is not reflected in the music. For example, he writes in *Trial by Jury* about 'a rich attorney's elderly, ugly daughter', but Sullivan's melody merely flows on pleasantly without any attempt to express that attitude in any musical form. It is true that Lady Jane's recitative about her 'disappearing beauty' at the beginning of Act II of *Patience* is accompanied by comic grunts on her 'violoncello' (or whatever the instrument really is), but Gilbert's words for the song that follows are perhaps the unkindest that he ever wrote for an ageing spinster; yet Sullivan sets them to a tender, gentle, compassionate melody ('Silver'd is the raven hair' ...).

Gilbert's portrayal of Katisha is unsympathetic, but the character of Sullivan's music in the Finale of Act I of *The Mikado* makes her almost a tragic figure; and in Act II, Koko, after forcing himself to woo her without music, eventually succeeds by singing the famous song *Titwillow*, the music of which is so pathetic as almost to bring tears to one's eyes, though we know that he is really only fulfilling his previous obligation—

> '... to take under my wing, trala,
> A most unattractive old thing, trala,
> With a caricature of a face'.

And even after *Titwillow*, Katisha admits to being 'just a little teeny weeny wee bit bloodthirsty'. Their final duet is musically as merry as can be—but look at Koko's words:—

> 'There is beauty in extreme old age—
> Do you fancy you are elderly enough?
> ... Is a maiden all the better when she's tough?'

> 'Are you old enough to marry, do you think?

63

Won't you wait till you are eighty in the shade?
There's a fascination frantic
In a ruin that's romantic
Do you think you are sufficiently decayed?'

Dame Carruthers, in *The Yeomen of the Guard*, has the most unattractive *character* of all Gilbert's elderly women; but her
unpleasantness is entirely in his libretto. Sullivan does not paint
her in unattractive *musical* colours; she has no sinister-sounding
passages to sing; on the contrary, her one great song with the
chorus of Yeomen, in Act I, is a fine, stirring, majestic melody,
and none of the music that she sings in concert with other persons in the drama discloses her unpleasant nature in the slightest
degree; and when at the end Sergeant Merrill braces himself to
ask 'the old witch'—as he had previously called her—to marry
him (really in order to hush up his complicity in Fairfax's escape),
and she accepts, they break into what is musically a happy duet,
'Rapture, rapture', in spite of all the mixed feelings that its words
convey. It is almost Koko and Katisha again!

We are not here concerned with Gilbert's personal character.
But we do know that Sullivan, who portrayed a very wide range
of emotions in these light operas of his, and who composed so
many lovely, sometimes touching and pathetic melodies as well
as joyous or witty ones, but who apparently could not—or anyhow did not—follow Gilbert's sinister or caustic lead in musical
terms, was himself a most lovable and charming person, loved
and admired by his contemporaries, and able to compose gay and
enchanting strains in spite of great pain and ill-health throughout
his life, which he concealed from all save his closest friends under
a demeanour of buoyancy, cheerfulness and humour. He was so
devoted to his parents and elder brother that he was broken-hearted
at their deaths (his father's and brother's were premature). He
charmed everybody, except the company of the Savoy Theatre,
who did not see so much of him as of Gilbert—though he was
always courteous to them and very generous to individual artists.
As he grew wealthy, he developed a love of gambling.

Hesketh Pearson[13] thought that Sullivan probably had Jewish
blood in his veins, and that his sense of 'isolation' and 'adaptability'
and devotion to his family were due to this. He also says that
Sullivan had 'a strong feminine strain in him', which was why

[13] *Gilbert and Sullivan* (1935).

'his best work was only produced under the spell of a dominating and masculine personality—Gilbert, as it happened, thought it might have been Irving: for he transmitted Irving's own 'croaks' into just what that great man wanted as incidental music for *Macbeth* and in fact was the perfect medium.' In middle age he became intimate with Mrs Ronalds, the American beauty who lived apart from her husband and was a great friend of the Empress Eugénie, and she had immense influence over him.

There was another conflict in Sullivan's career, besides the one which he had to wage against illness. He constantly hankered after composing serious music—symphonies or oratorios or 'grand opera' —and was urged by Queen Victoria herself and various newspaper critics to do so. Yet neither *The Golden Legend* nor *Ivanhoe* has survived in performance. And the explanation is not far to seek. Sullivan had no exceptional gifts for symphony or for such works as those, and in that field he was—or would have been—competing, so to speak, against some of the greatest geniuses in musical history. But his talent for light opera was so outstanding as to amount to genius. In this 'genre', at any rate, he could outshine all those who participated in it or who have attempted it since. This may have been a disappointment to him; but the world has cause to be grateful for the fact that in Gilbert he found the ideal artistic collaborator; their temperaments were so far apart that they could never be close friends, and, indeed, were at times estranged by some petty difference or quarrel, even though they were ultimately reconciled.

Sullivan, for all the apparent simplicity of his music, was a subtle composer, and a clever parodist. For instance, he parodied Handel in *Trial by Jury* (the jurymen's 'He'll tell us how he came to be a judge') and in *Princess Ida* ('This helmet, I suppose' in Act III); and Donizetti's sextet in Act II of *Lucia* in *Trial by Jury* ('A nice dilemma'). And he wittily quoted from Bach's *Great* organ fugue in G minor in the orchestral accompaniment of the *Mikado's* solo song.

In spite of all this, Arthur Jacobs in his book *Gilbert and Sullivan* (1951) declares that 'both then and now ... the Gilbert and Sullivan operas have appealed more to ordinary theatre-goers than to musical specialists' and that 'Gilbert and Sullivan audiences were mainly of play-goers, not opera-goers'.

Neither Mr Jacobs nor I was alive at the time of the original productions, but these two statements of his are, I suggest, misleading. Theatre-goers and *lovers of serious music*, at any rate, are not divided into watertight compartments. Many of the latter love 'the theatre' too. And there are plenty of them, including many distinguished professional musicians, who love 'G. and S.' For example, Ernest Newman, the greatest musical critic of his generation, devoted a whole series of enthusiastic articles to them in *The Sunday Times* and wrote of 'the glorious *Gondoliers*'. Francis Toye, author of two important books on Verdi and Rossini and former musical critic of *The Morning Post*, was a 'G. and S.' 'fan'. His brother, Geoffrey, not only conducted the 'G. and S.' operas at the Prince's Theatre but also serious operas at Covent Garden. Thomas F. Dunhill, a talented composer, was the author of a very good book *Sullivan's Comic Operas*. Sir Malcolm Sargent conducted many revivals of 'G. and S.' at the Savoy Theatre, was well-known as a lover of them, and performed 'G. and S.' concerts at the Proms. annually for many years. The various excellent artists mentioned earlier in this chapter, have not only sung excerpts from them on these occasions with obvious relish and recorded them for the gramophone, but are also famous in opera and oratorio. Witness, too, the Sadler's Wells peformances of *Iolanthe* and *The Mikado*, in which the same artists who normally interpreted great serious operas, ancient and modern, delighted to take part in those Gilbert and Sullivan works after the expiry of the Gilbert copyright enabled them to do so. I know scores and scores of keen lovers of serious music who revel in the lilt and beauty of Sullivan's music and its masterly and delicate orchestration and craftmanship. Indeed, it would be ridiculous if it were not so. Serious music lovers on the Continent love the light operas of Johann Strauss and Offenbach, and Weinberger's *Schwanda the Bagpiper*. Why on earth should not their opposite numbers in the English-speaking countries enjoy these brilliant and accomplished English comic operas, which, I suggest, are superior even to their foreign counterparts? *The Mikado* (always) and *Iolanthe* (more recently) have been popular also in certain continental countries too (and the whole series, in the U.S.A.) The others could, even at this stage, also find favour abroad. The point is, they are *works of art*, which have survived the test of time and continue to appeal to successive generations; they are not like the ephemeral 'musicals', English or American, which are here today and gone tomorrow.

It may be naughty of me, but I look upon it as a mark of a really great critic that he appreciates first-class, artistic, light music, and not only serious compositions—that he can feel the 'greatness' of 'great' light music such as Sullivan's. In one sense, it should be obvious to a 'musical specialist' that Bach, Mozart, Beethoven and the rest are great composers; critics may be able to throw interesting light on the works of these tremendous geniuses, and often do so, but they would soon lose their status if they did not perceive that *these* men are great; at least one real test of a good, broadminded, musical critic is whether he *also* appreciates the artistry of a Sullivan. Most of them pay tribute to Johann Strauss, as Brahms did, and even to some of Offenbach; yet as orchestrators, both of these are inferior to Sullivan, and a lot of Offenbach's music (apart from *Tales of Hoffman*) is trivial, compared to the infinite charm, fragrance and wit of Sullivan's. The audiences at the Promenade Concerts are predominantly youthful, and tremendously keen on serious music; is it to be supposed that those who have crowded the 'G. and S.' Proms are 6,000 entirely different individuals from those who flocked to the others? Of course not! A love of great, serious music and of the great, light music of Sullivan also, is to be found in the hearts of most healthy-minded music lovers. I am glad to say that I adore 'G. and S.' as much as ever! This adoration is fully compatible with my love for the music of the various great composers discussed in this book.

CHAPTER ELEVEN

Beethoven: controversy and glory

Prometheus is one of the heroes whose story, in different forms, has permeated Western culture from many centuries before Christ down to the 20th century A.D. It has haunted the imaginations of Hesiod, Aeschylus, Servius, Apollodorus, Ovid, Horace, Pausanias, Goethe, Beethoven, Shelley, Schubert, Hugo Wolf, Liszt, and Skriabin. In the *Theogony* of Hesiod (8th century B.C.) Prometheus was a son of the Titan, Iapetus, by Clymene; when Zeus hid fire from men, he went to Olympus and stole it, carried it down to earth in a fennel-stalk (a practice followed in modern times on certain Greek islands) and gave it to mankind. Zeus had originally turned against the human race because, when gods and men met at Mecone to decide what portions of slain animals the gods should receive in sacrifice, Prometheus arranged the best parts of the ox, covered with offal, in one heap, and made a second heap of the bones, artfully concealed with fat, and then invited Zeus to choose which he preferred. Zeus chose the bones and fat: being omniscient, he may have realised that Prometheus intended him to choose the worst portion, but could not protect himself against the risk of doing so. In revenge, Zeus withheld fire from mankind. Prometheus, philanthropically, stole it from him, and then Zeus punished him by chaining him to a rock, and sent an eagle to gnaw his liver every day, the liver being miraculously restored overnight. He was finally rescued by Heracles, who shot the eagle. Zeus permitted this, to let Heracles win fame, and eventually had a reconciliation, though a somewhat uneasy one, with Prometheus.

In Asychylus (*Prometheus Bound*), Prometheus is not a half-Titan, but a god, a prophet, a suffering hero, the friend of mankind, the teacher of arts, crafts and sciences, and, above all, the giver of fire. He is temporarily overmastered by the superior will of Zeus, but will not yield. He had originally helped Zeus against the Titans, but turned against him when Zeus, flushed with victory, planned to destroy the whole human race. Since he had defied Zeus, Prometheus was chained to a rock in Scythia: Hermes visits him and tells him to reveal what marriage threatens Zeus's throne, but Prometheus refuses to say, so Zeus flings him into Tartarus. (Ultimately Prometheus is brought up again, this time to the Caucasus, and is tormented by the eagle—a punishment to end only if some other god were to offer to take his place in Hades—which the incurably wounded Cheiron does.)

Another version, preserved by Servius and Apollodorus, and hinted at by Aeschylus, says that Zeus himself released Prometheus, who had warned Zeus that the woman he must avoid was the sea-nymph, Thetis.

Goethe's great ode is an extract from an unfinished drama begun in 1773-4, and makes Prometheus the son of Zeus, neither a god nor a Titan, nor a man, but the immortal prototype of man as the original rebel and affirmer of his fate, the original inhabitant of the earth, seen as an anti-god, as Lord of the Earth.

Beethoven was inspired by the Prometheus idea even in his early days. He composed a simple, charming melody which first appears in his ballet *The Men of Prometheus*, next becomes the theme of his so-called *Eroica* variations for pianoforte (op. 35)— still in his 'First Period'—and lastly is the theme on which the variations in the Finale of the *Eroica* Symphony (No. 3) are built. This was the first of his symphonies composed after Beethoven himself said (in 1802) that he was starting 'on a new road', and it was associated in the first place not only with the idea of Napoleon as a heroic benefactor of mankind (in accordance with Beethoven's *original* misconception of him) but with Prometheus: the simple theme of the Finale marks the elementary beginnings with which the hero started, and rises with increasing variety, complexity and grandeur to the apotheosis of the *Poco Andante*.[14]

It was perfectly natural that the Prometheus conception should have been a vital element in Beethoven, both as man and artist. Evidently Prometheus and unselfish heroism were connected in his mind. And his own character was Promethean and heroic. Just as politically he was a mighty republican, so in his art he was the great revolutionary composer, who brought untold riches and benefit to the souls of music lovers in all lands and for all time; the fiery creator, who introduced *fire* into *instrumental* art, which

[14] See my books 'The Soul of Music', p. 79, and 'The Divine Quest in Music', pp. 82-3.

previously had been tender, melancholy, grief-laden, joyous, energetic, witty, exquisite and delicate, even though it had also been majestic and sublime. Only the vocal music of his predecessors had, at times, actually been *fiery* in character—for instance in the aria 'Why do the nations ...?' in Handel's *Messiah* or the 'smiting of the first born' chorus in *Israel in Egypt*, or Bach's 'Thunder and Lightning' chorus in the *St. Matthew Passion*. Beethoven was a hero, who after the death of his mother when he was barely 17, took on his shoulders the responsibility for his family and the education of his two younger brothers—his father being unstable and addicted to heavy drinking; who pursued his revolutionary and independent career as a composer without ever falling from his high artistic ideals: who, when afflicted with the tragedy of growing, incurable deafness, endured with constant fortitude both this and the wretched general ill-health from which he suffered throughout his adult life; who maintained his courage both in his life and in the actual heroic quality of his music— heroic not only in the *Eroica* or the *Funeral March for a hero* in the pianoforte sonata in A flat (op. 26), but also in the C minor Symphony, where he 'seized Fate by the throat' and blazed his way to spiritual victory; in *Fidelio* and the *Leonora* overtures, where he tells in music the tale of a wife's heroic deliverance of her husband from tyranny and death; in the triumphant musical 'resurrection' which concludes the overture to *Egmont*; in the struggles, vigour, visions, and ultimate, heavenly joy and human brotherhood which the Ninth Symphony unfolds. When the moment came for Beethoven to die during a thunderstorm, he raised his hand with Promethean defiance towards the heavens, and then sank back, lifeless so far as his earthly body was concerned, but enshrined as a beloved hero in the hearts of men for evermore. Here, in real life, was a Prometheus, who was a personal hero, a culture hero, a bringer of fire, and one who in his own early 19th century fashion, 'visited' the 'other world' during his lifetime, when he penetrated to the mysteries of the world beyond this one in the visionary passages of the *Missa Solemnis*, the Ninth Symphony, the final sonatas and the last quartets. This brief account is, as we shall see, only a partial description of Beethoven—a man of complex personality in his life and an artist of almost 'infinite variety' in his creations. No composer, certainly, has surpassed him in profundity of emotion and thought, or in richness of imagination, or has ascended so far into the mystical heights. Only Bach's music—in very different fields for the most part—has equalled his in spiritual glory and in grandeur of conception and achievement.

The 19th century biographers, except Thayer, drew an almost entirely favourable portrait of Beethoven as a man (although even his devoted Schindler wrote about some of his personal faults). In the 20th century, following on Lytton Strachey's precedent for debunking the idols of the past, the pendulum has swung the other way—and swung too far, sometimes. We have had an example of this in Editha and Richard Sterba's controversial book *Beethoven and his nephew*.[15] The Sterbas have not a good word to say about the man Beethoven (as distinct from his music) from start to finish. One of the troubles about their book is that it does not start—or anyhow does not make a proper start—early enough. It selects the latter part of Beethoven's life, in which his relationships with his nephew Karl and with Karl's mother were the main purely biographical elements, as its principal subject, and treats all the earlier years as mere introductions to that. But it is impossible to form a true picture of a man in our minds unless we regard him as a whole. It is remarkable that as we read the life of Beethoven in the pages of Thayer, there is scarcely a word to be said against him for the first thirty years of the fifty-six which he was destined to spend in this world. He was brave, determined, kind in his actions to his fellow musicians and others, a devoted son and an affectionate brother, though he and his brothers had quarrels at certain stages of their lives. He probably indulged himself sexually in his youth, but only to a moderate degree, and the theory that he contacted syphilis is extremely doubtful. He was not a regular churchman, but was deeply religious. The faults in his character manifested themselves progressively from about the age of thirty onwards—that is, after he realised his deafness. Schindler[16] points out that Beethoven 'lacked the necessary persistence' to observe 'the dietary precautions' and the 'injunctions to take more rest and put as little strain on his hearing as possible', as advised in 1801 by Father Weiss, priest at St Stephen's Church, Vienna, who was 'familiar with the physiology of the ear' and had cured many cases of deafness; and that he 'little

---

[15] Originally published in the U.S.A. by Pantheon Books Inc. and in Great Britain by Dennis Dobson in 1957.
[16] 'Beethoven as I Knew Him' by A. F. Schindler, edited by D. W. MacArdle, translated by Constance S. Jolly (1966), pp. 62-3.

heeded the advice of his doctors': 'don't speak to me of rest!', he wrote to Dr Wegeler on 16th November, 1801. There is his personal tragedy. By rest and diet he might have cured, or anyhow helped, his deafness. But to rest, except in sleep, was incompatible with his artistic activities. He sacrificed his hearing and even his health, on the altar of his creative genius. If he had not done so, the world would not have inherited the legacy of his glorious music. Psychologically, his defects of irritability, unreasonableness, aggressiveness and arrogance are inherently attributable to this central tragedy in his life. The Sterbas do not take sufficient account of the fact that, though, as Ernest Newman pointed out, his deafness had the effect of 'turning him in upon himself' and thus, through an irony of fate, causing him indirectly to conceive in his inmost being the most profound, mystical creations of his artistic career, it was for him personally the most ghastly tragedy that could befall a musician. They mention his deafness often, of course, but, oddly enough, seem to feel little or no sympathy for him in his great affliction; if they do so, this does not appear in the book. On the other hand, they try to convince us that he was an unconscious homosexual, not only in his relations with good-looking young men like Holz and Weber, but towards his own brothers. The fact that he embraced them warmly means nothing—it is merely in accordance with a common practice on the continent of Europe. And the facts of Beethoven's life point the other way. He was essentially virile. Throughout his life he maintained his vigorous masculine, piano style.[17] He fell in love with one attractive girl after another, sometimes seriously, sometimes more superficially. The Sterbas seek to establish that he continuously renounced love and the erotic instincts towards women. Yet Ernest Newman in 'The Unconscious Beethoven' adduced some evidence that he caught venereal disease in his early manhood; and we have not only the passionate love letter to 'The Immortal Beloved' (which may not have been sent), but the sequence of ardent ones to the widowed Countess Josephine Dehm (née Brunswick) which have come to light since the Sterbas' book appeared and are included in Emily Anderson's three-volume edition of Beethoven's letters.

He was not a misogynist, as the Sterbas try to make out; for in addition to his love affairs with the other sex, he had a host of Platonic friendships with women all his life. On the basis of

[17] Schindler's 'Beethoven as I knew him', p. 413.

the actual evidence, rather than on that of the theories of psycho-
analysts like the Sterbas, Beethoven was a complete heterosexual.
And when they devote pages to establishing that his attitude towards his nephew was that of a 'mother', I am moved, in all
modesty, to ask 'so what?'! Beethoven was appointed as sole
guardian of his nephew in the first instance by the will of the
boy's father, and though by a codicil the mother was added
(apparently against the father's real wishes), he regarded himself
as *in loco parentis*; whether we choose to regard him as 'father'
or as 'mother' is, I suggest, unimportant. The guardianship question
was not an easy one to answer, and the fact that the various
tribunals differed over it, is significant. The Sterbas make great
play over Beethoven's 'hatred' of the mother, Joanna; but even
if some people today would have decided in her favour, just because she *was* Karl's mother, the facts remain that she had been
convicted of embezzlement against her own husband and was
sufficiently loose in her morals to give birth to an illegitimate
child during her son Karl's boyhood. Beethoven, therefore, had
some grounds for feeling that she would not have exerted a good
influence upon him.

My own view is that neither Beethoven nor Joanna was suited
to be the boy's guardian: Beethoven proved to be a terribly possessive 'father', jealous, suspicious and even tyrannical; he expected the unfortunate Karl to spend his time with him and run
errands for him when the boy was in reality doing his best to
work for his examinations; and he himself was so haphazard and,
indeed, insanitary in his own habits that it is not surprising that
Karl's physical needs were ill-cared for. The crisis came when
Karl, in despair, attempted suicide. The effect on Beethoven was
shattering, but whether the Sterbas are medically justified in saying
that it actually led to his death, which was in fact caused by
inflammation of the liver, accentuated by a severe chill contracted
during his return from Gneixendorf to Vienna in Arctic weather,
seems uncertain. Fortunately Karl's attempt to shoot himself was
unsuccessful; he recovered, he became an Army officer (and subsequently proved to be an excellent one); the day after Karl left
to join his regiment, Beethoven wrote to his lawyer, leaving all
his property 'to my beloved nephew', and Karl, though unable
to be with him in the final stages of his last illness, showed the
utmost concern for Beethoven's grave condition. Indeed, one merit
of the Sterba's book is that they rehabilitate the character of Karl,

73

which the 19th century biographers had unjustifiably blackened. And it is not inconsistent with the facts to say that Beethoven and his nephew were reconciled before his death.

My own reaction to the whole pathetic story, based on a careful study of Thayer's *Life* both in the Krehbiel (1921) edition and in the Elliot Forbes (1964) edition, Beethoven's letters in Emily Anderson's complete edition in three volumes, Schindler's biography, parts of the Conversation Books, and the Sterbas' book itself, not to mention many other biographies of the great man, is to feel the utmost compassion both for the uncle and the nephew. Beethoven was hopelessly unsuited by temperament to be the guardian of anyone; but he was actuated throughout by a devoted love for the boy and a profound concern for his welfare. The result was catastrophic, yet it did not end in unrelieved tragedy.

Beethoven had other personal faults besides those mentioned above: he was ill-mannered, sometimes inconsiderate of other people's feelings, contemptuous of many of his less gifted contemporaries; and he negotiated simultaneously with several publishers about the *Missa Solemnis*—though here we are bound to remember that there were no copyright laws and no Performing Rights Society to protect his interests, and that at that time he was in considerable financial difficulties.

The Sterbas[18] finally decide that 'the immense conflict which Beethoven was unable to solve in his personal life' was 'the polarity between the male and female principle', and they suggest that this corresponds to the tendency in his entire work as an artist 'to conceive and manipulate things in antithesis', which Ernest Newman had pointed out. But even if we were to accept a sexual 'polarity' in Beethoven's life as being a true assumption (which, as indicated above, I do not), their account here does not touch on the main problem which their utter denigration of his character involves:— if he was personally so bad a man as they make out, how does it come about that most of his music is not merely aesthetically 'beautiful' but essentially exalted and spiritual—that it expresses nobility and tenderness in such a marked degree? As they themselves say,[19] 'After all, it is the same personality which creates the works and reveals itself in human relationships; the same psychological motivations and drives impel the creator to produce his works and determine his conduct.' Part of the explanation of

[18] ibid., pp. 305-6.
[19] ibid., p. 305.

this problem, I suggest, is that their diagnosis of his personal character is faulty, because incomplete; by stressing his bad points and omitting to point out his good ones, they have drawn a picture of him as a man which is partially misleading.

The fact that a man with Beethoven's flaws of character produced music which is almost consistently noble or exalted, can, I think, be explained by the following considerations:—

(1) His personal defects are outweighed by his virtues. On balance, he was enormously courageous in adversity, benevolent, open-hearted, humorous and affectionate, even though he was also ill-tempered, arrogant, jealous and possessive. He could be suspicious of his friends, and even insulting, but afterwards he was so contrite, so frank and generous in confessing his fault, that they forgave him at once.

(2) Music deals with generalised emotions, rather than those of individuals; and Beethoven's music *idealises* the emotions of mankind.

(3) It is not at all uncommon for the great creative artist to 'rise above himself' in his art-works. We shall see how, and to what extent, this applies, for instance, in the case of Wagner. It certainly happened with Beethoven, who could speak more eloquently in music than in words.

(4) The tragedy of Beethoven's deafness largely caused the personal faults of the latter part of his life; but it also caused him, by an almost unconscious process of inward reflection, to penetrate, in his loneliness, the mysteries of human existence and to express the eternal verities, in the glorious music of his last period.

Marion Scott, in her excellent book *Beethoven*, analysed the composer's three 'periods' as follows: 'In the first, Beethoven saw the *material world* from the *material standpoint*; in the second he saw the *material world* from the *spiritual standpoint*; in the third he saw the *spiritual world* from the *spiritual standpoint*.'

This description is accepted by Burnett James in his penetrating study *Beethoven and Human Destiny*. But I think that it is an over-simplification and also misleading. The three 'periods' exist, but they overlap. Orchestrally, the 'second period' is foreshadowed markedly in the Finale of the Second Symphony and in the Third Pianoforte Concerto, though it only emerged completely in the

Eroica Symphony. And meanwhile Beethoven had been creating sonatas which, though 'First Period' in date, were surely 'Second Period' in character. Think, for instance, of the powerful Sonata *Pathétique*, op. 13, with its turbulent first movement, its noble and tender Adagio, and its whirlwind of a Finale; the deeply romantic op. 27, No. 2, in C sharp minor; or the profoundly spiritual sonata for violin and piano in C minor, op. 30, No. 2; or the sublime agitation and restlessness of the pianoforte sonata in D minor, op. 31, No. 2. And later in his career, certain works, such as the pianoforte sonata in A, op. 101, and perhaps even the gigantic *Hammerklavier* in B flat, op. 106, and the two works for 'cello and piano, op. 102, mark a transition from the human glories of the 'Second Period' to the transcendent mysticism of the 'Third'.

Moreover, I do not follow what Marion Scott meant by the 'material world' and 'the material standpoint', as applied to Beethoven's music at all (except insofar as he depicted Nature in parts of the *Pastoral* Symphony—for all his description of it as 'more an expression of feeling than a painting'.) The varied emotions of mankind—joy, sorrow, melancholy, gaiety, love, occasionally anger, and so on—are portrayed even in his early works, but *from the start* they are imbued with a spiritual quality, which deepened in his 'Second Period' and ultimately took on a mystical character in his final phase. The idealisation of emotions, which was to form so marked a characterisation of his later art, is present even in his 'First Period' compositions. The longer I 'live with' Beethoven, as I have done since my boyhood, the more impressed I become with this spiritual factor that existed in his music from first to last. There is little or none of the element of conflict in his very early work, but as his personal responsibilities and struggles and sorrows grew, so was his art deepened in significance and ultimately exalted in glory.

For in spite of the grandeur and beauty of the Second Period masterpieces—six of the symphonies, the Razoumovsky quartets and those numbered op. 74 and 95, the great trios, the *Leonora*, *Coriolan* and *Egmont* overtures, *Fidelio*, the Mass in C, the wonderful chain of Middle Period sonatas for pianoforte solo, the *Kreutzer* and G Major (op. 96) works for violin and piano and the one for 'cello and piano in A (op. 69), the concerto for violin and the fourth and fifth for piano and orchestra—all of them greater, in my estimation, than any works in each field by any of Beethoven's predecessors (except the Mass in C, which no one would place on a level with Bach's tremendous Mass in B minor)—even these are surpassed by the exaltation and sublimity of the supreme works of his 'Third Period'—the *Missa Solemnis*, the *Ninth Symphony*, the last sonatas for pianoforte, and the final quartets.

There is no fundamental inconsistency between Beethoven the man, with all his faults, and Beethoven the consummate and almost faultless artist. For in the first place, Ludwig, in spite of his personal failings and because of his great personal qualities, which his modern detractors choose to ignore, was a far better man, if we regard him as a whole, than they have portrayed him as having been, in the partial and distorted picture which they have drawn: to say the least, they have disclosed only a portion of his personality. Secondly, in his music, he rose above his personal weaknesses, and by his tremendous genius, his unsurpassed technical mastery, his artistic integrity, his immense and painstaking industry, and the divine inspiration of God, he exalted his art to such heights of spiritual vision that the world has never ceased to marvel at the outcome, to love the creator of such sublime masterpieces, and to be thankful for so wonderful a gift to mankind. Dear, glorious Beethoven!

CHAPTER TWELVE

War-Time Music

The continuity of my life as a music lover has been interrupted by
the two world-wide upheavals. I was an officer in the Army in both
World Wars, and all those of my readers who have participated in
that experience—even in one War—and who love *artistic* things,
will know what this meant, quite apart from the rigours, the suffering, the terrors, in which *all* members of the armed forces shared
in their various ways and degrees. To be cut off from music for so
long a time at a stretch, was a real hardship, even though the
severity of the 'desert' was occasionally relieved by small musical
oases. And the lack, or shortage, of music for those who served in
the forces, was not the only factor: another was the effect of war-
time conditions upon music-making generally—which was felt by
civilians as well: those were not the days for musical experiments; it
was as much as the organisations concerned could do, to carry on
with their concerts at all amid the disturbances and horrors of the
vast conflicts in which mankind was involved.

On the outbreak of war in 1914, most of my Oxford friends
volunteered for service in the forces, and I was on the point of
doing likewise immediately, when my father, supported by the
advice of Dr Poynton, strongly urged me to finish 'Greats' and the
Civil Service Examination first. He argued that if I intended to take
up the Civil Service as my career, and as the Commissioners were
not cancelling the 1915 examination, it was really my duty to do
this. I ultimately, though reluctantly, agreed, consoling myself
with the fact that the greatly diminished number of under
graduates, including myself, who returned to Oxford in October,
1914, after the Long Vacation, continued our training in the Oxford
University Officers' Training Corps every afternoon. (Actually, I and
the others were only anticipating, of our own volition, what was to
be Government policy in World War II, when University students
who were within a year of sitting for their Final examinations
were encouraged to wait and take them, their call-up being deferred

78

meanwhile.) The Musical Club continued its concerts at rarer intervals than in peace-time, and I remember that while the music of
Wagner and Richard Strauss was given a rest in London and other
parts of the country for the duration of the war, we had several
performances of Brahms' chamber music at the Club. Is it, perhaps, true that the art of Brahms is more universal in its appeal,
less specifiically Teutonic in its outlook, than that of his mighty
German contemporary or of their successor, 'the other Richard'?

I got a Second in 'Greats'; and only a few weeks before the Civil
Service Examination was due to start, the Commissioners announ-
ced that there would only be 13 vacancies, instead of the usual 80. I
was not among the first 13 in the Examination, and I was now free
to do what I was determined to do anyhow after taking the Examination (irrespective of the result), namely to join the Army—as a
subaltern in the Royal Field Artillery, which in those days was
horse-drawn. (I had been taught to ride in my early boyhood.) In
due course I went with a battery to Egypt and Palestine, where I
served in Allenby's campaigns.

It would take me far beyond the scope and purpose of this book
to describe the ordeals, perils and hardships of active service, or
the adventures of that arduous, but exciting, enterprise. I performed no special acts of bravery, did my job like any other gunner
subaltern, and tried to look after the health and welfare of the
men and animals under my charge to the best of my ability. I
must have been partly responsible for the deaths of many innocent
Asiatic Turks—a terrible thought to remember. But such is war, a
ghastly legacy from humanity's blood-stained history and an almost
insane method of settling international disputes. At that time we
were all 'caught up in it' and believed that this was the only method
of overcoming the aggressive spirit of Germany and her allies.

There were a few musical interludes. In the course of my service,
I was on more than one occasion located for a few days at the vast
British camp at Kantara, on the Suez Canal. Imagine my surprise,
when I found that in the large lounge tent of the Officers' Mess
there was a magnificent Bechstein grand piano—the noble gift of
some generous benefactor! Every effort was made to protect it
from the sand-storms which fairly frequently blew up from the
surrounding desert and seemed to penetrate everywhere, but no
one else appeared to be willing or able to play on this superb
instrument while I was there, so eventually I summoned up my
courage and resolved to 'have a go', though fully conscious of my

great limitations as a performer. I had, of course, to rely entirely on what I could reproduce by heart or by ear, but I regaled my fellow-officers with snippets from Chopin, Puccini, Sullivan, Anton Rubinstein, Tchaikovsky, and even Mozart and Beethoven. Encouraged by the warm applause, at the end of my first little selection, from my kindly listeners who, starved of music of any kind for so long, seemed willing to put up even with my inadequate ramblings on the keyboard, I repeated the experiment on subsequent occasions. When you are on active service, you have to depend largely on your own efforts and seize any opportunity that comes your way either for making or hearing music.

I had no further chance of indulging my interest in music until I was in bed in the Red Cross Hospital in Cairo with septic sores on my legs—one of those unpleasantnesses which various soldiers had to put up with in the Palestine campaigns—and I found myself willy-nilly listening to a band in the Zoological Gardens across the road discoursing what seemed to my Western European ears a very strange form of music : each piece seemed to go on and on, without the kind of melody or harmony to which I was accustomed, and to come to an abrupt, inconsequent and unexpected end. When I recovered sufficiently, I went with another officer to tea at the Continental Hotel, and again snatched an opportunity of playing on a piano in the hotel lounge; but it was not nearly so fine an instrument as the one in the camp at Kantara!

On one occasion when I was on leave from the front, at Alexandria, I noticed on a hoarding an announcement of an orchestral concert! I do not remember most of the programme, but I know that it contained Beethoven's Seventh Symphony. Alas!, however, when I got to the place, I found that it was a combination of enormous restaurant and concert hall, and I had to endure the afternoon anguish of listening to the clank of coffee cups and tea-trays and the loud buzz of conversation from an extremely cosmopolitan clientèle, with the immortal strains of Beethoven's masterpiece serving as a scarcely audible background! The actual programme may have been excellent, for all that I know.

The only other place where I 'met' a piano out there, was the Mena House Hotel, after a strange adventure on a camel which I cannot resist narrating, even though it has nothing to do with music. Another officer and I, on short week-end leave at Mena from a gunnery course at Zeitoun (on the other side of Cairo) decided to ride on camels for a short tour round the Pyramids. 'He very nice camel, he called Alice,' naïvely maintained the camel driver concerning the beast on which I was mounted. All went well, until we got off the sand on to a hard track which ran alongside the main road from Cairo to Mena; but at that point, Alice took it into her head to bolt! Now, I should explain for the benefit of those of my readers who have never ridden on one of these gigantic, single-humped dromedaries, there is a stirrup on its left flank into which you insert your left foot, and you cross your right leg over your left; there is a rope attached to a ring fastened beneath the animal's head, you hold this with your left hand, and when you wish the camel to go to the left, you pull in that direction; while if you want it to turn to the right, you simply push its neck rightwards. Apart from these elementary movements, you have no means of controlling the beast unless you know the right noises to make—and I, of course, didn't! Normally, the driver, who walks beside the camel on foot, utters certain sounds when he wants it to get up from its sitting position on the ground (when you have mounted on to the saddle), to move forward, to stop, and to sit down again. But Alice's driver was, of course, left far, far behind, bellowing his 'oo's' and 'ah's' to the air fruitlessly, while sundry other officers riding in horse-drawn gharries along the road laughed heartily at my plight as Alice sped on her way, shooting out her long legs at a breakneck speed, with me bumping up and down helplessly on her back and clinging desperately to the pummel to prevent myself from being pitched on to the hard surface so far—as it seemed—below me! However, all ended happily; for Alice stopped of her own accord, with rather alarming suddenness, when she got to her usual stable near the Mena House Hotel, sat down by the usual 'instalments', and thus permitted me to dismount. Eventually the breathless driver overtook us, followed by my fellow officer. After that, and after tea, I was quite relieved to soothe my excited nerves by playing a little music by ear on a not particularly good grand piano at the hotel.

During my 'active service' I managed to get a few days' leave with another officer to visit Jerusalem and Bethlehem, and—while at Kantara awaiting orders for my return to England and demobilisation—to go to Luxor and Aswan. All these experiences left indelible impressions on my mind.

Practically my only other 'musical' activity in the Middle East occurred after I had had dystentry and malignant malaria in turn in the early autumn of 1918, and was convalescing from the latter disease with the aid of 30 grains of quinine a day at a Stationary Hospital at Gaza. For it was there, during my enforced idleness so far as military duties was concerned, that I began to formulate my ideas for my first article on a musical subject (apart from my little efforts at Oxford mentioned previously). I somehow managed to buy a writing block and wrote and wrote—in indelible pencil—a long essay about 'Music and Life'; little did I think that when I eventually got home to England I would be able, after licking it into shape, to get it accepted for publication by 'The Musical Quarterly' of New York.

It took me several weeks to get back to England early in 1919, as I had to spend two weeks in a hospital at Taranto before travelling in a hospital coach on a ten or twelve days' train journey to Le Havre, *en route* for Southampton and London.

PART TWO

CHAPTER THIRTEEN

The Aftermath

Only three people could have shared with me completely the inexpressible feelings of joy and thankfulness with which I, like so many others, returned home to England after a long absence on active service in a terrible war and was reunited with my family. Those three were my mother, my father and my brother, Tom. I had not been able to let them know the date of my arrival. They knew only that I was *en route*, a rather sick man, and might turn up any day now. My brother and his wife, Bettie, whom he had married in December, 1917, and whom therefore I had never met, were staying with my parents at their house, 17 Hyde Park Street; he, having served on the Western front, where he had several almost miraculous escapes, had been demobilised before me. I travelled by train from Southampton to the demobilisation centre at Wimbledon: it was a kind of sausage-machine, for I entered as an officer by one door and shortly afterwards left by another door as a civilian, albeit still in uniform. When I reached Waterloo, the genial porter who heaved my valise on to a taxi exclaimed 'and very nice too!' The taxi drew up at our house at 6-30 p.m. Tom opened the door. ...

After very few days, I realised that my first task must be to do my best to restore my health. At Tom's suggestion, my mother and I went away together for a fortnight's holiday in March—to the Tors Hotel at Lynmouth, North Devon. The only music that I heard there was the music of the rushing river below my window: I used to lie awake and revel in the sound of it, after all those months in a parched land where horses had languished from lack of water and we men sometimes had to choose whether to clean our teeth at night or in the morning or even had to do without it. My mother, who had a room on the same side of the hotel, found the noise of the river disturbing to her night's rest, but she wouldn't mention this or ask to be moved to a different room, because she was so

84

anxious not to mar my pleasure in the slightest degree; I only discovered it long afterwards. I was supposed to have been cured of bacillary dysentery and malignant malaria in Palestine and Egypt, but complete recovery of health was slow in coming, and it was not until late in 1920 that a consultant sent me to that great specialist in tropical diseases, Philip Manson-Bahr, who discovered that I had faint symptoms of *amoebic* dysentery, and cured me of it permanently.

Meanwhile, I had had to decide on my future career. I drew a blank for the Home Civil Service (Service in India or the Colonies was ruled out by my medical experiences in Palestine): the Commissioners in 1919 had very few appointments available—many war-time temporary Civil Servants having been made permanent— and there were vast numbers of applicants; selection was made solely by means of short interviews, without any written examination. The small Mendl family grain firm had been 'killed' by the war. My father's work now consisted of certain part-time directorships and grain arbitrations in the City. So, after consulting the Oxford University Appointments Committee, I decided that, after all, I had better get 'called' to the Bar; the qualification might in any case be useful; I had 'eaten my dinners' at the Inner Temple while I was an undergraduate; I got exemption from two of the more academic Bar examination papers, on account of war service, passed the others, and was 'called' in June, 1920. I had one year's pupillage in the chambers of William A. Jowitt (the future Lord Chancellor) and two years as a tenant at 2 King's Bench Walk. I found the law rather fascinating, but that I was ill-suited to advocacy. The comfort was that I met various old friends at the Bar, and made several new ones, including that dear, charming man, R. A. B. Powell ('RAB') with whom I shared a room for those two years, and who was subsequently to be my best man at our wedding, and H. Trevor Morgan, that loyal and sympathetic friend, who ultimately became a County Court Judge.

In the summer of 1923, I had the opportunity—which I took— to join the London staff of the 'Shell' organisation. I was not really commercially minded, but the Group's scope was sufficiently wide to enable me to spend many years of my life working quite contentedly, and very hard, in its service: my admittedly short legal experience had some value both for the Company and for myself; above all, various forms of staff management and staff welfare, with an appeal both to my human sympathies and to my passion for justice, proved congenial; and I made some good friends among my colleagues.

It was a great joy to be able to go back to the world of music in my spare time, after my return from war service. I went to many concerts in the cheapest seats that I could get—either alone or with friends. I met Pat Shaw (younger brother of my Univ. friend Philip who had been killed at Loos). He was then a medical student in London, and he and a friend of his called Appleby shared my zeal for music; we three went to the Queen's Hall together on a number of occasions. Pat was the author of the superb suggestion that 'The Ring' should be played almost continuously, with relay orchestras and merely brief pauses for eating and sleeping—so that the unity of the whole cycle should be fully enjoyed by the audience. How this could be fitted in with the day-time hours of work of most amateur music-lovers, was a practical point which he had not thought out, but as an 'ideal', I could see what he meant, though I doubt whether he intended the idea to be taken seriously! He in due course became a doctor, and later emigrated to Canada.

One of my contemporaries at University College, Oxford, had been Robert Lorenz. I came to hold him in high regard and respect. His parents being of German origin, but not naturalised British subjects, though resident here for many years, he could not get a commission in the British Army; he was, however, born and educated in England (at Rugby and Univ.), and apart from his name no one could have detected, on meeting him, that he was not wholly British. When war came, he was as determined as anyone to play his part in the national effort against German militarism and aggression. So he voluntarily joined the ranks as a private soldier almost 'on the outbreak', and became a sergeant on the Western Front. I met him by chance at Queen's Hall soon after the war. He was a keen music lover, and was far from being more attuned to the music of Germany and Austria than to that of other nations; he loved the works of the great Teutonic masters, but frequently told me, for instance, that he considered Debussy's La Mer one of the finest scores of the 20th century; and he was, par excellence, a devotee of the music of Elgar. The two symphonies of Elgar had unaccountably run into a period of neglect even in their native land; it was Lorenz who, behind the scenes, worked so hard for a revival of the First Symphony, in A flat, after the war, and even wrote round to many friends and acquaintances (including myself) to persuade them to attend that memorable performance. Few people today realise how much we are all indebted to the efforts and devotion of Robert Lorenz, the amateur music lover, for the resuscitation of interest in the great English composer at that time. Lorenz also wrote articles on music in the Press and produced some attractive radio programmes of gramophone records of music that he loved, for the B.B.C. I was grateful to him, too, for introducing me to Ernest Newman and other distinguished personalities of the musical world. It was sad that some years later he died, prematurely, in his middle age.

Through my Aunt Alice, who was associated with her professionally, I got to know Mrs Duncan, the accompanist, who with her husband lived in Notting Hill; in the same house lived Thomas F. Dunhill, the talented musician and composer of the song *The Cloths of Heaven* and other works, including the music of the comic opera *Tantivy Towers*, written in collaboration with A. P. Herbert as librettist; and Lloyd Powell, the artistic pianist and brother of Dilys Powell (the well-known critic and broadcaster). Lloyd Powell used to give small musical parties at that house, and kindly invited me—and, after my subsequent marriage, my wife —to several of them. On one or two of these delightful occasions I met that great violinist, Jelly D'Aranyi, then a charming young woman, and had the satisfaction of telling her that she had first made me realise the glories of the Brahms violin concerto. Many years later, I rejoiced to find a similar reaction expressed by Neville Cardus;[20] though her performance of this work which I heard was at a different concert from that of which he wrote, she had evidently been able to carry her inspired interpretation of it from one occasion to another.

At 17 Hyde Park Street, my parents were in due course able to resume their occasional hospitalities in the form of small dinner parties, with music afterwards, and a few musical *soirées* with light refreshments. Most of the music was provided by Aunt Alice, who always sang artistically in various languages, and Dilys Jones,[21] who charmed everyone with her artistry and her beauty—and by my Uncle Charles when he was in England. They all arranged for professional accompanists on these special occasions. Carlotta de Feo was often there, and my Uncle Louis also introduced a new element into these gatherings, before his fatal

[20] *Ten Composers*, pp. 58-60.
[21] See Chapter 6.

illness began. He[22] brought to the *soirées* some of his friends from the musical and theatrical worlds, such as Francis Toye (the music critic of *The Morning Post* and subsequently author of admirable books on Verdi and Rossini), his wife, his brother Geoffrey Toye (the well-known conductor) and the latter's wife Doris Lytton, and the talented and attractive actress Cathleen Nesbitt, whom I always associate with her performances in H. M. Harwood's *A Grain of Mustard Seed* ('it has such a *kindly* cynicism', she said to me) and in Flecker's *Hassan*. Then there was Khoubitzsky, a Russian tenor with a lovely voice, whom Louis knew and who also sang at my parents' house. The only time I went to the Derby was with Louis, who backed the winner, Spion Kop (which I did not), and kindly paid all my expenses; Khoubitzsky had asked him to put something on the horse of his choice; at that time they were sharing digs; when Louis, with me, arrived there afterwards, and handed Khoubitzsky £10, the enormous Russian picked up my not very large uncle in his arms and kissed him on both cheeks! I completed the day by going with my friend Claude Anstice Brown (whom I had first met in the Inner Temple as a student) to a concert at Queen's Hall conducted by Albert Coates and consisting of Holst's Choral Symphony and Beethoven's Ninth—a memorable programme. Claude was one of the most versatile men I have ever known. A fine Rugger player in his day and a very good performer on the Lawn Tennis Court, he had an excellent brain and a great love of painting and of music. He left the Bar to become Secretary (later, Director) of the Institute of Incorporated Practitioners in Advertising. He had a very pleasant quality baritone voice, which he had had trained, and clear diction, and was sometimes persuaded to sing after an informal little dinner at my parents' Hyde Park Street house and at their subsequent flat (12 Cumberland Mansions, W.). The only non-vocal contributor, among my parents' friends, to a musical evening, was Harry Lewis, who was a solicitor and an exceptionally good amateur pianist; after dinner, my father might say 'Would you like to play to us?', and he would reply that he would be delighted, and sat down and played piano works by Beethoven, Schumann, Chopin, or Brahms, which he knew by heart.

I must mention a few of my girl friends with whom I had, in varying ways and degrees, musical associations, particularly at this

[22] See Chapter 2 about Aunt Alice, my two Mendl uncles, and Carlotta de Feo.

period. Marjorie Price was a talented amateur pianist; she and her family have remained close friends of my wife and mine throughout the years; so has Beatrice Reid, whose father was an old friend of my father's and who played the violin very well in an amateur string quartet and in an orchestra. Joyce Durrant had a deep contralto voice of fine quality and made rather a speciality of John Ireland's *Sea Fever* to her sister's accompaniment (her favourite composers, I remember, were Chopin and Tchaikovsky); she and her husband, Kenneth Playfair (the heart specialist) are also still among our life-long friends. I have referred (in Chapter 9) to Joan Green (née Elkin), one of my first cousins; another was Marjorie Martin, an extremely cultured woman, with whom I have not been able to share many musical experiences (as she has always lived in Hertfordshire), except ballet, for which she naturally had a special love—she herself at one stage taught ballroom dancing.

It was my mother, and not in this case my father or my maternal grandmother, who at this stage of my life first enabled me to become a Chopin enthusiast. I had never become completely attuned to his art—even at the hands of Paderewsky—but my mother took me to hear Pachmann in a Chopin recital at the Queen's Hall, because, she said (in effect) that she felt sure that when I heard that great interpreter of his music I would fall under the spell of the great Polish composer. How right she was! I do not say that Pachmann's performances were always perfect, or that they have not been equalled in subsequent years by such artists as Dinu Lipatti or Horowitz; but Pachmann undoubtedly had an uncanny insight into the subtleties of Chopin's mind and the varied emotions of his music; and with his exquisite touch—every note was like a pearl—and his consummate technique, he has never, in my experience, been surpassed as a Chopin player. Sometimes, in his eccentric way, he accompanied his performances by gentle comments to those of the audience in close proximity to the platform, but this did not seem to matter: one felt that it was all part of the natural expression of his sympathy with the music.

I am, however, not going to insert my chapter on Chopin at this point. For it is time for me to devote my attention—at last!— to four composers who entered my life at no *particular* stage of my music-loving career, for the simple reason that they have been, as it were, 'great personal friends' of mine all my life, if it be not presumptuous of me to use this expression! These four are Mozart, Schubert, Schumann and Mendelssohn. None of them made a *sudden* impact, or became the subject of an immediate or dramatic *schwärm*, or passion, albeit continuing afterwards. Rather do they seem to have crept into my existence almost unawares in my childhood, and to have remained there, with my love for their music constant but ever widening in scope as I heard more and more of their works.

In the ensuing chapters, therefore, I shall try to say something about the personalities and general artistic characteristics of these four great geniuses; I have deliberately postponed them until now, just because they are 'early loves' who have been with me for my entire life and who could therefore best be placed, I felt, in the midst of my narrative, rather than at the beginning or near the end of it. After them, it will be Chopin's turn!

CHAPTER FOURTEEN

Mozart, the disturbed genius

A musical lady acquaintance of mine—an old friend—once summed up the art of Haydn and Mozart to me as 'bread and butter music'. Well, I am very fond of bread and butter, so perhaps I ought to treat this remark as a tribute to their simplicity—which I regard as a good quality. Yet I know full well that it was not intended as a compliment, but rather implying that their works are, in her view, unexciting and (perhaps) rather uninteresting. In any case, I disagree with it. For it ignores the subtlety, the depth and the wide range of Mozart's astonishing genius and concentrates solely upon the apparent simplicity of his music. Concerning Haydn, with his many surprises, I shall have more to say in a later chapter.

Mozart's own ideal aspiration was towards the creation of opera. Now, unless an operatic composer has the gift of writing his own librettos, as Berlioz and Wagner had, or the benefit of a librettist of genius, as Verdi in his last years found in Boito or Richard Strauss in Hugo von Hofmannsthal, he is, so to speak, 'at the mercy' of his collaborator. In some cases this has proved a real obstacle—as, for example, with Weber's *Euryanthe*, which contains some of his finest music but has, to so large an extent, been kept from the stage by the badness of its libretto. As a generalisation, I would say that the librettos of Mozart's operas have both merits and defects, but the astonishing thing is that this does not seem to matter. *Idomeneo*, *Die Entführung aus dem Serail*, *Figaro*, *Don Giovanni*, *Cosi fan tutte* and *Die Zauberflöte* are all great masterpieces, whether or not we find fault with this or that feature of their librettos; Mozart's genius completely transmutes and transcends the character of the script which he is setting. Although opera is a composite art, and in theory we may think that either a defective or distasteful plot or libretto would detract from our total enjoyment, with Mozart the whole work becomes a delight, thanks to the magical way in which his music transforms, or even glorifies, the work of his librettists. Such, at any rate, has been my experience.

Idomeneo is really an *opera seria*, only saved from a sad ending by divine intervention, like so many of the tragedies of Euripides. Its libretto based on Greek mythology, yet reminiscent of the Biblical story of Jephtha, is a perfect setting for Mozart's glorious music, which is 'correspondingly' exalted, passionate and tragic, though, as usual, transcending the literary quality of the words. Nor can one point to any incompatibility in *Die Entführung* between its romantic and comic libretto and the music with its profound emotions and its humour. It is in the other four great Mozart operas that some music lovers have found a 'discord' between the libretto and the score.

The story of *Figaro* is all based on the 18th century *droit du Seigneur*—the lord's 'right' to sleep with a female employee; and though da Ponte's libretto—like Beaumarchais' comedy on which it was founded—shows how Figaro and Susanna outwitted the Count Almaviva, pursues its way amusingly through an almost incredibly series of 'love' intrigues and comic situations and ends with the Count asking forgiveness of the Countess (who herself has had rather a *tendresse* for the page, Cherubino), and in their complete reconciliation, some people find the basis of the plot distasteful and the story unworthy of the beautiful and enchanting music which Mozart composed for it. But the point, surely, is that in any case this music completely transcends both Beaumarchais and da Ponte. The Countess, thanks to Mozart, is, until the happy ending, almost a tragic figure; Cherubino's two great arias embody anxiety and love in a universal fashion; the last Act is filled with the witchery and romance of a summer night in a garden; the Count's final pleading with the Countess is couched in most moving tones; and their reconciliation is almost transformed into an epiphany by Mozart's genius. The admixture of these features with the spirit of pure comedy, in musical terms, makes *Figaro* as nearly the perfect comic opera as we are likely to get in this imperfect world.

Don Giovanni really is more of a problem. It is easy to understand what a fascination the legend had for certain creative artists before Mozart,[23] with its fantastic protagonist and his sensational, supernatural downfall. But one can also sympathise with those

[23] Tirso de Molina (the reputed author of a Spanish play on the subject), Molière, Shadwell, Goldini, and Gluck (with his ballet 'Don Juan').

who, in spite of the final 'moral' of the punishment of wickedness, feel a certain revulsion from the story: a thoroughly unsympathetic character, a murderer, a man who boasts about his innumerable amorous conquests, tries to seduce an innocent girl just before her wedding, behaves very badly to other women in the opera, and is ultimately swept off to Hell by the demons summoned up by the weirdly vitalised statue of the murdered Commendatore. It might be said 'Macbeth for example, is an even greater villain, yet you enjoy Shakespeare's play without any qualifications.' Yes, but that tragedy is the picture of a man who starts as a loyal and gallant general, is tempted by criminal ambition, and eventually meets his doom; we can even admire his desperate courage at the end, and his overthrow is brought about by the forces of good, gathering across the border under the leadership of the gallant Macduff. Don Giovanni is merely a scalliwag from start to finish, who is swept off to eternal damnation. There is nothing funny about his amatorial adventures, and nothing romantic in him. All this is true, and yet the opera is a great and enjoyable masterpiece. How on earth did Mozart achieve this result? He called the work a *dramma giocoso*, but it is really a tragi-comedy, the first of its kind in operatic history. And part of its fascination, as a music-drama, lies not in the manner of Giovanni's death, but in the way in which the composer became caught up in the tragic implications of the story and produced a tragi-comic masterpiece hovering between comedy and horror. When we add to this the bewitching melodies like 'La ci darem', 'Deh! vieni a la finestra', 'Batti, batti', and the rest, the pathetic music assigned to Donna Anna and Donna Elvira (the two most appealing characters in the work), the superb concerted numbers, and the tragic grandeur of the scenes with the Statue, we cease to be 'appalled' by the legend: we listen to Leporello's comic account of the catastrophe and the happy sextet in which he and the other characters settle their future lives, and we depart to our beds, thankful, once more, for the genius of the brilliant young man who created such a wonderful score and could transform *that* story into a great work of art.

For some people, there is an obstacle in the case of *Cosi fan tutte*, arising from the artificiality, and excessive symmetry, of da Ponte's libretto, in which the main characters are two sisters, two young officers engaged to be married to them, and two conspirators who seek to prove to the officers that all women are unfaithful: *Cosi fan tutte*—'all women behave like that!' Of course

93

it all ends happily, though who is to marry which, remains obscure. All this is true, but Mozart's music is delicious—emotional as well as witty. Dorabella's grief at her fiancés departure sounds utterly genuine at the outset, but becomes burlesque; Fiordiligi's song of fidelity 'Come scoglio' is clearly a parody. I do not pretend to love this opera as much as *Figaro*, but Mozart's music is not merely beautiful on the surface; it expresses human character, and in so doing transcends the artificiality of the plot.

The libretto of *Die Zauberflöte* is, for some critics and listeners, a muddle and a lot of nonsense, only made bearable by Mozart's incomparable art. What are we to make of the Queen of the Night, who turns out to be one of the villains of the story and yet is the person who in the First Act has sent her three ladies to present the magic flute to Tamino and the chime of bells to his servant, Papageno? My answer is that this is symbolical of the fact that out of evil, good may come (and often does);[24] and that in consequence we have the enchanting melody which Tamino sings to the accompaniment of the flute in the last scene of this Act, and that the flute again, with its utter simplicity, guides Tamino and Pamino, in their last ordeal, to happiness at the end. Papageno's music, with his bell instrument, is so magical that *we* want to dance with him, too, and are ourselves bewitched, like Monostatos and the slaves, by that delicate 'polka' that he plays! There is no incongruity in the juxtaposition of the homely, comic Papageno (who is a kind of operatic Sancho Panza) and the solemnity of Sarastro, the High Priest, and the scenes in the Temple. This is no 'pantomime' mixed with the Freemasonry. It simply shows that earth-bound, heart-warming humour exists quite naturally in this world side by side with the sacred aspects of life. The *words* of Schikaneder's libretto are not great art; but its ideas are, in my eyes, both true and satisfying; and the music, whether grave or gay, whether humorous or spiritual, reveals Mozart at the height of his powers.

Although this book is more concerned with the general characteristics of a composer's art than with any detailed consideration of individual works, I have written about each of Mozart's greatest operas partly because of his personal preference for opera as an art-form and partly because there has been some controversy about his approach to it. Yet when all is said and done, none of these

---

[24] 'There is some soul of goodness in things evil, Would men observingly distil it out'. Shakespeare: Henry V, Act IV, Scene i.

wonderful compositions *surpasses* in greatness the peaks of Mozart's achievement in the instrumental field—think of the unblemished artistry of his finest symphonies, such as the *Little G minor* (K.183), the A major (K.201), the *Haffner* (K.385), and, above all, the *Linz* (K.425), the *Prague* (K.504) and the perfection of his three last symphonic masterpieces in E flat, G minor, and C major (K.543, 550, and 551) which he miraculously created in a matter of weeks; the chain of great piano concertos; the two fantasies for pianoforte in D minor (K.397) and C minor (K.475), or such sonatas as those in A minor (K.310) and C minor (K.457); the quartet for piano and strings in G minor (K.478), and the loveliest of his string quartets (such as the six dedicated to Haydn) and quintets, (especially the one in G minor, K.516); the noble *Masonic Funeral Music* and the exquisite serenade *Eine kleine Nachtmusik*; or the beautiful compositions for clarinet in concert with other instruments; and (in spite of the operatic character of certain portions) think, too, of the great Mass in C minor, and the Requiem, even though unfortunately neither of these works was completed by him.

Mozart was neither a mere weaver of delicious patterns in sound, nor only a portrayer of the feelings of the characters in his operas. He was, himself, a 'disturbed' genius. There is a suppressed emotion, an undercurrent of melancholy, or even of agony (rather than a 'demonic element' as often alleged), underlying the beauty of much of his instrumental music when it is in a minor key. (In fact, these emotions are not always suppressed in the music). When we consider the G minor Symphony (K.550), the string quintet in the same key, the D minor pianoforte concerto, his use of the key of C minor in the Fantasia for piano (K.475) and the piano concerto K.491, we cannot fail to sense, in works which have no association with any fictitious, operatic characters, a current of profound disturbance and sadness in the composer's own nature, though it is controlled by a feeling of resignation.

Mozart was a devoted son to both his parents. He did all he could for his mother in her last, brief illness, when they were living together in Paris, and he broke the news of her death to his father and sister most delicately: she was really dead before he wrote to Leopold (on July 3rd, 1778) to tell him how ill she was; I cannot agree with Eric Blom, who, in his notes to his admirable selection of Mozart's letters translated by Emily Anderson, wrote that this letter, whilst showing 'great tact and presence of mind', also reveals 'a certain callousness—the callousness of a great artist to whom nothing matters and whom nothing touches quite so much as his art'. It was, I suggest, at least partly from a desire to take his father's and sister's minds away from the sadness of his news that he also wrote, in the same letter, about his new *Paris* Symphony and its excellent reception by the audience. His consideration for their feelings is further shown by his writing by the same post to ask the Abbé Bullinger (at Salzburg) to prepare Leopold 'very gently for this sad news', and by waiting till July 9th before writing to his father to tell him that his mother had died. He wrote most frequently and in great detail to his father up till the time of the latter's death, and when this event occurred late in May, 1787, he wrote most sympathetic and affectionate letters to his sister, of whom he was very fond; the one of 2nd June was not in Emily Anderson's original edition, but she supplied it to Eric Blom: in this, Mozart expresses his grief very briefly at the outset and then goes on to discuss the handling of the estate; but we cannot be sure that this was his first letter to her after Leopold's death; the next one, dated 16th June, is full of tenderness towards her.

He could be difficult, but the outrageous behaviour of Archbishop Colloredo to him even at the age of 25 and when (at last) he realised Mozart's stature as a musician, certainly reflects on the Archbishop's character rather than on the composer's. Mozart was a high-spirited fellow, and fully justified in not lying down to Colloredo's insults any longer. He was apt to despise unduly fellow musicians of smaller calibre than himself, but was a patient teacher. He was a devoted husband, though he had some grounds for thinking that his wife showed signs of not remaining completely faithful to him when his professional work took him away from her. The admixture of a theatrical element with devoutly religious feelings even in his greatest liturgical works—the Mass in C minor and the Requiem—may be related both to his personal idealisation of opera and to the fact that Freemasonry in his last year meant even more to him than the Church in which he was brought up.

An outward gaiety in his temperament, shown in his love of the society of people, in his enthusiasm for dancing, and even in his great liking for billiards and skittles, concealed an inward nervousness and a tendency to depression. Thus we can understand his composing a joyous work like the great E flat Symphony No.

39 (K.543) or a light-hearted comedy such as *Cosi fan tutte* at a time when he was beset by anxiety over his financial position. The same period gave us the troubled, but glorious, G minor Symphony (K.550) and the triumphant C major (K.551—misnamed the *Jupiter*); just as the last year of his life saw the humour, the fairyland and the spiritual glory of *Die Zauberflöte* on the one hand and the final sadness of the Requiem on the other. He was to the end a Christian and religious in the broad sense, and he never renounced Roman Catholicism, though he ultimately got more solace from Freemasonry. Unlike the 'integrated' Haydn, he was an (equally human) amalgam of seeming cheerfulness and sorrow, of resignation and rebellion, of personal disturbance and consciousness of artistic mastery. An observant listener can discern all this in his music, just as we can read about it in the records of his life and in his letters; a man whom a sympathetic person can scarcely fail to love, a composer whose art is adored by the vast majority of music lovers.

CHAPTER FIFTEEN

Interlude on Musical Romanticism

Before I embark on writing (at very varying lengths!) about such composers as Schubert, Berlioz, Mendelssohn, Chopin, Schumann, Wagner, Franck, Bruckner, Brahms and Mahler, I had better set out my thoughts on the meaning of the word 'romanticism', as applied to music. So much confusion arises in criticism from failing to think out, or to make clear, what is really meant by such terms as 'classical' and 'romantic'.

Walter Pater said 'the essence of romanticism is the blending of strangeness with the beautiful'. Frankly, I do not think that this will do. Some art generally regarded as 'romantic' is not 'strange'; moreover, a blending of strangeness with beauty does not always or necessarily produce a romantic result. So far as music is concerned, in all humility I stick to the description in my book *The Soul of Music* (p. 204): 'when we feel that music faithfully expresses the passion of love; or is dreamy in character; or tells a fairy tale; or sings of the deeds of a hero; we can appropriately call it "romantic".'

'Romantic' is often opposed to 'classical'—a term which, however, in different senses, is also contrasted with 'modern' or with 'popular' music.[25] But it just isn't true that in 'classical' music, as against 'romantic' music, 'form is first and emotional content subordinated, whereas in "romantic" music, content is first and form subordinate'.[26] A lot of music which is 'romantic' in feeling is strong in structure; and some music which is weak as regards form is not intrinsically 'romantic' either.

Romanticism is a fundamental quality of human nature. And in music it has a long history. There is romanticism in Monteverdi, in Purcell (*Dido and Aeneas* and *The Fairy Queen*), in Couperin,

[25] For a full account of these contrasts I would refer the reader to chapter 15 of 'The Soul of Music', pp. 197-211.

[26] J. C. Fillmore: 'Pianoforte Music', as quoted in the New English Dictionary. See 'The Soul of Music', p. 198.

in Handel's operas and in his *Atalanta* and the oratorio *Solomon*; not much in Bach; quite a lot in Gluck; perhaps more in Mozart than in Haydn. There is, of course, a large romantic streak in Beethoven, and still more in Schubert, partly on account of his special gift for composing songs to poetry which was often itself romantic; but the span of Beethoven's art, and even of Schubert's, is too wide for the word 'romantic' to be adequate to express its character. 'In Beethoven you get everything', my cousin Gladys (the writer 'Henrietta Leslie') once said to me; and Schubert would have been entitled to be called almost as universal as Beethoven if he had composed Masses equal in calibre to Beethoven's two, or operas of the quality of Beethoven's *Fidelio* or the six great operas of Mozart.

It is true, however, to say that romanticism first began to be a *predominant* feature of music in the nineteenth century: the romantic parts of Beethoven's art—*Adelaide*, for instance, and the *Leonora* overtures, the slow movements of the Fourth Symphony and of the Violin Concerto; the Fourth Piano Concerto; many elements in the Seventh Symphony, in the sonatas, and so on; Weber's *Der Freischütz*, *Euryanthe* and *Oberon* (with its fairy music), which are romantic through and through, and even his *Concertstück* for pianoforte and orchestra, which is based on a romantic story; Schubert, in so many of his *lieder*, and in the passionate or idyllic portions of the *Unfinished* and the *Great C major* Symphonies and of his chamber music and works for pianoforte.

And then come—chronologically—Berlioz, who is considered to be one of the great romantics, but is—as I hope to show—more than that besides; Mendelssohn, who is only partly romantic; Chopin; Schumann, who is romantic to the core; and Liszt, whose music is often romantic but also contains an unromantic element of glitter and superficial ornament. The art of Franck and Bruckner is romantic to some extent, but also deeply religious.

The growth of romanticism synchronised, by a natural process, with the development of instrumental 'colour'. Wagner is predominantly a romantic, if ever there was one, yet his mature music-dramas have often been called 'symphonic' partly because of the enormous importance of the orchestra and partly because the leitmotives are symphonically, as well as dramatically, varied and developed. Verdi, though largely a man of the theatre, was only a romantic to a limited extent. Tchaikovsky and Dvořák were pre-eminently romantic. When the sixth (and last) volume of the

99

original edition of 'The Oxford History of Music', by Edward Dannreuther, appeared, it was entitled *The Romantic Period*, and one of the reviewers criticised it for saying so little about Brahms, 'that great romantic composer'; many years later, in *The Times* of November 18th, 1966, their music critic wrote an article on *Brahms the Romantic*, began it by asking 'Is it really true that Brahms is to be admired as the champion of classicism in a romantic age?' and answered that question in the negative. Old fallacies die hard. There is no reason why the nebulous term 'classical' or any other expression, should be opposed to 'romanticism' at all. Romanticism is an identifiable spirit in art. And Brahms is not only romantic, besides being a master of structure; he is more of the *type* of Beethoven and Schubert—a great genius whose music embraces most of the emotions, thoughts and aspirations of humanity, and only falls short of the supreme heights of Beethoven's art in that he does not, even in the *Requiem* or in the greatest moments of his instrumental and his other vocal works, reach the level of the most profound 'middle period' compositions of Beethoven or penetrate into the eternal verities with the mystic vision with which Beethoven did in the masterpieces of his last period.

Finally, the *predominantly* romantic age continued till the end of the 19th century in the *lieder* of Hugo Wolf, bowed itself out in the songs and some portions of the symphonies of Mahler, declined to some extent in Richard Strauss, and even more in the early works of Schoenberg, during the first part of the 20th century. But romanticism, that ever-recurring trait in human nature, continued to find its place, though not a leading one, in the music of other (non-Teutonic) masters—Elgar, Sibelius, Nielsen, Janáček, Falla, even Debussy (in *Pelléas et Mélisande*), Delius, Vaughan Williams, William Walton and Benjamin Britten.

The question whether a period is to be called 'romantic', is thus largely a matter of degree. The 19th century, after its early years, is hitherto the only one in which romanticism has, on the whole, dominated the musical scene.

CHAPTER SIXTEEN

The Range of Schubert

In some ways, Schubert is the most astonishing miracle among all the great composers. Dying at 31, he did not attain the heights of mysticism reached (in his last period) by Beethoven, who, however, at least lived to the age of 56. Mozart was a child prodigy, but his really youthful compositions were greatly surpassed in character and emotional depth by his more mature ones. Mendelssohn produced the lovely *Octet* at 16 and the marvellous overture to *A Midsummer Night's Dream* a year later. But Schubert, by the time he was 21, had already composed eight of his very greatest *lieder*: *Gretchen am Spinnrade, Der Erlkönig, Ganymed, Gruppe aus dem Tartarus, Die Forelle, An die Musik, Der Tod und das Mädchen,* and *Prometheus: above all,* the second, fourth, seventh and eighth of these are imbued with a tragic grandeur amazing in one so young; and even if we consider these eight songs alone, we are astounded at the range of emotion and imagination that they reveal, coming from a man so inexperienced of the world. Schubert in his short life composed over 600 songs, and is widely held to be the supreme song-writer in musical history. He is the author of two of the world's most glorious symphonies, and of some of its greatest chamber-music and works for pianoforte solo. How does all this fit in with his simple, easy-going, good-tempered, affectionate, mainly cheerful, modest, guileless character? It is easy to utter the pass-word 'genius' and leave it at that. The three real answers to the problem, I believe, lie in the width and depth of his imagination and the consequent ability to put himself inside the skin of the immense variety of human characters who figure in his songs—an ability which can truthfully be compared to Shakespeare's astonishing penetration into all the different personalities who walked upon the stage of his plays; in his love for the beauties of nature, which he instinctively transformed into musical terms—the sound of the brook, the ripple of water, the rustle of the trees, the songs of birds, the violence of a storm, the loveliness of flowers, the stillness of a moonlit night; and in his apparently innate capacity for expressing the most varied human emotions, profound, delicate, sorrowful, tragic, gay, loving, joyful, and triumphant, not only in song, but by means of instruments alone. It was his sympathetic character, his love of his friends and of human beings in general and of the sights and sounds of the countryside, allied to his exceptional, natural gift for music—his sheer power of invention, combined with his industrious care in composition, that united to make him one of the supreme composers.

He was utterly sincere and simple; so is his music; his gift for writing beautiful melodies is one of his most appealing qualities; but another feature of his art that takes one's breath away is his apparently instinctive use of subtle, surprising modulations and of sudden changes between major and minor.

There was a crisis in his career. As his fame grew in the early 1820's, his head was, perhaps, turned a little. He became, for a time, aloof from his father and brothers (his mother had died when he was 15), and his attitude towards his old friends tended to cool off. Then, in the autumn of 1822, he contracted venereal disease—an easy thing for a young bachelor to do at that stage of medical history. The shock had, in one, strange sense, a wholesome effect in restoring him to his real, genial self: his affection for his family and his friends returned, and so did his natural cheerfulness and his creative activity; yet his health had been undermined; during his last six years he often felt ill and depressed; it is probable that the disease largely contributed to his early death in 1828, though the immediate cause of this was typhoid fever.

However that may be, those final years saw the composition of *most* of his supreme masterpieces: all the greatest instrumental works except the superb Quartett-Satz in C minor of 1820; the two fine settings of the Mass in A flat and E flat, spiritual in character, though not mystical; a whole world of lovely songs, including those two wonderful cycles, *Die Schöne Müllerin*, with its immense variety of emotions and pictures of nature, and the tragic sequence of *Die Winterreise*; the gay *Der Musensohn*; the delicate *Geheimes*; the serene idealisation of love in *Due bist die Ruh'*; the charming *Auf dem Wasser zu singen*; the majestic *Die Allmacht*; the sublime *Im Abendrot*; and the final collection of masterpieces (not really a cycle) which together are known as the

Schwanengesang—to name only some examples.

The crisis in Schubert's life to which I have referred, deeply though it must arouse one's compassion if it caused him pain or remorse and ultimately shortened his life, does seem to have sounded fresh depths in his nature and exalted his imagination into the heights. Without it, one wonders whether we should have been blessed with the most profoundly beautiful of the songs of his last years; the glorious *Unfinished* Symphony in B minor, which he seems to have forgotten to complete; the immortal Impromptus for pianoforte and the finest of his sonatas; the three magnificent last quartets in A minor, D minor, and G major; the sublime *Great* C major Symphony, which has its passages of terror as well as of vigour, melancholy loveliness, and spiritual victory; and that consummation of all his chamber music, the Quintet for Strings in C, which ranges from resignation, through celestial beauty, dreaminess, anguish, peaceful visions, energy, and solemnity, to ultimate joy.

This son of a schoolmaster of peasant stock was brought up in a devout household, but became an unorthodox Catholic. He was capable of composing beautiful music for the Church, but his mind and his aspirations ranged over so wide a field that he enriched the world with a succession of masterpieces unsurpassed in variety when one reflects on the brevity of his life.

Schubert, like Beethoven, stands at the entrance to the predominantly 'romantic' age of the 19th century. There is more actual 'romanticism' in his art than in Beethoven's, possibly because he was more of a song-writer; but, like his even mightier contemporary, he transcended the 'romantic' in music; though he did not reach middle age, his range of imagination and emotion embraced humanity to an extent only equalled afterwards, in my view, by Brahms and, perhaps, Berlioz.

CHAPTER SEVENTEEN

Mendelssohn, the underrated Master

Felix Mendelssohn was of Jewish blood, baptised in infancy into the Lutheran faith, a loyal and patriotic German, a good European, and a profound humanist, like his distinguished grandfather Moses Mendelssohn, the great philosopher, who was a deep thinker not only about the Jewish religion but about religion in general. Abraham Mendelssohn, Felix's father, reared his children as Christians, because, though indifferent to established religions and yet deeply and philosophically religious in the widest sense, he believed Christianity to be the most purified form of religion and Judaism to be antiquated; he eventually adopted Christianity himself, because he felt it his duty to do for himself that which he had recognised as best for his children.

Felix was intensely religious and was a faithful and serious Christian; he also felt a strong bond of kinship with individual Jews, although the concepts of Judaism, insofar as they differed from Christianity, meant little to him. He was devoted to his father and loyal to his father's and grandfather's humanistic ideals. He showed himself extremely sensitive to any anti-semitic experiences —as when a royal Prussian prince stopped him in the street when he was aged ten, spat at his feet, and called him 'Jew-boy', during the little 'pogrom' known as the 'Judensturm'; or when some street-urchins insulted him (aged fifteen) and his sister Fanny, shouted 'Jew-boy' and threw stones at them; and when in 1832 the Berlin *Singakademie*, because he was a 'Jew-boy', refused to elect him at the age of 23 to the position of director, in spite of his brilliance[27] (they retained, however, the valuable collection of manuscripts which had largely been presented to them by his father and his aunt-by-marriage, because they did not want to appear ungrateful; and they tried to make amends in after-years

[27] This is according to Eric Werner's account in his book 'Mendelssohn'; H. E. Jacob ('Felix Mendelssohn and his times') thinks that the rejection of him for the post was really due to his youth.

by appointing him an honorary member and by regular performances of several of his compositions).

As a youth, he was not only sensitive, but occasionally moody;
he was intellectual, dreamy, and imaginative. He had a brilliant
mind, a sense of humour, a happy, resilient nature, and a warm
heart.

His tastes were simple, he hated drunkenness and all other forms
of excess; a handsome man, with charming manners, cultured,
well-read, and witty, it is not surprising that he was popular both
in the English Court and elsewhere.

He was very fond of Schumann, as a man, was friendly with
Chopin, liked Berlioz personally very much but neither appreciated
nor understood the music which Berlioz composed during his lifetime. There were, even, cordial relations between him and Wagner
in the latter's younger days, and Mendelssohn, the elder of the
two, was very welcoming to Wagner, who, later in life, was not
deterred by this from declaring in his pamphlet 'Judaism in music',
published some years after Mendelssohn's death, that Mendelssohn
was precluded by his 'Jewish nature' from 'calling forth in us that
deep, heart-searching effect which we await from Art'; and in 1881-2,
Wagner wrote far more violently against Jews generally and against
Mendelssohn.

It is ironical that Wagner should have thought that Mendelssohn's
'Jewish nature' prevented him from evoking a 'deep, heart-
searching effect'. The one eminent composer of Jewish blood who
does convey in his music 'the Jewish soul', as he once wrote himself (and who appeared after both Mendelssohn and Wagner), is
Ernest Bloch, whose art no one could describe as lacking in emotional depth. And to suggest that Jewish writers, artists or philo-
sophers have lacked profundity, does not bear scrutiny for a
moment; this, however, would open up a much wider subject. I
have never been able to see anything intrinsically Hebraic in the
music of Mendelssohn. Wagner was deceiving himself; if he had
been constitutionally able to listen to it with unprejudiced ears,
he would have found it purely European, subject, where appropriate, to the influences of Italy, England and Scotland, but mainly
in the great tradition of German music, to which, indeed, it made
an important contribution. Yet Mendelssohn was against any narrowly nationalistic conception of music; in his eyes, the art transcended national boundaries.

Mendelssohn consistently tried to help practising musicians and composers; and though he came of a prosperous family he shunned class distinctions and was, like his forebears, philanthropic without discrimination of religion, race, or nation.

He and his sister Fanny were particularly devoted to one another, and though failing health and a severe stroke led to his premature death, it was her sudden death that precipitated his own, six months afterwards.

Before his marriage, Mendelssohn enjoyed flirting, but he was restrained in the expression of passionate emotions. He married Cécile Jeanrenaud, a beautiful girl of Huguenot extraction, who was a young woman of lovely character and became his beloved wife and companion, though she was not musical and could not rise to his intellectual or artistic level. Mendelssohn was not a romantic lover. He was, indeed, not a man of the most profound emotions—unless you call religious feeling an 'emotion', which I do not.

Now, this leads me to a consideration of the relationship between this remarkable man's personal character and his music, to an explanation of what I mean by entitling this short chapter *Mendelssohn, the underrated master*, and to a reflection upon the extent to which he was a romantic composer.

It has been said that he was a great composer, *in spite* of the fact that in his art he did not express great depth of emotion. On the contrary, I believe that one of the reasons why he deserves the attribute of greatness is that it was one of his special qualities to convey, with eloquence and unsurpassed art, emotions which were *not* very profound, but tender, gentle, brave and vigorous yet not heroic, melancholy yet not intensely sad. You will not find in his music the heartbreaking sadness of some of Chopin's creations, the deeply disturbed, though restrained, grief of Mozart's greatest movements in a minor key, the radiant happiness often shining in the scores of Haydn, the tragedy or the *innigste empfindung* or the spiritual triumph that appear in the music of Beethoven or Schubert, nor the deep, surging emotions of much of Brahms's music. But it is precisely because Mendelssohn voiced the feelings of so many human beings who—unlike others —do not experience profound emotions but gentler, more restrained, less disturbing ones, that he has been a popular composer. He is, so to speak, their prophet—and a very eloquent and delightful prophet, too! He had the most perfect technique and craftsmanship for expressing this kind of human nature, which was also his own nature as a man. He was a consummate master of instrumentation and, as a matter of sheer skill, he wrote most beautifully for human voices—particularly for a choir.

The only *profundity* in Mendelssohn's art is to be found in his religious music—in *St. Paul* and its successor, the great, and at times dramatic, oratorio *Elijah*, in the *Hymn of Praise*, in his settings of the psalms and of various Christian liturgical texts—just as his Christian faith, coupled with his loyalty to his family and to others of Jewish blood and to his native Germany, and his humanitarian outlook, were the most profound features in his personality. His sacred music is deeply religious, but it is not mystical, like Beethoven's, nor does it rise to the exalted heights of the liturgical art of Bach. It is, however, to him that the world is to a large extent indebted for the re-discovery of Bach's supreme masterpiece, the *St. Matthew Passion*, and for a general awakening of the love for the art of that mighty genius.

To what extent, then, was Mendelssohn a romantic composer? In his instrumental works he followed, broadly speaking, the structure evolved for sonata, chamber music, concerto and symphony by Haydn, Mozart, Beethoven and Schubert. But there *is* a romantic streak in his music, though it is not so pronounced as the romanticism of Berlioz, Schumann, Chopin or Wagner. The tenderness of his slow movements, such as those in the *Scotch* and *Italian* Symphonies, in the Violin Concerto in E minor, and in his chamber music works, is gently romantic; and so are his *Variations sérieuses* and many of the short pieces which, like Schubert and Chopin, he wrote for pianoforte and which he called *Songs without words*—provided that these are played simply and without sentimentality. He sensed the romanticism and glamour of Scotland, which so many of us Southerners experience when we cross the Border, the haunting beauty of that 'land of the mountain and the flood', with its lochs and waterfalls, its rushing streams and its magnificent Western coast, its heather and its rhododendrons growing wild on the hill-sides, and its background of romantic, albeit bloodstained, history. He gave musical expression to this Scottish atmosphere in his wonderful *Hebrides* overture and in the *Scotch* Symphony. And in the wild grandeur of *The First Walpurgis Night* there is something of the fantastic romanticism that recurs in Berlioz.

The other romantic feature in Mendelssohn's music is the fairy element. This is obvious in his marvellous overture to *A Midsummer*

Night's Dream and in the incidental music to the play, but the fairies in Mendelssohn are not confined to Shakespeare: they are present in the *Fair Melusine* overture, too, in scherzo after scherzo of his chamber music from the Octet for strings onwards, and, for instance, in the *Song without words* popularly known as *The Bees' wedding*, which has nothing to do with bees, but is a delicate piece of fairy music for the piano, as light and airy as gossamer. If—or as—fairyland is essentially romantic, Mendelssohn's ever recurring fairies and elves are another facet of the romantic side of his art.

During World War II, I was for a while somewhat closely associated in the War Office with a particularly charming English, Staff Colonel, who was very fond of music and a great lover of Mendelssohn. I remember his saying to me 'What grand music the old fellow wrote!' I could not help smiling inwardly, because, apart from *Elijah* and *The First Walpurgis Night*, Mendelssohn's music is not conspicuous for its 'grandeur' so much as for its other qualities, and he certainly was not 'old' when he died. But I know exactly what the Colonel meant: 'old fellow' was, of course, just a term of affection, and 'grand' was simply a sign of his recognition of the beauty of Mendelssohn's music.

Mendelssohn—who was, it seems, somewhat overrated during his lifetime—has been underrated sometimes in the 20th century, and though there has been a revival of love and esteem for his art, the undervaluing recurs in some quarters, but is due, I suggest, to a failure to appreciate the qualities which I have tried to indicate and a mistaken idea that, because the emotions in his music are not so profound as in that of some other great composers and because even his sacred music is not so sublime as that of the supreme creators of religious art, therefore he is not in the front rank. That depends on how many composers you are prepared to put in that exalted class! Mendelssohn was certainly a great and individual and unique artist.

CHAPTER EIGHTEEN

Romantic Schumann

By nature, Robert Schumann was romantic to the core, both in himself and in his art. No composer has expressed his own character and temperament in his music more completely. From his father, who was the son of a poor clergyman and who became a cultured bookseller, he inherited his great interest in literature; from his mother, his intense emotional sensitivity and his profound streak of melancholy. Thus, though as a schoolboy at his native Zwickau in Saxony he was full of vigour and bonhommie, he was morbidly affected by his sister's suicide and his father's death, both occurring when he was only sixteen. Yet he was fully capable of enjoying himself on excursions into the country with his friends, dancing and flirting with peasant girls at an inn, and in drinking champagne and smoking cigars—he had not got an instinct for economy. His mother induced him to study law at Leipzig, but he was not happy in it either there or at Heidelberg, and with the moral support of Friedrich Wieck, the eminent teacher of the piano in Leipzig, he returned there when he was 20, to become a professional musician under Wieck's tutelage.

Of course, this romantic young man had several love affairs: he had two calf-loves in his adolescence, and at 24 became engaged to the charming and beautiful Ernestine von Frickine. That, however, was a short-lived matter. There was something irresponsible and unstable in his temperament; but as time went by, he came to realise that he was seriously in love with Wieck's daughter, Clara, though she was then (early in 1836) only 16; she was, however, very mature for her years. Her father strenuously opposed the match, but they remained deeply as well as passionately devoted to one another; eventually they married in September, 1840, when he was 30 and on the day before her 21st birthday. Ultimately, Wieck became reconciled to the marriage, which proved to be an ideal one. Schumann had in 1832 crippled his right hand with a mechanical contrivance which he had himself invented, but had stoically faced the realisation that his career as a pianist was finished and that his true future lay in composition. Clara was a marvellous virtuoso, and with her art as a great pianist and his as a composer of genius, theirs would have been a long as well as a perfect union if only his health had held out. The years just after his marriage were the happiest in his life. In their sixteen years of married life they had eight children (though one died in early childhood), but his nervous weakness and exhaustion gradually developed into mental instability, until the dreadful day in February, 1854, when he tried to drown himself in the Rhine. He spent 2½ years in a private asylum before he died in July, 1856.

In spite of his introspective nature, he was tender-hearted, deeply sympathetic, and enthusiastically interested in the welfare of his fellow-musicians and in the art of other composers—not only his great contemporaries such as Berlioz, Chopin and Mendelssohn (for whom he had a warm personal affection), but also that of the younger generation. He sensed the greatness of Brahms when the latter was only 20.

His was a complex nature. Even in his youth, he represented two, or even three, contrasted sides of his personality in the articles which he wrote under pseudonyms in the *Neue Zeitschrift für Musik*, the magazine which he and some of his friends started in 1834, to combat superficiality, vulgarity and mediocrity in music. There was 'Florestan', the vigorous stormy character, and 'Eusebius', the gentle, dreamy one; whilst 'Raro' was either a (rare) combination of the two or (at other times) an impersonation of the level-headed Wieck.

It was natural that he should in his most characteristic works have regarded music as a vehicle for the expression of emotions and dreams. His love for Clara was his greatest inspiration. To this we are indebted for such masterpieces as the *Phantasie* (op. 17), the *Kreisleriana* (op. 16), the *Davidsbündlertänze* (op. 6), the *Noveletten* (op. 21), the *Phantasie-stücke* (op. 12) and the *Kinderscenen* (op. 15). Whereas Chopin called his pieces simply *Préludes*, *Études*, 'Ballades', and so on, Schumann gave to his piano compositions names which, even though attached afterwards, were surely present in his imagination beforehand; this happened even with such early works as *Papillons* and *Carnaval*, with its pictures of Florestan, Eusebius, Chiarina (Clara as a child in her 'teens), Estrella (Ernestine), Chopin, Paganini, Pierrot and Columbine, Harlequin and Pantaloon. He *could* write 'absolute' music for the piano as well, but the three sonatas are not so typical of his mentality, and the *Études Symphoniques* are, I think, the one great pianoforte composition of his which does not seem to have stimulated by any non-musical influence: it is largely a set of variations, with a powerful Finale based on a fresh theme.

After he had produced some of the loveliest music for pianoforte solo in the world, Schumann's married happiness and his love of poetry found vent in the world of song. He became one of the greatest of the great series of German *lieder*-writers. The *Liederkreis* (op. 24) and the *Dichterliebe*, set to poems by Heine, and *Frauenliebe und-leben* to words by Chamisso, are among the glories of 19th century romantic art, and so are many other songs, whether grouped in cycles or more or less independent, inspired by poets as varied as Eichendorff, Mörike, Lenau, or Byron. He was gifted with a genius for word-painting, and for conveying love and joy and sorrow and patriotism and dreaminess, as well as the beauties of nature. The piano part is as important as the voice, so that an equal partnership between singer and 'accompanist' is vital for the interpretation of these lyrical masterpieces.

It was quite natural for Schumann to turn to orchestral music after hearing the *Great C major* Symphony of Schubert, which he himself had discovered in Vienna in 1838. Schumann did not become a great master of the development section of sonata or symphony, and orchestration was not his strong point. Nevertheless, I have never felt that his orchestration was as bad as it has been made out to be, though no doubt Mahler's re-scoring of the symphonies was technically an improvement. But though Schumann was embarking on an orchestral and symphonic phase of his career, so different from his groups of short piano pieces and his poetical *lieder*, his works in this genre always seem to me to possess an *intrinsically* romantic character, with the ardour, the tenderness, or the manliness which (for instance) imbue their different movements. The *Spring* Symphony, No. 1 in B flat, was inspired by Böttger's poem on the subject of spring, and even though Schumann subsequently discarded the titles *Spring's Awakening*, *Evening*, *Merry Playmates* and *Spring's Farewell* from the four movements, the fact remains that they are singularly apt for the actual character of the music. The D Minor Symphony, which followed next (though revised later and published as No. 4), is intensely romantic in feeling and its slow movement is appropriately entitled *Romanze*. The

Symphony in C major is deeply emotional, especially its glorious Adagio; and the *Rhenish*, E flat, Symphony in five movements is essentially atmospheric and lyrical, though more organically constructed than the others; the solemn fourth movement represents the ceremony in Cologne Cathedral when Archbishop von Geissel was installed as Cardinal.

Whatever may be said against Schumann's scoring in his symphonies, the Piano Concerto in A minor is faultless in all respects, and is, indeed, one of the greatest concertos ever written, with its romantically passionate first movement, its enchanting and delicate Andante, and its virile, splendid Finale. This lovely work towers over Schumann's other compositions for solo instruments with orchestra, though the 'Introduction and Allegro appassionato' is a delightful companion piece to it, and the first two movements of the Cello Concerto are beautiful and characteristic of his art.

In his chamber music Schumann concentrated more on structure than in his symphonies, but the three string quartets contain many romantic beauties, particularly in the slow movements; the Third Quartet, in A major, is surely the finest of the three. The Piano Quintet, however, is the greatest of all his chamber music works and is one of his loveliest compositions, with its warmly emotional first Allegro, its deeply-felt slow movement, and its richly varied Finale.

This versatile composer also won considerable achievements in the world of vocal music with orchestra. *Paradies and the Peri* may not be an unqualified masterpiece, but it contains some fine descriptive passages and beautiful arias for solo voices, though its choruses are more conventional. The *Scenes from Goethe's Faust* is striking for the fact that it is one of the few attempts by a composer to embody any of Goethe's *Part II* in music—the other notable one being the last movement of Mahler's Eighth Symphony. From Goethe's *Part I*, Schumann does set the garden scene (briefly), 'Margaret before the image of the Mater Dolorosa', and the scene between her and Mephistopheles and the chorus in the Cathedral, both beautifully and dramatically. But his other two Parts are devoted to the Second Part of Goethe's great work. Schumann's *Part II* is not especially remarkable, but his Third Part is a sublime setting of the whole of Goethe's last scene—the hermits, the choruses of angels, the three women, the 'penitent' (formerly Margaret), the Mater Gloriosa, and the Mystic Chorus—all of it seraphic, serene, and exalted music.

I have never heard Schumann's only opera, *Genoveva*, which is very rarely performed and does not seem to have been very successful, but the fine poetic overture is fairly often given at concerts. The overture to Byron's dramatic poem *Manfred* is full of tragic grandeur, and the incidental music, consisting of fifteen numbers, most of them quite short, is wonderfully expressive of the words and ideas of the drama; though some of it is sung by a chorus, there are several eloquent orchestral passages to be performed against speaking voices.

Only at the end of his creative career did Schumann turn towards liturgical music—a Mass and a Requiem. He was not religious in the narrower sense of the term. But his music, like the man himself, is full of nobility, freshness, and deep sincerity; many other composers rose in their art above the faults of their personal characters; in Schumann's case, his own liability to morbid introspection does not appear in his music. He was a lovable man, and a great and lovable composer.

CHAPTER NINETEEN

Chopin, the poet of the piano

From the language of some of Chopin's letters in his adolescence to his friends Yan Bialobloki and Titus Voitsyekhovski it might be thought that he was going to become a homosexual. Actually it was no more than youthful exuberance, accentuated by the difference between Polish and English habits of expression; it is scarcely necessary to attribute it to the fact that many boys have homosexual impulses, which they outgrow. Anyhow, Chopin soon started to fall in love with girls. He had a calf-love for Konstantsya Gladovska, which he lacked words to express to her. After that, he had a serious affair with Marie Wodzinska and asked her to marry him. They became engaged, but she changed her mind—or rather, her parents changed it for her (on account of Chopin's health); he never really recovered from this, but his next and final attachment was his famous liaison with Aurore Dudevant (George Sand, the eminent writer). Meanwhile, he had left his native Poland on his musical travels—to Vienna, and eventually to Paris. When, in Vienna, he heard of the outbreak of the Poles against the invading Russians, he was divided in his mind as to whether he should return and fight for his country, but his parents dissuaded him because of his uncertain health. Any man less suited to being a soldier, it is hard to imagine: a frail, indecisive fellow, in whom the feminine instincts that in varying degrees are present, even if unconsciously, in every male, seem to have predominated. Guy de Pourtales[28] even goes so far as to speak of 'Mr' Sand and 'Miss' Chopin, but this is an oversimplification. There was certainly something markedly masculine in George Sand. Her attitude towards him was not merely quasi-maternal, but even domineering. The liaison ended sadly, and Chopin's long period of tuberculosis resulted in his death at the age of 39.

[28] 'Chopin, a man of *solitude*', translated by Charles Bayly, Jnr.

His father was French, his mother Polish; he was devoted both to Poland and to France—and to his family and his friends; he loved his sister Louise dearly, and the affection between them was a comfort to him in the closing stages of his illness.

This attractive man was idolised in the Paris salons both as a personality and as pianist and composer. But he was sad at heart for most of his short life, and his own sorrows are often apparent in his music. There is only one aspect of his character which might seem to detract from his charm—his anti-semitism, and I think that even this has been emphasised unduly by some of his biographers, for it was largely a facet of his youthful days: at that time of life he did, it is true, give vent to prejudice against 'the Jews'—a not uncommon feature of immaturity; but in the 'Selected Correspondence of Chopin' edited by Arthur Hedley, which contains all the letters of any importance whatever, the anti-semitic references are insignificant and very few in number. It is far more material that he included several people of Jewish blood among his friends—Mendelssohn, Meyerbeer, the Rothschilds, Heine, Schlesinger, the publisher, and the banker, Auguste Leo. I never feel that anti-semitism went very deep in Chopin or was at all a leading feature in his make-up.

There is a certain paradox in the fact that this man of extremely refined manners, so sensitive, so aristocratic in his bearing, a dandy in his dress, should have composed music which has such a wide appeal, even to not very musical people. I remember how one of the senior lady-secretaries in the Head Office of the industrial firm for which I worked for so many years, though she had very little interest in serious music (and did not pronounce French very well—bless her!), once said to me 'But I *do* like Showpang'! And this is typical. Chopin's art is immensely popular throughout the civilised world. It is *not* music just for the cultured few (or principally loved by its author's compatriots rather than by the men and women of other nations). Yet, like Chopin the man, the music is, so to speak, frequently aristocratic, never showy or vulgar, and utterly refined—even fastidious—to an unusual degree, though expressive of the most varied human emotions. Its ornaments are never mere appendages, but as natural, as essential, as the leaves or blossoms on a beautiful tree. He is a consummate master of pianistic technique, of the colours that can be wrought from the character of the piano as an instrument. And his structures are masterly, too. He does not often, or even usually, compose in

inherited 'sonata' form, but more frequently, and more characteristically, in shorter forms of his own creation—whether he calls
them *préludes*, *études*, *ballades*, *impromptus*, or *nocturnes*, or
whether he is employing the dance rhythms and lilt of waltz,
polonaise, or mazurka. It has been said that his nocturnes—like
Mendelssohn's *Songs without words*—are salon pieces, almost as
if that were a term of reproach; but why should there not be
music which is eminently suited to be played on a pianoforte in
the sitting- or drawing-room of a private house, as well as music
appropriate to a church or to a large or small concert-hall? To say
that Chopin was chiefly a miniaturist, and therefore less great
than a composer of operas or oratorios or symphonies, is rather
pointless criticism. Chopin never created a music-drama, but Wagner could not have composed chamber-music or short pieces for the
piano. Different composers excel in different media. It is the intrinsic quality of the music itself that matters. It is not even true
to assert that Chopin could not create large forms or extended structures (as some critics have said). His second and third sonatas for
pianoforte solo are two of the greatest ever composed for that in-
instrument; and their form is perfect. The Finale that follows the
Funeral March in the B flat minor sonata is a stroke of sheer
genius: it sounds a note of utter desolation as the *immediate* after-
effect of the burial of a beloved person on the soul of at least
one mourner who had been present at the funeral; it is a completely artistic finish to the work, but no one other than Chopin
could have produced just that brief expression of bleak, lonely,
whirling despair in musical terms. Each of those two sonatas and
the two (early) concertos takes roughly half-an-hour to perform;
and though Chopin was no more than a competent orchestrator,
the pianoforte parts of the two concertos are music of great beauty
and of deep, human emotions. The four romantic Ballades, the
magnificent Fantasy in F minor, the lovely Barcarolle, are all instances of, at any rate, fairly extended forms, constructed by the
hand of a master. Detractors of Chopin seem, almost, to criticise
his works because they are not so long as a Mahler symphony or a
Wagner opera! Is Wolf not entitled to be called a great genius
because most of his wonderful songs are short?

Both as a person and as an artist, Chopin was sensitive and delicate to an unusual degree; but his music goes far beyond that:
within the medium of the pianoforte he expresses grief, resignation, pathos, despair and courage, turbulence of spirit and gaiety,

116

love and tenderness, serenity and religious devotion[29]. And all these moods and emotions were reflections of those which he experienced in his own life.

In his grandest moments, Chopin's music can be tremendous—in the C minor Prelude, in the A minor and C minor Études (Nos. 11, and 12 of op. 25), in the *Revolutionary* Étude (op. 10, No. 12), in the Finales of both the later sonatas. And though *scherzo* means 'Joke', Chopin's Scherzos are certainly not funny!

Chopin was *par excellence* a poet of the piano. But his songs are not to be despised, and the sonata for 'cello and pianoforte has many beauties. Of course he is not on a level with Bach and Handel, with Haydn and Mozart, with Beethoven and Schubert, with Wagner or Brahms, or, *I* would add, Berlioz. Chopin was the romantic creator of much of the loveliest romantic music for his instrument that has hitherto been composed. At times, also, he rises to tragic grandeur. And some of his melodies are unutterably beautiful, even though they do not soar to the sublime heights of the greatest of those of Beethoven, Bach and Handel. No wonder that he is one of those who are loved best and most widely of all the great masters of music, and that his appeal seems to continue undiminished through successive generations of music lovers.

[29] I have drawn attention to some of the religious moments in Chopin's works and life, in my book 'The Divine Quest in Music'.

CHAPTER TWENTY

Until Marriage (including Franck, Delius, Debussy and Richard Strauss)

In Chapter 13 (*The Aftermath*) I tried to set the scene for the musical side of my life in the period immediately following World War I. I must now resume the narrative, but it will take a somewhat different shape from the one in which I have framed it hitherto. In preceding chapters it has been possible to divide it into distinct, successive periods such as early childhood, Harrow, Germany, Oxford, and the First War. But after my return home in 1919, I have remained in London (apart from holidays, some of my Army Service in 1939-41, and short visits abroad); and the tenor of my life, though by no means always smooth, has only been changed in any dramatic way by a few events, two of them, for example, personal, and a third world-wide—my conversion to Christianity, my marriage, and the Second World War.

From this point onwards, therefore, although certain composers will require separate chapters, my reflections on others will—I feel—fall quite naturally into their place within my autobiographical narrative itself.

One of the first composers for whom I developed a special love after the First War was César Franck. He and his art do not occupy so much of my time and attention now, in my old age, as they did then—any more than Tchaikovsky does today as compared with his place in my boyhood; but I have always retained an affection for both of them. In the days of which I am speaking (soon after World War I) there were plenty of opportunities to hear many of Franck's works, and I became increasingly fascinated by a certain dichotomy in his music, which had its parallel in his personal character. On the one hand, we have Franck the organist of Sainte-Clotilde in Paris, kind-hearted, charitable, unselfish, modest, with a strong sense of duty and family affection, concerned with paying the debts of his father, who had been distinctly des-

118

potic before César's marriage, and with helping those two extravagant relatives, his brother and his brother-in-law; a believing Christian, but not a devout Roman Catholic churchman. He was, however, also passionate, impatient and occasionally ill-tempered.

These two contrasted aspects of his nature are, to a large extent, reflected in his music, which is sometimes religious in feeling, sometimes romantic, tempestuous, and even picturesque in its portrayal either of evil or of pagan forces. The religious side appears not only in the *Béatitudes*, *Rédemption*, his early Biblical eclogue *Ruth*, the Mass for three voices (which contains the popular *Panis Angelicus*), the song *La Procession*, and the two short oratorios— *The Tower of Babel* and *The Complaint of the Israelites*—but in some of his purely instrumental works as well: quite naturally it is present in his three Chorales for organ—his final works—but the Prelude, Chorale, and Fugue and the Prelude, Aria and Finale, though written for the pianoforte, an instrument not normally associated with church worship, are strongly religious in character; there is definitely a spiritual character, as well as deep emotions, inherent in the violin and piano sonata[30], the Symphony, and the Quartet, even though they are also in parts romantic, as are the Symphonic Variations for piano and orchestra. The passionate, tempestuous element in Franck is most strongly evident in the Pianoforte Quintet, which his benevolently domineering wife disliked and found disturbing. And even though the portrayal of Satan in the *Béatitudes* is less convincing than the lovely music which he composed for Christ, he showed his ability to depict diabolical forces, at least for a short time at a stretch, in *Le Chasseur Maudit* and *Les Djinns* for piano and orchestra; and he had enough imagination to convey a pagan, picturesque legend in his tone-poem *Psyche*.

Thus Franck was not, as Vincent d'Indy, his pupil and biographer depicted him, a purely saintly person who composed religious music. He was an intriguing mixture: the good qualities certainly predominate in his personal character; his music, in which a strong vein of chromaticism is mingled with a mainly diatonic technique,

[30] This sonata was originally written for 'cello and piano, but Ysaye persuaded Franck to transfer the 'cello part to violin; the ms., however, is headed for violin or 'cello alternatively; not until 1967 did I hear it played on the 'cello (an octave lower than the violin) and pianoforte, by the sisters Joan and Hester Dickson: the effect was so noble that I almost wish Ysaye had not exercised his powers of persuasion! But it is a noble and lovely work—in either form.

is on occasions profoundly religious or spiritual, at other times deeply emotional, even stormy, or vividly descriptive.

In Chapter 10, I wrote that, in the field of light music, only Messager's *Véronique* and *Monsieur Beaucaire* approached the Gilbert and Sullivan operas in my affections. *Véronique* appeared in London when I was a boy; for *Monsieur Beaucaire* we had to wait until soon after World War I. It was, I think, equally charming and delightful. Maggie Teyte created the leading lady's part, and I well remember how enchanting she was. How versatile, to be the perfect artist in a light opera, as well as in the works of Mozart, Debussy, Fauré and other French masters! Speaking of light music, I have not yet mentioned Edward German: he was, in my view, the greatest British composer in this 'genre' since Sullivan: *Merrie England* and *Tom Jones*, and the various dances for *Henry VIII* and *Nell Gwyn* are full of graceful, expressive melodies, skilfully orchestrated, and retain the freshness of their appeal whenever we are given the opportunity of hearing them.

It was at some date between 1919 and 1923 that I met Delius at a small party at the house of my old friend Cedric Glover, and had an interesting conversation with him, partly on the subject of ballet. I mentioned *Schéhérazade* as being a masterly piece of choreography, but he objected to it on the ground that it told quite a different story from the tales in the *Arabian Nights* on which Rimsky-Korsakov's colourful score was based. I have often reflected how fully I agree with him. At that time, I knew *comparatively* little of Delius's music, but from then onwards I took every chance that presented itself of hearing it. Delius is another composer whose art aroused my enthusiasm for a period, and of whom I can still say that I have never lost my enjoyment for it, though it does not hold the specially high place in my affections that it held formerly. This seems a suitable point at which to reflect briefly upon Delius as man and artist.

He was a curious mixture: he could be charming, and even kind towards young artists if he thought them talented; but if not, he was ruthless. He was so egocentric that in his eyes it was an 'outrageous interruption' of his work (according to his sister) when during World War I he had to leave his house at Grez-sur-Loing for no more than three weeks. Compared with other Englishmen who had to endure great hardships and suffering in those grim days even if for reasons of health or age they were spared the perils and terrors of service in the Forces, he ought really to have considered himself very lucky to have been practically immune from the effects of war, except for the damage done to his house by French officers. He was intolerant, and perhaps it was his struggle for independence against his parents in his youth that hardened his character. He was anti-Christian, a pantheistic pagan in his outlook, and a follower of Nietzsche. He had no financial difficulties, being comfortably off, and despised 'the herd'. Nevertheless, he appreciated the warmth of the reception given to him in London at the extended festival of his works organised by Beecham in 1929, the bestowal of the Companionship of Honour, and the Freedom of his native city, Bradford. And he showed great courage in enduring the paralysis and blindness of his last years.

He was, perhaps, the most cosmopolitan of all eminent composers, anyhow from the biographical standpoint. His parentage was German, he was born in England, but spent most of his life in other countries: in Florida, to which he escaped in his youth, but where he devoted himself to music instead of cultivating the orange grove as his father had intended; in Danville, Virginia, teaching music to the daughters of a professor; studying music in Leipzig, where he was befriended by Grieg; living with his generous and kindly uncle Theodore in Paris, where he met his devoted future wife, the Norwegian artist Jelka Rosen; and finally, in the house at Grez-sur-Loing, with its charming garden sloping down to the river, where together they lived until his death.

In consequence, so it has always seemed to me, the music of Delius does not for the most part reflect the character of any particular country, except where it sings 'the song of a great city', Paris, in an orchestral nocturne, or reflects in *Appalachia* the heartache of the negro slaves in America parted from their wives and children. *Brigg Fair* is an English Rhapsody, based on a Lincolnshire folk-song, but this and the *North Country Sketches*, three of which portray seasons rather than places, are music of Western Europe, and not specifically 'British' in their intrinsic character; and the exquisite nature studies *On Hearing the First Cuckoo in Spring, Summer Night on the River, In a Summer Garden, A Song of Summer, A Song before Sunrise*, depict scenes which belong as much to France, for example, as to England. And their idiom is, simply and uniquely, *Delius*. *Sea Drift* is a picture of the sea and a heart-rending expression of a bird's grief for the loss of its mate. *The Song of the High Hills*, with its wordless voices used as part of the orchestra, represents man's vision of great mountains, with man and nature in contrast. *The Songs of Farewell* picture land and sea, joy and farewell—anywhere in the world. There is nothing English (or Italian) about *A Village Romeo and Juliet*, that beautiful, pathetic, opera-story of two star-crossed lovers. By his evanescent, shifting harmonies and his rich yet delicate colouring, Delius portrays the beauties of nature and also something of its mysticism. It is all pantheistic, as is *A Mass of Life*, in which the pictures of nature are just as important as the expression of the Nietzschean 'will to live' or the dancing choruses. Delius's music is often mystical, but it is not spiritual. In the *Requiem* his attitude to death was too negative to inspire him to the composition of great music.

It is, I think, this lack of a spiritual quality which causes me now to be less enthusiastic than I used to be about Delius's art, and to place him far below his great contemporary, Elgar, in my affections. Nevertheless, I can still enjoy the many beauties of his finest works, and I believe that they will continue to appeal to future generations of music lovers. Some people dislike the absence of any astringency in his music. The best answer to such criticism is to admit the fact. In Delius's art, as in much of his contemporary Mahler's, there is a strong vein of nostalgia for the passing of a predominantly romantic epoch. He was a lover of nature, a dreamer of dreams, who in an idiom all his own and therefore new and original, nevertheless looked back regretfully to the past.

During the greater part of my adult life, no enthusiastic music lover who attended concerts or operas at all frequently could fail to become acquainted with many of the creations of Debussy and Richard Strauss or, therefore, to be influenced by them. Both these composers figured over and over again in the programmes of concerts which contained works by other composers that one wished to hear anyhow, and as for their operas, anyone young in age, or young at heart though no longer in age, would seek to hear them, if only out of curiosity. With two composers so prominent among my contemporaries, I could not honestly pretend that their music did not mean a good deal to me. This is especially the case with Debussy, whose art I have for the most part enjoyed throughout. At the start I was puzzled by it. My father used to call it 'elusive', and I found the 'whole-tone scale' idiom a difficult one to which to acclimatize myself at first. But as time went on, I became fully accustomed to it. The orchestral works—*L'Après-midi d'un faune*, the *Three Nocturnes*, the three parts of *Images*, and, perhaps, above all, *La Mer*—came to be among my favourite modern pieces for orchestra. They were so genuinely poetical and expressive, and free from artificiality. So, too, were the piano works, which evince a special feeling for the subtle colour possibilities of the instrument —though I was even more conscious of this in the orchestral works, with their almost infinite nuances and atmospheric tints inherent in the varying characteristics of the different instruments. As for the songs, I have had the advantage of hearing a number of these exquisite creations sung by Maggie Teyte, the wonderful English artist who was an unsurpassed interpreter of modern French music. She, above all the other performers won me to appreciation of that unique and lovely opera *Pelléas et Mélisande*. In the instrumental works, nature and legend play a larger part than human emotion; but *Pélleas*, quiet, reticent, subtle as it is, is as moving an expression of human pathos as anything composed in this century; to see and hear it performed in the Maggie Teyte days— which I did twice—was an unforgettable experience. Since World War II it has been memorably and beautifully revived in this country, at Glyndebourne. Another Debussy work which I have always loved particularly is the String Quartet in G minor, so unlike any other string quartet ever written, yet, I have always found, so easy to understand.

Debussy was not a man of great strength of character, although he was strong-willed. He was poorly off, yet extravagant and a hedonist, at any rate until his last years. He loved the pleasures of the table and was of sensual, yet refined, nature; both soft hearted and ruthless. After various affairs he married Lily Texier, a pretty, innocent, simple young girl of good character; but—as in the case of Wagner and his first wife, Minna—she could not rise to his artistic or intellectual level, and after less than five years he left her for the wife of another man, by whom he had a daughter and whom he subsequently married. His first wife had shot and wounded herself badly, near the heart. One cannot sit in judgment on these cases of incompatability, but Debussy, like so many geniuses, had a difficult temperament, and an exceptionally incoherent and conflicting character.

He was extremely sensitive, and his musical soul was, for the most part, inspired by the beauties of nature, by poetry, by mythology, and by the ancient age of chivalry. After the comparatively early string quartet (1893) and until we come to the final sonatas, these features were typical of his most characteristic

123

works, whether for voice of instruments, apart from the pathos and other emotions of *Pelléas et Mélisande*.

At the end, this richly imaginative, poetical musician became a composer who simply expressed human feelings, though in an entirely refined, 20th century idiom peculiar to himself—and to France. He had moved away from the essentially German influence of Wagner, with its quasi-philosophical undertones and its symbolic profundities, and just as in World War I he was in himself a fervently patriotic Frenchman, so in his music he had become the embodiment of at least one side of French culture, though in marked contrast to the more direct, less elusive art of his great contemporary and compatriot, Gabriel Fauré. He showed great compassion for his suffering fellow-countrymen in the war, but was deeply depressed by the knowledge that he had cancer. He died in March, 1918, during the last great German offensive.

Debussy was 'not a practising Catholic nor a believer', as he said to a representative of *Comoedia*. 'Mysterious Nature is my religion', he wrote. And this attitude is reflected in his music, not only in the compositions already mentioned, but even in *La Cathédrale engloutie*, which conveys the dignity of the building submerged in the depths of the sea rather than anything intrinsically religious. *The Blessed Damozel* was an early work (1887) and delicately reflects the gently Christian character of D. G. Rossetti's words (in a French version) and an imaginative picture of Heaven. The incidental music for d'Annunzio's *Le Martyre de Saint-Sébastien* (1911) is a remarkable mixture of Christianity and paganism, in consonance with the play, and is characteristic of Debussy's fascinatingly ambivalent mysticism.

I have never loved Richard Strauss's music as I have Debussy's. He had been the stormy petrel at the turn of the century, and came fully into his own again in England after the passions of war had subsided. Elsewhere[31] I have discussed many individual compositions of his: all the symphonic poems; three of his operas; and *Metamorphosen*. Here I can only indicate certain general features of his music and personality.

In my young days, there was a saying that went the rounds in music-loving circles: 'If Richard, why not Wagner? If Strauss, why not Johann?' Absurd, of course. Richard Strauss certainly had his own individuality and his own important place in musical

---

[31] In 'The Soul of Music', pp. 94-101, 134, 159-160; in 'The Divine Quest in Music', pp. 173-4; in 'Adventure in Music', chapter 11 and p. 113.

history. His claim to greatness, I think, rests on his exceptional gift of characterisation (which in music can only be generalised, not, strictly, individualistic), his brilliance in sheer description both of human situations and of the external world, and his mastery of orchestration. These are assets indeed; but I confess that I find the emotions often rather shallow or sophisticated, the view of human nature frequently either superficial or debased.

Let us consider, first, the symphonic poems. *Macbeth* does contain fine portraits of the cruel king and his fiendish queen. *Don Juan* is vigorous rather than truly ardent, and (following Lenau's poem) omits altogether the climax of the visit of the Statue and the final seizure of the Don by the demons—which, for most creative artists who have treated the subject, has been the feature that captured their imagination most strongly: in Strauss's work, Don Juan rushes from one passion to another, in pursuit of beauty, and dies in a duel. In *Death and Transfiguration*, the sick chamber is graphically described by this master of psychopathic unhealthiness, but the 'Transfiguration' scene after the death is a piece of gaudy tinsel, lacking in any truly religious insight. *Till Eulenspiegel* is an exceedingly clever picture of a rascal, though the actual orchestral representation of the hanging is one of Strauss's typical lapses of taste. '*Thus spake Zarathustra*', for all its richness, power and mastery somehow fails to rise to the bigness of its subject—not that Nietzsche's ideals are very exalted anyhow! The greatest of the symphonic poems is *Don Quixote*, with its kindly portraits of the crazy, fantastic knight and the homely, earth-bound Sancho Panza, and in spite of the insignificant lapses into short-lived sensationalism in the bleatings of sheep and the wind machine. In *Ein Heldenleben*, the 'hero', after a striking beginning and various adventures, vividly depicted, turns out to be none other than Strauss himself, with his critics portrayed as 'the enemies'; 'the hero's works of peace' are a pot-pourri from Strauss's earlier compositions, and 'the hero's wife' is a musical representation of Frau Strauss. The later works in this genre—the *Sinfonia Domestica* and the *Alpine Symphony*—are brilliantly scored, but emptier than their predecessors. The *Domestica*, however, contains a detailed description of Strauss's own sexual relations with his wife!

It is a somewhat similar tale when we turn to the operas. *Salome* is a vivid setting of a revolting subject, for all its mastery in telling a grim story. *Elektra* debases the ancient Greek dramas of

Aeschylus, Sophocles and Euripides, for there is no sense of the performance of a dreadful duty on the part of Elektra or Orestes: she *exults* in the contemplation of the deed, and dances in ecstasy at the murder of her mother and of Aegisthus, until she falls dead; this is a piece of musical sadism, as was the climax of *Salome*; but there is great beauty in the Recognition scene between Elektra and her brother.

Der Rosenkavalier is an extremely popular operatic comedy, but I confess that, except for a period about 1926-7, I have not cared for it very much. There is genuine beauty in the Marschallin's soliloquy in Act I, in Oktavian's entry in Act II, and above all, in the trio for women's voices near the end of a long evening. But for the most part the music seems to me to be sophisticated and shallow, and its emotions rather superficial. The Waltz fragments are continually and irritatingly interrupted: the waltz, I feel, is a dance form which calls for a completed melody (or series of completed melodies), like a minuet; but of course that would not have fitted into the continuous fabric of Strauss's score; no doubt, he had to get the waltz rhythm 'out of his system', so to speak, and on to paper. (The fact that his waltz themes are, strictly, anachronistic in an opera set in the time of Maria Theresa, is irrelevant, so long as their presence is artistically successful.) Norman Del Mar, in his perceptive book on Richard Strauss, draws a parallel between the Marschallin and Hans Sachs in the *Meistersinger*: both, it is true, are unsuccessful lovers; but Eva in Wagner's opera is in love with Walther before Sachs is presented to us, and has come to regard the latter simply as a dear old friend; not until Act II is his unrequited passion for her revealed to us, and his chief role in the story is to help Walther to win the contest of song, and thereby the hand of Eva, with his *Preislied*. The prelude to the Strauss opera depicts the *mutual* passion of the Marschallin and Oktavian, who is only 17 and has not yet broken his voice, and when the curtain rises she is either in bed or on a sofa in her bedroom, with Oktavian kneeling on a footstool beside her. Her husband is away, hunting. Oktavian is not the first young lover with whom she has consoled herself, and in due course she gives him up to Sophie, who is certainly more suited to him in age and with whom he has fallen in love. That is the Marschallin's claim to nobility of character, though she is certainly a pathetic figure. But the *Meistersinger* story is of romantic, innocent love, and Sach's nobility does not consist so much in giving up Eva to Walther as in showing his love for her and at the same time his breadth of view about Walther's efforts to musical and poetical composition in face of the hostility and rivalry of Beckmesser, and his warm, genial, and helpful friendship towards the young man. The Marschallin may be a great lady, but Hans Sachs is, surely, a greater man.

There is a certain charm in *Arabella* and *Ariadne in Naxos*, but the charm is chiefly on the surface, and the incidental music for *Le Bourgeois Gentilhomme*, though attractive, is somewhat artificial. In *Capriccio*, the composer discusses the aesthetics of opera as an art-form, the rival importance of words and music (linked with the rival appeals of poet and musician for the Countess's love); there is no drama in it, and no final solution; the music is mellifluous, scored (as usual) in masterly fashion, but mediocre, and the total effect is very boring. In *Intermezzo*, Strauss washes dirty linen in public, the husband being more or less a self-portrait and the wife a disagreeable representation of Frau Strauss; in this work, his bad taste reaches its nadir .

His finest opera, I think, is *Die Frau ohne Schatten*. Its scoring is superb, rich and sonorous; and it flows on in a wonderful, melodic stream. Its leitmotives are not overdone (as sometimes in Wagner), and its musical characterisation of the various *dramatis personae* is masterly. Apart from some loud dissonant clashes in appropriate places, it is mostly diatonic—not even chromatic. Though the central ideas of the libretto are basically simple, the story and the symbolism are complex; but fairy tales and symbolism are specially suited to opera. The plot, which is not only imaginative but fundamentally noble, and ends happily, seems to me to have inspired Strauss to compose his most beautiful operatic music.

Strauss wrote a number of lovely songs: *Traum durch die Dämmerung, Morgen, Heimliche Aufforderung, Ständchen, Wiegenlied, Du Meines Krönelein, Ruhe meine Seele, Cäcilie, Ach weh mir, verglückhaften Mann, Ich schwebe, Allerseelen*, and his Four Last Songs with orchestral accompaniment. They are unblemished beautiful *lieder*, in the tradition of his greater predecessors, particularly Brahms and Wolf. *Metamorphosen*, for 23 solo strings, nobly laments his fellow-countrymen who had fallen in World War II and whose leaders had deceived them.

He adored Mozart and often conducted his music, with great delicacy, but he prettified it and thereby missed half the point. One of the best things that he did was to recognise and acclaim

127

the genius of Elgar in his early days: Elgar was to become a much greater composer than Strauss ever was, but these acts of generosity have not occurred so very often among eminent composers.

Norman Del Mar's book gives us insight into the personal character of Strauss. He was a conceited man, wrapped up in his work of composition, and also pre-occupied with his own finances, increasingly as time went on. No wonder he looked more like a business man than a musician! Even as early as *Feuersnot* (his second opera), at the first performance of which in Dresden he and his wife shared a box with Gustav and Alma Mahler, he 'thought of nothing but money ... the whole time he had a pencil in his hand and was calculating his profits to the last penny', wrote Frau Mahler. He was, of course, also a pagan, which accounts for his choosing *Salome*, of all subjects, for an opera based fundamentally on the Biblical story, and for his attitude towards John the Baptist. Romain Rolland (who came to know Strauss very well) suggested to the composer in the most tactful manner possible that he had represented the Baptist's faith in a 'somewhat detached' manner and 'without a really personal emphasis'. Strauss at first denied this, but later confessed—'I didn't want to treat him too seriously. You know, Jochanaan is an imbecile. I've got no sympathy at all for that kind of man. I would have preferred above all that he would appear a bit grotesque'.[32] Yet this was not Wilde's view of John the Baptist, and Strauss's opera is based on Wilde's play. And in the New Testament, Jesus Christ himself is recorded as having said 'I tell you this: never has there appeared on earth a mother's son greater than John the Baptist'. (New English Bible translation: Matthew 11, v. 11.) Indeed, the whole Gospel narrative of the life and martyrdom of the Baptist is that of one of the greatest and noblest men in history. Norman Del Mar[33] recorded that Romain Rolland 'at first saw Strauss as a personification of the domineering Germany of the post-Bismarck era ... a man more strong than inspired; of vital energy, nervy, morbidly over-excited, unbalanced but controlled by an effort of will power....'

But two years later, Rolland wrote that 'the lower part of Strauss's face grimaced a little, the mouth often in a horrid pout either ironical or discontented.... He behaves thoroughly badly

[32] Norman Del Mar: 'Richard Strauss', vol. I, pp. 236, 249-250.
[33] Ibid., pp. 284-6.

at the table, sitting with his legs crossed at the side, holds his plate near his chin to eat, stuffs himself with sweets like a baby.... Cordial and nicely behaved with us, he is short with others; he scarcely listens to what they say.... "*Was?*" he mutters. "Ach! So, so", and that's all.' At the end of the first performance of *Salome* in Paris 'he showed himself on the stage ... to let himself be applauded. The curtain was raised two or three times. But he was used to a different sort of enthusiasm; someone whispered to him: "I am able to inform you that the President intends to decorate you with the Légion d'Honneur". "I have well deserved it", was his reply.'

Rolland goes on to say that Strauss was 'the artist-type of this new German empire, the powerful reflection of this heroic pride, near to delirium with this mistaken Nietzscheism, with this egoism and practical ideology, which preaches the cult of force and the disdain of weakness. But attached to this are certain characteristics which I had certainly not seen before, and which are more properly of the people of Munich, of Southern Germany; that is to say, an age-old depth of humorous buffoonery, paradoxical and satirical. of a spoilt child or of Till Eulenspiegel—it is necessary to remember this if one is not to find some of his opinions odious'.[34]

Strauss is not an attractive personality, and the music is, on the whole, consistent with the man. In *The Soul of Music* I contended that even after Beethoven, Schubert and Weber, the Teutonic *leadership* in music started to decline. Mahler was the last of the German/Austrian composers who can be called definitely great, and even he was not on a level with his predecessors. In Strauss we have German music in its decadence; he was extraordinarily accomplished, but only on the borderline of greatness. He was, so far as we can judge, the last of the old order in Germany (or Austria) before the advent of Schoenberg, Webern and Berg, with their new musical language, but he was not a romantic; there was something cynical and degenerate in his artistic make-up, and though in his very last works he certainly did something to restore the image of German music to its former level of beauty, none of his countrymen, nor any Austrian composer, has appeared to follow in that direction. That may yet happen; but the Teutonic glory faded out, nostalgically, with Mahler. Meanwhile, other nations took the place once occupied by Germany and Austria in the art of musical composition.

[34] Norman Del Mar, ibid.

In the latter part of my short sojourn at the Bar, I met Jack Penn, who had been a friend of mine at Harrow and also at Oxford (though in a different college, Hertford). I had introduced him to another barrister, my old Univ. friend Theobald ('Theo') R. Fitz-walter Butler, and the three of us did many delightful country walks in the Home Counties at week-ends and shared our mutual love of Shakespeare by frequent visits to the Old Vic, where we saw most of the Bard's plays. In December 1922, Jack suddenly said to me 'Shall we go to Rome?' and I at once replied 'Yes, let's!' As this was to be my only visit to the Eternal City, a brief mention of it is perhaps justifiable. I had so often heard glowing accounts of it from my parents and my grandmother, who at this time was—alas!—gradually weakening in her last illness. (My paternal grandfather had died during my last year at school.) Jack was the perfect companion, for he had a great love of architecture and considerable knowledge of it. This was a wonderful way of spending the Christmas Law Vacation, and we included a day or two in Pisa at the end of our fortnight in Rome. I shall not dilate upon our sight-seeing, but it is relevant to this book to mention that we also enjoyed a fine Concert in the 'Augusteo' in Rome, a rotunda which reminded me of the Albert Hall on a smaller scale. The main work in the programme, I remember, was Berlioz's *Symphonie Fantastique*. On our return home, in January 1923, I was in time to see my grandmother before her death; she had been anxious for me to go to Rome, and could just murmur the name 'Rome' faintly, when I visited her, and seemed happy when I simply replied 'Yes, Rome was lovely'.

In the Easter vacation (1923), I spent ten days at Bournemouth and was able to do some walking with Theo Butler on the cliffs above Studland and elsewhere, and also to see something of Lloyd Powell and his family: Dilys Powell accompanied me to a concert at which the *Enigma Variations* were very well performed. How few of my musical experiences subsequent to World War I have taken place outside London!

Staying in the same hotel as I was, were Mr and Mrs Robert Burnett and their daughter, Dorothy. (He was Northumbrian; his wife was American by birth and came from Kentucky. Dorothy was born in Boston, Massachusetts, when he was working there.)

I had been in and out of love before, but those earlier episodes had never produced anything beyond loyal and lasting friendships. Dorothy and I became engaged in the autumn of 1924. That winter

130

she accompanied her father on his business visit to U.S.A. and Canada, as already arranged, thus being able to see her brother in Vancouver. They returned in the spring of 1925, and we were married on October 5th, 1925.

Meanwhile, I had maintained my friendship with George Owen, who had been at Univ. with me, and whose father, the Rev. Everard Owen, had been a master at Harrow in my days there. Seeing that at this stage of my life I owed no allegiance to any institutional form of religion, Mr Owen, then a vicar in London, asked me whether I would like to discuss the subject with him. I accepted, and this gradually led me to becoming a convinced believer in Christianity—though eventually the light dawned suddenly. (Another clergyman friend also helped me towards this conclusion.)

Dorothy and I were married in St James's, Piccadilly. I selected the music with great care. As I still disliked Wagner, there was to be no Bridal March from *Lohengrin*! The bride entered the church with her father to the strains of Parry's Bridal March, originally written as a piece in the incidental music for *The Birds* of Aristophanes. Something by Beethoven was essential, and for a short item, *just* suitable for the organ, I could think of nothing better than the March from my beloved *Fidelio*—not one of the greatest numbers in that immortal score and actually associated in the opera with the entrance of the villain, Pizarro, and his guard! Still, it is a cheerful little composition. The *musical* highlight of the service was the beautiful singing by our dear friend Dilys Rhys-Roberts (Dilys Jones) of Bach's *My heart ever faithful*, with her lovely voice sounding the eloquent melody from the organ-loft. She sang another aria as well, but I cannot remember what it was, partly because this came while the signing of the register was taking place in the vestry. Our procession out of the church was made to Mendelssohn's Wedding March from *A Midsummer Night's Dream*, not exactly an original choice on my part, but as welcome as ever! Afterwards, my parents-in-law received the guests at the Hyde Park Hotel. These included all members and close relatives of both our families who were available in or near London, and many of our friends. There was dancing at the reception, and I had arranged with the leader of the little orchestra beforehand, among other things to adapt a selection of suitable tunes from among the Harrow School songs, which proved to be excellent dance music as a change from the more usual types of waltzes and fox-trots. We spent most of our honeymoon at Cadenabbia, on the Lake of Como, in lovely weather, staying at the same hotel at which my parents, Tom and I had stayed in my boyhood, but we also visited Stresa, on Lago Maggiore; in between we had two or three days in Milan, and witnessed a very good performance of *Aida* (not at *La Scala*, which was closed); my wife had never been to this opera before; it has remained one of our favourite ones—on its intrinsic merits, and not only because of that happy association!

On our way home, we were the guests of my Uncle Charles in Paris, and then settled in the first abode of our married life, a small flat in Hyde Park Mansions, Marylebone Road.

CHAPTER TWENTY-ONE

From 1926 onwards (including Holst)

Certain non-musical events stand out in my life between our wedding and the outbreak of World War II in 1939. The first was national—the General Strike of 1926, when I was temporarily released from my work in Shell-Mex to serve as a special constable; (my only personal hardships in that mercifully short and anxious period, were guarding '2 LO', the B.B.C.'s installation, on the roof of Selfridge's in a tremendous thunderstorm, and guarding the power station in Lisson Grove in an all-day downpour of rain! I was, fortunately, not called upon to use my truncheon at all). The second 'event' was domestic—the birth of our son, Jim, in October, 1927, which caused exceptional concern to our parents and me for my wife's welfare, but had a happy issue. The third 'happening' was more protracted, for the World economic crisis of 1929-31 not only necessitated economies involving general reductions in salaries throughout the Shell organisation, but resulted in redundancies of staff and finally a merger between Shell-Mex (my own employers) and the British Petroleum Company for the purposes of the business within the U.K., to form Shell-Mex and B.P. Ltd., in consequence of which there were further dismissals of staff. All these things were necessary both in the interests of the Companies and of the welfare of the survivors; but employees looked distressed and anxious, wondering whose turn would come next. Further natural effects were a slowing-down of promotion, and, of course, standstills in increases of pay. After that, the infamous Nazi régime in Germany caught us all up, as it were, in a swelling torrent of disastrous international events and finally plunged humanity into the abyss of another world war.

When our son was about two years old, we moved from our little flat into a small house in St John's Wood, with a garden:

this enabled us to have a dog, known as Jumbo, a black cocker spaniel, of sweet disposition, though he was not very clever, The other 'great dog' in my life had been a white, wire-haired terrier calls 'Socs'—short for Socrates because of his intelligence (a name given to him by his previous owner)—who had brought real joy to Tom and myself in our boyhood, as well as to our parents. Jumbo was a splendid negotiator: several cats in the neighbourhood who eyed one another with suspicion, if not hostility, were induced by their mutual friendship for Jumbo to reconcile their differences. Believing, as I do, in the immortality of the souls of animals who have a moral sense, I look forward to renewing contact with Socs and Jumbo in the after-life.

My wife is not nearly so keen on music (or Shakespeare) as I am. She enjoys chamber-music, pianoforte music and songs performed by great artists, a few operas and orchestral masterpieces, provided that they are not too loud—but not most choral works. It has always been understood between us that she would accompany me to occasional musical performances of the kind that she likes, but not to all those that I have attended in the course of our long, happy, married life. And she has accustomed herself either to listen to music on the radio (if she does not wish to concentrate on it) as a pleasant background to reading a book, or even to pay no attention to it at all. For some people, married happiness depends *partly* on complete sharing of interests. For others—my wife and myself among them—the *essential* things are mutual devotion, identity of outlook on the fundamental issues of life, and the very fact that the wife and the husband have aptitudes or tastes that are complementary to one another. My wife, for instance, has a splendid practical brain—far better than mine! On the other hand, we are fond of the same kind of places for holidays—lovely scenery, beautiful and interesting architecture, and good walking (though for reasons of health and age I am now very limited in this respect). She has taught me something, at least about *objets d'art* and old furniture. We have shared pleasure in ballet, though I am now rather 'choosey' where that is concerned and our son has sometimes been her companion in recent years at ballet performances, in lieu of, rather than in addition to, myself. From all this, it may be gathered that we have been a very closely united trio.

I should be misleading my readers if I were to create the impression that my life has been particularly smooth and serene. My wife and I have had at least our fair share of hardships, sorrows and anxieties, which we have shared in complete partnership ever since we became (privately) engaged to be married, but many of which are not mentioned in this book. It is this ideal married partnership, plus religion, mutual devotion between my parents and myself all through our joint lives, and between us two and our son, affection for various relatives, the formation of many close and delightful friendships, and the satisfaction of at least trying, and sometimes succeeding, in helping other people, that have sustained me throughout and conduced to my happiness.

The composers whom I propose to discuss in connection with the period 1926-1939 are Holst; Handel; those four great 16th and 17th century masters, Palestrina, Byrd, Monteverdi and Purcell; Wagner; Elgar; and Brahms. I begin with Holst in this chapter. The others will follow in subsequent chapters. Handel was the first of the *supreme* composers for whom I developed a special (and abiding) love after my marriage; I had not had sufficient opportunities of hearing more than 'Messiah' and a few other works of his, before then, nor the music of his predecessors. I became a convert to Wagner. My devotion to Elgar rose to its climax in this period—and has continued, unabated, ever since. I was already familiar with most of the compositions of Brahms earlier than 1939; but just as Beethoven seemed the right composer to sum up the account of my music-loving life just before the First World War, so the tremendously great musical personality of Brahms is, I feel, a suitable one with which to conclude my narrative of the interval between the two wars.

I have always loved the music of Gustav Holst, that shy, Gloucestershire-born son, grandson, great-grandson of professional musicians, whose art is so largely steeped in the spirit of England and the English countryside, but who had Scandinavian blood in his veins and was deeply influenced by non-English cultures. He adored Bach *and* Gilbert and Sullivan, the beauties of nature, the Parthenon and lovely churches. He was a great walker, whether in the country in England or in cities. He was an unorthodox Christian, to whom Christ and Christ-like conduct were more important than Christian liturgy. And he loved to give a helping hand (even during his last illness in bed!) to young composers and to friends in need and to his pupils in St Paul's Girls School and Morley College. Indeed, he was a most kindly man, deeply interested in other people. He fought courageously against neuritis and bad sight. In his early manhood he had to struggle to earn a living, and the struggle continued into the first part of his ideally happy marriage to Isobel Harrison, a sweet-natured and beautiful young chorister in the Hammersmith Socialist Club Choir which he was conducting. Unfit for the Forces in World War I, and having been unable to get any kind of war work, he was in 1918 ultimately appointed Musical Organiser in the Educational Department of the Y.M.C.A. in the Near East, until June 1919, and served in Salonica and elsewhere. He had a strong sense of humour and a strong vein of mysticism, revealed in his profound absorption in Sanskrit literature and finding musical expression both in 'Sanskrit' compositions and in Christian works of art. His daughter Imogen[35] tells us that 'he was never converted to any religion, Hindu or otherwise'. Holst is, for me, one of the most interesting and most attractive personalities of the twentieth century in the musical world.

His Hindu period came early in his career. Yet Savitri is a little gem, and unlike any other opera ever written—a strange, intimate setting of a weird, symbolic tale from the Indian epic, Mahabharata: after the death of Satyavan, his wife Savitri welcomes Death in simple music, with the distant sound of women's voices blending with the notes of a flute; in her dialogue with Death her love and her entreaties for the restoration of Satyavan's life are victorious; he comes back to her, she tells him how one of the Holy Ones has visited her and blessed them, and the work ends in calm, mystical harmonies, as Death fades into the darkness. The Choral Hymns from the Rig Veda are not quite on this exalted level, but they catch something of the spirit of the old oriental nature worship and the warmth of the sun that shines on the land of the ancient Indian bards, though with modern rhythms like 5/4 and 20th century harmonies and discords.

The Planets is described as a suite for orchestra. Most suites have consisted chiefly of a series of dances, but this work is really a cycle of contrasted symphonic poems, the planets being treated in their astrological significance. Thus Mars, with its relentless 5/4 rhythm, conveys the primitive, tragic cruelty of war (though Holst began the composition of it before World War I broke out); Venus, the restfulness of peace; Mercury is the winged messenger, with quick, bewitching, interlacing rhythms; Jupiter is the spirit of jollity—it must be said, a very English jollity, with its hearty good fellowship and its alternating folk-song-like melody; Saturn, the

[35] Imogen Holst: 'Gustav Holst, a biography' (1938), p. 21

mellow wisdom of old age; *Uranus*, the weird, fantastic magician; and *Neptune*, the mystic, ultimately fading into the Infinite.

In the *Hymn of Jesus*, Holst voices the ageless spirit of the Christian religion. It is both archaic and modern. Its harmonies are of the 20th century, its rhythms belong to no particular period. It is spiritually identical with the ancient Byzantine Hymn, which it expresses in deeply religious, mystical music. This mystical quality recurs in the *Ode to Death*, which is set to Walt Whitman's poem and brings the musical comfort of 'lovely and soothing death'.

The short opera *The Perfect Fool* begins with a ballet in three parts: the Wizard first invokes the Spirits of the Earth, which Holst aptly portrays by means of clumsy rhythms; then, the Spirits of Water, whose music unmistakably trickles; and lastly, the Spirits of Fire, with a keen, vigorous dance and gorgeous orchestral colouring. The remainder of the work is very amusing, especially the gentle skits upon the styles of Wagner and Verdi in the music associated with the Traveller and the Troubadour, and the solemn mockery of the conception of the Wizard himself. *At the Boar's Head*, however, does not quite come off: Holst clearly enjoyed setting a comic subject from Shakespeare and indulging his love of English folk music, but the extraction of the various Falstaff scenes from *Henry IV* in isolation from their setting in the historical drama seems automatically to rob them of the artistic quality of contrast with which Shakespeare imbues them in the play.

There was also a so-called neo-classical strain in Holst, connected with his devotion to Bach: this is shown in the *St Paul's Suite*, which in its form reminds us of Bach's overtures, the *Fugal Concerto* and the *Fugal Overture*, in both of which Holst goes back to the contrapuntal methods of Bach. Yet all of these have a peculiarly English charm.

In his *Choral Symphony*, Holst continued the idea of linking a chorus with the symphonic structure, which was begun by Beethoven and followed by Berlioz, Mendelssohn, Liszt, Mahler, Vaughan-Williams, Britten and others in their devious ways. Even if we do not feel that Holst's contribution is quite on the same level as the poetry of Keats to which it is set, the work has many beauties and is of great interest both by reason of its somewhat unusual form and of the affinity of the music to the spirit of the selected poems.

The orchestral *Egdon Heath* shows the composer reaching out into a new world, and is one of his greatest works. Its mysterious, unearthly character, so relevant to the passage from Thomas Hardy's 'The Return of the Native', which is printed in the score, seems to stretch Holst's imagination, and with this, his technique, into a more remote sphere than any into which he had penetrated before.

The Wandering Scholar, to a libretto by Clifford Bax—the last of Holst's short operas—is good fun, in a splendidly robust way, and brilliantly orchestrated. The *Choral Fantasia*, set to verses from Robert Bridge's *Ode to Music*, is one of his most profound compositions, ranging from a vision of creation to tragedy and bitterness, human love, infinite mystery, and ultimate tranquillity. The Prelude and Scherzo for orchestra, *Hammersmith*, presents a masterly contrast between the calm of the slow-moving river Thames and the colourful, human scenes in Hammersmith Broadway; the music returns at the end to the peace of the opening Prelude.

This brief description of some of his leading works may perhaps indicate the wide scope of Holst's art, the catholicity of his mind, and show how various aspects of his music are entirely in harmony with corresponding facets of his personal character.

In 1926 my first book was published, a selection of essays on various musical subjects, contributed by me to certain magazines and journals in the U.K. and U.S.A., to which I gave the title *From a Music Lover's Armchair*. Just afterwards, its publishers asked me to write a book on jazz. I agreed, on the understanding that I was free to write exactly as I liked on the subject. It appeared in 1927, under the title *The Appeal of Jazz*, and was the first book to be published about rag-time and jazz-music in this country. It went back to the earlier days of syncopation—whether in the works of great composers or elsewhere—and I made some attempt to describe the qualities and defects of jazz, as I saw them, and to account for its popularity at that period of history, as a social phenomenon. The book met with an excellent reception from the Press, and to write it was an interesting experience for me. After that, however, I gradually wandered away from jazz, except as an incentive to dancing, though I have always admired the skill of its performers. In the world of popular light music, I could not help feeling a sense of satisfaction at the way in which, by way of contrast, Ivor Novello, with his romantic, charming melodies, always free from vulgarity and skilfully composed, captured the hearts of the people about the time of World War II and just afterwards.

In 1937, my mother-in-law died. Her health had not been good for some time. I shared my wife's and my father-in-law's grief, and felt the loss myself personally, because I had a great affection for 'Little Ma', as I called her! There was also a musical bond between us: she had been a pupil of Busoni, and had at one time been a teacher of the piano herself. She had, however, not kept up her music very much in recent years: (her husband had no particular interest in the subject). But sometimes we shared musical experiences: for instance, she took my wife and me to a fine performance of *Don Giovanni* at Covent Garden, and accompanied me to a splendid concert at Queen's Hall, when Weingartner conducted Beethoven's *Leonora No. 3* overture and the 2nd Symphony of Brahms among other things: she was greatly impressed by the performances.

It was, however, in the late-middle nineteen-twenties (as mentioned earlier in this chapter) that I developed my special love, which has continued ever since, for the art of one of the mightiest musical figures of the 18th century, George Frederick Handel, who will accordingly form the subject of the next chapter.

CHAPTER TWENTY-TWO

Many-sided Handel

I first heard *Messiah* in the form of selections, at a concert in the Speech Room at Harrow School when I was a boy. The effect on me was instantaneous and electrifying. Since then I have listened to it in almost every conceivable kind of version, but for years I have only been satisfied with a performance of it in its entirety. This is my inclination with regard to most musical (and dramatic) works, but in the case of *Messiah* I am unwilling to miss a single item. For the whole composition is a masterpiece, and should not be cut at all. It is, moreover, one of the supreme non-operatic music dramas. Whereas Bach in his *Passions*, following Lutheran tradition, concentrated on the story of our Lord's last days and hours as unfolded in the Gospel narratives, Handel saw that the whole career of Jesus from the prophecies of His birth to His Crucifixion, Resurrection and Ascension, was the greatest of all dramas, and expressed this design in wondrous music. Basing himself on a selection of quotations from the Old and New Testaments, he set forth the story as a mighty drama, conveyed by eloquent recitatives, instrumental passages, solo arias, concerted numbers, and choruses of extraordinary beauty, power and variety.

Sir Thomas Beecham, in a cut version, unjustifiably transposed the Hallelujah Chorus to the end. John Tobin performed the complete work with a choir of only about one hundred, and arranged for the soloists to introduce ornaments of their own. His object was thus to revert to the practices of Handel's own day so far as possible; but this, I felt, did not 'come off'; a choir of only one hundred in a large hall (such as the Royal Festival Hall or Royal Albert Hall) robs some of the choruses of their weight and impressiveness —though I am far from approving of the 'monster' choirs of earlier generations. Ornaments added by performers to the composer's arias were, like the cadenzas of the 18th and early 19th centuries in concertos, bad practices, which I see no reason to revive or perpetuate just because they were an old habit. Mozart's

140

orchestral accompaniments to *Messiah* are intrinsically attractive, but introduce an alien element; neither they nor anyone else's alterations of Handel's score should be used. Only in those works where the composer has left his score incomplete—as Handel often did elsewhere—are any additions or alterations permissible, in my view.

From my schooldays onward, I have steadily added to my happiness by 'discovering' fresh compositions of Handel—the clavier and organ works, the sonatas for clavier and other instruments combined, the oratorios other than *Messiah*, the Chandos Anthems, the Dettingen Te Deum, 'Alexander's Feast', and the other *Ode for St Cecilia's Day*, *L'Allegro, Il Penseroso ed il Moderato, Hercules, Acis and Galatea*, the *Concerti Grossi* (for which I have a special affection), and several of his operas. Though Bach reached even greater heights, in some respects Handel's art was more many-sided. His style is simpler and more direct; it is mainly (though not entirely) diatonic, whereas Bach so often used a chromatic idiom and wide, unexpected intervals, to express mysticism, grief or suffering. The straightforwardness of Handel's own nature is matched by the simplicity of his music, which combines grandeur and gracefulness to an unsurpassed degree.

After the first London performance of *Messiah*, Lord Kinnoul complimented Handel on the noble 'entertainment' which he had provided. The composer answered 'My lord, I should be sorry if I only entertained them; I wished to make them better.' Beecham expressed the view that art is entertainment and nothing else : history does not record his reactions to this remark of one of his favourite composers. Many music lovers may have been put off by so frankly 'reformatory' an attitude as Handel here evinced, but it is undeniable that some manifestations of music and of the other arts do have an uplifting, and therefore, ethical, effect. To describe great religious or liturgical works of art, or many of the supreme instrumental compositions of the world, as 'entertainment' and nothing else, is clearly a misnomer. They are not only aesthetically beautiful, but spiritual in character, and affect us accordingly.

The important *dramatic* element in *Messiah* is present also in his other oratorios. Indeed, paradoxically enough, these works are more dramatic in character than his operas, which preceded them. Into the operas Handel poured a vast wealth of lovely melodies, truly expressive of the emotions of the persons who sing them in the situations in which they find themselves, but, somehow, not combining to build the whole work into a drama as Gluck's and Mozart's do. But the Handel oratorios are essentially dramatic, and some of them have been mounted successfully on the stage. Oddly enough, Beecham, who was *par excellence* an operatic conductor, did not apparently sense the dramatic quality of Handel's oratorio *Solomon*. For his method of bringing it to what he evidently considered a reasonable length (about two hours) for 20th century concert performance in 1951 and 1955 was to leave out Part II entirely—in which Solomon's famous judgment between the two women, each of whom claimed the baby as hers, was set by Handel to most moving music. The result was to lose the effect of the contrast between the joyous festive parts of the work and the solemn mood of Part II and to ignore this side of Solomon's character altogether.

Handel's gift for descriptive music is shown, for example, in the superb series of choruses depicting the plagues in *Israel in Egypt*. He expressed the fatherly goodness of a loving God in *But as for his people, He led them forth like sheep* and in the duet *Thou in thy mercy*. His dramatic sense, and his realistic understanding of the earlier part of the Old Testament, enabled him also to convey the idea of God as 'a man of war' and to voice the feelings of the children of Israel who rejoiced that the Lord had thrown the horse and his rider into the sea, in accordance with the words of the Book of Exodus. This dramatic and realistic instinct permitted him in the cantata 'Acis and Galatea' to portray the lust of the Cyclops Polyphemus for the fair body of the nymph, in the aria *O ruddier than the cherry*. In other words, Handel, as a true dramatist, could get inside the skin of his characters. But he did so for dramatic reasons, depicting sin in order to point a contrast with the nobility or the spiritual nature of the soul expressed elsewhere.

In the art of Palestrina and Byrd there is unutterable spiritual beauty, amounting at times to sublimity. But Bach and Handel are the first two composers, I suggest, in whom we of today can find that particular quality of *grandeur* which is present in varying degrees in the music of other great masters of succeeding generations, such as Gluck, Haydn, Mozart, Beethoven (supremely), Schubert, Berlioz, Wagner and Brahms, and which, among English creators, did not appear until Elgar. Of course, grandeur is not the only hall-mark of towering greatness, but those who are gifted with it are among the giants.

Handel was a man of a very different kind from Bach. He developed into a confirmed bachelor; for though he had two love affairs, neither of them materialised into matrimony, because objection was taken to his being a 'mere musician'. The only woman to whom he remained really devoted, was his old, widowed mother. He travelled to Italy, he came to England, settled here and became a naturalised Englishman. Kings and princes welcomed him, the people and the nobility acclaimed him. He was a *bon viveur*, ambitious, and loved the applause of the multitude. He took great risks and had at times to face such rivalries, opposition and financial difficulties that he was almost reduced to despair. He contended against ill-health, and, in his last years, blindness. He was, by instinct, robust and hearty in demeanour, occasionally impetuous and hot-tempered, but witty; honourable in his dealings, exceedingly generous in his actions, for example, towards the Foundling Hospital and towards the son of his old friend J. C. Christopher Smith, whose education he took on and who afterwards became his amanuensis and confidential friend.

He was capable of deeply religious feeling, but he was not so consistently devout as Bach, nor do we find in his music that mysticism which is present in the work of his mighty contemporary.

Bach and Handel resembled one author in their great benevolence, their hospitality, sense of humour and courage. In other ways, they were utterly different in their characters and their careers. These two great men, both born in Germany in 1685, never met, though they very nearly did so when Handel returned from England to Halle on a visit in 1719. Handel, however, did receive a visit, in London in 1747, from his younger contemporary, Gluck.

Handel was, I think, the first composer who expressed actual heroism in music—in *Judas Maccabaeus* and in the victorious sections of 'Israel in Egypt' (which is at times heroic, even though the heroism is quite appropriately tinged with a ruthlessness faithfully reflecting the parts of the Book of Exodus with which this oratorio is concerned). In this respect he was a forerunner of Beethoven and of Wagner and of Richard Strauss, though both Wagner's and Strauss's conceptions of a hero were very different from either Handel's or Beethoven's. Handel was able to compose truly heroic music, because, like Beethoven, he was, among other things, a hero himself. So, no doubt, was Wagner in his own way, but Wagner's kind of courage, iron will, determination and perseverance, which together made up his heroism, were almost the only likeable traits in his personal character; whereas both Beethoven and Handel, though they had their human faults, had attractive features in their personalities in addition to their heroism. Handel, the man, was a hero in the way in which he faced up to adversity again and again. The resilience of his bravery was amazing. He never gave in. But he was not only heroic. He was, in spite of his bad tempers, a man of loving charity, tenderness, and forgiving disposition. He and his old friend John Christopher Smith (the elder), walking together in a street of Tunbridge Wells, had a quarrel when Handel had gone totally blind. Smith, though he knew that Handel could not 'see' without his help, left Handel standing there and returned to London. Handel was so deeply wounded that he cut Smith's name out of his will. But a few years later—shortly before his death—Smith's son, Christopher junior, who was then looking after Handel's affairs, was horrified when he found that Handel meant to put his name in the will in place of his father's. He interceded with Handel, who not only restored the original legacy of £500 in favour of the father, but added £1,500 more!

It was this love for his fellow-men, this glorious forgiveness, which enabled the genius of Handel, in *Messiah* supremely, but elsewhere too, to have the vision of the loving God, embodied in Christ, which he translated into sublime music. Heroism in a good cause is one part, one aspect of the Christian conception of love. In *Messiah*, Handel, as nearly as any man could, expressed that love in its most complete form.

CHAPTER TWENTY-THREE

The 16th and 17th centuries (Palestrina, Byrd, Monteverdi, and Purcell)

I will begin this chapter by confessing that I have not had *very much* personal experience of composers earlier than Palestrina or our own Elizabethans—not enough, anyhow, to write about them in a book largely concerned with the composers who have exerted the most influence upon me. I have heard some medieval music and I have read a good deal about it and indeed about the music of the ancients from the Sumerians onwards. But this is a book based on full and actual experience—and by experience I mean listening to or playing or singing music. Silent score-reading by itself is, for me, not enough for my purpose here. Vaughan Williams described it as a very difficult process; and though, obviously, composers, conductors and professional singers and players must be expert at it, and to some critics such as Ernest Newman it comes quite naturally and easily, a humble music lover such as myself would, I suggest, feel diffident about expressing a very definite judgment, or even comment, about a work which he had never heard. There are some people, I know, who have declared that music (like little boys) should be seen and not heard; and poor Beethoven's increasing deafness prevented him from listening to much of the music on which he expressed his views; but Beethoven was a gigantic genius, to whom the written notes spoke with as much vividness as the printed word does to you and me. For us ordinary lovers of music, I believe that, though a quiet perusal of the score (assuming that we can manage this) is of great value, it is only a means to an end—a way of helping us to imagine what the music would sound like if we could hear it. Actual audible performance is, for us, the ideal method of apprehending it.

Therefore, as—like many others—I have not had sufficiently frequent opportunities of hearing music preceding that of the 16th century A.D., Palestrina and Byrd are the two earliest composers whom I propose to discuss.

Before E. H. Fellowes revealed to us the riches of Elizabethan music, it was customary for musical historians and writers about the art to start their list of great composers with Palestrina. And indeed, no music composed before or since is more deeply religious than his: it is devout, mystical and serene, and seems to float through the spaces of a beautiful church to our ears and to our very souls; I have usually heard it in a church or broadcast from a church by sound radio: the concert hall is no place for music which is so essentially ecclesiastical in character; this does not mean that it is not sometimes emotional, for there is plenty of joy and pathos where the text calls for this; but the time for actual drama in religious music, or for the profound or vivid expression of momentous events like the Crucifixion and Resurrection, such as Bach and later masters embodied in their art, had not yet arrived; one must not expect to find this in the masses or other liturgical works of Palestrina or Byrd, or their predecessors and contemporaries.

Palestrina's music is almost entirely religious, in the strict sense of the term. Even his secular madrigals do not differ greatly in intrinsic character from his far more numerous sacred works.

He was himself a modest, generous, devoutly religious man, deeply devoted to the service of the Church, in which he held official appointments, and to his first wife and his sons: it was bitter grief to him to lose her and the two elder ones and one of his brothers in the epidemics which swept over Rome and Central Italy in the train of the continual wars of that time. After her death, he even thought of entering the priesthood, but changed his mind when he met a wealthy widow, whom he married eight months after the death of his first wife. Rather surprisingly, he entered into the business of his second wife's furriery, and made money out of it, whilst continuing his duties at St Peter's and his composition of great musical masterpiece—masses, motets, hymns and other liturgical works and the 'Stabat Mater'. The only things that have been said against his character have been that he may have married the widow for mercenary reasons; that he may have been a party to an intrigue for securing for himself the director-ship of the papal choir a few years later, though there is no real evidence of this; and that at the height of his fame he sent to his patron, an amateur, a group of motets before publication, for 'sug-gestions as to improvements'—a piece of mere flattery which did not come off! The suspicions as to the first two of these accusa-

146

tions may be well-founded, and the third is obviously true. Even so, perhaps they may be regarded as human failings in a character otherwise apparently unblemished! In any case, they do not detract from the deeply felt purity and sanctity of his beautiful music.

William Byrd, the foremost representative of the 'Golden Age' of English music which included such geniuses as Dunstable, Dowland, and Tallis, Morley, Weelkes, Wilbye, and Orlando Gibbons, was, in one sense, an even greater composer than Palestrina: for he was, I suggest, equal to him as a creator of religious music, and he shone also in every other field of composition then in existence. His three settings of the Mass—those in three parts, four parts, and five parts respectively—are as glorious as the Masses of his distinguished Italian contemporary, and, though himself a Roman Catholic, he was broad enough in his outlook to compose a great deal of Anglican Church music. This was not done merely to placate the newly established Church; for the *Great Service*, which contains *Venite, Kyrie,* and *Credo*, as well as the morning and evening canticles, all set to English words, is not only one of Byrd's finest works, but one of the glories of English music, and, indeed, one of the supreme liturgical masterpieces in musical history. And he wrote large quantities of other lovely music for the English liturgy as well as his famous Latin Church compositions.

In addition to his religious art, he was the creator of some of the most beautiful madrigals and secular songs ever written. In his great works for viols he was a pioneer of chamber music for strings, and in his voluminous and exquisite pieces for virginal—preludes, fantasies, dances, marches and others—he laid the foundations of all the keyboard music that the great masters to come were to vouchsafe to the world.

It is this astonishing versatility, wedded to almost unflagging inspiration and skill, that make Byrd appear to me today as the supreme composer of his epoch.

He was greatly revered, and held in 'unfeigned affection' by his contemporaries, and was a man of profoundly religious devotion, though also of austere temperament. He was just as sincere in his setting of the words of the new Anglican liturgy as in that of the Roman Catholic Church to which he faithfully adhered throughout his long life (1543-1623). He was born about ten years after the dissolution of the monasteries and the consequent breaking-up of many choirs, and so did not have to endure the loss of home and employment which had afflicted numberless musicians at that time. The replacement of Latin by English in the services of the Reformed Church of England occurred when he was only a child. He became in turn organist at Lincoln Cathedral and the Chapel Royal in London, and came to live at Harlington in Middlesex, and finally at Stondon in Essex. In his old age, he *seems* to have become somewhat disagreeable. He was in litigation with the lady who previously owned his house at Stondon, and with others, including the local rector (about a right of way over his land), and even omitted one of his children from his will for 'undutiful obstinacy', though he was 'unwilling to name' who it was. These incidents may have been symptoms of the irritability of an old or ageing man, but we cannot judge the rights and wrongs of each of them today. There is no evidence of his being ill-tempered in his youth or early middle age and he was evidently a very kind-hearted man: witness the trouble which he took to help Mrs Michael Tempest, whose husband had fled to France after being attainted for his part in the North Catholic Rebellion in 1570, leaving his wife and five children very badly off in England. Queen Elizabeth had granted an annuity to her, but it had fallen into arrears. Byrd rectified this by writing to an official of the Court of Exchequer who was a friend of his. If there was a quarrelsome streak in him, this would be yet another instance of the great creative genius rising in his art above his lower self as manifested in some of his human relationships. But his sincerity, his breadth of mind, his devotion to his religion, to his wife and to all except one of his five children, and the immense veneration in which he was held in his lifetime, are in harmony with the nobility, spiritual beauty, and grace of his music.

After Byrd, I leap on to the 17th century—to some reflections on Monteverdi and Purcell. (Though the former began his life in the later 16th century, most of the work by which he is known dates from the 17th century).

Monteverdi was born in mid-May, 1567, at Cremona, and was the son of a doctor. After his schooldays he became one of the court musicians (a string player) in the household of Vincenzo I, Duke of Mantua, and began composing the wonderful series of madrigals which were to become a central feature of his art. He accompanied the Duke on a journey to Hungary, married Claudia Cattaneo (a court singer) in 1599, and made another journey with the Duke to various towns in Flanders. In 1602 he was appointed 'maestro della musica' to the Duke on the death of the holder of that office. Denis Arnold[36] surmises that after about ten years at Mantua he had become 'rather jealous of others, conscious of every imagined slight on his worth and well aware that gossip could undermine his position'. However, his new appointment naturally helped, but the Duke was irregular in his payments. Claudia continued to work after her marriage, but gave birth to three sons, only two of whom survived to maturity. When she became ill in November, 1606, Monteverdi's father cared for her in Cremona, but in September, 1607, she died. We do not know much about Monteverdi's character, for certain, but Follino, the court chronicler at Mantua, out of his 'affection' for him, advised him to return there quickly, because of the scope for his genius which his position opened up. He seems, indeed, to have been very popular personally, as well as highly esteemed, wherever he was located. Nevertheless, he had become angry and unhappy, until his pay was at last raised and a pension arrangement made for him.

When the Duke died in 1612, his son and successor suddenly dismissed Monteverdi, who returned to Cremona. But his luck turned: for on the death of the *maestro di capella* at St Mark's, Venice, in 1613, Monteverdi was appointed to fill the post. He was robbed of all his money by highwaymen on his way there, but that was the end of his chain of misfortunes. He remained happily at Venice until the end of his life in November, 1643, the only set-back of a personal kind being the occasion in 1627 when his son Massimiliano, who was in the priesthood, was imprisoned for having read a book which he did not know to be prohibited; six months elapsed before the young man was proved innocent at the final examination. The war in Northern Italy in that year resulted in the invasion of the imperial troops from beyond the Alps bringing plague into that part of the country. But Monteverdi and his son Francesco (anyhow) survived. The emotional strain, however, affected the ageing composer physically; yet not only did he become a priest, but in his seventies he composed a series of stage works, culminating in *L'Incoronazione di Poppea* at the age of 75! He was also able to revisit his friends in Cremona and Mantua before his death. He was clearly a man of great determination and courage.

Opera, though it arose from the liturgical dramas of the middle ages and, indeed, originated from the ancient Athenian dramas which were partly accompanied by music, came into existence as a

[36] *Monteverdi* (The Master Musicians), p. 13

distinctive art-form about the end of the 16th and beginning of the 17th century at the hands of Peri and Caccini. But Monteverdi was its first great exponent, and 'Orfeo' was an early opera of his. It was a revolutionary one, for in addition to recitative, expressive 'da capo' arias for the soloists, and vivid choruses, he caused the orchestra to make important contributions to the drama and the evocation of the emotions of the characters. The story is a variant on the traditional one, for though Orpheus loses Eurydice, Apollo bears him up to eternal rest in Heaven[37].

Il Combattimento di Tancredi e Clorinda, to a text from Tasso's Gerusalemme liberata, contains vivid orchestral effects for the fight between the crusader and the maiden warrior, and has a moving ending when he wounds her mortally, finds (on removing her armour) that she is a woman, baptises her into Christianity at her request, and is grief-stricken at her death. It was published in Monteverdi's 8th book of madrigals, but is neither a madrigal nor an opera, for Monteverdi wished it to be sung during a musical evening after madrigals, with no scenery or action; it is more like a short cantata.

In his last opera, Poppea (based on history, in accordance with Tacitus), Monteverdi made further innovations (as compared with Orfeo) in bel canto, da capa aria and recitativo secco, reduced the orchestra to strings and continuo instruments, and eliminated the chorus. This opera has become a popular success at Glyndebourne and elsewhere, and it is undoubtedly a splendid entertainment. Yet for me, personally, it can never be one of my favourites. It is, I suppose, one of my peculiarities that if I find the subject or the libretto of an opera (or the story of a play) actually repellent or even distasteful, my enjoyment is impaired, however much I may appreciate the melodies or the music in general or the skill with which it is composed. The works that I love best are never merely 'entertainment'; they must be, in some sense, nourishing to the soul; and I cannot take great pleasure in the presentation of evil actually victorious at the end. In this work, Nero plans to divorce his wife, Octavia, in order to marry his mistress, Poppea. Octavia plots with Otto, Poppea's husband, to murder Poppea, but is herself found out and banished. Nero is free to marry Poppea, and the opera ends with her coronation, amid general rejoicing. The story leaves a nasty taste in one's mouth, and affects my attitude

[37] I have written more fully about Monteverdi's 'Orfeo' in my book, 'The Divine Quest in Music', p. 192

to the whole opera. I cannot help this, and I am not likely to change my reactions at my time of life. But the score of this opera is masterly and contains so many beauties that one must recognise that it is a great work, though I personally enjoy his 'Orfeo' more wholeheartedly. Monteverdi's madrigals, with their marvellous wealth and depth of emotion, their beauty and their charm, spanned most of his creative life. His church music is also very varied in character. The 'Vespers' music (1610) is not entirely religious in feeling; some of it is secular or operatic in character; but it is mainly devotional and is a great masterpiece, though with a curious combination of styles. The *Gloria* for seven voices, two violins and four trombones, almost anticipates Bach and Handel in grandeur.

Purcell was a most original, versatile, and prolific composer. In a life of about thirty-five years, he wrote music for the church, incidental music for the theatre in rich profusion, music for five plays which approximated to being operas in the full, modern sense, and one great, though short, work which was definitely an opera (*Dido and Aeneas*), odes for royal occasions and for St Cecilia's Day, a large number of solo songs and duets, a chain of works for strings with and without continuo, and music for harpsichord! He was born into an age in which England had had enough of Puritanism, at any rate for the time being, and under the Restoration, Charles II asked Pelham Humphrey, the 'master of the children' of the Chapel Royal, and the other composers, to add 'symphonys etc. with their instruments to their anthems' when he came to the chapel himself.

Purcell grew up in that atmosphere. His father[38], Henry (senior) was 'Master of the Choristers' at Westminister Abbey, his uncle Thomas was a tenor in the Chapel Royal, and he himself sang in the Chapel Royal as a choir-boy and eventually became organist of Westminster Abbey. He was an extremely busy man, for in addition he became one of the three organists at the Chapel Royal, and 'organ-maker and keeper etc.' (i.e. repairer and keeper of the organs and other instruments) at the Royal Court.

The Church of England, in spite of the King's own taste for brightening up its music, still maintained its links with pre-Crom-

[38] Franklin B. Zimmerman (*Henry Purcell, 1659-1695, His Life and Times*) has shown by means of freshly discovered documents, that the composer was not, as Sir Jack Westrup and other writers had thought, the son of Thomas Purcell, but evidently of Thomas's brother Henry (senior).

wellian and Elizabethan traditions, and it came natural to Purcell to produce liturgical music which was intrinsically religious, yet always melodious, without being either austere or mystical. In the finest of his anthems, hymns, and setting of the Psalms, he expressed the prayers and emotions in sincere and even dramatic strains—sometimes very moving, elsewhere conveying joy or thanksgiving.

Purcell's lovely fantasies for strings, the gravely beautiful chaconne in G minor, his 'sonnatas' for strings and continuo (which latter show Italian influence) present great variety and contrasts of feeling and tempo. The greatest of the Odes is, surely, 'Hail, Bright Cecilia', a glorious work with most striking choruses and lovely solo parts.

In those days an opera in England meant a play with a lot of incidental music. *The Fairy Queen* was Shakespeare's *A Midsummer Night's Dream* with the text mutilated, like the version of *The Tempest*—for both of which Purcell wrote beautiful and appropriate music, as he did for Dryden's *King Arthur* and for *The Indian Queen*. But *Dido and Aeneas* was a true opera in the modern sense. How typical of England that the first real English opera should have been written for performance by a girls' school! It is a great work—with its expressive arias and duets, its vivid choruses for witches and for the sailors of Aeneas, and Dido's glorious final lament, 'When I am laid in earth'. My own first experience of it was a notable one, with my old friend Denne Parker (Mrs Gilkes) in the part of Dido. Much more recently—though long ago now!—Kirsten Flagstad sang this, with that great artist Maggie Teyte as Belinda, in a memorable performance at the original little Mermaid Theatre in St John's Wood.

In spite of all the exhaustive researches of Franklin B. Zimmerman and Sir Jack Westrup, we know next to nothing about Purcell's personal character. Roger North described him as 'the noble Purcell' and 'the divine Purcell', but these enthusiastic terms may well have referred to his qualities as a composer, rather than as a man. In his short span, he lived through the times of Charles II, James II, the 'Glorious Revolution' and the reign of William and Mary. The Great Plague and the Great Fire of London occurred in his boyhood. His life was certainly not uneventful. He was, we may infer, a man capable of being either melancholy or robust, sensitive and imaginative in a pronounced degree. There is abundant evidence in his music of a deep love of humanity.

CHAPTER TWENTY-FOUR

The Complex Case of Wagner

As a man, Richard Wagner was, I suppose, the most unlikeable of all the great composers. So let us first consider his good points. He was sometimes generous to fellow-musicians, especially to fellow-sufferers, even when he was enduring great misfortunes himself. He achieved a great deal for the artistic, political and social position of German musicians generally. Although he and Minna Planer ought never to have married—since she was quite incapable of rising to the artistic and intellectual level of the stupendous and turbulent genius to whom she was wedded—and although he was unfaithful to her and they grew further and further apart, he did feel pity for her (when he was away from her) and grief over her troubled existence and her death. Above all, throughout his life he showed tremendous courage and determination in pursuit of his artistic ideals. He suffered setbacks over and over again, discouragement, hostility, hardships and poverty. He never gave in. He was, indeed, more *truly* heroic than the mighty hero of *The Ring*, Siegfried, who never has to conquer fear because he does not know what fear is.

But when we have said these things in Wagner's favour, we are still faced with a formidable array of unpleasant personal features. He was an egoist through and through—from his boyhood onwards; in spite of his love of animals, he angrily followed a dog through the town, because it had taken a bone which the boy Wagner considered as his own. He was a borrower by nature. He thought himself entitled to financial help in order to have leisure and comfort in creating masterpieces. He even borrowed from strangers. His idea of friendship was entirely one-sided. His friends existed in order that they might serve him. They were expected to drop everything else and fly to his aid, no matter how their own concerns might be affected by doing so; this applied, for instance, even to so eminent an artist as Liszt, and to Cornelius, who was a talented composer in his own right. For them, Wagner

might have been expected to show some vestige of understanding
and unselfishness; but unselfishness towards other individuals did
not come easily to Wagner. Everyone was expected to sacrifice
himself—or herself—on the Wagnerian altar.

Minna was not at all eager for the marriage, but he urged her
into it. He expected her to share all his privations for the sake of
his great artistic *future*, and he even needed her purely as a house-
keeper. He was not merely unfaithful to her, but meanly denigrated her in *Mein Leben* which he dictated to Cosima after her
death. During his marriage to Minna, he tried (unsuccessfully) to
elope with Madame Jessie Lausson, and had affairs with Mathilde
Wesendonck (and several other pretty women) and finally with
Cosima von Bülow. On each occasion he shows up in an un-
favourable light. A woman who was attractive in his eyes existed
to satisfy both his ardent passion and his personal longing for a
mate, either temporarily or permanently. The fact that she was
another man's wife—even (as in Cosima's case) the wife of a
devoted friend such as Hans von Bülow—was as irrelevant from
his standpoint as the fact that he was married himself. It may be
that he had earlier fallen in love with Mathilde Wesendonck because his mind was full of *Tristan und Isolde*, and not the other
way round; she became, for a time, infatuated with him; Otto her
husband, continued to behave with extraordinary kindness to
Wagner, who meanwhile seems to have been so absorbed in his
passion for her that he was oblivious of Otto's grief and Minna's
anguish; but when Richard had finished *Tristan*, he had finished
with Mathilde. She had played her part in his creation of a masterpiece. In a very different way he was later to fall temporarily 'in
love' with Madame Judith Gautier, whose youthful beauty and
sympathy were apparently necessary (even though he had at last
found his ideal mate in Cosima) to inspire him to create *Parsifal*
(of all works!), the great 'sacred', Christian masterpiece of his old
age. The two cases are, of course, quite unlike one another: there
is *some* similarity between the 'triangle' of Wagner and the Wesen-
doncks, and the *Tristan* story; but Judith Gautier had not the re-
motest counterpart in *Parsifal*—she was merely the spark which
ignited the fire of creation: I do not think that Kundry was her
counterpart.

He had many Jewish friends, who either helped him greatly
and loyally or were dedicated interpreters of his operas. Meyerbeer was personally kind to him as a young man, and Wagner

was artistically indebted to his Grand Opera style. But Wagner was always an anti-semite and became a venomous one. In the revised (1869) edition of his essay *Judiaism in Music*, he specifically attacked Mendelssohn many years after the latter's death; this may leave a somewhat unpleasant taste in one's mouth; but though Mendelssohn was a strong Lutheran and a far better Christian than Wagner was, Wagner, in a letter to King Ludwig II of Bavaria written in the autumn of 1872, contrasted the Jews with 'the rest of us' who had had a Christian upbringing, and contended, not merely that no one who was of Jewish blood could really belong to German culture, but that the Jewish race is 'the born enemy of pure humanity and everything that is noble in it'. Wagner's own anti-semitism was doubtless fanned by Cosima, who regarded the Jews as the source of all evil. In his article *Know Thyself!*, Wagner praised the massacres of the Jews in the Russian pogroms, which he thought should be imitated, and advocated the elimination of all the Jews in Germany. Ernest Newman, his brilliant and fair-minded biographer[39], wrote that Wagner here anticipated in words the thoughts which Hitler and the Nazis were later to put into hideous practice so far as it lay in their power. Wagner's anti-semitism increased in venom as he grew older, and was at its worst when he was creating his 'Christian' drama *Parsifal*. The inconsistency between his Christianity and hatred of the Jews scarcely seemed to occur to him.

In various biographies we read of Wagner's 'charm'. Today, we, who never knew him as a man, have to take this on trust. In my eyes, there are, broadly speaking, two kinds of charm—the one that is a natural, outward manifestation of an inward sweetness and gentleness, and the other a superficial attractiveness of manner which even a person of unpleasant character can turn on and off like water from a tap. I am very much afraid that Wagner's 'charm' must have been of this latter sort, for I find it hard to trace that it had any roots in his basic nature. And he was apt to be rude, tactless, ill-tempered, and even violent in his manner.

He was ungrateful, grossly extravagant, and luxurious. He craved luxury in all its forms, whether in his personal surroundings or in his sexual relationships. Yet his head was full of his artistic theories and his creative ideas. Without his arrogance—which was the ob-

---

[39] *The Life of Richard Wagner*, vol. IV, pp. 634-9. See also chapter 17 of the present book. Robert W. Gutman's 'Richard Wagner' discusses the subject very fully.

verse of his determination and his iron will—he would never have achieved what he did. He had, really, a split personality, but the cleavage was not in a straight line, either with good ethical points on one side and bad on the other or with a predominantly unattractive personal character divided from an exalted and noble artistic creation. It was a jagged split, with vices and a few virtues inextricably mixed in Wagner the human being and a musical/dramatic outpouring which, partly, at any rate, reproduced his personal complexity.

His 'charm' was a kind of enchantment, which fascinated even when it repelled. His friends could not help bowing to his imperious will. He seemed to engender a sort of love/hate in them. He lost friend after friend through his egoism. But he achieved all his artistic aims by his indomitable will:—the completion of the vast enterprise of 'The Ring' after interrupting it two-thirds of the way through for twelve years to compose two other masterpieces, *Tristan* and the *Meistersinger*; the construction of the opera house at Bayreuth entirely for the performance of his works; and the fulfilment of his ambition in the creation of 'Parsifal'. Living to the age of about 70, he finished his task, and died as a kind of Teutonic emperor of the music drama.

Of all the masters of opera, Wagner was the most autobiographical in his art. Other composers largely sank their personalities when they turned to operatic creation, and either simply conveyed the emotions of the characters in the libretto or actually got inside their skins—just as Shakespeare could. The man Wagner constantly appears in his work, even though it was written for theatrical performance.

The Flying Dutchman is also Wagner, the lonely wayfarer, seeking, at that stage of his life, for recognition. Tannhäuser is Wagner, divided between voluptuousness and the longing for the love of a devoted woman. Even Lohengrin is actuated by that kind of longing—though here for a woman who would accept him unquestioningly. In 'The Ring', various aspects of Wagner's own nature are present in Wotan, Siegmund, and Siegfried. Wotan haranguing Fricka resembles Wagner haranguing Minna. Wotan as the Wanderer is again Wagner, the misunderstood genius. Siegmund, whose story of his life in Act I of *Die Walküre* shows him as a misfit in society hitherto, is a self-portrait of Wagner, who could not adapt himself to the world of normal humanity. Siegfried is the aggressive, undaunted, determined Wagner, who pursued his artistic aims in spite of all obstacles and without regard to others who crossed his path. Siegfried is also Wagner as the imperfect 'hero', seeking for his ideal mate. Tristan is Wagner's idealised self-portrait. Mathilde appeared to him as Isolde, and even his three illegitimate children by Cosima bore the name of characters in his works—Isolde, Eva and Siegfried. And in the reverse direction, so to speak, Jessie Lausson had offered him, he said, his 'salvation', like the various 'redeeming' women of his operas. Walther in Die Meistersinger is Wagner, the architect of 'the music of the future', battling against old conventions and what he considered to be the academic pedantries of his contemporary critics.

An important question is, to what extent did Wagner's essentially theatrical art benefit or suffer from this persistent autobiographical vein? Not at all, I suggest, in *The Flying Dutchman*, composed when he was a young, struggling artist: it is a perfectly integrated product of that period of his life, even though with its 'set pieces' it is naturally a long way from the 'unending melody' and subtly changing leitmotives of his mature works. *Tannhäuser* presents Christian feeling in the music of the Pilgrims and the better side of Tannhäuser in his love for Elizabeth; the only lopsidedness —if we may call it that—arises from the fact that the Venusberg scene was revised at a later stage of the composer's life, when he had advanced to the far more developed style and artistry of *Tristan*, with the result that the gorgeous allurements of Venus and her companions are expressed with greater mastery than the other aspects of the story and of its principal characters. Lohengrin is a more spiritual person than his creator; the religious tone of the opera is nowhere more completely revealed than in the Prelude, which is a mystical vision in music and nothing else; Lohengrin is a mysterious figure until we reach his 'narration' in the last scene; but I always feel that the defect of the story is that it was, to say the least, unreasonable for a girl to be expected to marry a man—even though he had championed her—without knowing who he was, whence he came, or, indeed, anything about him!

Many out-and-out Wagnerians—especially among his fellow-countrymen—have idolised Wagner to the extent of claiming that he was not merely a tremendous musical genius, but also a great poet, dramatist and philosopher. It is sufficiently marvellous to find a great composer who is capable of writing his own libretti at all, but because Wagner did this, and did it, on the whole, successfully, we are not bound to fall down and worship all aspects of him as a creator. In reality, he was a moonshiny thinker, an indifferent writer of verse (it is scarcely worthy of the name of poetry), and at times a capable, or even a skilful, dramatist: at any rate, he knew, broadly, what was required in the way of drama for his operatic purposes. I propose at this point to look at some aspects of his mature operas subsequent to Lohengrin.

The 'book' of The Ring, allowing for all its symbolism and mythological qualities, has certain very odd features. Alberich, the evil dwarf, steals the gold from the Rhinemaidens and fashions from it a ring which gives its possessor power over the whole world, and a magic helmet (Tarnhelm), which enables him to assume any shape he likes. Wotan, the king of the gods, is completely a-moral, and decides to steal the ring from him. So, accompanied by the wily fire-god, Loge, he makes his way down to Nibelheim, where Alberich lives with his attendant Nibelungs. Alberich, though a villain, is stupid enough to show off the powers of the magic helmet, and when he turns himself into a toad, Loge puts his foot on him, seizes the helmet, and they take him prisoner and lead him up to the valley above, where Wotan gets the ring from him; we have to accept that the usurpation of world-power depends on an obvious and insignificant trick like that! Alberich curses the ring, and anyhow Wotan's possession of it is short-lived: he has to pay the two giants, Fasolt and Fafner, for building the castle of Valhalla for him and his fellow-deities, and though the giants are supposed to represent the laborious, rather dull-witted, creatures of the earth, they have sufficient sense not only to demand that enough ingots of gold shall be piled up to cover the figure of Freia, the life-enhancing goddess of love and beauty, whom they had seized as a pawn, but that Wotan should add the magic helmet and stop up a tiny chink in the pile by including the ring too. Of course all this is symbolic, like the rest of the story, and the ownership of the accursed ring does not bring any luck to Fasolt, for the two brothers quarrel over it and he is killed by Fafner. (What advantage it is for Fafner subsequently to turn himself into a dragon and live in a cave, to guard the treasure, is not explained!).

Now let us consider the characters of the 'heroes' in the subsequent operas of The Ring. I suppose that most people would say that Siegmund is the hero of Die Walküre, and Siegfried of the two final dramas of the cycle. Siegmund is in some ways a more attractive character than his son, and before the curtain rises he has been truly heroic in going to the rescue of an unknown maiden and slaying her attackers, though their servants subsequently over-whelmed and disarmed him and slew her. His passionate love for his sister Sieglinde is both incestuous and adulterous, but it might be said that he could not help the former disadvantage (!) and anyhow he is a legendary figure, only half human and half the son of the god Wotan (who is himself a most promiscuous lover); while Siegmund's adultery is softened by the fact that Sieglinde had been forced into marriage with a harsh husband, Hunding, from which her elopement with Siegmund seemed likely to rescue her. Sieg-mund has no opportunity to show heroism during the action of the opera itself. He is immensely strong, and thus able to wrest Wotan's sword, Nothung, from the tree, and, helped by Brünnhilde, the Valkyrie or warrior goddess, and armed with Nothung, he would certainly have been able to conquer Hunding in the fight, if Wotan (under severe moral pressure from his wife, Fricka) had not inter-vened. But there is otherwise nothing in fact specially heroic in his conduct on the stage. (And he is only alive during the first two Acts.)

We must, however, decide what we mean by heroism. Surely it is an essential element in it that the hero conquers fear (or bravely endures great suffering or hardship). But—unlike Siegmund —Siegfried is a creature who literally does not know what fear is. In real life, there are people who are much less sensitive to fear than most, but a *completely* fearless being such as Siegfried has, I dare assert, never existed in human history. If, however, we accept—as we readily can in a legend or fairy story—that Siegfried simply does not know what fear is, then there is nothing very heroic in what he does. He is tremendously strong, like his father, he forges the sword which Mime (the dwarf who has brought him up) has failed to do, and with it he splits the anvil from top to bottom. He kills the dragon, largely because he has been born without the sensation of fear in his make-up; for the same reason, he is not afraid of the flames that encircle Brünnhilde's rock, and he is allowed by a supernatural influence to pass through them un-scathed—which seems to imply that they are symbolical or appar-ent rather than real. And he does nothing heroic in *Götterdäm-merung* from start to finish—though he is supposed to have learnt what fear is (in the previous opera, *Siegfried*) at the sight of Brünn-hilde—the first woman he had ever seen—a strange conception! One would have understood his feeling a trifle nervous at such a moment, but fear is a curious emotion for any man—especially a hero—to feel at his first glimpse of a member of the opposite sex! One cannot avoid contrasting him with Miranda in *The Tempest*, who, when she first sees Ferdinand, having previously met no man except her father, is lost in admiration for him! It has been suggested that Siegfried does not experience fear at all, that his symptoms—dizziness, a trembling hand, a pounding heart—are quite consistent with those of a man falling in love at first sight, and that he confuses this with the sensation of fear, of which he has no previous knowledge. I have myself experienced both fear and falling in love, and must confess that I cannot see that there is much resemblance between them. It seems to me that Wagner's notion of Siegfried learning what fear is from his first sight of the sleeping Brünnhilde is, simply, one of those silly episodes which occur now and again in his libretti!

I can therefore, find nothing heroic in the Siegfried of the libretto, and it will be appreciated that I am not, for the moment, discussing the music. But in addition to the absence in him of *real* courage—which must involve the conquest of fear or suffering— Siegfried reveals several unpleasant characteristics. In the opera *Siegfried* he loathes Mime, who has brought him up from infancy, and cannot believe that he (Siegfried) is the son of an ugly creature so unlike himself, but in Act I his treatment of the dwarf is simply the behaviour of a contemptuous aggressive bully, when we bear in mind that he does not know that Mime is secretly planning to kill him. There is also something of this same aggressive, contemptuous character in the impatient, insolent manner in which he defies old Wotan in Act III scene i for getting in his way and smashes the spear—even though we know that this is a symbolical act and is a vital link in the story and that Siegfried is unaware that Wotan is his grandfather (whilst realising from Wotan's *last* words that the latter was largely responsible for the death of Siegfried's father, Siegmund; it is only at the very end of their wrangle that Wotan reveals that it was his spear that had broken the sword which Siegfried now carries. All Siegfried's offensive, insolent words are uttered before this).

Siegfried is not even intelligent. On the contrary, he is a perfect example of brainless brawn. After he has ascended the rock—to music of beauty unsurpassed in all *The Ring*—he finds his extremely youthful-looking aunt Brünnhilde on the summit, still wearing her armour and helmet. (I have often wondered why she had to wear the helmet, or even the armour, during her years of sleep—it sounds dreadfully uncomfortable!) Robert Donington[40] thinks it is quite natural that Siegfried should imagine the sleeping figure to be that of a man—a comrade. I, frankly, do not. Siegfried has been told by the woodbird, and by Wotan too, that he will find a beautiful maid asleep on the hill-top—this, indeed, was the whole object of the exercise, so to speak! Yet he has not the wit to imagine for one moment that this may be a warrior maiden, and only when he removes her helmet and her hair falls over her shoulders does it dawn upon him: 'Das ist kein Mann!' ('That is no man!'), he exclaims in excited tones. No wonder the audience tittered, at some performances which I have attended!

His conduct when he encounters the Gibichungs is both obtuse and unpleasant. Hagen and Gunther twist him round their little fingers. Hagen thinks that Brünnhilde would be a suitable bride for Gunther, and Gutrune for Siegfried; so they induce him to drink a magic potion, which he does without question and which makes him fall in love with Gutrune instantly and 'forget' his love for Brünnhilde. He readily swears 'blood brotherhood' with Gunther, and is persuaded to undertake, with the aid of the Tarnhelm, to disguise himself as Gunther, to ascend the rock through the flames again, to bring Brünnhilde back with him and then to hand her over to Gunther as his bride. He threatens her with being 'wedded' to him that night in her cave, and when she counter-threatens him with the might of the ring, which he had given her by way of plighting her his troth, he treats her with the utmost roughness, struggles with her, and wrests the ring from her (incidentally, Hagen had not asked him for it). Because of the blood brotherhood pledge, he places Nothung between himself and her in the cave, but he forces her to go with him next day to the hall of the Gibichungs. How can we have any respect for a 'hero' who behaves—even under the influence of a potion—in so outrageous a fashion? He adds treachery to his offensiveness. It is impossible for us to *shed any tears* when Hagen plunges the spear into Siegfried's back in Act III, and—to do him justice—Wagner does not introduce any *pathetic* music either into the moment of his murder or into the tremendous Funeral March which follows, as the vassals carry the body of this tough, unchivalrous, unheroic 'hero' over the hills. There is nothing glorious about him, although other persons in the drama call him so, and though Wagner himself

---

[40] *Wagner's 'Ring' and its symbols*, p. 208

wrote of him in 'A Communication to my friends', in effect, as the ideal, perfect, human being!

All this, I submit, is true of the character of Siegfried as contained in the libretto. Yet Wagner has written some truly heroic, grand and beautiful music for him. And the explanation of this, I suggest, is partly that it is not within the scope of music to differentiate between mere fearlessness and true courage, as words can. If we feel that Wagner's various Siegfried leitmotives, and his constant and wonderful transmutations of them, suit a truly heroic character, but do not convey mere lack of a sense of fear, that is because music cannot embody a purely negative conception. Wagner's Siegfried music is thus perfectly appropriate either for an impossibly fearless man or for a brave man who feels fear but overcomes it. And when we come to the scenes of Siegfried's treachery and so on, the music is entirely suited to these, also, with its dark, sombre colours and clashing discords. As for his stupidity, Wagner's music does not depict that: music can express emotions and portray character (in generalised terms), but it is hard to see how he could have conveyed to our minds in musical terms the idea of Siegfried's foolishness, even if he wanted to do so—for music can only do that by being silly in itself, and Wagner's genius did not lie in the direction of musical insipidity.

In reality, however, there is no complete, male hero of *The Ring*, in spite of Siegmund's *past* heroic conduct, his staunchness in Act II of *Die Walküre*, and the constant verbal descriptions both of him and of Siegfried as mighty heroes, and in spite, too, of the heroic music which Wagner composed for Siegmund and the sword in Act I, and for Siegfried throughout the two subsequent evenings. The real heroism—in libretto and music combined—is to be found in Brünnhilde. She is the true hero or, rather, heroine, of *The Ring*, even in spite of her grave lapse in Act II of *Götterdämmerung*, when, owing to the evil intrigues of Hagen, she joins in the conspiracy to murder Siegfried, whom she not unnaturally believes to have betrayed her. Moreover, although she does not appear till Act II of *Die Walküre* and not at all in the first two Acts of *Siegfried*, she is the leading figure in the three main operas of the cycle; she is, as it were, the climax to which all the action and music of Acts I and II of *Siegfried* and the first scene of its third Act have been leading; and she dominates the whole of *Götterdämmerung* and particularly its impressive closing scene.

In *Die Walküre*, Wotan first orders her, as the instrument of his will, to protect Siegmund in the coming fight with Hunding. She warns Wotan to guard against the bidding of his wife Fricka, who now enters and insists on the punishment of Siegmund by death at the hands of Hunding; Siegmund's and Sieglinde's love for one another is both incestuous and adulterous; Wotan himself has been guilty of past infidelities; Nothung must be made to lose its magic power; the moral superiority of the gods must be preserved. Fricka makes a strong case for marital fidelity, yet naturally our sympathies are with the lovers, because Sieglinde's loveless marriage with a despotic husband has been forced upon her, and anyhow, death, we feel, is too severe a penalty for Siegmunds' offences. Nevertheless, Wotan gives Brünnhilde her new orders in accordance with Fricka's wishes—and we love her for trying to disobey them. She is really aiming at fulfilling Wotan's own desires, when she decides to defy him and to save Siegmund and Sieglinde. She fails in her efforts to protect Siegmund, because Wotan intervenes in the fight and Nothung breaks on his spear, leaving Hunding free to kill Siegmund, though Wotan contemptuously slays Hunding as well. Brünnhilde carries Sieglinde away to the Valkyries' rock and, giving her the pieces of the broken sword, bids her flee before Wotan arrives in vengeance, take refuge in the forest, where she will give birth to a mighty hero, and keep the pieces of sword for him. When Wotan comes and threatens to send Brünnhilde to sleep, to become the obedient wife of any man who wakes her, she pleads with him that she has acted out of compassion for Siegmund and in fulfilment of Wotan's inmost will; ultimately she prevails to the extent that he agrees to ring the rock with magic fire which only a fearless hero will dare to penetrate. He puts her to sleep and kisses her godhead away. Throughout this opera, she is an entirely noble, heroic and tender character. And she maintains that character throughout the Third Act of Siegfried and right on into Götterdämmerung until in Act II she realises that Siegfried has betrayed her, when in despair she enters into the conspiracy with Hagen and Gunther for his projected murder. (She has, in her anguish, even falsely accused him of having forced 'delight' and 'love' from her, which would have involved a breach of his vow of blood-brotherhood to Gunther.) Thus she becomes, in revenge, one of his murderers; but the world of The Ring is a pagan, pre-Christian (and legendary) world, and we can hardly judge her conduct at this juncture by Christian standards. After his dead body has been brought back into the Gibichungs' Hall, she gives as gentle an answer as she can to Gutrune's reproaches, and then resumes her former spiritual greatness. She orders a funeral pyre to be built to Siegfried, prays for the repose of Wotan's soul, and rides her horse, Grane (poor beast!) into the flames in the bliss of self-sacrificing love. The Rhine overflows its banks, and the Rhinemaidens recover the Ring. The fire consumes Valhalla. Earth and Heaven are purified by Brünnhilde's redeeming action.

Let us return to Wotan. In the libretto, he is obviously a very imperfect king of the gods. Even apart from his immoralities, he is, for all his dignified bearing, rather a weak character, and in the third Act of *Siegfried*, for instance, he cuts a pretty poor figure. He enters and summons Erda, the earth-goddess and mother, by him, of Brünnhilde and the other Valkyries, to advise him on what is in store for the gods. But Erda, who is supposed to be the fount of all wisdom and had played a vital part in the drama when in the *Rheingold* she had urged Wotan to give up the ring to the giants, has, it turns out, been asleep *at least* for all the twenty years or so that Brünnhilde has been slumbering on the rock surrounded by a wall of fire, and is therefore scarcely in a position to give him either well-founded advice or up-to-date information! No 'stop-press' news for her! Yet Wotan knew perfectly well that she had been asleep all that time, and he might have known, therefore, that it would be useless to consult her. So it is hardly surprising (if I may be pardoned the expression) that she tries to pass the buck! She first suggests that Wotan should ask advice from the Norns, or goddesses of fate—only to meet with his retort that they were of no use and that the rope of destiny is going to snap soon anyway (which it duly does in the prologue of *Götterdämmerung*). Next, she bids him ask Brünnhilde—and is astonished to learn for the first time that the latter has been asleep too, and has lost her godhead. So Wotan dismisses the useless Erda to her life of slumber in the depths of earth—leaving us wondering from where she had got her reputation for profound wisdom and why he had woken her up and summoned her for advice at all! *Dramatically*, this is a completely pointless scene —redeemed, of course, by the profundity and grandeur of the music. Wotan, purely dramatically considered again, continues to cut a poor figure when confronted with his insolent grandson, Siegfried, who now enters, guided by the woodbird—though he tries to maintain his dignity; but when Siegfried shatters Wotan's spear upon his sword, the game is up; Wotan picks up the pieces of the spear, acknowledges defeat, and disappears from our sight for the last time.

Wotan's stature depends on three factors: (1) the symbolical nature of his words and actions (which Robert Donington[41] has so lucidly expounded; (2) the manner in which the role is performed: it takes a singer and actor of the calibre of Anton van Rooy, Friedrich Schorr, Rudolf Bockelmann, or Hans Hotter, to invest the character, both musically and dramatically, with that dignity which Wagner evidently intended and to make us overlook or ignore the little deficiences to which I have drawn attention as regards the non-musical aspect of him. I once saw a young man play the part, who skipped up and down the steps which the Covent Garden production had provided on the stage, with the agility of a mountain-goat. This was, no doubt, very beneficial for his health, but somehow it did not suit the personality of Wotan! (3) The grandeur and beauty of the vocal and orchestral music which Wagner associated with him. Wotan's *Farewell* to Brünnhilde in the third Act of *Die Walküre*, with its nobility and pathos, is his greatest musical passage. It is, indeed, one of the supreme passages in *The Ring*. But it is not the only occasion on which the music of Wotan—or for that matter, the music generally —transcends the words.

There are certain incoherences in *The Ring*. Erda in *Das Rheingold* bade Wotan give up the ring to the giants, and Wagner originally intended that this would avert the doom of the gods; but he altered the passage to read that doom awaits them anyhow— yet Erda still advises Wotan to surrender the ring; in that case, the object of his doing so is wrapped in mystery. Wagner had, of course, changed his mind in the course of the years of creation of his immense drama, and had decided to end it with the downfall of the gods (hence *Götterdämmerung*). Another obscurity in the libretto arises from the fact that Wagner at one time meant both his words and his music at the end of the whole cycle to convey the idea not merely of redemption or transformation, but of redemption *by love*. The reference to love, however—the conception of Brünnhilde's suicide as a *loving self-sacrifice*—was subsequently omitted from the libretto. The great musical theme to which the name *Redemption by love* is commonly given by writers and commentators, has appeared in Act III of *Die Walküre*,

[41] Robert Donington: *Wagner's 'Ring' and its symbols.*

when Sieglinde hears from Brünnhilde the prophecy that she is to give birth to Siegfried and receives from her the fragments of Siegmund's sword; she replies with a cry of rapture and thankfulness to Brünnhilde, set to this melody; there is no association of it there with redemption by love, but this title is quite rightly bestowed on it by critics when it re-appears at the end of *Götterdämmerung*, not by reason of any words in the final version of the libretto, but in virtue of the intrinsic character of the music itself. The verse tells us that the fire which is to burn her will cleanse the curse from the ring, and that she longs to embrace Siegfried in mightiest love; but the redemption—whether of him or of the world—by means of her love, is all in the music, not in the libretto as we have it. This is another instance of the music transcending the verse.

My third problem in *The Ring* arises when it is all over and the old order of gods is finished. The leading characters, except one, are all dead (including Hagen, who has been drowned). The three Rhinemaidens have recovered the ring; so far, so good. But Alberich is still alive—Alberich, the embodiment of evil. What is to stop him *now* from stealing the ring and really obtaining mastery of the world? No doubt, the Rhinemaidens will take great care of it, but there are no Valhalla gods or giants to hinder him this time. It might seem almost as though Satan/Alberich were lurking in the background, biding his opportunity. Did Wagner mean us to be conscious of the evil which—whether embodied in an Alberich or in a personal Devil or present only in ourselves—continues to exist in the world and is only countered by the goodness and loving influence which in the end has enabled Brünnhilde, in spite of her previous complicity in Siegfried's murder (before she realised the truth), to bring redemption? It is true that Alberich, in his colloquy with Hagen at the beginning of Act II of *Götterdämmerung*, has said that if ever Brünnhilde advised Siegfried to restore the ring to the Rhinemaidens, his (Alberich's) gold would be lost and no cunning of his would ever get it back. But can we rely on that? I think that the answer is to be found—as usual—in the music. Wagner really believed in redemption by the love of a woman, both for himself and in his art: the idea recurs in his operas and is expressed in the final music of *Götterdämmerung*. Of course it is not an orthodox Christian idea, even when it appears in an apparently Christian drama such as *Tannhäuser*. For Christians, the only true Redeemer is Christ, and no man or woman can win 'redemption' through a woman's (or another woman's) love; we each have to win it ourselves, through our own repentance for our sins and through Christ's (or, for members of other God-worshipping religions, God's) forgiveness. But for Wagner, the idea was indeed a leading motive.

In spite of Wagner's theories about opera and drama and the importance which he attached to the libretto (not to mention the scenery, costumes and lighting), the music is paramount. He was a far greater composer than dramatist. It is the music of *The Ring*, and of his other masterpieces too, which has excited the wonder of the world, and has held audiences enthralled for 100 years or more and looks like continuing to do so for generations to come —even though the music is wedded to the drama as unfolded in the verse. The music takes the story into itself, and the result is a marriage of arts in which the music is, surely, the dominant partner.

In my view, the *greatest* music directly associated with Siegfried himself is his ascent of the rock in the third Act of *Siegfried*— Wagner at his grandest—and the Funeral March, in which most of the leitmotives previously connected with him appear in an exalted and idealised form; this is almost an apotheosis; never, surely, has a rather unattractive character been accorded so magnificent an obituary as Wagner has presented to us here! Wagner regarded Siegfried as the perfect human being; we can scarcely agree with him so far as the Siegfried of the libretto is concerned, but in such purely orchestral passages as these he reveals his own musical idealisation of a great hero. Apart from such mighty instances as these two, or the closing scenes of *Das Rheingold*, or *Die Walküre*, and of *Götterdämmerung*, the features which we prize in *The Ring*, I suggest, are its immense emotional range, the vast sweep of its structural span, its marvellous musical representations of water and sky, of storms and wind and rainbow, of spring in moonlight and the rustle of leaves in the forest, of magical and supernatural forces, of superhuman and sub-human creatures, of destiny and death, of abysmal evil and loving redemption. We shall not find in *The Ring* the *spiritual grandeur* of works like *King Lear* or the Ninth Symphony or the big choral masterpieces of Bach and Handel, or the very greatest achievements of Brahms, or even the highest mystical heights attained by Elgar—a very great composer, who was, nevertheless, not of the same overall stature as Wagner. But we do find in *The Ring an* almost complete sense of musical

167

architecture applied to what is in sheer length the most gigantic musical composition ever created; this is wrought, of course, by the wondrous and continuous transformation of a net-work of expressive leitmotives, allied to a prodigious mastery of the whole colossal design. I say *almost*, because I always feel that in *The Ring*, as in his other mature masterpieces with the exception of *Tristan*, Wagner was inclined to over-repetitiveness. It was not necessary, surely, to bring in the relevant motive on every single occasion that the various characters and ideas are mentioned in the text; or to reproduce the same narrative *quite* so often! We know what happened in *Das Rheingold*; could Wagner not have left it to our imagination that Wotan would have recounted it to Brünnhilde off-stage, without telling it all to her in a twenty-minute narration in Act II of *Die Walküre*? Over and over again, the past history is repeated to us in each opera of the cycle subsequent to *Das Rheingold* in some form or other. The reason for this is partly that Wagner began his libretti with *Siegfried's Death* (which became *Götterdämmerung*) and then realised, step by step, that he must precede this by the operas which now constitute the three previous evenings. He could not fully harmonise his sense of the unity of the whole with his typically Teutonic desire to make each drama comprehensible by itself. He apparently could not bring himself to use the blue pencil—or anyhow, not sufficiently for our comfort! He lacked the highly self-critical approach of Brahms, who destroyed quantities of works which were not up to the very high standards that he set himself; or of Beethoven, who hammered and chiselled at what was sometimes initially insignificant material until he had sculpted it into a perfect whole. Beethoven and Brahms, in all their greater works, scarcely wrote a superfluous note. In Wagner's mature operas, except *Tristan*, superfluous —even long-winded—portions are, unfortunately, all too frequent.

Tristan und Isolde is, I feel, the greatest and most perfect of Wagner's works. Isolde's *Narration* to Brangäne in Act I, unlike the repeated narratives of past events in *The Ring*, is an absolutely necessary story of the previous relationship between her and Tristan—how he had killed Morold, her betrothed, in combat and she had cherished the idea of revenge against him; yet when she found that the wounded man whom she was nursing was indeed Tristan and she had him at her mercy, his piteous look into her eyes overcame her with compassion, and so on. That had been the beginning of their love for one another. Therefore, when in this

Act he is bringing her on the ship to King Marke to become the King's wife, and Brangäne gives them the love potion instead of the expected potion of death, the magic liquid only serves to open the floodgates of a mutual love already begun. Out of the many versions of the old legend, Wagner has constructed a much simplified, and also a nobler, tale; for in his opera, Isolde does not marry Marke, and there is thus no adultery between the two lovers and no infidelity on Tristan's part towards his royal master —for he could not help the effect of the potion; in Act III, after Tristan has been wounded by Melot at the end of the second Act, the King, having heard the truth, arrives on the Breton coast, intending to unite the lovers in marriage; but he is too late; Tristan is dead, and Isolde sings her Liebestod and dies upon his body. For this great story, Wagner has composed some of the most beautiful love music ever written, and some noble music for the King; whilst Brangäne and Kurvenal are devoted companions and friends to Isolde and Tristan respectively, portrayed in most moving musical terms. (Kurvenal, as a character, always reminds me, somehow, of Kent in *King Lear*.) There is no redundant music in this tremendous score. The whole work is a wondrous expression of tragic love. And in the love duet of the second Act and the *Liebestod* there is also a touch of mysticism—for these lovers live in an ecstatic dream world, and at the end Isolde's words and music *seem* to be transporting her to a mystical union with Tristan after death.

And yet, and yet—something even in this masterpiece prevents me from hailing it as *the greatest* portrayal of the love of man and woman in music. I believe that this something is the lack of a real idealisation of such love. The words and the music aspire to the heights, yes, but somehow they remain on earth. There is nothing truly *idyllic* in this love. That, for me, is to be found, rather, in some of the love music of Beethoven, Berlioz, and the great 19th century German and Austrian composers of *lieder*. In the slow movement of Beethoven's Fourth Symphony; in the music of Leonora and Florestan in *Fidelio*, culminating in their great duet of joyous love triumphant after all their suffering and perils, 'O namen—namenlose—Freude!'; in the second movement of the Sonata in E minor, op. 90, which Beethoven himself said represented a conversation between Prince Lichnowsky (to whom the work was dedicated) and his beloved; in the *Scene d'Amour* of Berlioz's dramatic symphony, *Romeo and Juliet*, where in purely orchestral strains he perfectly expresses the pure, innocent, idyllic love voiced

in Shakespeare's tragic drama; in the love duet between Dido and
Aeneas in *The Trojans*, where Berlioz distils the very essence of
their mutual devotion in a moonlit setting near the sea; the facts
that duty is shortly to call Aeneas away to fulfil the divine com-
mand of founding Imperial Rome, and that Dido will, in her
bewildered failure to understand this, invoke curses upon him before she takes her own life—these facts are in the future; at the
moment, we are listening to the glorious, ideal, love music. And
then I think of the innumerable unutterably beautiful love songs
composed by Schubert, Schumann, Brahms, and Hugo Wolf, and
I feel that in these instances, and not, after all, in *Tristan*, the true
love of man and woman is to be found. There is no 'magic potion'
in them. But the basic reason, I believe, is that Wagner, the man,
for all his love affairs, did not really know what *true* love is—the
utter, unselfish devotion, in soul as well as in body, between man
and woman; too often, perhaps, he expresses mere allurement;
when he came to compose *Tristan*, for all its mastery, its passion,
its emotion, its attempt even at mysticism, he could not attain to
the musical portrayal of ideal, idyllic love, because he himself
was incapable of experiencing it. He was too much of an egoist.
His union with Cosima was a perfect partnership, of course; but
it was, after all, a partnership between two very imperfect persons!

Perhaps the nearest approach to true love in Wagner's operas
is Hans Sach's profound love for Eva in *Die Meistersinger*. Here,
after all, is a noble soul who has loved a sweet girl for many years
of her life; and she frankly confesses that she had loved him,
romantically. But he is an elderly widower, whereas she is a young
girl, for whom a marriage between two people so far apart in age
would surely have been less suitable than the mutual love between
her and the youthful, ardent Walther. *Die Meistersinger*, though
it has an undercurrent of melancholy and resignation in the heart
of Hans Sachs, is a happy opera, with a very skilfully contrived
libretto, and a golden score. And Hans Sachs, both in his words
and music, is not only noble, but broadminded and tender-hearted.
He is the most lovable of the leading characters in the Wagner
operas.

There is, nevertheless, a flaw in the story, in my eyes. I cannot
reconcile myself to one of the central ideas, whereby Pogner offers
his daughter in marriage to the winner of the song competition
to be held on the following day. It is true that Eva is to have the

right to refuse the victor, though if she exercises that right she must take no other lover. But can we accept Pogner as the kind, loving father that he is presented to us as being, a Master not only rich but 'high-souled' (as Sachs describes him in the final scene) if he is prepared to give her away to the winner of a contest of any kind? Wagner did not invent the idea—it occurs, for example, in E. T. A. Hoffman's *Master Martin the Cooper* and elsewhere—but he adopted it as his own, and it is basic to the whole conception of the opera. However, we must accept the story as we find it, including also the portrait of Beckmesser. Wagner originally called the marker *Hanslich*; and Hanslick, the eminent musical critic and opponent of Wagner, is obviously burlesqued in the part. Some people have called the character of Beckmesser a gentle satire; but according to Hanslick himself, it is an untrue and unfair one; for he maintained that, whereas Beckmesser is a typical pedant with no sense of beauty, chalking down every departure from the rigid rules of the Mastersingers, he himself had no such foot-rule of formal correctness and was only concerned with big issues and fundamental considerations.[42] However, the real point for us today is that, in the hands of a gifted artist, Beckmesser, whatever his origins, can be a figure of real fun. I shall never forget Geraint Evans's brilliant performance at Covent Garden.

Sachs's monologue 'Wahn! Wahn!' is, in its own way, an example of the superiority of Wagner's music to his libretti. *Musically*, it is one of the truly noble passages in his scores—and an expression not only of Sachs's nobility, but of his wisdom: it is music of broad, wide significance, applicable to humanity as a whole. Yet the words that come from Sachs's lips here arise out of reflection on a petty brawl in a Nuremberg street: it seems disproportionate that so trivial an incident should cause him to dwell upon the craziness and quarrelsome nature of mankind in general. Yet this discrepancy scarcely troubles us, as we listen to the profoundly beautiful music.

Sachs undeniably *tricks* Beckmesser into thinking that the poem which he has found in Sachs's room is by Sachs himself, whereas in fact Walther had just dictated it to him: by this means, he causes Beckmesser to make an utter fool of himself before the

---

[42] I am indebted for this information to an article by Stewart Deas, in 'County Life' (January 11, 1968). See also Robert W. Gutman's book 'Richard Wagner'. pp. 217-222.

Nuremberg folk in the next scene. The result for most of us, I fancy, is a certain sympathy for Beckmesser at the end; but I doubt whether Wagner intended this: for Hanslick, after all, had criticised *Lohengrin* unfavourably (but not pedantically), even though he had praised *Tannhäuser*; and he was half-Jewish in blood.

The opera is of somewhat excessive length. If Wagner had been a less prolix composer, he would have shortened David's catalogue of *Tones* in Act I, and prevented the closing scene from going on quite so long. However, in spite of its enormous length (the last Act alone lasts two hours), *Die Meistersinger* is musically a sheer delight, though I never regard the *Preislied* as one of Wagner's finest efforts. Hans Sachs's emphatic nationalism inherent in his final insistence on the honour due to German Masters and 'holy German art' and, above all, his attack on 'foreign' influence, were added in response to Cosima's vehement demand; the ending of the opera would have been better without this passage: it is a Wagnerian anticipation of the excessively nationalistic outlook in Germany which was to follow in the 20th century and from which the world has suffered so much.

This extraordinary man, Wagner, in his late sixties, could not resist planting an ardent kiss on the lips of a Flower Maiden at a rehearsal of his sacred opera, *Parsifal*, nor can one forget the link between its creation and his temporary passion for another man's beautiful young wife. Yet neither of these things, nor Wagner's distinctly un-Christian personal character, affect either the beauty or the sincerity of the great work itself. Wagner, as usual, was utterly wrapped up in the subject. But it does contain, for me, one or two rather unsatisfying features. Parsifal himself is the pure fool: now, his purity was essential for the story; but why must he be foolish? One would have thought that a man who was to become Head of the monastery of the Holy Grail at Monsalvat would require some wisdom, or at least some administrative ability, in addition to his chastity! Another point is the character of Gurnemanz, who acts as Parsifal's guide, philosopher and friend in the first scene, and yet behaves, as it seems to me, in a most un-Christian way towards him when he finds at the end of Act I that Parsifal has not understood in the least what the service of the Holy Eucharist was all about, and therefore turns him out of the place angrily, with the words 'Thou art but a fool, then'. Surely he might have understood that Parsifal had not had the advantage of a Christian upbringing, and might have explained the significance of the ritual to him in a patient, Christian way. Admittedly, if he had done so, and unless Wagner could have persuaded himself to shorten some of Gurnemanz's very long-drawn-out passages in the First Scene, the Act would have been even longer than it is already and the subsequent story would have taken a very different course from the one that it did. But perhaps Gurnemanz, like Polonius in *Hamlet*, is really the 'tedious old fool'; and certainly Parsifal turns out to be not such a fool as he was alleged to be.

The second Act gave Wagner a glorious opportunity to depict evil, for which he had a special gift. Klingsor is its very embodiment, and the Flower Maidens and Kundry, in her seductive shape under his wizardry, are Wagner's final and consummating gift to the music of allurement, which he had already portrayed so eloquently in the Venusberg scenes of *Tannhäuser* and the Rhinemaidens of *The Ring*. Not until Parsifal catches Klingsor's spear and makes the sign of the Cross at the end of the Act is the spell broken. After that, the coast is clear for the healing serenity and religious feeling of Act III.

Wagner was, first and last, a man of the theatre. The *Kaiser-marsch* and the *Huldigungsmarsch* are unimportant. The *Wesen-donck Lieder* are associated with *Tristan*, and the *Siegfried Idyll* with *The Ring*, though the *Idyll* was inspired by the birth of Wagner's son. It was characteristic of Wagner that even these two, strictly-speaking, non-operatic works, were essentially autobiographical and at the same time linked to his music-dramas. His early *Faust Overture*, though originally intended to be the first movement of a symphony, was, of course, associated with Goethe's great dramatic poem. Wagner, the man, appeared in Wagner, the creative artist, throughout his career. He was an unpleasant person. Perhaps this was itself one reason, at least, why he was the greatest master of the expression of evil in music that has ever lived.

I once asked an old friend of ours, an ardent Wagnerian, whether she thought that even Wagner's sacred music in *Tannhäuser*, *Lohengrin* and *Parsifal* is as truly religious as, say, Bach's *St. Matthew Passion*. She replied, 'No, it is theatrical'. Now, I have written two chapters on 'religion in the opera house' in my book *The Divine Quest in Music*, and I do not wish to add anything to the subject here, except to say that, if Wagner had really had it in him to compose music so sublimely and utterly religious as that of Bach, of Beethoven in the *Missa Solemnis* and elsewhere, of Brahms in his *Requiem*, of Handel and his *Messiah* and church music, of Palestrina and the Elizabethan masters in their liturgical music, or of Elgar in his three great choral masterpieces, there is no reason why he should not have done so just because his medium was the theatre. Oratorios, after all, are normally performed in secular concert halls. The truth, as I see it, is that Wagner was not, for all his gifts, able to reach to the sublime essence of true religion in his music—not even in *Parsifal*; but that his range in all other directions was so immense that we must be grateful for the manifold heritage of his gigantic genius.

CHAPTER TWENTY-FIVE

The Nobility and Charm of Elgar

It is a relief to me to turn from the ambivalent, though gigantic, figure of Wagner, to the nobility, tenderness and charm of Elgar. I never met him; but he must have been a most delightful person.

He came of modest, but artistic, parentage. His father, the son of a builder, was a man of attractive personality, and intensely musical, who started by tuning pianos, and then opened a music shop in Worcester. His mother was a sweet-natured country girl, whose father was described in her baptismal entry as a 'labourer' but in a later census return as a 'farmer'; she wrote poetry and had a gift for delicate sewing in coloured silks and for sketching; she had a refined and cultured mind. It is not surprising that Edward (the fifth of their seven children) should have become a musician; but his eventual towering transcendence as a composer and the high and innumerable honours which were bestowed upon him were simply the outcome of his genius, his industry and his own achievements—and of the inspiration of a supremely happy marriage. The father of his wife, Caroline Alice (née Roberts) was a Major-General with a distinguished record of service in India, who had died when she was ten; and her mother was the daughter of a clergyman and a member of a well-known Gloucestershire family. Socially, according to the temper of those days, Alice was considered by her relatives to have married beneath her, and one of her aunts cut her out of a settlement which she had intended to make upon her.

None of the great composers developed so slowly as Elgar from talented creation to real greatness. For he was forty-one when he wrote the *Enigma* Variations. His supreme masterpieces began with that, and ended with the death of his wife after a short illness in 1920; she was then 71, and eight years older than Elgar. He was—to use his own words—'stunned' and 'broken' by the event, and at first felt that his career as a composer was over. But his creative activity did not cease completely; for after it he not only composed such attractive, though light, works as the *Severn Suite* and the *Nursery Suite*, but some years later made copious notes for an opera, to be called *The Devil is an ass*, based on a Ben Jonson play, and for a Third Symphony. He also began a piano concerto. These compositions were, however, left uncompleted as a result of his fairly long last illness and his death in 1934 at the age of 76. Meanwhile, in the years after Lady Elgar's death, his many friendships and hobbies, conducting, a sea voyage, and various other activities had occupied most of his time.

He was intensely kind-hearted, sympathetic, and generous. He gave presents to friends and fellow-musicians who were ill or in need, and constantly performed kind actions to help them. He had, indeed, a great love of humanity, and was a true Christian not only in belief but in his conduct towards others. He was very wide in his outlook and sympathies, and had many friends who were foreigners as well as British ones. One of the closest of these was A. J. Jaeger, of Novello and Co. Ltd.—*Nimrod* in the Variations— who was a native of Düsseldorf. Elgar lived long enough to witness the beginning of the Nazi régime, and was horrified at it: he wrote to Miss Adela Schuster on March 17, 1933, 'I am in a maze regarding events in Germany—what are they doing? In this morning's paper it is said that the greatest conductor Bruno Walter and, stranger still, Einstein are ostracised; are we all mad? The Jews have always been my best and kindest friends—the pain of these news is unbearable and I do not know what it really means'. He was, however, shy and could at times be tactless or even apparently rude; but he never *intended* to hurt anyone's feelings. His estrangement from Charles Villiers Stanford—ultimately reconciled[43]—was really due to mutual incompatibility of temperament.

He and his wife were utterly devoted to one another, and to their daughter Carice (so-called by combining the first syllable of Caroline and the last syllable of Alice). Both of them were Roman Catholics. His wife was converted to that Church four years after their marriage, and he had been brought up as one: his mother

---

[43] See Diana McVeagh: *Edward Elgar—His Life and Music*, p. 95. The ultimate reconciliation of 1922 is not mentioned in Percy M. Young's *Elgar O. M.* (1955) but her book (1955) is slightly later than his, for his preface was dated October, 1954, whereas hers bears the date April, 1955. Michael Kennedy's account in *Portrait of Elgar*, pp. 124-5, makes one wonder whether Elgar even then felt truly reconciled to Stanford, though the latter evidently wanted 'to forget all about it'.

had become a Catholic through worshipping in the Catholic church where his father was organist (the father, however, was an Anglican until soon before he died). Elgar never talked about his religion; he often neglected to go to church, especially during his last years, and was more sceptical about some of its doctrines after his wife's death than before. Charity and a broad Christianity became more important in his eyes than actual participation in the worship of the Roman Catholic Church. All his life, however, he remained faithful to it, maintained in old age his donations to its charities, confirmed his loyalty to it during his last illness, but refused to see a priest on his deathbed, and received extreme unction at the end while unconscious. He had definitely intended to complete his great sacred trilogy of oratorios, of which *The Apostles* and *The Kingdom* were the two parts that had come to fruition; but creation of the third oratorio of the cycle, *The Judgment* (or *The Saints*) was postponed, at first, it would seem, through his turning to the composition of the two symphonies and the violin concerto and *Falstaff*, and then by the First World War. W. H. Reed failed to persuade him to take it up again—though he toyed with the idea in 1921—and he finally abandoned it in 1927, partly because he was convinced that a sacred oratorio was no longer wanted by the public, and partly, no doubt, because of the scepticism to which I have referred. Insofar as he had any urge left to compose, his muse had, so to speak, become secularised.

Elgar had many hobbies and interests apart from music. For instance, he loved racing, and a certain amount of betting, and billiards, and he enjoyed good food and wine, the theatre (including a good revue), amateur chemistry, the visual arts and literature, especially Shakespeare and R. L. Stevenson. He loved dogs and horses and birds and the sea, and took delight in puns and playing on words. He was, as Mrs Richard Powell tells us,[44] 'a brilliant and amusing person', with a keen sense of humour and fun, and though highly-strung, he was full of exuberance as well as being subject to periods of dejection and even of despair. He was extremely sensitive and greatly discouraged by the initial lack of appreciation of his genius. He adored the countryside, especially his native Worcestershire and its neighbouring counties and also Sussex where he came to live for a time. He was fond of fishing, golf, walking, cycling, and even flying kites! In fact, he loved the good things of life, and was a man of

[44] *Edward Elgar, Memories of a Variation*, p. 108.

extremely wide tastes and outlook; he lived for certain periods in London, but at heart he was a great countryman.

The music of this great-hearted man was an entirely natural product of his personal character. To a large extent he was self-taught. Music for him was 'written in the sky'; or it was 'in the air, all around us; the world is full of it, and you simply take as much of it as you require'.[45] Psychologically, this meant that in Elgar's case, the musical ideas sprang spontaneously from his inmost soul or subconscious self—under God's inspiration.

Those who do not appreciate Elgar's art always point scornfully to the *Pomp and Circumstance* Marches. 'Imperial', 'jingoistic', even 'vulgar', they have called them. Actually, I think they are jolly good military marches—neither more nor less than that. The trio melody in No. 1 March was afterwards used as a chorus by the composer in his *Coronation Ode*, with the words beginning 'Land of Hope and Glory'. It soon became popular, and caught on with the troops in World War I. Anyone who marched to it in uniform, as I did, in those grim days, knows what a splendid march tune it was for them. We all thought we were engaged in a righteous war—and so we were. *Land of Hope and Glory* was an inspiration to us and its popularity with the British public has continued to this day. Another early piece of his at which his detractors turned up their superior noses was *Salut d'Amour*. 'A mere salon piece', they said. It is a rather charming, unpretentious little work, dating from 1888/9, originally written for violin and piano, and later orchestrated. *Of course* it is a salon piece. Why not? Salon pieces have their place in good music, as Mendelssohn and Chopin have also shown.

Artistically, Elgar's music for children is more important. The two early *Wand of Youth* suites, and the much later *Nursery Suite*, are refined, delicate and utterly charming. Very attractive, too, is the incidental music written for the fantasy play *The Starlight Express*, which has some reminders of the *Wand of Youth*.

The *Cockaigne* overture is a splendid picture of London life, and the *Alassio* overture ('In the South') is a fine, romantic piece. But the real *greatness* of Elgar is to be found in the *Enigma Variations*, *The Dream of Gerontius*, *The Apostles*, *The Kingdom*, the two symphonies, the Introduction and Allegro for strings—and, I would

[45] See Neville Cardus: *Ten Composers*, p. 125; William Reed: *Elgar as I knew him*, p. 129.

add, the early Serenade for Strings—*For the Fallen*, the concertos for violin and for 'cello, the symphonic study *Falstaff*, and the three chamber works. On your reaction to these compositions, I suggest, can depend your opinion whether you think Elgar to be a major or a minor figure in the world of music. Personally, I not merely love his music, at its best, more than that of any composer subsequent to Brahms, but hold that it reveals Elgar as a great and original genius.

The *Enigma Variations* and the Brahms Variations on the St Anthony Chorale are, I think, the two greatest sets of *independent* variations for orchestra yet composed. Prior to Brahms, the variation form had mainly appeared either as one of several movements in sonata, or symphony, concerto or chamber music work, or as a separate composition *for a solo instrument*. Elgar was thus doing something fairly unusual[46] in composing a purely orchestral set of variations as a self-contained work at all. He was even more original in using the variation form for a composition not merely dedicated to, but really to sketch 'my friends pictured within'. The first one is more than a friend. It is his own beloved wife; and the Finale is a self-portrait. Some are portraits of friends of his; others, more like caricatures; three are based on incidents. It is possible to get rich enjoyment from listening to them all simply as a glorious piece of music in variation form; but our understanding of them is immensely enhanced by knowing something about the personalities—or stories—depicted, and there is no better way of doing this than by reading *Edward Elgar, Memories of a Variation* by Mrs Richard Powell—'Dorabella' of Variation X, the charming and intensely musical friend who as a young woman was so much in the confidence of Elgar and his wife and was so closely in touch with him at the time of the creation of this work—and of his other great compositions which followed it, at least until the time of her marriage in January, 1914. 'Programme music'? Yes, if you like to use that term; but how original to apply the variation form in relation to people whom he loved in real life, in the way in which Elgar has done here! Thus his

---

[46] Strauss's *Don Quixote* (1897), described as 'fantastic variations for 'cello and orchestra', is a symphonic poem cast in variation form, but also partaking of the nature of a concerto, like Franck's *Variations Symphoniques* for piano and orchestra and Tchaikovsky's *Variations on a rococo theme* for 'cello and orchestra. Both Dvořák and Parry wrote fine sets of symphonic variations for orchestra.

first great masterpiece is at once uniquely autobiographical: the link between the man and the artist has never been stronger.

The Dream of Gerontius is not, of course, Gerontius's dream, but Elgar's and Cardinal Newman's vision of the death of Gerontius and, thereafter, of the actual journey of his soul, through the next world into Heaven itself. And as this second part of the oratorio is far the longer of the two, this makes it, so far as I know, unique in the history of music and certainly the first of its kind. Hell and Heaven, and transfiguration, had been pictured musically, but nothing approaching this in its completeness. Newman's poem is essentially Roman Catholic in its atmosphere and character. But Elgar's conception, just because it is music—which deals in universals and is not tied to the concreteness of words or the visual arts —is sufficiently wide in its appeal to be loved by the British public to an extent comparable with *Messiah*, *The Creation*, and *Elijah* among sacred (non-liturgical) oratorios. This is especially remarkable in this materialistic second half of the 20th century. The younger generation, at least in the U.K., seems to cherish *Gerontius* as much as its parents and grandparents have done. The reason is that Elgar's genius is to be found here at its most sublime. He himself wrote on the manuscript 'This is the best of me ...', and among his previous works, certainly the *Variations* alone had approached it in greatness, and one cannot compare that warmly human, purely orchestral, work with a highly mystical oratorio such as *Gerontius*, for they are too different in kind.

Gerontius was succeeded by a chain of masterpieces. In *The Apostles* and *The Kingdom* Elgar again adopted the *Leitmotive* system that he had applied so eloquently to oratorio in *Gerontius*. But, for these works, instead of setting the visionary poem of a great 19th century prelate and writer, he selected texts from the Bible in order to embody musically the whole history of Jesus Christ on earth and the early days of His Church, and intended to follow them with a concluding oratorio depicting Antichrist, the Last Judgment, and the Heavenly Kingdom. It was a tremendously ambitious project: we can sympathise with him in finding in due course that he could not complete it, though it is very sad that he did not do so. The two oratorios of the cycle that we have got, are works of great beauty; but in spite of this, and although they reflect Elgar's personal faith at that time most sincerely and devoutly, the public have never held them in such great affection as *Gerontius*. It may be that their episodic nature

180

Apotheosis of Handel

Sir Edward Elgar, 1932

and the fact that the trilogy was left unfinished have something to do with this.[47]

The *Introduction and Allegro* for string orchestra and quartet has been described as the most abstract of Elgar's great works. Certainly it is not highly charged with emotion, nor is it in any sense programme music. It has a delightfully breezy, vigorous, open-air feeling, offset by the memory of Welsh songs sounding in his ears from the distance across the border. The First Symphony opens with a truly noble melody, which recurs in different forms throughout the work; the Allegro is full of struggle and grief; the ensuing Allegro molto hurries along with energy, or hovers gracefully in fantasy, until it merges into an Adagio so sublime that it is not surprising that Landon Ronald, that unsurpassed conductor of Elgar's orchestral compositions (I never heard him perform the oratorios), reverently told Lady Elgar that he always wanted to cross himself after interpreting it. The doubts and storms of the Finale culminate in the opening melody of the symphony, which returns in a blaze of glory. Hans Richter described this work at the first rehearsal for its earliest London performance in December, 1908, as 'the greatest symphony of modern times, written by the greatest modern composer—and not only in this country.'[48] Yet it was at least equalled by the gloriously beautiful Second Symphony, completed in February, 1911, and inscribed with Shelley's words:—

> 'Rarely, rarely comest thou,
> Spirit of Delight'.

That 'spirit' begins the work and often returns, but sometimes mingled with regret, as though for the passing of a splendid epoch. The slow movement is a solemn expression of grief, and even the 'Rondo: Presto' has an uneasy atmosphere. The Finale, however, is mainly serene, though with a slightly wistful conclusion.

Between these two symphonies came the violin concerto, for ever associated in my memories with Kreisler, Sammons, and Menuhin. On the title page Elgar wrote in Spanish 'Herein is enshrined the soul of .....' and Mrs Richard Powell[49] has declared that

[47] I have described these three greatest of Elgar's choral compositions that have come down to us, more fully in my book *The Divine Quest in Music*.

[48] Diana McVeagh, ibid., p. 50.

[49] Ibid., p. 86. Michael Kennedy, however, in *Portrait of Elgar*, p. 129, produces strong evidence that the unnamed person was Alice Stuart-Wortley, on the basis of some newly published letters.

the five dots denoted Mrs Julian H. Worthington, a most charming and kind American friend—yet another autobiographical touch. This is a contemplative work of great beauty, and the Cadenza in the Finale is unique, with its dreamy recollections of the themes of the concerto, accompanied by the soft notes of the strings of the orchestra.

Elgar's last great orchestral composition before the war was *Falstaff*, in my opinion the most masterly of all symphonic poems. It is typical Elgar, who was not really suited to the portrayal of evil and had made his demons in *Gerontius* less ferocious than Berlioz or Wagner would have done. And so the principal character, who is the Falstaff of Shakespeare's *Histories*, not of *The Merry Wives of Windsor*, is here a 'knight and a gentleman and a soldier', as in Morgann's essay, in contrast with the picture of Prince Henry, who is at first courtly but ultimately stern. Elgar plays down the fat man's faults, clearly sympathises with his humanity and his downfall, introduces two exquisite interludes, one to portray Falstaff's dream of his youth while he is asleep behind the arras at *The Boar's Head* and the other to describe Shallow's orchard, and ends the work with an infinitely pathetic musical description of Falstaff's death.

The best of Elgar's works associated by him with World War I is *The Spirit of England*, set to words by Laurence Binyon. Of its three movements, *The Fourth of August* seems to have dropped out of the repertory, and even *To Women*, fine though it is, is seldom performed nowadays, but *For the Fallen*, the longest of the three, is a deeply moving and noble tribute.

In 1918, Elgar turned to chamber music. He had often had thoughts in that direction, and ultimately they came to fruition in three works more intimate and also, on the whole, more resigned, than the great creations which had preceded them. He did not appreciate the piano as an instrument, and so in the violin and piano sonata it is the string instrument (which had been Elgar's own medium as a performer) that has the more eloquent share of the two. The quartet is beautifully written for the four strings, though the quintet is a bigger, if less perfect, creation. In all three, there are slow movements of outstanding loveliness.

The cello concerto was his last really great work. It, too, has a chamber music quality. There is an autumn sorrow in it, a sweet, tender emotion, yet exalted, never morbidly nostalgic.

It was, to me, remarkable that when Harriet Cohen was asked

in a radio interview which was the modern composer whose music appealed to her most, she replied, without hesitation, 'Elgar'. She herself performed the pianoforte part in the Quintet with great distinction; but that a fine pianist should so love the art of a composer who did not greatly care for her instrument as compared with others or write much for it, was, I feel, both a tribute to his stature as a creator and a symptom of hers as a dedicated musician.

Elgar, a composer with a wide and deep range of emotions, was also a mystic and a dreamer. He has been regarded as a prophet honoured chiefly in his own country: he was, both as man and artist, essentially English, indebted though he was, in the spirit rather than in the letter, to several of the great German and French masters of the past. The first people to recognise his genius fully, when it matured in the *Enigma* and *Gerontius*, were, in fact, the Germans, and it is significant that Richter, Richard Strauss, Jaeger, Kreisler, Casals and other eminent musicians abroad appreciated his stature as soon as they encountered his great masterpieces, and that Menuhin and other famous foreign performers of younger generations revere his music and rejoice in interpreting it to modern audiences. If the nations other than Elgar's own do not enjoy his works except *Cockaigne* and the *Variations*, I am afraid that I can only suggest that they do not realise what they are missing! For Elgar, in all the creations to which I have drawn attention, and also in his life, showed himself to be a truly great composer and a great man.

CHAPTER TWENTY-SIX

The Stature of Brahms

Wagner made 'Renunciation of Love' one of the leading motives of *The Ring*, but he certainly did not renounce love in his private life! In a sense, Brahms did not do so either, but he did renounce the fulfilment of it in marriage. The reason why he did this was largely, though not quite entirely, that he decided that marriage would have interfered with his complete fulfilment as a creative artist; whereas Wagner required a mate—whether married to him or not—in order to consummate his artistic self. Moreover, love, for Wagner the man, was something passionate, absorbing, but basically egotistical. For Brahms, love was devoted, self-sacrificing, tender. His conception of love was Christian, while Wagner's (in his private life) was pagan, for all the 'redemption by a woman's self-sacrificing love' that he sought to portray in some of his operas.

Johannes Brahms inherited from his father excellent health (until his last illness), his gift for music, and his resolve to rise in the world. His father, a professional musician with some executive talent, was of humble origin. His mother was the daughter of a tailor and was herself a seamstress, who earned her own living from the age of 13, but she had socially higher ancestry, for her mother's family, on the father's side, included many people of professional standing. She was not highly educated, but very shrewd and immensely kind-hearted. From her or her forebears, Brahms derived his unselfish warm-heartedness and also his intellectual powers. He inherited from both of his parents his exceptional love of Nature, and his happiness in the smaller joys of life. Yet he was not, on the whole, happy. How many great creative geniuses have been? There was a deep, inward melancholy in his make-up, which increased as the years went by.

He was a devoted son. His father was 17 years younger than his mother, and when she became old while her husband was middle-aged and still active, relations between them became strained; Elise, their daughter, was too frail to help, and Fritz, their other son, did nothing to mend the situation; it was Johannes who tried again and again, alas!, unsuccessfully, to reconcile them, and who eventually, when they parted, took a room for his father (who was gradually retiring from his musical profession) elsewhere in Hamburg, and supported both his mother and sister. He was profoundly shaken by his mother's death, remained a loyal and affectionate son of his father both during the latter's widowhood and after his happy re-marriage, and invited him to Vienna, to the Rhineland and to Switzerland. He became very fond of his stepmother (who was 18 years younger than his father) and was generous to her too.

Brahms was a staunch friend of Schumann and admirer of his music. When the successive tragedies of Schumann's insanity and death occurred, he rallied to Clara's side, and became deeply attached to her; his help and sympathy sustained her, but they decided against marriage; on her side, the fact that she was 14 years older than he and had seven children by Schumann, and, so far as Brahms was concerned, his conviction that his art demanded his complete dedication, proved decisive. Personally, this was for him his first and greatest instance of renunciation of marriage; he believed that 'bitter experiences give the artist material for his work' (as he had written earlier and in another connection to Joachim), and yet he never really reconciled himself to his celibacy. This was, in great measure, the anguish of soul which he had to endure throughout his life.

Brahms renounced matrimony, but he did not renounce love. On the contrary, he came to love Clara utterly, and she remained his ideal of womanhood throughout his life, and through and in spite of his successive loves for other women; at her death he wept bitterly, as though his heart would break. He loved Agathe Siebold, but decided that he could not 'wear fetters', that he must dedicate himself to his music; it was she who then broke off relations, and both of them long endured the wound; only after ten years did she marry another man, and only in her old age did she forgive Brahms (replying to his greeting conveyed through Joachim), though in the end she came to understand the deep wisdom of his choice completely. He was very fond of the girls of a small ladies' choir in Hamburg (in 1859-61), but especially Bertha Porubsky, who came from Vienna; she and Luise Dustmann-Meyer, the singer, told him about the beauty of that lovely city, which gradually, as it were, became his home; one of its attractions was that he enjoyed

185

flirting with its beautiful women. He was very friendly with Luise, kept up with Bertha, who had just got engaged, and was specially attracted to Ottilie Hauer, a very pretty girl, who, however, married another man. Brahm's love for her was, characteristically, transformed into a lasting friendship. So it was throughout his life; his lovely pupil, Elizabeth von Stockhausen, who married Heinrich von Herzogenberg and thereafter became one of his closest friends; Clara's beautiful third daughter, Julie, for whom his feelings ran very deep, but who married an Italian count; Hermine Spies, who was not only a brilliant young contralto, but a very charming, pretty girl, to whom he was strongly attracted but who died only a year after marriage to another man. Thus, after his deep, initial love for Clara—a woman so much older than he was—he fell in love successively with girls much younger than himself. And the reason that they all married other men was largely because Brahms's dedication to his art constantly withheld him from embarking on matrimony, in spite of his passionate and affectionate nature; it was an inward conflict, lasting until his old age.

But a consequence of this was an *inward* bitterness, which resulted in sarcasms, roughness and even rudeness; these were, however, only surface symptoms and did not obliterate his deep humanity, warm-heartedness, kindness and generosity. And another cause of the bitterness was Hamburg's lack of appreciation of him, which he never forgave: the city of his birth 'repented' too late. His love of his fellow human beings was matched by an exceptional love of the beauties of Nature. He loved children; he had many dear friends, and was very good to them and to mere acquaintances and to fellow-musicians, especially to those younger than himself, and even to strangers. And he was very religious, in the broad sense of the term, was a convinced Lutheran, and had a tremendous knowledge of the Bible, to which he resorted constantly. He wrote to Clara once that he was 'a difficult person to deal with', and it is true, as Karl Geiringer [50] has said, that he did not try to clear up a misunderstanding or to see other people's points of view; this caused him to lose some of his best friends. The rift between him and Joachim, however, was really due to Joachim's misguided suspicion of his wife's fidelity. Brahms sought to disillusion him, but Joachim felt that Brahms was taking her

---

[50] Karl Geiringer: *Brahms: his Life and Work*, p. 133.

side against him; years elapsed before the great friendship was restored. In the normal way, Brahms was the staunchest of friends with those to whom he had grown attached.

It may appear to us strange that the musical world in Germany and Austria should for their contemporaries have been divided into two camps, representing Wagner and Brahms; for today these two giants seem to us to be directly complementary to one another, each pre-eminent in his own field, and there is no reason why the broadminded music lover should not enjoy the art of both of them. Wagner was essentially a man of the theatre: the musical drama was all-in-all to him, and even the only non-theatrical works of his which really count, the *Siegfried Idyll* and the five settings of poems by Mathilde Wesendonk (related to *Tristan*), are largely associated with his operas. Brahms, on the contrary, excelled in almost every contemporary form of music except opera, which he did not touch, and the symphonic poem, to which he was utterly opposed; he had no use for 'programme music', such as Liszt and Berlioz created. Yet he was partly, and to an important extent, a romantic composer, as in the three early piano sonatas, the ballade *Edward*, and the songs in which he reflected so beautifully the moods, emotions, and atmosphere of the many German poems which he set to music.

His art has often been described as a mixture of romanticism and classicism. It is, in my view, truer to say that, whilst there is a strong romantic vein in his music, the term is too narrow to be applied to it as a whole. In his work he expressed a tremendously wide range of emotions (including romantic ones) and also of spiritual and religious conceptions. In his instrumental compositions he found it perfectly natural to convey these mainly in and through the traditional forms of the sonata and of chamber-music and the concerto and the symphony, though he altered these according to his needs and introduced, for instance, in some of his works, a movement of intermezzo-like character, dreamy or contemplative perhaps, in place of the scherzo or minuet of his predecessors; and he treated the variation form as an independent composition, whereas previously it had usually been one of the movements in a larger whole. Moreover, he went back to the contrapuntal structures of previous centuries, yet employed them for novel purposes: to take one example, only a composer of tremendous genius and imagination could convey tragic grandeur by means of the ancient *passacaglia*, as Brahms did in the Finale of his Fourth Symphony.

The music of Brahms is both universal and autobiographical. In the sombre opening movement of his First Piano Concerto, he was expressing his own grief at the Schumann tragedy; in the lovely Adagio, he was painting a portrait of Clara[51]. In the Requiem, his emotions at his mother's death were reflected, even though the *idea* of composing it may have started some years earlier as a result of the loss of Schumann. All through his life, Brahms voiced his own feelings and thoughts and religion and his love of Nature, in his art. It was natural for him to celebrate the victory of Germany over France in 1870-1 and the foundation of the German Empire, in his splendid *Triumphlied*, for he was a great patriot, and he did not realise the truth about the Ems telegram or the fact that Bismarck was the real aggressor.

But just because he was a man of such wide and deep sympathy and so profound in his mind and outlook, his music is not only personal to himself, but conveys the emotions, aspirations and reflections of mankind. The Requiem is not based on the Roman liturgy, but on passages from the Old and New Testaments and the Apocrypha, selected by Brahms himself out of his intimate knowledge of the Bible. It is a *Deutsches* Requiem, only in the sense that he naturally used Luther's German translation. So concerned was he to make it as universal as he could, that its text does not even mention the name of Christ, although it is, in the broadest and deepest sense, Christian in character; it contains no 'Dies Irae', but constantly sounds the note of comfort and the peace that passes all understanding.

This is characteristic of Brahms. For all his inward personal unhappiness, he could not bring himself to compose works of inspissated gloom. There is always some relief, some ray of light amid the darkness. Even in the funereal *Begräbnisgesang* there is the hope of resurrection after death. In the beautiful *Alto Rhapsody*, Brahms could follow Goethe's picture of the unhappy young misanthrope in his *Harzreise im Winter*, by the third stanza, in which the *Father of Love* is besought to enlighten the young man's soul—in musical as well as poetic terms. In the *Song of Destiny*, though Hölderlin's poem ends with a description of the suffering of Man, contrasted with the happiness of the gods, Brahms finishes

[51] As Karl Geiringer (ibid., p. 249) points out, this is almost certainly the right interpretation of a sentence in Brahms' letter to Clara of December 30th, 1851.

with a serene instrumental epilogue, repeating the introduction, though in the key of C major instead of E flat, and thus bringing his music to a tranquil conclusion. Schiller's allegorical ode *Nänie* was set by Brahms in memory of his friend Feuerbach, the painter, who had recently died, to music of tender sorrow, comfort and peace. Even in his setting of Goethe's *Gesang der Parzen*—which contained no relief for suffering and condemned humanity— Brahms ends on a note of compassion. The tragedy of the Finale of the Fourth Symphony is so far from being depressing that the spiritual grandeur of the whole conception is exalting to the mind and soul of the listener—a kind of Aristotelian catharsis (purification) through suffering.

Brahms's love of little children seems to fit in with the charm and graciousness, and even playfulness, of some of his music. The titanic genius who created the great symphonies, the Tragic overture, the glorious chamber music works, the *Four Serious Songs* and the choral masterpieces, could unbend to let us enjoy light-heartedly the waltzes for piano duet, the Hungarian dances for two pianos, the *Liebeslieder* and the *Neue Liebeslieder*. The Finale to that most gigantic of all piano concertos, Brahms' No. 2 in B flat, is the music of playful happiness.

In the short pieces for pianoforte which he composed at the end of his life, in the four works for clarinet and other instruments (the Trio, the Quintet and the two sonatas), he revealed a mellow tranquillity, a spirit of resignation and serene wisdom.

Brahms seems to me to have covered a more comprehensive and more profound range of the moods, emotions, thoughts and prayers of humanity than any composer since Beethoven. He did not touch the fantastic—that, among many other aspects, was the province of Berlioz. But the far-reaching greatness and grandeur of Brahms's music are the artistic embodiment of his greatness as a man.

CHAPTER TWENTY-SEVEN

War-time music again

World War II saw me back in the Army in the first month of the war, at the age of forty-seven. This time I was posted from the Army Officers' Emergency Reserve to the Royal Army Service Corps. On my way to a Drivers' Training Unit—a place for which I was not ideally suited, as I could not even drive a car and have never done so!—I was stationed for a few days at Aldershot; and I remember, one evening in the Mess Lounge, an excellent military band was playing good light music with great rhythmic precision and exhilarating sonority. I could not resist the lilt of the Johann Strauss waltzes, and almost involuntarily started dancing gently to the entrancing strains. No wonder that the charming Brigadier, who was Commandant, murmured to a fellow-officer in amused accents which I could not help overhearing, 'Look, there's old Mendl, footing it like a wood-nymph, all by himself!'

After a bit, I was posted to a Staff Captain's appointment at the War Office in London, but there was not much chance for me to gain musical experiences then, owing to the long hours of work —in spite of Henry Wood's gallant effort in keeping the Proms going at Queen's Hall. My War Office job came to an end after about a year, and I found myself back on the regimental side of the Corps, in a mechanical transport unit at Bradford. The Major was old enough to be my nephew, and the other officers were young enough to have been sons of mine; none of them was interested in music, except a jolly fellow who in civilian life had conducted a professional jazz orchestra in variety shows, and in his private life enjoyed opera. The most musical man in the unit, I think, was one of the officers' batmen, with whom I used to discuss musical subjects seriously while I was putting on my boots and gaiters after breakfast and he was making the 'beds' in our unfurnished billet at Warwick (to which place we subsequently moved in a 15-hours' drive by convoy through pouring rain). There was a memorable oasis in the musical desert of war-time Bradford, when Irene Scharrer gave a Chopin recital in the Town Hall. You bet I was there! I shall never forget how beautifully she played those pieces of Chopin—a composer in whose works she specialised —and how grateful I was to her for bringing an afternoon of artistic refreshment into my music-starved existence and into the lives of the rest of her enthusiastic audience on that Saturday afternoon.

During a short refresher course at Boscombe, I managed to go to a fine orchestral concert given by the Wessex Philharmonic Orchestra in the Winter Garden at Bournemouth: one of the main works was Bach's D minor pianoforte concerto, but I cannot remember who was the soloist. After that, there was another musical desert while I was officer in charge of a holding wing near Chesterfield, and in the Spring of 1941 I was released from military duties to take up 'work of national importance' as a temporary civil servant at the Ministry of Economic Warfare in London. I arrived there in time for the worst blitz of the war, May 10th—when, among other precious buildings, the dear old Queen's Hall, with its wonderful memories and associations, was destroyed. I spent that night—like a good many others—in an air-raid shelter, and I remember that the next morning I received a telegram from my father, who with my mother, my wife and my aged father-in-law, was at that time in South Devon—intimating that they would like to hear news of me: I replied 'Flourishing, after a dirty night. Love.'

There was music to be heard in London from then onwards, broadcast from elsewhere or in the Albert Hall; but, with one notable exception, it was not a time for 'fresh woods and pastures new.' I recall one period of several weeks in which Tchaikovsky's First Pianoforte Concerto and Beethoven's Seventh Symphony were performed over and over again: one never tires of them, of course, and one had no right to expect much variety of musical experiences amid the horrors of war. The exception to which I have referred was Myra Hess's splendid enterprise in starting and maintaining the lunch-time concerts at the National Gallery. I found it difficult to get to them from the Ministry's offices in Berkeley Square in the time available; but when, following D-day and the return of the Allied Forces to Europe, the work of blockading Germany started to diminish, and my own duties likewise, I returned in October, 1944, to Shell-Mex House to fill a position in the Petroleum Board (into which the various companies distributing petroleum products in the U.K. had pooled their resources

and their staff as a war-effort), I—like others—was able to take
my lunch interval at the National Gallery occasionally and to hear
masterpieces of chamber music, song, and pianoforte music, performed under memorable conditions in beautiful surroundings.
What a wonderful benefit Dame Myra Hess conferred on us all in
those days! I remember also with great pleasure one Saturday afternoon when Frederick Lamond played Beethoven sonatas to an
enthralled audience in the Wigmore Hall and neither he nor we
paid any attention to the warning sirens which ominously told us
that V.1 bombs were flying over London.

My wife and our son Jim, then a schoolboy, made their temporary home for the first four years of the war at Shaldon, near
Teignmouth, South Devon; he went there in his holidays; my
father-in-law stayed in a small hotel in the same village, and I
occupied his London flat meanwhile, our own little house in St
John's Wood having been rendered unsuitable by neighbouring
bombs. I visited them when on leave. My parents moved to Berk-
hamsted, and it was a great shock to us all when my mother, to
whom I was devoted, died there suddenly from a heart attack in
March, 1943, aged seventy-four. My father took a fresh flat in
London and I moved into it to keep him company; London was
during that period free from air-raids, and my father-in-law moved
back to the metropolis, followed by my wife after she had handed
over her various war-time duties at Shaldon (she then worked for
the Red Cross in London until the war ended). This naturally
brought me back to my father-in-law's flat; my brother, who, after
serving in the R.A.F. early in the war, was in the Ministry of Food
at Colwyn Bay, was soon afterwards transferred to London and
took my place in my father's flat until the latter's death at the
age of seventy-eight-and-a-half in July, 1945, after a long illness,
which the old man endured with characteristic bravery and even
cheerfulness. He was able to rejoice in our victory over Nazi Germany in May of that year; but he certainly did not foresee that
the war with Japan was to end so dramatically and suddenly as it
did, in the following August.

So at last the long ordeal reached an end. And in the years that
followed, Vaughan Williams came into his own again, and Benjamin Britten and Michael Tippett were to win the recognition that
was their due, in ever increasing measure.

PART THREE

CHAPTER TWENTY-EIGHT

What happened afterwards

In this chapter I will go on with my autobiographical narrative, covering events from the summer of 1945 onwards, largely in relation to music, but also to matters unconnected with it, insofar as these are necessary for continuity. In the ensuing chapters, I shall discuss various composers, but in most cases without much reference to their personal characters and simply as important artistic figures in my music-loving life.

My father-in-law lived until early September, 1946, when he died at the age of eighty-eight, after a gradual decline in health, during which my wife looked after him with devoted care. That autumn, we moved from his flat to a small one in Marylebone, which some friends of ours were quitting and which we have continued to occupy ever since. Our son had grown up, and after leaving Harrow was called up for his two years of national service in the Army; through the ranks, he subsequently got a commission and served in the Suez Canal Zone; he was demobilised in 1948, and went to University College, Oxford, following in the footsteps of seven earlier Mendls. In due course, he was called to the Bar, but, unlike his father and grandfather, continued to practise in that profession, and became also concerned in politics. He wisely moved from the small room in our little flat into an abode of his own. Throughout his life he has been, like me, a keen lover of music and interested in other arts as well.

The Government did not assent to the break-up of the Petroleum Board until July, 1948, when I was offered and accepted a position with my former Company, Shell-Mex and B.P. Ltd., connected with staff management and staff welfare. By that time I had only four years to go, as the Company's normal age for retirement was sixty, and though in 1952 a tentative suggestion of a short continuance beyond that age was made to me, I declined this, as it would have brought no increase either in salary or in pension, I was anxious to be of some help to my wife, who had already had trouble with her eyes, and I wanted to write. I celebrated by sixtieth birthday by going to a Promenade Concert—alone! My wife was in hospital, and our son was not in London. The programme was glorious—Haydn and Brahms, with the B.B.C. Symphony Orchestra conducted by Malcolm Sargent, and that superb artist, Solomon, playing the solo part in Brahms's 2nd piano concerto in B flat. It was, alas! to be the last occasion on which I heard him. In Brahms, Beethoven, and Schumann, at any rate, he has remained unsurpassed, in my experience.

Since the appearance of my two early books, my literary work had consisted only of magazine and newspaper articles, but it had recently occurred to me that some of these might form part of the raw materials for another book, which was eventually published in 1950 under the title of *The Soul of Music*; Ernest Newman most kindly wrote a foreword to it. I also had ideas for two companion volumes on the spiritual aspects of my two great artistic loves—music and Shakespeare. These appeared in 1957 and 1964 respectively as *The Divine Quest in Music* and *Revelation in Shakespeare*; for the former, the then Dean of Windsor, Bishop Eric Hamilton (another old 'Univ.' man, though senior to me) was good enough to contribute a foreword, whilst that great conductor, Sir Adrian Boult, very kindly wrote a preface. Both the Church and the musical profession were thus represented, in bestowing a blessing, as it were, on my modest effort at an ambitious subject. My book *Adventure in Music* (1964) was a companion volume to *The Soul of Music*.

My Aunt Alice, who has figured earlier in this narrative, was the last of my mother's sisters to survive; she lived till 1952. My uncle Charles Mendl lost his first wife (the well-known Elsie de Wolfe), who was older than he was, and married *en seconde noce* the charming Madame Yvonne Reilly, whom he had known for many years, but who was considerably younger than himself; she was a talented violinist; but alas! she pre-deceased my uncle, who survived her by 15 months and died at his home in Paris in February, 1958.

My brother, who had a difficult time in his late middle age and a protracted fatal illness, lived until January, 1962.

Meanwhile, in spite of our deep involvement in these sad events, my wife and I managed to enjoy some pleasant holidays both on the Continent and in the U.K. She had not had many opportunities

195

of continental trips in her life, and so I was delighted to be able to escort her to the French Riviera, the Lakes of Orta and Garda, Florence, Siena, Venice and Verona, and, on the first occasions in her experience, to Switzerland—the Lakes of Thun and Lucerne, Wengen, Pontresina, and Zermatt. In this post-World War II period, also, we have not only kept up our old friendships, but have made new ones. Two of these have musical associations: Maurice Jackson, whom we met with his old father and his sister at the Isaak Walton Hotel in Dovedale, is a keen music lover; and so was Mrs Anne Kent, whom I met at a performance of Gluck's *Alceste* at Glyndebourne. My second cousin, Madame Ghita Schapira (née Mendl) who was my immediate contemporary, but whom I had not met since we were both seven, entered into our lives only a few years before her death; (the contact occurred through a mutual cousin in London, with whom she had kept in touch). Her husband had died many years before, she had found herself having to bring up her three children in Roumania through the Nazi regime and World War II and subsequently behind the Iron Curtain, and only in 1959 managed to make her way through Italy, where some Italian cousins on her mother's side welcomed her, to Israel. Her daughter got a job in Paris. Her two sons, their wives and her grandson followed her to Israel. She herself was a gifted pianist and teacher of the piano. She paid two or three visits to England after her sojourn in Israel, and my wife and I and our son found her a most charming friend. She was intensely musical and artistic, and this formed a strong bond between us.

Among our old friends, Dilys Rhys Roberts and (Mrs) Barbara Tylor (an American lady) were back in London; they were great friends of one another, having originally met through my family, and after Barbara had lost her second husband, they occupied flats in the same building. Dilys, however, moved to South Wales in her early eighties, in order to be near her son and daughter-in-law, and died there in 1967. During all these years in London, we have seen a lot of both these dear friends. Dilys maintained her keen interest in music, and Barbara Tylor has always been an enthusiastic music lover.

R.A.B. Powell, who had been best man at our wedding, died in his sixties. I have kept up with his family (who live outside London), mainly through his son, Guy, who is especially fond of opera.

It is now time for me to turn to the composers whose music has meant so much to me, other than those already discussed. Gluck,

Ludwig van Beethoven

geb. in Bonn, am 17? December 1770,
gest. in Wien, am 26? März 1827.

Beethoven

Lady seated at the virginals by Vermeer

Haydn, and Berlioz must come first, for they are, in a sense, overdue. The reasons why I have not written about them earlier in this book, will appear in the chapters which follow.

In *The Soul of Music* I included a chapter entitled *The Decline of the Teutonic Leadership in Music*. This leads me here to group certain composers of other nations or races together—three Czechoslovaks, three Scandinavians, three Spaniards, and some modern British composers apart from those covered in earlier chapters. Weber, Verdi, Mussorgsky and three Austrians will also come into the picture, and reference must be made to various other creators not treated elsewhere in this book. Finally, I cannot burke the difficult issue of the *avant garde*, even though some of its representatives are not among those who have meant most to me.

CHAPTER TWENTY-NINE

Gluck, musical dramatist

Gluck enters late into my story, simply because so many of my opportunities of hearing his operas have occurred since 1945. Following my introduction to his *Orfeo ed Eurydice* at the Savoy Theatre in my boyhood, mentioned in Chapter 6, I have heard and seen this opera a number of times, but the only performance which has equalled that one in my estimation was at Glyndebourne soon after World War II, when Kathleen Ferrier was memorable in the principal part. I have heard *Alceste* several times either at Glyndebourne (where Richard Lewis was magnificent as Admetus) or at Covent Garden or on the radio, *Iphigeneia in Aulis* and *Paris and Helen* twice each, *Iphigeneia in Tauris* on a number of occasions, and 'Armide' only once. Yet I have scarcely ever lost the chance of hearing and/or seeing these lovely works. They are far too seldom performed, anyhow in the U.K., for they, like the three Berlioz operas, deserve, on their artistic merits, to be in the regular repertoire of every great city in the world that has an opera house.

The historical importance of Gluck's operatic reforms is always stressed in books and articles—how he did away with the superfluous musical embellishments of the existing Italian opera with its trills and roulades, and the non-dramatic recitatives and 'da capo' repetitions on the orchestra, fusing words and music into a dramatic whole, and indeed aiming even at making the music subservient to the verse. This latter object, however, was a piece of confused thinking on Gluck's part, for in opera the music is bound, by its association with a libretto designed for music, to take the words up, as it were, into itself: the audience goes to the opera house to hear the musical embodiment of the words and the story; if the libretto were really the dominant partner, we should surely prefer a play—either with or without incidental music. But Gluck was perfectly right in seeking to make these six operas more dramatic than all his previous ones had been, or than those of his immediate contemporaries or predecessors. In this respect, he was following the example of Monteverdi and anticipating Mozart, Beethoven, Weber, Berlioz, Wagner, Verdi at his greatest, and Debussy.

198

What, however, is sometimes forgotten is that Gluck himself was, as he wrote in his Preface to *Alceste*, anxious 'to strengthen the expression of the sentiments' and to voice 'the passion involved'. His operas have been described as classical, in contrast with the romantic ones of Weber and the 19th century. As I have, however, pointed out in my book *The Soul of Music* (Chapter 15), these distinctions between classical and romantic music are apt to be misleading. No one, so far as I am aware, has yet produced an adequate definition of what classical means: it is sometimes contrasted with popular, sometimes with romantic, and often used to denote that which has become established once the composer has become an old master. It is possible to give a description of romantic, as applicable to music.[52] As I have suggested, romanticism has existed as a fundamental quality of art and of human nature from the earliest times. Those of us who had a so-called classical education, know that, whilst it meant learning ancient Greek and Latin literature, we found ourselves reading the extremely romantic adventures of Odysseus in the pages of Homer, the impassioned, tragic stories of legendary characters such as Orpheus and Eurydice, Alcestis, Iphigeneia, Agamemnon, Electra and Orestes, and Oedipus, whether in the dramas of Aeschylus, Sophocles and Euripides, or elsewhere; the romantic conflict between duty and passionate love in the tales of Aeneas and Dido as recounted in the poetry of Virgil, and romance as present in the love poems of Theocritus and Catullus and many of the odes of Horace. So much for ancient classical literature: it was as romantic as anything can be. Therefore we need not be surprised when we find that Gluck's music was romantic in the same sense as that of his successors: the real distinctions are those of idiom and of degree. Gluck wrote in an 18th century musical style, and before the days of rich orchestral colour which, starting with Beethoven and Weber, was developed into a wonderful instrument of romantic art at the hands of Berlioz and Wagner. And in the romantic stories of *Armide* and of *Paris and Helen* he was able to give fuller rein to his instinct for lyrical beauty and passionate emotion than was feasible in the more formal structures of his other, Hellenic, operas. But he was, basically, not only a dramatic, but, as I see it, a romantic composer, particularly when we take into account the period in which he lived.

[52] See Chapter 15 of this book.

Gluck inherited the toughness of his forester-huntsman father, and his upbringing in the woodlands strengthened his will-power, energy and independence of spirit. Although he appears to have caught a venereal disease from a single encounter, this did not prevent him, later on, from making a marriage which, though childless, proved completely happy, and also brought him a considerable dowry, thus enabling him to pursue his artistic ideals without financial anxieties. He was a jolly, manly fellow, frankly fond of money and of the pleasures of the table; indeed it was his liking for liqueur—against which his doctor had warned him—that caused his death: when his wife left the room and one of his friends had declined a glass, Gluck, pretending to be annoyed, drank its contents himself; and died within a matter of hours after an apoplectic seizure. Apart from that tendency, he was prudent, vigorous, and autocratic, though he was also capable of being diplomatic and adept at publicity. He was deeply affected by the death of his niece and adopted daughter from smallpox when he was sixty-two; yet he behaved badly towards his colleague, Calzabigi, the librettist, by handing the manuscript of the latter's *Le Danaidi* to two other writers for translation into French and adaptation, without Calzabigi's knowledge or consent, and allowing his name to appear as joint composer of 'Les Danaides' with that of Salieri, though in fact he had done no more than give a few hints and a little advice to that former pupil of his.

Although it was his robust determination that enabled him to triumph over obstacles and to put through the reforms for which he is justly famous, his personal character *itself* does not appear in his music, in the way that the composer's personality is autobiographically revealed in varying degrees in the art of Bach, Beethoven, Berlioz, Chopin or Elgar, for instance, and even a mainly operatic composer such as Wagner. Gluck sunk himself in his operatic characters. You could not possibly tell from his operas or from his music for the *Don Juan* ballet that his personal nature was as I have described it. In his case, the man and his music inhabit different worlds. So far from being integrated, they have virtually nothing to do with one another. We can appreciate to the full all the quality of Gluck's masterpieces, without having the smallest knowledge of the man himself; whereas in the case of the other composers mentioned above, a knowledge of their personal characteristics enriches our *understanding* of their music, even if it does not increase our enjoyment of it.

CHAPTER THIRTY

Haydn—at last

I came to Haydn gradually, and, on the whole, relatively late in my music-loving career. As indicated in Chapter 4, my father professed to have little use for his music, when I was young. More recently, I converted an elderly lady, who had had *The Creation* rather forced down her throat in her childhood, by taking her to an all-Haydn Prom. at the Albert Hall on September 4th, 1964: she said she had never enjoyed a concert so much! This may have been a pardonable overstatement, but there was no mistaking her enthusiasm.

The result of my father's indifference to Haydn, however, was that I heard practically none of his music until I came across some of the string quartets in the concerts of the Oxford University Music Club when I was an undergraduate before World War I. I loved them, and since then I have gradually built up my experience of Haydn's quartets, piano sonatas, trios, symphonies, concertos, and choral works—with the result that he has become one of my supremely favourite composers. And the fact that there has been a great revival of interest in the music of this wonderful creator since World War II has, of course, given me increased opportunities for widening my knowledge of his art. My critical sense does not, indeed, allow me to regard him as any less great than his contemporary, Mozart, with whom he has so often been coupled. The finest of Haydn's quartets are equal even to the six beautiful ones which Mozart dedicated to him; and whereas only a relatively small proportion of Mozart's forty-one symphonies, such as the *Little* G minor (No. 25), the A major (No. 29), the *Linz*, the *Prague* and the marvellous last three in E flat, G minor, and C major, are really *very great* music, Haydn's 104 in this genre comprise a far larger number of real masterpieces, even if some people would say that none of them quite equals the last three of Mozart. It was Mozart, of course, who shone in the piano concerto and the opera, but Haydn composed a whole series of great settings of the Mass which have none of the quasi-operatic character of parts even of Mozart's inspired, unfinished Mass in C minor and of his also uncompleted Requiem. Haydn re-created the early chapters of *Genesis* in simple, eloquent, musical terms into his glorious oratorio *The Creation*, transformed a German version of Thompson's *The Seasons* into a musical masterpiece, and gave us a unique expression of Christ's Seven Last Words on the Cross in the form of a series of profound slow movements followed by an earthquake. Mozart achieved nothing corresponding to these particular enrichments of our civilisation.

What a man! Haydn started his career as a chorister and went on to being a player on the *klavier* and a teacher of music, and, later, the director of music in the establishment of a rich nobleman, composing works to please the tastes of his master, so that he was virtually a servant; he ended his long life as a beloved and honoured international artist.

In his middle twenties, he fell in love with a girl pupil, who took the veil, and was then persuaded by her father to marry her sister, Maria, who took no interest in his career. It is small wonder that the marriage turned out unhappily. His wife proved to be 'quarrelsome, jealous, bigoted',[53] and even uneconomical. Haydn was a susceptible man, and several times was greatly attracted to other women; it has even been suspected that he was the father of Luigia Polzelli's younger son, though this has never been proved. Haydn's marriage gradually ceased to have any reality for him. He bought a house in Vienna in 1793, which remained his property, but from 1797, when he lived in it, his wife was hardly ever there, as owing to severe rheumatism she spent most of her time at the Baden sulphur springs until her death in 1800. He had remained remarkably unembittered during their married life, and devoted all his art 'to the glory of God'.

He is called 'The Father of the Symphony'. But he did not sit down like a kind of 18th century Schoenberg and scratch his head to invent a new language of music. The symphony or sonata (or string quartet) form evolved—'just growed' (as they say!)—out of the old operatic overture, and Haydn developed it into a marvellous instrument for the expression of contrasting emotions, humour, and gaiety. Unlike Mozart, he loved the country—and he could

---

[53] Karl Geiringer : *Haydn, a creative life in music*, p. 41.

not, otherwise, have composed *The Seasons*. So his music is not only divine, but fresh with the fragrance and open-air feeling of a fine spring morning. He was one of the greatest melodists in the world's history, but these wondrous tunes are never left as self-contained things: they are developed or varied, apparently in the most natural way possible, but really, of course, with the art that conceals art. He may have been the greatest pioneer in the origins of the sonata form, but he often departs from its formal structure when his imagination prompts him to do so, and he springs more actual *surprises* upon us than Mozart or perhaps even than Beethoven, though this may be due to the fact that Beethoven's output was less voluminous and that most of his music is so very familiar to us today.

There was a merry twinkle in Haydn's eye, one feels. He loved his little joke. There is no more *lovable* composer, and no more lovable *man* among the great composers. Obviously his character was not completely unblemished (whose is?), but he was extraordinarily benevolent, generous to needy relatives, helpful to his fellow-musicians, kindly and humorous, meticulous and regular in his habits, and deeply religious. The man and the artist are one. The more we study his life and his character, the more clearly we can see that, like Bach and Elgar and certain others whom I have mentioned, he is one of those in whom there is no conflict, no inconsistency between the man and the composer. He is to be contrasted with Gluck, because his operas are the least significant part of his work; whereas Gluck was essentially a man of the theatre and (largely for that very reason) his personal character throws little or no light upon his art, whilst Haydn's personality is reflected vividly in his music, of which the most important manifestations were non-operatic.

CHAPTER THIRTY-ONE

The Imagination of Berlioz

I have loved the music of Berlioz consistently all my life, from the days when, as a boy, I used to hear the usual three excerpts from *La Damnation de Faust*, played with great delicacy in the case of *Dance of the Sylphs* and *Minuet of the Will-o-the-Wisps* and with fire and gusto in the *Marche hongroise* (the Rákóczy March) by the old Queen's Hall Orchestra under Henry J. Wood, down to recent times when, as an elderly man, I have listened with rapture to the three great operas and the wonderful choral works.[54] Only since World War II has it been possible to complete my delightful experience of the masterpieces of this giant among French composers, the mighty prophet of 19th century musical romanticism. Hence it is only in this comparatively late place in my narrative that I can fittingly embark upon a brief discussion of Berlioz, as man and musician. I have said that my love for his art has been consistent all my life; but I should add that it has increased with the years and with deeper and wider knowledge of his works.

As a man, he is, in my eyes, an extraordinarily attractive and fascinating creature. In my book *The Divine Quest in Music* (p. 103) I wrote a short description of his personal character, based on Berlioz's own Memoirs and Professor Jacques Barzun's splendid book *Berlioz and the Romantic Century* (especially, Chapter 20, in Vol. II): 'He was passionate, daring, impetuous, sensitive, impressionable, susceptible to despair, but with a strong will and lucid mind; modest and shy, yet conscious of his superiority, so that he did not suffer fools gladly; gay and humorous, grateful and tender-hearted, and a good friend; an exceptionally fair-minded critic; devoted to his affectionate, unorthodox father (who was a doctor), and only prevented from being attached to his harsh, de-

[54] Since Wood, the great advocates of Berlioz's music among conductors whom I have heard have been Hamilton Harty, Thomas Beecham, Rafael Kubelik, Pierre Monteux, Malcolm Sargent, and Colin Davis.

vout mother by her denial of love from him' (consequent on his choice of music as a profession in preference to medicine). Of course there were blemishes. When his youthful love for Harriet Smithson, the Irish actress, failed to prosper at first, he fell in love with Camille Moke, the piano teacher, actually in response to her initiative. Her mother publicly acknowledged their engagement, but while he was in Italy after winning the *Prix de Rome*, he heard from her the news that Camille was about to marry M. Pleyel, the piano manufacturer. He was furious at the faithlessness of the two women, and set off for home with murder in his heart. Of course the tender-hearted Berlioz could not possibly have carried out that initial impulse. He tried, instead, to drown himself in the sea, but most fortunately for all of us, was rescued, and recovered his equilibrium under the influence of the beauty of Nature on the Riviera, and of his love for his family and for his art. He made a great mistake in subsequently marrying Harriet Smithson after all, for the marriage gradually broke up unhappily. She became a shrew and a drunkard. And during the long agony, he neglected their son, Louis, in his boyhood, though he was, in reality, utterly devoted to him. Berlioz's genius won a good deal of recognition in his lifetime, but throughout he had to endure great sadness through the deaths of his beloved sister Adele, of many dear friends, and, above all, of Louis from yellow fever at the age of thirty-three—an event which made Berlioz temporarily prostrate with grief. He suffered, too, from endless disappointments and intrigues with regard to his musical compositions, and from recurrent ill-health, largely due to worry and anxiety. On Harriet's death, he married Marie Recio, who had long been his mistress; he tried to do his best for both these women; his second wife also predeceased him—by nearly seven years.

He remained to the end a faithful friend and an artist of unswerving integrity. He was not only one of the greatest composers, but also a brilliant writer and critic, and a man of wide reading and culture. He idolised Virgil, Shakespeare, and Beethoven, and was a great admirer and lover of the art of Gluck. He had a superb intellect, so that, romantic as he was, his romanticism was, so to speak, controlled. This, I think, is a more truthful way of describing the quality of his mind and spirit than to call him 'romantic and classic', as Ernest Newman did at one stage.[55] One illustration of his personal romanticism was his constant, idealised remembrance

[55] Ernest Newman: *Musical Studies*, 1st essay.

of his boyhood love for Estelle Duboeuf, whom, as Mme. Fornier, he re-visited her in her old age, and with whom he exchanged letters; he still loved her.

The romantic element in his music is controlled in the sense that he never lets it run away with him. The master-mind is always magnificently in control. Moreover, the *Symphonie Fantastique* and *Harold in Italy*, for instance, romantic as they are, were built, fundamentally, according to the symphonic structure which Berlioz inherited from his predecessors. They do not depart from the form (or forms) of Beethoven's symphonies any more drastically than Beethoven diverges from the Haydn/Mozart inheritance. Haydn himself altered and adapted the symphonic structure which he had largely built up, as he moved through his career, constantly springing surprises upon us in the process. We call Haydn 'classical', but today we could just as well apply the term to those two symphonies of Berlioz, as compared with some of those of later composers such as Mahler, Sibelius or Nielsen. The word has, anyhow, very little meaning—or, if you like, too many meanings—as I have pointed out before.[56] Virgil's *Aeneid* is as romantic as anything in more recent European poetry, and it is upon the second and fourth books of that great work that Berlioz based his epic music-drama, *The Trojans*.

The reviewer of my book *The Divine Quest in Music* in 'Oxford'[57] criticised me for what I had written on Berlioz's attitude to religion, which related both to the man and the artist. 'But what of Berlioz,' he wrote, 'an articulate, self-professed infidel? Simple! Berlioz, it seems, had "unconscious faith"! This facile formula will commend itself no more to honest believers than to honest doubters'. I would not have thought that the idea of 'unconscious faith', which is recognised by the theology of the Christian Churches, was either very simple or facile. In any case, this criticism was purely destructive. Of Berlioz's *major* works, two are settings of the liturgy, one is a sacred oratorio, and several others (which I had mentioned) have religious associations in varying degrees. Berlioz, both as man and artist, was of the utmost sincerity. The problem is, what is the explanation of the apparent inconsistency? Berlioz in his Memoirs[58] gives us a partial clue. He was

[56] See above, Chapters 15 and 29, and Chapter 15 of my book *The Soul of Music*.

[57] The Oxford Society's magazine, December 1957, Vol. XV.

[58] Chapter 1, translated by Rachel (Scott Russell) Holmes and Eleanor Holmes, annotated, and the translation revised, by Ernest Newman.

brought up as a Roman Catholic. 'Since she (the Church) has ceased to inculcate the burning of heretics,' he wrote, 'her creeds are charming. I held them happily for seven years; and though we quarrelled long ago, I still retain the tenderest recollections of that form of religious belief. Indeed, I feel such sympathy for it that had I had the misfortune to be born into the midst of one of those ponderous schisms evolved by Luther or Calvin, my first rush of poetical enthusiasms would have driven me straight into the arms of the beautiful Roman faith.' He goes on to describe his first communion in most moving terms and how he went on as he had been, 'for several years'. At twenty, he wrote the words and music of a Biblical oratorio, 'The Crossing of the Red Sea', and composed a Mass about two years afterwards. The great *Requiem* and *Te Deum* followed in later years and eventually the deeply devotional *Enfance du Christ*. There are religious elements in the *Symphonie Fantastique* and *Harold in Italy*, in *La Damnation de Faust*, and even in the *Grande Symphonie Funébre et Triomphale*. The theme of death was part of Berlioz's spiritual outlook—witness this work, the funeral marches for Juliet and Hamlet, and the ballad on the death of Ophelia; he composed a beautiful *Méditation religieuse*, and gave religious music a central position in *Euphonia*, his plan for a Utopian city of music. Clearly, religion—whether Roman Catholic, or broadly Christian, or interpreted in the widest sense of the term—formed an important part of Berlioz's *artistic* mentality, and inasmuch as Berlioz the man was dedicated to music, it is not too much to apply to him, though he professed himself an 'unbeliever', the well-known Christian conception of 'unconscious faith'. Indeed, it is difficult otherwise to account for many of the actual facts of his creative life. In his Memoirs, he often speaks of God in terms which show that he was at least no atheist. Obviously he ceased to be a practising Roman Catholic or churchgoer, but that is a very different thing from being 'godless' and certainly does not preclude him from having remained Christian in his subconscious being. Of course, religion is only one of the facets of Berlioz, whether as man or as artist. It is not without significance that his first great masterpiece was named *Symphonie Fantastique*[59] for there was something fantastic about him as a person—with

---

[59] For the *Symphonie Fantastique*, Berlioz wrote a 'programme', though afterwards he gave instructions that this should not be given out except when the sequel 'Lélio' was being performed after it. As Jacques Barzun says in 'Berlioz and the Romantic Century' (Vol. I, p. 157), the 'programme'

his deep-set, piercing eyes, his aquiline nose, his shock of reddish hair, and his strange, though youthful, behaviour in the Camille Moke affair—and as a composer. He excelled in depicting demonic or violent scenes, and visions of supernatural terror and wrath— the nightmare in *March to the Scaffold* and the *Witches' Sabbath* in the *Fantastique*, the *Orgy of Brigands* in *Harold*, the *Ride to the Abyss* and the *Pandemonium* in *La Damnation de Faust*—yes, and even the *Dies Irae* and *Rex Tremendae* sections of the *Requiem*. But as with most creative artists, it is necessary to consider his work as a whole, in order to have a comprehensive view of its quality.

Berlioz was just as much a master of delicate and idyllic effects as of fortissimo or fantastic ones. The graceful waltz movement in the *Symphonie Fantastique* and the serene *Scène aux champs*— even though they are interrupted by the theme of the *idée fixe* and (in the latter movement) the sound of distant thunder; the exquisite *March of Pilgrims singing the Evening Hymn* and the *Serenade of a mountaineer of the Abruzzi to his sweetheart* in *Harold in Italy*; the bewitching fairy music of the *Queen Mab* scherzo in *Romeo and Juliet*—that perfect orchestral transmutation of Shakespeare's magical poetry; the enchanting *Danse des Sylphes* and *Menuet des Follets* in *Faust*; the way in which the vast forces of the *Requiem* are used as much for piano or pianissimo effects as for sonorous or thrilling ones, and also for music of the utmost serenity, peace, ethereal quality and gentleness; the atmosphere of quiet religion and pastoral beauty which pervades so much of *L'Enfance du Christ*; the deep tranquillity of the vocal and orchestral sounds in Dido and Aeneas's love duet in *The Trojans*; the grace, delicacy, wit, and charm of *Béatrice et Bénedict*—these are as characteristic of Berlioz as are his more clamorous or fiery passages.

He was the author of some of the most beautiful love music ever created: *Absence*, that song of yearning for the departed lover (the performance of this musical gem by that unsurpassed interpre-

<hr>

cannot be identified *in detail* with the facts of the composer's (at first, unrequited) love for Harriet Smithson. Nevertheless, the work had an autobiographical reference, for Berlioz tells us so himself in his Memoirs (Ernest Newman edition, as above, p. 190): 'The subject of this musical drama is, as everybody knows, the history of my love for Miss Smithson, my anguish and my distressing dreams'. Newman's note on pp. 98-99 also deals with the point.

ter of French song, Dame Maggie Teyte, is one of my most trea-
sured memories); the wonderful setting of the Balcony Scene from
Romeo and Juliet by purely orchestral means in the *Scene d'Amour*
of his *Dramatic Symphony* based on Shakespeare's tragedy; the
love duet in the First Act of *Benvenuto Cellini*; the glorious,
idyllic love music for *Aeneas and Dido* just mentioned—set to
words which Berlioz adapted from Shakespeare's exquisite scene
between Lorenzo and Jessica in the last Act of *The Merchant of
Venice* and which he introduced, by a stroke of genius, at this
point of his great Virgilian music-drama.

Berlioz's gifts for expressing emotions, deep religious feeling,
supernatural or fantastic scenes, and the varied moods of Nature,
were rendered possible by his supreme mastery of the orchestra
and his innate sense of the quality of the human voice. He was a
tremendous pioneer of orchestral colour, to whom Wagner and
many other later composers were greatly indebted. He did not
employ anything approaching the elaborate Wagnerian system of
leitmotives, but in his three great operas, in his cantata-version of
the First Part of Goethe's mighty *Faust* drama, and in his *Romeo
and Juliet*, he believed in high-lighting, as it were, contrasted musical and pictorial scenes which, nevertheless, when each work is
viewed as a whole, cohere into an imaginative unity—so that Faust
can, without incongruity, watch the soldiers of Hungary marching
to their stirring strains, the vivid carnival music can so fittingly
intervene in *Cellini*, and Mercutio's lovely description of Queen
Mab can play a larger part in Berlioz's score of *Romeo and Juliet*
than in Shakespeare's play; and *The Royal Hunt and the Storm* in
The Trojans is no mere interlude but becomes the masterly setting
for the consummation of the love of Dido and Aeneas as they take
refuge in the cave. None of these examples is in any sense an in-
truding element in the work; rather are they episodes at once
dramatic and descriptive, yet apt to the unity of the whole composition. Berlioz used recurring themes, but he did so economic-
ally: the *idée fixe* in the *Fantastique*, the *Harold* theme in *Harold
in Italy*, return in appropriately altered guises in the subsequent
movements; the Trojan March in *The Trojans* recurs in transmuted
forms, now in the major, now in the minor key, at different points
of the vast epic drama.

Truly we can say that Berlioz, the creator of wonderful and
original operas, overtures, symphonies, songs, devotional works, a
unique cantata and a long, dramatic, orchestral and vocal 'sym-

phony', was one of the most many-sided and universal geniuses in the history of music. Whilst we can recognise that he was one of the great romantics, he was much besides. We can hardly call religious feeling *romantic*, and if it be agreed that his *Requiem*, *Te Deum*, and *L'Enfance du Christ* are intrinsically religious in quality, obviously 'romantic' is too narrow a term for him. And some of the non-religious elements in his music are not actually romantic, but rather expressions of emotions which are common to human nature. Romantic, emotional, fantastic, serene, idyllic, magical, religious (whether consciously as in some of his works or unconsciously in his personal character), intellectual, vividly pictorial and utterly sincere—the artist and the man were completely integrated. Berlioz never uttered a false note. His contribution to the *history* of music (both in the technical and in the widest sense) is unsurpassed by any other innovators; but the inherent quality of his art is even more important. He was one of the greatest men that France has ever produced, one of the supreme artistic figures of the 19th century.

CHAPTER THIRTY-TWO

Widening Horizons (I)—Mainly Operatic (Weber, Verdi, and Mussorgsky)

Recognition of the importance of Berlioz as a pioneer of predominant romanticism in music should not blind us to the fact that
Weber was first in the field. Even in his instrumental works the
romantic element, combined with charm and a certain amount of
bravura, is prominent. We are in a different world from Haydn
and Mozart and even from early Beethoven. The 'Konzertstück'
for pianoforte and orchestra, though in three movements like a
concerto, is based on a romantic programme. And even elsewhere
in his non-operatic art there is a strong vein of romance. But
these purely instrumental compositions tend to be overshadowed
by those of his great contemporaries, Beethoven and Schubert.
When we think of clarinet quintets, it is those of Mozart on the
one hand and Brahms on the other that come to mind, in spite of
the beauty of Weber's in B flat. The *Concertino* and the two other
concertos for clarinet and orchestra are charming; and Weber, himself a very fine pianist, composed several delightful piano sonatas
beside the enchanting *Invitation à la valse* which Berlioz orchestrated so artistically.

But the real greatness of Weber lies in his operas—the first *predominantly* romantic operas in musical history.[60] I have had full
experience only of *Der Freischütz*, *Euryanthe*, and *Oberon*,
(though of course, their overtures and two or three numbers are
often performed at concerts). It is only since World War II that

[60] Obviously, there is romance in 'Fidelio', but Beethoven's genius is too
wide and vast to be confined within the word 'romantic'.

Euryanthe, as a whole, and some of the instrumental works have come into my ken. That is why I have not mentioned Weber, except briefly, earlier in these *Reflections*. Nowadays, some people seem to regard even *Der Freischütz* as *vieux jeu*, and the *Wolf's Glen* as outdated. So far as I am concerned, the entire opera, if well performed, never fails to thrill me to this day, and the *Wolf's Glen* scene remains a masterpiece of supernatural terror in musical terms; the early 19th century idiom and the reliance on diminished sevenths do not detract from this; and throughout the work, the masterly orchestration, the vivid writing for the voices and the romantic conception of the composer, combine to keep its appeal fresh, its loveliness untarnished and unaffected by the excitements that have happened in the world of opera since 1820 when it was completed. The music of *Euryanthe* is romantic, dramatic, and beautiful: the score is one of Weber's finest. The reason always given for not performing it (apart from the familiar overture) is the complicated and absurd libretto: this *is* rather involved, but not more so than those of many other operas which remain in the repertoire, and though there is a certain absurdity, it is not unique in this respect! I suspect that the neglect of this splendid opera is due to lack of enterprise, rather than to any intrinsic defects in it. As for *Oberon*, I count myself lucky to have seen and heard it several times at Frankfurt in 1911, once at Buenos Aires in 1913, and to have listened to it on the radio once since World War II. Most British music lovers, I fancy, know only the glorious overture and *Ocean, thou mighty monster*, both of which have been popular in concert-halls all my life. But the whole opera is a delight—if you like fairy tales. It is not dramatic. It is, literally, a fairy story in music, full of beautiful melodies and set forth in a succession of scenes which cry out for artistic stage settings. All of these three operas of Weber ought, on their merits, to be performed frequently. His operatic art is not only of great importance in the history of music, but is immensely enjoyable for its intrinsic qualities of romantic beauty, melodic charm, and wizardry of orchestration.

Is it chance, or is there some mysterious Providential influence, that deals with the brevity or length of the lives of geniuses? This rather absurd conundrum forces itself upon my attention when I reflect on the fates of some of the great composers. Purcell, Mozart, Schubert, Weber, Mendelssohn, Chopin, and Bizet, all died under the age of forty. This was a personal tragedy for each of them and a grievous loss for those of their contemporaries who loved them. Nevertheless, what a rich legacy every one of these men left to the world of music lovers, in spite of the short span of life allotted to them! The one great exception which occurs to me is Purcell: what operatic masterpieces might not the creator of 'Dido and Aeneas' have bequeathed to us, if death had not carried him off in his thirty-seventh year—to say nothing of his potentialities in other fields of music? Purcell is assuredly a composer who attained greatness but did not live long enough to consummate it. At the other end of the scale, Haydn started writing beautiful music in his youth, outlived his much younger contemporary Mozart, reached the age of seventy-seven, and finished his career with some of his greatest masterpieces; Wagner just managed, as it were, to complete his mighty achievements before dying at seventy; Elgar did not begin to compose really great music until he was past forty, and who can tell whether that third oratorio of the projected trilogy would have been up to the level of its two beautiful predecessors, if he had felt moved to compose it, or whether the third symphony would have equalled the two magnificent ones that we have, if death had not come to him in his seventy-seventh year?

The most astonishing paradox is the case of Verdi. He lived to the age of eighty-seven. Until his middle age he composed tragic operas which were good in parts, and great only in occasional passages, and created his supreme operatic masterpieces and five great pieces of sacred choral music, in the latter part of his long life! If *he* had died at thirty-five, like Mozart, he would have been no more than on the threshold of his genius. *Nabucco* (1842), with its vivid character-drawing, its musical drama and its Biblical splendour, is almost alone among his early operas in giving a foretaste of what was to come. His *Macbeth*, composed a few years later, falls far short of the tremendous poetic drama on which it was based, and is a long way below the level of the two consummate Shakespearean masterpieces with which Verdi was to end his operatic career many years later. Yet much of Lady Macbeth's music is very fine, and her sleep-walking scene is masterly. I confess that I am not enthusiastic about the 'rum-te-tum' accompaniments which occur in various Verdi operas before the *Don Carlos* and *Aida* period, and that to me they appear to be unequal. *Rigoletto* has wonderful moments and a superb last act, including the great quartet. *Il Trovatore* is hampered by a poor libretto, but the music

213

rises above it—particularly in the Convent Scene and the moving final act, with the ever fresh *Miserere*. *La Traviata* (1853) is, I suggest, the first of Verdi's operas which is a great work of art *as a whole*. It is full of deep compassion and humanity, and contains passages of great beauty such as *Ah fors' è lui* and *Dite alla giovine*, and of delicacy and refinement like the prelude to the third act. But fine though this work is, and in spite of much beautiful music in the operas which intervened, it is with *Don Carlos* (produced in 1867, when Verdi was in his fifty-fourth year) that we enter upon the greatest (and culminating) period of this astonishing man's career. With its dramatic grandeur and its wonderful character-drawing, it surpasses all its predecessors; only the *auto-da-fé* scene falls below the high level of the rest. Presumably its length and the complexity of the plot were the causes of its comparative neglect as compared with some of the earlier, more popular Verdi operas. I myself have only known it since its triumphant revivals at Covent Garden in 1958 and subsequently, with a brilliant cast, conducted by Guilini, and produced by Visconti.

Aida is a tragic music-drama, with a continuous melodic tissue, richly orchestrated, and eloquently expressing the mutual love of Radames, the victorious Egyptian general, and Aida, the gentle Ethiopian girl who has been captured and is really the King's daughter, the pressure put on her by her father to renounce her love for Radames, their loyalty, the passion and jealousy of Amneris, the imprisonment and deaths of the lovers in the vault, with the chanting of the priests and priestesses above. The marches and processions, the dancing of the Egyptian girls, are far less important than the deeply moving music of the leading characters, the nobility of the whole subject, and the serenity of the ending.

Simon Boccanegra was originally written in 1857, but its libretto was revised by Boito in 1881 at the request of Verdi, who made radical alterations in the score. So it virtually belongs to his late period—midway between *Aida* and *Otello*. The plot is complicated, but not more so than those of many other great operas. Musically, there is not a weak spot in it anywhere. Even *Don Carlos* has its one scene that marks a falling-off, and the marches in *Aida*, good and stirring though they are, are hardly great music. *Boccanegra* is consistently dramatic and beautiful, sometimes pathetic, sometimes noble, with an eloquent ending in tragedy, relieved by reconciliation. Apart from the complications of the story, the score is an unblemished masterpiece.

214

Otello is as near an approach to Shakespearean tragedy at the height of Shakespeare's powers as has been achieved in any opera hitherto. Boito provided Verdi with a marvellous libretto in adaptation of the play. The work opens in Cyprus, with one of the greatest tempests in all music. The Bard's first act in Venice is omitted; so are the murder of Emilia and the order for the torturing of Iago. This ghastly, human villain of the play is transformed, in the operatic *Credo*, into an emissary of the Devil in the form of a man. Desdemona's sad, exquisite *Willow Song* is followed by a gentle *Ave Maria*. The beautiful love duet between Othello and her is echoed piteously at the end, as he falls on her body 'to die upon a kiss'. Grandeur, infinite pathos, a stream of melodic beauty, masterly orchestration which never overpowers the loveliness of the writing for the voices—all combine to make *Otello* the crowning summit of Verdi's chain of tragic music dramas. Yet, as he approached eighty, he finished his work for the stage with one of the most brilliant of operatic comedies. *Falstaff* surpasses Shakespeare's farcical *Merry Wives of Windsor*, partly because this is not one of the poet's best plays, but partly because comedy, which portrays characters, is a finer art-form than farce, which depends mainly on situations. Boito added the speech decrying honour from *Henry IV*, and Verdi transmuted it into witty music, with trills and grunts on the woodwind and basses. The whole opera is imbued with wit and charm. Even the warming-up of Falstaff's system with wine after his ducking in the Thames is conveyed musically, with a prolonged trill and crescendo on the orchestra. Some of Shakespeare's characters are cut out, and his Anne Page becomes Nanetta, the daughter of Ford. There is a most tender love duet between her and Fenton, and a powerful monologue by Ford about jealousy. In the last scene the fairies are depicted by enchanting music, and the work ends with a humorous fugue in which everybody—even Falstaff—treats the whole story and the whole world as one big joke.

Verdi's one string quartet is so charming, refined, tender and (in the last two movements) so vigorous that I always wish that he had written more chamber music. However, we must be grateful for our varied legacy from him! Between *Aida* and *Otello* this great-hearted, generous, charitable man, who was for a long time anti-clerical, yet a Christian, even in allegiance, at least in his later years, composed his beautiful *Requiem* in memory of Manzoni. This is *not* his finest opera, as has been said, but a dramatic, truly Italian, embodiment of the liturgy, even though it does show signs of having been composed by a man who had devoted his life to opera. It is as vividly pictorial as Dante's *Divine Comedy*. I, personally, could do without the big drum in the *Dies Irae*, but there is no denying the thrill and terror of the movement generally. The essence of the work as a whole is that it is a prayer for peace —voiced in the *Lux aeterna* and the final entreaty for deliverance from eternal death.

Verdi's last works, created when he was an octogenarian, were the *Quattro Pezzi Sacri*—the unaccompanied choruses *Ave Maria* and *Laudi alla Vergine Maria* and the choral and orchestral *Stabat Mater* and *Te Deum*. Whatever some people may have said about the theatrical character of the *Requiem*, there is in these pieces simply a deeply religious expression of faith.

What an amazing career! From early works which showed more talent than genius, Verdi advanced steadily through the 19th century to a *final* period which conclusively established him as one of the greatest composers. Eighty years were needed, in his case, to accomplish this consummation.

My experiences of performances of Verdi have been spread over my lifetime, but several of them date only from the post-World War II period. I did not make the acquaintance of Mussorgsky until the interval between the Wars, and it is only from 1958 onwards that I have heard *Boris Godunov* in its complete, or nearly complete, form, or *Khovanshchina* at all. I was lucky enough to see and hear Chaliapin as Boris (an artist equally great as actor and singer), but less fortunate in hearing the opera then with Rimsky-Korsakov's entirely unnecessary and unsuitable alterations of the score. Sadler's Wells (with Ronald Stear in the leading part) were pioneers in reviving it in London with Mussorgsky's original instrumentation, and this admirable example was followed in 1958 by Covent Garden, which, moreover, performed both the scene in front of the St Basil Cathedral preceding that of Boris's death and the Revolution scene in the Forest of Kromy to conclude the work. Later, unfortunately, they reverted to the *Rimsky* version: a pity! I did not go, though Boris Christoff in 1958 and 1961 had been comparable to Chaliapin; he is also memorable for having worn a magnificent embroidered robe in the Coronation Scene!

Mussorgsky is no more a one-opera-composer than Bizet. He created (among other songs) two fine song-cycles, *Sunless* and *Songs and Dances of Death* (including the famous *Trepak*); the attractive fragments of the opera *Sorotchintsi Fair*; a powerful and vivid tone-poem *A Night on the Bare Mountain*; *Pictures from an exhibition*, which is frankly more interesting in Ravel's brilliant orchestral version than in Mussorgsky's original score for piano solo; and, above all these, the unfinished opera *Khovanshchina*: whatever we may think of Rimsky-Korsakov's tampering with the score of *Boris*, we are bound to be thankful that he orchestrated *Khovanshchina*, for otherwise its performance might never have taken place, though others have since composed versions of it as well. The musical world would certainly have been poorer without hearing this stirring drama of religious strife and tragic love, with its many beautiful passages and its striking choruses. The orchestration used at Covent Garden in 1963 was by Shostakovich.

Yet when we speak of Mussorgsky as a great composer, we think essentially of *Boris Godunov*, which is one of the supreme operatic masterpieces of all time. It is a mighty historical drama, though the real Boris was not guilty of the murder of Dmitri, the young son of Ivan the Terrible, which in the opera haunts Boris, as king, with terrifying visions caused by his guilty conscience and leads to his tragic death. But it is a tragedy of the Russian people even more than of Boris himself. The hallucination scene in Act II and the scene of the King's death, are tremendous both as drama and music; the anguish of the people, typified finally by the lament of the Simpleton, is most moving; and the orchestration, simple and direct to the verge of austerity and only spoilt if Rimsky-Korsakov's highly-coloured version is used, is perfectly suited to the powerful story.

Mussorgsky was both a dreamer and a sceptic, and as M.D. Calvocoressi remarks, [61] he was 'sensitive, impulsive, demonstrative and excitable; amenable to influences in certain respects, in others, thoroughly impervious'. It was a tragedy that he took to heavy drinking and died of alcoholic epilepsy, at 42. Yet there was, somehow, a strong vein of optimism in his nature. He was 'kind, honest and affectionate' (wrote Ludmila Shestakova in a letter to Stassov, March 23rd, 1881),[62] and loved children and the beauties of nature. He had been, in his youth, an army officer, and it was his Russian patriotism and his deep humanity that enabled him, with his great gifts of musical expression, to create and complete that one outstanding work of genius, *Boris Godunov*.

[61] *Modest Mussorgsky: his Life and Works*, p. 48 (Rockliff, 1956)
[62] M. D. Calvocoressi: ibid., p. 209.

CHAPTER THIRTY-THREE

Widening Horizons (II)—From Austria to Czechoslovakia (Bruckner, Wolf and Mahler; Smetana, Dvořák and Janáček)

It has been said that both Bruckner and Hugo Wolf had something Wagnerian about them. Certainly they were great admirers of Wagner's art. Bruckner, indeed, was set up by his contemporary champions as a kind of Wagnerian symphonist, in rivalry with Brahms. There is, of course, plenty of room for both Bruckner and Brahms in the musical firmament, and the antithesis has no meaning for music lovers today. Each of them wrote symphonies and choral works, though Bruckner's symphonies are far more discursive than those of Brahms. This discursiveness, however, is a trait which began, in Teutonic music, with some of the works of Schubert, and continued through Bruckner and Wagner to Mahler. Otherwise, there was little or no resemblance between Bruckner and Wagner, either as man or as artist. Wagner was almost entirely a man of the theatre; Bruckner left opera untouched. Wagner was addicted to ever-recurring leitmotives, whereas Bruckner did no more than repeat or echo themes of previous movements, as, for example, Berlioz, Franck and Elgar did. Wagner, as a man, was utterly egotistical, and (though brave and determined) he was self-confident to the point of arrogance; he sometimes called himself a Christian, particularly when he wanted to decry Mendelssohn for his 'Jewishness', but he was certainly not Christ-like in his conduct. Bruckner, on the other hand, was a profoundly religious Roman Catholic, began as a modest village schoolmaster, and remained a man of deep humility throughout his life. He dedicated his gifts to God. And though there is a strong element of romanticism and a wide range of emotions in his symphonies, they, and not only his liturgical works, are frequently religious in quality. Some of the melodies in his symphonies resemble chorales or are intrinsically devotional. His final, Ninth, Symphony was inscribed 'An mein lieben Gott', and its Adagio—the last movement of it that he lived to complete—is music of most exalted beauty.

He wrote long symphonies largely because he had a great deal to say and a wealth of melody to develop. There is a tendency in them to excessive repetitiveness of phrases. But how rich is our reward if we are only patient with him! And in his Masses and *Te Deum* there is no prolixity whatever; they are at least as terse as Brahms, and through their deeply religious character are perfectly suited for church performance.

Bruckner and Mahler are often coupled together. They were both Austrian, both Roman Catholics (though Mahler was of Jewish origin) and both of them wrote long symphonies; there is a vein of religion in Mahler's also; but there the resemblances end. Bruckner belonged to a different, and earlier, period in musical history, and he was, I think, much the greater composer of the two, by virtue of the grandeur of his art, the profoundity and exaltation of his vision. I do not say that these qualities are absent from Mahler; but there was something schizophrenic about him, whereas Bruckner's was a completely integrated personality both as man and artist.

Though I heard a few performances of Bruckner symphonies between the wars, most of my experiences of his works, as has been the case with the majority of British music lovers, have occurred since 1945. Bruckner's art took a long time to establish itself in the U.K. Perhaps it has now come to stay.

By contrast, Wolf's music has been with me, on and off, for most of my life. I heard his *lieder* sung by Julia Culp, Elena Gerhardt (when she was young) and others. Opportunities to hear them since World War II have, however, been even more frequent, and the charming *Italian Serenade* for strings remains a popular favourite. His opera *Der Corregidor* is a succession of beautiful vocal numbers rather than a dramatic whole. Apart from this and his fine tone-poem, *Penthesilea*, he was, first and foremost, a miniaturist. This does not mean that he only excelled in exquisite music—though that is certainly the adjective to apply to some of his perfect songs, particularly in the *Italienisches Liederbuch*—but he

219

was also capable of producing music of immense power within the confines of a song with piano accompaniment. *Prometheus, Grenzen der Menschheit, Anakreon's Grab,* and *Der Feuerreiter* are each of them examples of *tremendous* music lasting for a short period of time.

Ernest Newman, in his book on Hugo Wolf, evidently felt that Wolf was an even more wonderful song-writer than Schubert. I cannot quite agree. It is true that Wolf, more than any of the great composers of *lieder,* had such an acute sense of poetry that he was able to evoke music which perfectly expressed every line of the poem, and not merely its general mood or atmosphere. But he had not Schubert's *lyrical* gift, or that of Schumann or Brahms. Just as Wagner had passed from the complete tunes of his earlier operas, *The Flying Dutchman, Tannhäuser,* and *Lohengrin,* to the 'unending melody' of his mature dramas, so Wolf eloquently set *all* the phrases of a poem, as it were, to musical phrases which suited them to perfection, rather than giving us the lovely melodies that poured from the minds of the other three great Teutonic song-composers. It may be a matter of taste which type you prefer—the *detailed* musical expressiveness of Wolf, or the essentially melodic settings of the others. I love both kinds, but I am not prepared to dethrone Schubert from his place as the prince of song-writers! Be that as it may, Wolf's *lieder* are among the greatest gifts that the art of music has vouchsafed to the world, and the variety and scope of the emotions and moods and natural scenes which he calls forth are astonishing. And though, after a Catholic upbringing, he came (like Berlioz) to describe himself as an unbeliever, this did not prevent him from setting religious poems in the *Spanisches Liederbuch,* and elsewhere too, with as much artistry, imagination, and insight, as secular ones.

He was a devoted son and brother, a passionate, impetuous, utterly sincere man, whose dedication to his art came to override practically every other purpose. Like another great composer of *lieder,* Schumann, he ended his days tragically in an asylum.

Mahler overlapped the turn of the century not only in his life but in his musical outlook. He was born in Bohemia in July, 1860, and died in Vienna in May, 1911. He was of Jewish blood, but became a Roman Catholic in 1895. As Artistic Director of the Court Opera in Vienna, he did not spare himself in securing perfection of production of each work in all its details. Indeed, his very thoroughness and enthusiasm made him an exacting manager, and his leadership, inspiring though it was to many, was too over-bearing for others. It was a good thing that he gave up the position a few years before his death, though he had undoubtedly achieved great things for operatic production and had proved himself to be a masterly conductor.

His childhood was unhappy, and though he was fervently religious and deeply compassionate, he was profoundly conscious of man's inhumanity to man, of the cruelty in nature, of the troubles and sorrows of mankind. So his faith was never serene; he found it difficult to reconcile the afflictions of the world with his belief in a loving God.

These conflicts within his soul found expression in his music. In his symphonies we find struggle, disturbance, nostalgia, and regret—as it were, for the passing of an epoch—grief, charm, idealism, religion, yet also irony, exultation, and mysticism. I began my experience of Mahler by hearing William Mengelberg conduct the Fourth Symphony at Frankfurt in 1911, when I was very intrigued by it. I did not meet with the First (or any other) until after World War I, in London. Other performances of Mahler's symphonies and songs followed occasionally in the interval between the Wars, but it was not until after 1945 that they became at all frequent here. I was lucky enough to hear Bruno Walter conducting Mahler; he had, of course, exceptional insight into their character, so that his performances were authentic to the nth degree.

During this time, my attitude towards Mahler's art has fluctuated, but in recent years I have warmed up to it. There is so much that is beautiful, exalted, profound, or exquisite, that one accepts the banal moments or (even) passages, and the long-drawn-out periods, for the sake of this. The range of moods and emotions in these works is remarkable, but that is a quality of many of his greater predecessors; what distinguishes his symphonic compositions from theirs particularly is the extraordinary contrasts within the scope of one work. A minuet or a sarcastic burlesque or a rustic *Ländler* in slow waltz time will occur in the midst of a symphony which begins with strife and ends either with spiritual victory or with heartfelt regret or even despair. This may at first seem an oddity, but one comes to realise that it does not impair the unity of the whole.

Until Deryck Cook orchestrated so masterfully the unfinished score of the Tenth Symphony, I had believed—as, I suppose, many

221

other music lovers had—that Mahler's creative career had ended with the slow, poignant fading-out of the Finale of his Ninth and the exquisite nostalgia of *Das Lied von der Erde*. But the Tenth Symphony comprises most of the human emotions and ends in complete serenity. It is a reassuring thought that after all that had passed in his anxious soul and in his earlier life and his earlier compositions he could end his life's work with such a peaceful affirmation.

Some of his symphonies are entirely orchestral; others introduce solo voices or chorus. The Eighth is a gigantic work beginning with a Christian prayer and concluding with a visionary setting of the mystic chorus which ends the Second Part of Goethe's *Faust*. Mahler's songs are an important part of his artistic gift to the world, not only because they are beautiful in themselves, but because they help to explain the song-like quality of so many of the melodies in his symphonies. In this respect he was an inheritor of the tradition of Schubert, Schumann, and Brahms—all of them great *lieder*-writers whose symphonies often sing lovely songs to us in the form of instrumental subjects. Mahler was, also, a master of orchestration. I have no doubt, now, that he was a great composer, the last of the line of the great German and Austrian creators of music hitherto—though I am no prophet of what the future may bring forth! Nevertheless, I do not feel that he is on a level with his famous Teutonic predecessors. There are those occasional banalities; and the discursiveness which now and again appears in Schubert's instrumental works and in Bruckner's symphonies has become long-windedness sometimes in those of Mahler. Yet actual deterioration of the Teutonic greatness in musical creation did not begin with him, but with Richard Strauss.

If the Teutonic *leadership* in music started to decline in the latter half of the 19th century, the cause of that was, obviously, not that Germany and Austria were ceasing to produce very great composers—to make any such suggestion about the age of Wagner, Bruckner, Brahms and Hugo Wolf would be preposterous—but simply that other nations had given, or were starting to give, birth to creative musical geniuses of their own. I will conclude this chapter by considering briefly the Czeckoslovak contribution in the persons of Smetana, Dvořák, and Janáček.

As with most British music lovers who have not been able to visit Czechoslovakia, my experience of Smetana's works has been limited to what I have heard in England. His beautiful string quartet No. 1 in E minor *From my Life* (1876) used to be played at the Oxford University Musical Club when I was an undergraduate, and has remained in the British repertory. It is frankly autobiographical, reflecting his youthful aspirations and happiness, his love of the Czech dancing rhythms, his passionate love for his first wife, Kateřina, who died prematurely in 1859, and his personal development; he had memories of a happy childhood, and in this and other works his natural tendency was to convey happiness in his music rather than sorrow—in spite of the tragic affliction of total deafness which overtook him in October, 1874. It is amazing to think that most of his remarkable cycle of six symphonic poems, *My Country*, was composed after that event. He was a great patriot, and the opening poem, *Vysehrad*—in ancient times the palace of the Premyslid kings—depicts the majesty of past Czech glory, and ultimately the crash of the palace into ruins, with the harp of the bard Lumir sounding a gentler note at the end. *Vltava* opens with the tiny stream at its source and grows into the mighty river of Prague; it cunningly combines the structure of a rondo with the illustrative character of a symphonic poem. *Sarka* is a sinister picture of the legendary woman, who captivated a knight by her beauty and, with the aid of her fellow-Amazons, slaughtered him and his companions in satisfaction of their hatred of men. After this, it is a relief to hear the cheerful strains of *From Bohemia's Woods and Fields*, with its pastoral effects, its polka rhythms, and its stately chorale. *Tábor* is an orchestral song of praise for the bravery of the Hussites, and *Blanik*—the mountain inside which they were, according to legend, sleeping after their defeat—represents their entrance within it and their ultimate re-emergence in glory.

Smetana was by nature and temperament an optimist, and in his most popular opera, *The Bartered Bride* (the only one which has been performed in England in my experience, and which I have thoroughly enjoyed several times) is one of the most delightful operatic comedies ever written. Marenca, the heroine, has her moments of anxiety and even of sorrow, and she and Jenik are given some tender love music to sing; and Vasek, with his shyness and stammering, is pathetic in his foolishness; but for the most part, it is a joyous opera, with its buoyant overture, the marriage broker treated as a figure of fun, and the score replete with irresistible Czech dance rhythms, the gaiety of the circus performers, and the cheerful choruses of villagers. *The Bartered Bride* gives us one of the happiest evenings that it is possible to spend in the theatre.

Dvořák is an old friend to British music lovers of my generation. I think that is just the word for him. There is no friendlier music in the world. Of course it sometimes expresses the griefs and conflicts of humanity as well as its joys and aspirations. That is the natural outcome of so warm-hearted, genial, and sympathetic a personality. He was utterly sincere. His music is never gaudy or showy or merely rhetorical. It is fresh, melodious, natural. And as he loved nature, and his native Bohemian countryside, it often reveals an open-air feeling as well as his love of the Czech and Slavonic folk-music and dance rhythms among which he was brought up. But his musical sympathies were wide enough to enable him to absorb the spirit of negro melodies and spirituals during his three years in the U.S.A. and to embody this, also, in the String Quartet in F (op. 96), the Quintet in E flat (op. 97), and the *New World* Symphony.

He was extremely popular wherever he went—with his own people, in England, America, Germany, and Russia. Brahms liked him and admired his gifts so much that he helped him in his youth with a warm recommendation to Simrock, the publisher. Tchaikovsky and he became warm friends and each loved the other's music. He was very friendly with Seidl, a former secretary of Wagner, and became a keen Wagnerian. In those days it was most unusual for one great composer to love the music of Wagner *and* Brahms *and* Tchaikovsky, in spite of the differences and even hostility between those three and among their respective supporters.

Everybody seemed to love Dvořák and his music. They loved his Slavonic dances, with their irresistible lilt and rhythms, and his art appealed to other nations as much as to his own compatriots, just because it was intrinsically and genuinely Czech as well as possessing warm, human qualities.

His humanity and love of nature were part of his devout character. Whether he was composing chamber music or concertos or symphonies or works which were specifically and deeply religious such as the *Stabat Mater*, the *Requiem*, or the *Te Deum*, he regarded his art as God's gift. The Symphony in D minor (No. 7) is the greatest of all his symphonies, and though it is imbued with tragic grandeur, it is also the product of his deep humanity and sympathy with the struggles of mankind. Elsewhere his music

224

radiates happiness, geniality, and the profound conviction of his simple Catholic faith.

But his versatility was astonishing. I have only heard one of his operas, *Rusalka*, reputedly the finest of them. It is a sad fairy-tale, full of beautiful melody, rich orchestration, and a sense of drama. His contribution to the art of solo songs reached its climax in his ten *Biblical Songs* (1894)—noble settings of texts from the Psalms.

Dvořák was of humble origin, and became a happily married man, with six children. His innate gifts developed in many directions, but though his Austrian friends tried to persuade him to become more international by composing an opera with a German libretto, he remained Bohemian, Czechoslovak, through and through, and yet his art won the affection of nations other than his own. Music may be utterly national in character—such as that of Verdi, or Mussorgsky, or Couperin, or Schumann, or Manuel de Falla, or Elgar; but it knows no frontiers, and if a composer's genius is great enough, it belongs to the world.

So far as I am concerned, Leoš Janáček has been a discovery of my old age. Although he was born in 1854 and died in 1928, and was thus a contemporary of Elgar, this is not altogether so surprising at it might appear; for not only did his greatness mature slowly (like that of the great Englishman), so that he was in middle age before producing real masterpieces, but appreciation of his gifts was slow to come even in his own country and he was turned sixty before any of his operas were performed in Prague. Only since World War II have there been opportunities to hear much of his music in the United Kingdom.

What a discovery it has been! At any rate, I have heard five of his operas, his two string quartets, the orchestral Rhapsody *Taras Bulba*, the *Glagolitic Mass*, and certain other works. But the real point is that I have realised that he is one of the greatest composers with whom I have been, at least partly, contemporary.

Several features of his art have struck me. One is his absorption of the spirit of the folksongs of Eastern Moravia, where he was born, which are modal in character, as contrasted with the mainly diatonic folk tunes of the rest of Moravia and of Bohemia. Another is the extraordinary terseness of his utterance—by which I do not mean that his works are particularly brief in duration, but that they are built up of short, expressive phrases, repeated and developed with the utmost economy, and with sudden changes

225

of key. Janáček was no great melodist in the ordinary sense of the term. His music is direct in its impact, deeply felt, dramatic, at times passionate, and utterly individual. Because of its terse idiom, it *seems* to belong to the post-World War I era rather than to the more expansive age which preceded this, though about three-quarters of his life was lived in the 19th century. In his own day, he must have seemed very 'modern' or indeed 'avant-garde'.

He wrote 'I felt that in the *speech-motive* lay the consequences of inner secret happenings ... I felt the enigmas of the soul'. And in his operas from *Jenufa* onwards, he developed this conception: his speech-motive is an attempt to express in terse musical phrases (rather than in melodies or even themes or Wagnerian *leitmotives*) the basic emotions and ideas of men and women and even the instincts of animals. He observed the rhythms and inflections of speech and the sounds of nature and embodied them in musical terms. His music is, as it were, realistic even when the subject is a fantastic one.

Both *Jenufa* (set in the peasant world of Janáček's native Eastern Moravia) and *Kátà Kabanová* (based on a Russian drama) are tragic operas dealing with ordinary people. There is nothing symbolic or fantastic about them. Jenufa has a bastard child by a man who refuses to marry her, and is loved by another man, Laca, who jealously wounds her, but repents. The nobility of the story lies in the fact that her foster-mother, though she has killed the baby in her agony at Jenufa's shame, has done so out of her love for Jenufa and her desire for her happiness; the foster-mother, having confessed, is led away for trial, but Jenufa forgives her, and she and Laca are reunited in happiness. The music is lyrical and contains some Czech dance-rhythms, but is intense and dramatic. *Kátà Kabanová* is even more tragic; for Kátà is cruelly treated by her husband, Tichon, and his mother; she is religious, but in her unhappy state loves Boris and commits adultery with him; she confesses publicly, they agree to part, and she drowns herself in the river. The music has a poignant beauty; it is tense, terse, moving, and powerful.

By contrast, *The Makropulos Case* is a fantastic tale, with libretto by Karel Čapek. Elina Makropulos has been given by the Emperor Rudolf II an elixir of life and youth for 300 years, and re-appears at intervals under different names but always bearing the initials 'E.M.' In the end, having been charged with fraud and forgery, she tells her story and offers the formula to others, but

226

they refuse it; when the paper is burnt, she dies. In spite of the callousness of 'E.M.' (who voices no concern when Baron Prus tells her that his son Janek has killed himself out of hopeless love for her), Janáček expresses compassion for the basic pathos in the story of 'E.M.', and the other characters by his imaginative, evocative music. It is a gripping opera.

The Cunning Little Vixen is also fantastic. The characters are partly human beings, partly animals. There is tenderness in the love and adept human characterisation elsewhere; the beauties of Nature and the varied musical embodiments of animal, bird and insect life, without any actual copying of the *sounds* of Nature or her creatures, are, to me, most attractive. These analogies between humans and animals seem to be characteristic of Czech art, though Karel Čapek's *The Insect Play* is a satire, which this opera is not. It is a fascinating, enchanting, imaginative fantasy, with a masterly, impressionistic, and subtle score. It is neither a comedy nor a tragedy, for one cannot take very tragically the death of a sly little vixen, even though she is also loving and motherly.

The House of the Dead, an opera in three acts, based on Dostoevsky's diary in which he recorded life in a Siberian prison, might be expected to be gloomy, but it is not. Dostoevsky himself had a basically Christian outlook; and Janáček's opera is *not* depressing. His music, though it has its grim, tragic passages, also has its lyrical ones; above all, it is transfused with a radiance which illumines the whole work with a spiritual beauty. 'In every creature there is a divine spark', he wrote on the score, and he seems to bring this out not only in Petrovič, the political prisoner, and in the youth Aljeja, but in the other characters as well, even in the three main criminal prisoners, and in the chorus at the end when those who are not being set free summon up enough tentative courage and unselfishness to sing with uneasy, mixed feelings at the release of Petrovič and of the eagle, with its wounds now healed. There is a Christian symbolism in all this, even though the opera is *prima facie* realistic. The score is moving, pathetic, brave. Janáček left it partially unfinished. Two of his pupils lovingly filled in the gaps, but their 'happy' ending would be really out of place : the composer's original conclusion, as described above, is artistically right. This was his last work, and it is a unique masterpiece.

The Diary of a Man who disappeared is a cycle of vocal music for tenor, contralto, and three other female voices, with pianoforte accompaniment, about a young man who disappeared in Moravia before World War I and had thrown in his lot with a gipsy girl with whom he he had fallen in love, had a baby son by her, and decided to leave his parents and sister. It is (again) terse, powerful, eloquent and deeply felt—as it were, a development of the Wagner/Hugo Wolf unending melody idiom, in the form of unending short phrases. And the narrative is marvellously entwined with musical pictures of Nature, which seem to correspond to the human elements in the story.

Janáček composed four striking pieces of chamber music. The Concertino for piano and six other instruments is very attractive and genuine in its emotion. The Capriccio for pianoforte (left hand) and seven wind instruments is both beautiful and thoughtful. The First String Quartet, inspired by Tolstoy's The Kreutzer Sonata, wastes not a single note in its deeply felt, in parts eerie, melancholy, and exciting moods. The Second Quartet, Intimate Letters, is a passionate expression of his love for Madame Kamilla Stoesslová—profound, intense, absorbing, tender, joyous, tragic.

The Sinfonietta was described by Janáček in terms which suggest a kind of orchestral vision of Brno, the capital of Moravia, and the fanfare which begins and ends it was originally composed for a rally of the national sports movement. It is in several short, connected movements, culminating in a blaze of glory—a masterly work, in which vigour, dancing, pathos, and humour, are all expressed with conciseness and brilliant orchestration.

Taras Bulba is a dramatic, colourful Rhapsody for orchestra in three movements, depicting the tragic deaths of the two sons of Taras Bulba, the legendary Cossack general in the 17th century wars against the dominant Poles, his own capture and death after prophesying ultimate triumph for the Russian people. It is a great tone-poem, ending in spiritual victory.

The Eternal Gospel (for soprano and tenor soloists, choir, and orchestra) is a noble, deeply religious work, sonorous in its colour which is 'rich not gaudy'.[63] The Glagolitic Mass is the most astonishing setting of the liturgy of the Mass that I have ever heard—partly, perhaps, because the text is a vernacular version of the Latin Mass in the Old Slavonic language of the 9th century, but chiefly because of Janáček's intensely individual utterance—with its cross-rhythms, its rapid, repeated Amens, its vividness, power and imagination. It is an 'open-air' kind of worship, not ecclesiastical

[63] Shakespeare : 'Hamlet', I, iii (Polonius's advice to Laertes about clothing).

to Western ears, but assuredly religious in its essential character.

Hans Holländer[64] tells us that, as a man, Janáček was restless, impetuous, and intense; explosive, dynamic, and impulsive. He was essentially a countryman devoted to the very soil of his native land and to its folk-music and its people, and to the beauties of Nature. He came of a family of quite humble schoolmasters and organists. He married Zdenka Schultz when she was sixteen; she was higher in the social scale—upper middle class, urban, and of a reserved nature, German in her sympathies; her mother was of good Prussian-Silesian stock, her father the son of a North Bohemian doctor. Janáček's daughter died in her twenty-first year, and his younger child, a son, only survived birth for two and a half years. It is not altogether surprising that his early romantic love for his wife did not last into his old age. She had always found it difficult to acclimatise herself to his very different background and temperament, and ultimately she became a lonely, tragic figure. In his early sixties he became passionately attached to Kamilla Stoesslová, a Moravian merchant's wife, who was thirty-eight years younger than Leoš, with her 'robustness and gaiety, her true femininity and sensuous warmth',[65] and he produced all his great works after *Jenufa* under this stimulating influence. He was unorthodox in religion, but benign in character, profoundly humane, a lover of Russia, but a warm supporter of the new Czechoslovak republic which came to birth in 1918. We can discern all these personal characteristics in his music.

I have written more about Janáček than about Dvořák; the latter has long been generally recognised as one of the great 19th century composers, and has a comparatively simple musical personality; whereas Janáček's art has only recently reached full appreciation outside his own country. He was in advance of his time and a genius of great originality.

[63] 'Leoš Janáček: his Life and Work', by Hans Holländer, translated by Paul Hamburger, p. 33.
[65] Hans Holländer, ibid., p. 68.

CHAPTER THIRTY-FOUR

Widening Horizons (III)—From Spain to Scandinavia (Albeniz, Granados and Falla; Grieg, Sibelius and Nielsen)

In all the early part of my life, Spanish music meant to me, as (I fancy) to most other lovers of the art, music in Spanish idiom written by other nations, especially France: Domenico Scarlatti, the 18th century Italian who lived for many years in Spain, was the father of a Spanish style in music for keyboard, and was to influence Albeniz, Granados and Falla in years to come; Edouard Lalo, the French composer of Spanish descent, who was born and lived in France, and whose *Symphonie espagnole* for violin and orchestra is one of his best-known works; Bizet, who never set foot in Spain, but reproduced its atmosphere and some, at least, of the rhythms of its national music in parts of *Carmen*; Chabrier, in his exuberant Rhapsody *España*; Debussy, with his brilliant evocations of Spanish scenes in *Iberia*, and the Spanish elements elsewhere in his music to which Falla drew attention (the opening of the Scherzo in the string quartet, *La Soirée dans Grenade* for pianoforte, *La Puerta del Vino* and *La Sérénade interrompue* among the Préludes, and the *Seven Spanish Songs* in which the tunes are actually Spanish but the accompaniments are Debussy's own); Moszkovsky (a German of Polish origin), with his Spanish dances for piano duet; Ravel (who was born in the Basses-Pyrénées, and whose mother came of a Basque family), in his delightful comic opera *L'heure espagnole* and his popular *Bolero*; and the Russian, Rimsky-Korsakov, a denizen of a country much farther away from Spain than is either France or Italy, with his exhilarating *Spanish Capriccio* for orchestra. In those days we ordinary music lovers knew virtually nothing of the magnificent church music of the great 17th century Spanish composer, Vittoria.

Not until the period between the wars did we make the acquaintance of three eminent modern composers who were themselves Spaniards and expressed the essential spirit and atmosphere of their native land in music which is authentically Spanish in character. Both Albeniz (1860-1909) and Granados (1867-1916) were, *par excellence*, composers for the piano. Albeniz was by birth a Catalan, but as J. B. Trend pointed out,[66] caught the feeling of Andalusian music with its vigorous, contrasted rhythms, its harmonic effects derived from instruments tuned in fourths, and its richly ornamental melodies, in his enchanting series of twelve pieces for piano entitled *Iberia*. Granados charmed us all with his characteristically Spanish pianoforte compositions, especially in the two books of *Goyescas*, based on scenes from the paintings and tapestries of Goya. It was a great tragedy that he and his wife were drowned in January, 1916, when the *Sussex* was sunk in the English Channel by a torpedo from a German submarine on their way back to Spain from the U.S.A., after he had played at a reception given by the president in Washington and had missed the boat on which he had intended to travel.[67]

Manuel de Falla was the greatest of these 19th/20th century Spanish composers, and the most distinguished pupil of Felipe Pedrell, to whom the renaissance of genuine Spanish music was so deeply indebted. I have loved Falla's music from the start. *Nights in the Gardens of Spain* are not a piano concerto, for the piano is simply one instrument in the orchestral score, though admittedly an important one, and they are not structurally akin to any concerto ever written, but rather a series of three symphonic poems, not of a detailed kind, but conveying in turn the composer's impressions in a garden on a hill overlooking Granada, *A Dance in the Distance*, and *In the Gardens of the Sierra de Córdoba*. The first is calm and dreamy, the second livelier and more markedly rhythmical, and the third (though entirely instrumental) suggests the wild music of a group of gipsies, playing, dancing, and singing at an evening party in the garden of a villa. The enchanting music is not descriptive, but expresses human moods as well as the open-air atmosphere of three contrasted nocturnal scenes in Spanish gardens.

The ballet *El Amor Brujo* (which, J. B. Trend[68] felt, might be

[66] Article on Albeniz in *Grove's Dictionary of Music and Musicians*, 5th edition, vol. I, p. 89.

[67] J. B. Trend: article on Granados in *Grove's Dictionary*, 5th edition, vol. III, p. 755.

[68] J. B. Trend: 'Manuel de Falla and Spanish Music,' pp. 79-80.

translated *The Demon Lover*) was based on a folk-story found in many countries, 'in which the ghost of the dead lover always appears at the moment when a new lover tries to take his place.' This in turn may have come from *The Ring given to Venus*, in which the lover put a ring on the finger of a statue in church, thinking it to be that of the Virgin Mary, whereas it originally represented Venus: 'the finger bent and kept the ring', and the statue kept on coming to life, as it were (like the Commendatore's statue in *Don Giovanni*) to prevent an earthly marriage.[69]

In Falla's ballet, with scenario by Martinez Sierra, Candélas, a beautiful gipsy girl, loves another gipsy, a dissolute and jealous man. She has been unhappy with him, and consults a sorceress, who correctly foretells his death in a fight, but Candélas fears his ghost after his death. Young Carmélo now loves her, but the ghost continually frightens her away from him. She believes herself to be bewitched, but the sorceress and Carmélo decide to lay the ghost, and Candélas, agreeing, executes the Ritual Fire Dance. Carmélo induces Lucia, Candélas's friend, to let the ghost make love to her instead. The plan succeeds, the ghost is finally overcome, and Carmélo and Candélas are happily united. I had known the suite from the music of this ballet for many years, but my wife and I counted ourselves lucky in being able to see and hear the work as a composite whole, danced and played on the orchestra, with a mezzo-soprano singing behind the stage, as performed by Antonio's company at the Palace Theatre, London, in 1956. For it is a completely integrated work of art, in which the haunting music, with its Spanish rhythms, melodic beauty, and delicate orchestration, is perfectly matched to the fantastic scenario. This wonderful ballet, like the much more frequently performed *Three-cornered Hat*, ought to be in the regular repertoire of every ballet company. These are two of the greatest masterpieces, both musically and choreographically, in the world of ballet.

I originally saw *The Three-cornered Hat* at the Alhambra Theatre, London, in 1919, with Massine as the miller, Karsavina as his wife, and Woizikovsky as the Corregidor. Martinez Sierra wrote the book, Massine himself was the choreographer, and the scenery was by Picasso. Ansermet conducted. It is based on a story by Alarcón (used by Hugo Wolf in his opera *Der Corregidor*) and is about a devoted miller and his wife; they are visited at their mill

---

[69] Ibid., pp. 79-80.

in Andalusia by the magistrate, the Corregidor, who wears the three-cornered hat. He is much attracted by her, and returns, hoping to find her alone. As, however, the miller is still there, the Corregidor arranges for him to be arrested and taken away by the police. The Corregidor tries to embrace her, but she extracts herself from his arms and pushes him into the river; after he has emerged, she points a musket at him and walks away through the gorge. He hangs his clothes up to dry, puts on the miller's coat, and wearily throws himself on the miller's bed. Meanwhile the miller has escaped, and on returning home, snatches the Corregidor's cloak, knocks him down, writes on the wall 'Your wife is no less beautiful than mine', picks up the wet clothes and leaves. The Corregidor reads the words on the wall and is terrified at the probable outcome. The miller and his wife return, followed by a crowd of villagers who join in buffetting the tyrannical Corregidor. Policemen drag the wretched man away, and the crowd toss his effigy up and down in a blanket. The music is absolutely brilliant—witty, lively and charming—and the whole ballet, if well performed both by orchestra and dancers, is sheer delight from beginning to end.

My wife and I were also fortunate in seeing *Master Peter's Puppet-Show* in London early in our married life, for opportunities to do so are very rare. Falla composed it in the years soon after World War I at the invitation of the Princesse de Polignac for her puppet-theatre. He himself wrote the libretto, based on an adventure of Don Quixote (in Part II of Cervantes' novel). The Don and Sancho Panza are resting at an inn, where they see a performance given by a travelling showman with his puppets. The play tells how the Christian princess, Melisendra, is rescued from captivity among the Moors in Spain by Don Gaiferos, a knight of the court of Charlemagne. Muslim horsemen ride in pursuit of the lovers. But Don Quixote's mad knight-errantry cannot tolerate this: he attacks the Moorish puppets with his sword, imagining them to be real persons, and hacks them all to pieces—thus ruining the unfortunate showman's business. In the Princesse de Polignac's theatre, not only the characters in the puppet play, but also Don Quixote, Sancho Panza, Master Peter (the showman) and his boy, and the innkeeper, were themselves represented by puppets. It was a puppet-play within a puppet play. In other, later, productions, only the figures in the inner show have been puppets, the Don and the others being played by living performers, three of whom were singers. Falla's opera is, so far as I know, unique in its kind, and the score is entrancing. There are only about thirty instruments, with a large proportion of them wind instruments, but the trumpet and horns are frequently muted, thus transporting us into a world of romance and fairyland. Though the work contains few elements that are ordinarily regarded as specifically Spanish, compared with his earlier compositions, its blend of humour and basic seriousness, which is characteristic of Cervantes' great novel, is essentially Spanish in a deeper sense. We have seen in his other creations how humorous Falla's mind was and how he could convey romantic love, pathos and fantasy, and give us the poetry of night in an open-air Spanish setting. Through all these compositions there is a kind of profound charm, which, not being confined to a superficial attractiveness, seems to have penetrated into the composer's soul and to make us love both him and his music. J. B. Trend,[70] who knew him well, tells us that as a man Falla was 'passionately serious and yet, at the same time, one who has a sense of humour which is quite irresistible.' Evidently, the man and the artist were completely integrated.

From Spain I travel, in imagination, to Scandinavia—to Norway, Finland and Denmark.

Grieg has sometimes been described as a *petit maître*. That may be true, in the sense that he is not among the giants of music. But if, as I maintain, the continued appeal of several of a creator's works for many generations is a symptom of greatness, Grieg was a great composer. I used to hear the First *Peer Gynt* suite and *Solveig's Song* and the Piano Concerto over and over again under Henry Wood when I was a boy and a youth, and they still make their impact on music lovers. Soon after World War I, my uncle Louis Mendl and I saw Ibsen's *Peer Gynt* at the Old Vic, with Grieg's complete incidental music. These twenty-two pieces seemed to be an integral part of the haunting drama. The Old Vic revived the play some years later, but Grieg's music was not quite so completely performed then—to my disappointment. The Piano Concerto in A minor, though a comparatively early work (op. 16, composed when Greig was about twenty-five) always seems to me to be among the most beautiful romantic concertos. Grieg was, *par excellence,* a romantic, and nationalistic, composer. He was influenced by the art of composers of other nations, but he was steeped in Norwegian folk music, and his works reflect the roman-

[70] Ibid., p. 117.

tic beauty of the fiords of his native land and the characteristic atmosphere of its countryside and its mountains, its legends and fairy tales. Besides the two *Peer Gynt* suites, the *Holberg* Suite and the 'Norwegian Dances' have always been among my favourites; and one of my cherished memories is of hearing Kirsten Flagstad, who was one of the greatest Wagnerian sopranos, but who frankly did not excel as a performer of German *lieder*, singing groups of lovely songs by Grieg at a recital in the Royal Opera House, Covent Garden, some years ago; with her glorious voice and magnificent production, she was unsurpassed in interpreting the songs of her great compatriot.

Sibelius was one of the great modern influences on my music loving life between the wars. From this angle, it might be thought that I should have discussed him earlier in this book. But he did not die until September, 1957, and though he produced no major work after *Tapiola* in 1926, he fits suitably into this section about Scandinavian composers—one of whom is Nielsen, whose music I never encountered until after World War II; and they all illustrate the widening horizons which accompanied or followed the decline of the Teutonic leadership in music. Sibelius's art does not at present seem to attract the same wide acclaim outside his own country that it did during his lifetime, or that it still maintains in his native Finland. I believe that his stock will go up again, internationally; these swings of the pendulum often occur, and a temporary drop in popularity frequently happens to the work of a great creative artist soon after his death. Anyhow, as this book is concerned so much with my own reflections, and as I love and admire the music of Sibelius as much as I did when I first became acquainted with it, I make no apology for devoting some space to him at this point, in my old age.

Jean (originally Johan) Sibelius was born into a Swedish-speaking home in Finland in December, 1865 (though that country was then an autonomous duchy of Russia, Swedish had remained the language of most well-educated people, Sweden having ruled it from before the 18th century until early in the 19th). His father was a doctor, and his mother came from a family whose members were of the professional classes. He became completely bi-lingual, and was a devoted son of Finland throughout his life. He lost his father when he was only two and a half, yet had a happy childhood, thanks largely to his mother's loving care. As a small boy, he was 'something of a dreamer', had a great love of nature and a vivid imagina-

235

tion; his moods were liable to change 'from a playful exuberance to the deepest melancholy'; he was 'easily moved' and very affectionate.[71] In June, 1892, he married Aino Järnefelt, a member of an aristocratic Finnish-speaking family. He had given up his law studies at Helsinki University and embarked on a musical career, in 1886, and by 1897 had acquired a sufficient reputation as a composer to be granted a modest State pension by the enlightened Senate, which assured him at least a minimum income for life. He was a deeply cultured man, who always loved ancient Greek and Latin literature. In 1904 he moved from Helsinki into a small village, Järvenpää, near the city; this satisfied both his love for the lonely Finnish forests and his desire to be able to visit Helsinki easily. In 1908, a malignant tumour was removed from his throat; and he lived to the age of ninety! He was a 'shy, reserved' man, but beneath that exterior he was 'impulsive, generous and unselfconscious'[72] and an excellent host. He greatly enjoyed the pleasures of the table, but after his operation he was obliged to give up cigars and alcohol. He was kindly in his encouragement of young composers. The reason why he composed so little after 1926 is obscure; it may have been either 'the simple drying up of the mainspring of his creative powers' or 'some purely physical decline'.[72] Cecil Gray, who visited him, described him as uniting 'the traditional charm, affability, and *bonhomie* of the Swede, and the fiercely independent spirit, the sturdy self-reliance, the love of isolation and solitude, the extreme reserve, of the Finn. In the luxurious hotels and restaurants of Helsingfors (Helsinki) he is the man of the world, an epicure with a refined and highly developed sense for all the graces and amenities of civilised life; in the austere and primitive surroundings of Järvenpää, he is the mystic, the anchorite, the aloof and solitary dreamer'. He combined 'a quite astonishing power, vigour and overflowing vitality' with 'balance, serenity, and poise'.[73]

It has been said of Sibelius's music that it is not much concerned with humanity, but predominantly with nature and myth. Thus, Neville Cardus[74] wrote: 'We leave the world of men and women .... when we enter the world of Sibelius.... The world of Sibelius is unpeopled; there are no men and women in it, not a single living human being. The hedges are bare and no birds sing. Nobody loves

[71] Robert Layton: *Sibelius*, p. 4, reproducing the description of him given by his school friend, Walter von Konow.

[72] Ibid. pp. 24, 15, 25, 26, 27.

[73] Cecil Gray: *Sibelius*, pp. 56, 57 and 60.

[74] Neville Cardus: *Ten Composers*, pp. 155 and 156.

and dies like a rose in aromatic pain. The scene and the drama of Sibelius are nature.... The characters, the forces, the emotions expressed, are of the elements—wind and storm, the mists and night and dawn, the vacant landscape, the rustling grasses, the wailing of traditional ghosts, the menace of the dark and backward abyss. We hear the echo of old battles; and over everything Sibelius casts the dim light of legendary awe. Sibelius can exult, of course. But it is not man's high spirits that shake the orchestra now....'

I am not sure that there is not a slight confusion of thought here; for 'the elements' of nature do not *feel* any emotions for a composer to express; and Cardus admits that Sibelius 'can exult', but contends that this is not the exultation of 'a man's high spirits'; and if it is not that, what is it? The natural world of winds and landscape and sea does not exult: it is man that exults in it.

Robert Layton[75] wrote: 'Sibelius has an acutely developed sense of identification with nature and a pre-occupation with myth.... These pre-occupations override his involvement in the human predicament, except in so far as it affects man's relationships with nature.'

Now, all this is to a large extent a true account of Sibelius's symphonic poems, which are clearly concerned with myth, with various episodes in the *Kalevala*, and with the manifestations of nature, rather than with real, or even realistic, human characters. But I do not think we are entitled to draw any such definite conclusions as regards his symphonies, which are his other greatest contribution to the world of music, and which are more fully discussed by Neville Cardus in his Sibelius chapter of *Ten Composers* than any other of Sibelius's works. Sibelius did not, like Beethoven, give descriptive names for any of his symphonies: he composed no *Pastoral Symphony*, with sub-titles for its individual movements; he did not write on *Eroica*, with a funeral march. He made no remark such as Beethoven did about the opening of the C minor, 'Thus Fate knocks at the door.' He left it entirely to us to feel and interpret his symphonies as best we may. And there is no authority *from him* for us to declare that *these* works of his (as distinct from his symphonic poems) are concerned with myth or Nature either predominantly, or even at all. When Neville Cardus[76] asserts that 'Sibelius.is never concerned with the soul of mankind', I think that he overlooks the spiritual grandeur of the Third, Fifth, and Seventh Symphonies, and the tragedy of the Fourth.

[75] Robert Layton: 'Sibelius', p. 153.   [76] 'Ten Composers', p. 154.

Music, as I have often pointed out, deals with *generalised* emotions—joy, gaiety, sorrow, anger, fear, exultation, religious feeling, and so on. When it seeks to depict these as experienced by *individual* men and women in opera, oratorio, cantata, song, or symphonic poem, it does so only by producing musical equivalents of these general emotions common to mankind in ways which are felt to be *appropriate* to the individuals in the literary or dramatic story. A dramatist, a poet, a novelist, a painter, a sculptor, can produce an actual, recognizable portrait of a real or fictitious or legendary figure in words, colours, or stone. A composer can only write music *suitable* for them; for apart from representations of sounds in the external world which have regular vibrations and are therefore musical themselves (such as the notes of a bird's song), or have a musical rhythm, it does not *copy* that world at all; nor is its language that by which we normally communicate with one another—the language of words which literature uses. But Sibelius's symphonies, and his violin concerto and his string quartet, *Voces Intimae*, abound in 'human' music of the generalised kind which I have described. They are not only masterpieces of musical structure (as Beethoven's are, too). They are full of the deep, rich music of humanity.

It would be pure fancy to tack on to any of the symphonies of Sibelius either a programme or even a brief description purporting to relate them either to the manifestations of Nature or to myth. And they are certainly not mere sound patterns. Of course, Sibelius does not wear his heart on his sleeve, as it has been said that Tchaikovsky did. Nor did he portray the impassioned emotions which we find in the operas of Verdi. He came from a Northern country, and his natural instinct was to convey human feelings in a more controlled idiom. They never run away with him. They are always embodied in a firmly knit structure, even if that structure is of his own devising and often departs substantially from the traditional symphonic form of Haydn, Mozart, Beethoven, and Brahms.

In Sibelius's First Symphony, we are still in the predominantly romantic world of 19th century music. And this applies also to the Second Symphony, though in both there are anticipations of the typical, terse, athletic art of the later Sibelius symphonies. With the Third, he took 'a new road', just as Beethoven said he did in his Third (*Eroica*) Symphony, though Beethoven's first two also contained foretastes of his mature, second period. There, the analogy between the two Third Symphonies ceases. Sibelius's 'No.

3' is less highly charged with emotion than its two predecessors; the first movement is dynamic and powerful; the second, soothing, charming, yet wistful; the Finale is highly original in comprising two parts, in the first of which two brave little themes are expounded and developed, whilst in the second, instead of a recapitulation, a big new theme appears, beginning majestically and growing in excitement to a triumphant conclusion.

The Fourth Symphony is a masterpiece of tragic and austere grandeur. Its first movement passes through conflict, to end in exhaustion. The scherzo is quick and uneasy, with a trio twice as slow but increasingly tense. The slow movement is a profound meditation, and the Finale, though allegro in tempo, is sombre in mood until the last terrific battle and the final tragedy. The Fifth Symphony (in three movements) is a complete contrast. Its main key is E flat, its general character heroic but happy. The first movement opens with a horn calling us to action, though in 'piano' tones; it is an intricate movement, with a second part in which the trumpet heralds approaching victory, and it ends in a blaze of glory. The andante is a gentle and charming 'theme and variations'—a kind of interlude, before the exciting Finale (allegro), with its grand, swinging theme on the horns, its change to slow time, and its triumphant climax.

The Sixth Symphony is, again, utterly different from its predecessors. It is mainly quiet, serene, and economical in its orchestration. After the storm and stress of the Fourth and the exultant heroism of the Fifth, it provides, as it were, a welcome point of repose before we come to the gigantic single movement which constitutes the Seventh Symphony (gigantic in quality, not in duration). The first movement is cool and pure, yet subtle. The *allegretto moderato* is graceful and quiet, but scarcely a slow movement at all. There follows a fascinating scherzo, but without a trio section. The Finale has a beautifully poised main theme; after a time the music becomes more turbulent, but it ends with a coda of the utmost serenity and loveliness.

Sibelius's Seventh, and last, symphony is a continuous piece of music, lasting about twenty-three minutes in performance, and comprising within its scope four sections which roughly correspond to the more traditional four-movement structure of earlier composers, but with a slow section first, then a fairly quick one, then a kind of short scherzo, and, lastly, a majestic Finale. But the whole work is majestic—an inspired and inspiring culmination of his wonderful series of symphonies. It is perhaps not surprising that, after all, the once hoped-for Eighth Symphony never materialised.

The violin concerto was composed between the Second and Third Symphonies, and has always been popular both with soloists and the public. Certain writers have tended to decry it, though Tovey had a very high opinion of it. Personally, I love it; and one thing is undeniable—that it is music of great warmth and full-blooded humanity.

When we survey the whole range of Sibelius's symphonies and this concerto, they seem to me to give the lie to the theory that his art is solely pre-occupied with myth and nature, except in so far as the human predicament affects man's relationship with nature. On the other hand, these works are not abstract affairs of structure only, masterly though Sibelius's structural sense is. They are intrinsically bound up with the emotions, aspirations, and spiritual stature of mankind. But it is time now to turn to a brief consideration of Sibelius's contribution to the art of the symphonic poem, for his works in this genre stand, as it were, side by side, with his great chain of symphonies. About the symphonic poems there has been no controversy. They are highly imaginative musical embodiments of the myths and legends and natural scenes to which they are related.

He started the series with one that has no detailed programme. He called it simply *En Saga*, and it is a fitting prelude to its successors just because it is concerned with no particular legend but with the idea of Nordic myth in general. It is a work of rugged grandeur, with a variety of themes and changes of key. After that, he turned to the *Kalevala* legends, opening his cycle of four with *The Swan of Tuonela*, in which he depicts the Swan floating majestically on the great, black river surrounding Tuonela, the hell of Finnish mythology. The elusive melody of the cor anglais drifts on a surface of string music with shifting harmonies. But though this piece was the first of the *Four Legends* to be composed by Sibelius, *Lemminkäinen and the Maidens of Saari* is the earliest in the original legendary story and should be played first if the four are being performed together: Lemminkäinen, the fearless hero, seeks Kylliki and finds her in the land of the Saari; his love for her seems at first to be unrequited, but eventually he carries her off by sleigh to his home. The slow introduction, with cool wood-wind effects against quiet strings, gives place to a quick tempo, charming and atmospheric, with crescendos and diminuendos; the lovely score combines strength and delicacy. But *Lemminkäinen in Tuonela* is finer still; the hero is killed, and his body is borne away by the river to Tuonela, where it is hewn to pieces. The music is intensely descriptive, with its ominous shudders on the strings, the cries on the wood-wind and brass, the recurrent crescendos and climaxes, and the soft, sad ending. 'The Return of Lemminkäinen' depicts his magical resurrection and the exhilaration of his gallop homeward: the music races along excitedly, triumphantly, joyfully, and makes a magnificent finish to the cycle.

Sibelius's next symphonic poem was *Finlandia*, a good piece of patriotic music but not comparable in quality with his great works. After that came the *Symphonic Fantasia, Pohjola's Daughter*, in which he returned to the *Kalevala* legends. It is minutely descriptive, yet its programme enables it to follow the traditional structure of the first movement of a symphony, with the exposition of two themes (representing Väinämöinen and the Maid of Pohjola), development, and recapitulation. Väinämöinen, the hero, meets the beautiful maid, seated on a rainbow, spinning. He begs her to join him, but she imposes impossible conditions: he must make a boat out of the pieces of the spindle and tie an egg into invisible knots. Even he, with his magical arts, fails, so he continues his journey in his sledge, alone. The music is extraordinarily vivid and powerful and richly coloured, but begins and ends in utter darkness.

Like *En Saga* and *Nightride and Sunrise* (which is a musical image of a journey through a landscape at night and during the rising of the sun), *The Bard* has no story: its music is soft, suggesting a world of old legends, with a prominent part for harp. *Luonnotar* is a 'tone poem for (soprano) voice and orchestra' and returns to the *Kalevala*: it tells how Luonnotar, 'air's young daughter', became the Water-Mother on the sea and lifted her knee so that a teal might establish its nest, found it getting hot, and rolled the eggs into the water; the eggs broke into fragments, one of which rose to form the arch of heaven, another—the white upper portion —became the moon, and the mottled parts of the egg were transformed into the stars. It is an allegory of the creation of the world, told in difficult writing for the voice and imaginative, finally mysterious, orchestration.

In *The Oceanides*, Sibelius turns to Homer, for these are the ancient Greek water nymphs. It has a quiet opening—woodwind, flutes, soft brass—depicting the sea at dawn; the sunlight breaks on the dark expanse of the water, and there is a gradual crescendo, until the climax comes as clouds appear on the horizon. It is a marvellously atmospheric work. But the greatest and last of his symphonic poems is *Tapiola*, prefixed by this motto:—

'Widespread they stand, the Northland's dusky forests,
Ancient, mysterious, brooding savage dreams,
Within them dwells the Forest's mighty God
And woodsprites in the gloom weave magic secrets.'

Almost the whole work is based on the simple, short, opening phrase on the strings. Transmutations of this theme and orchestral changes portray the infinite variety of moods and colours in the Scandinavian forests, and culminate in 'a mighty, rushing wind' and a tremendous storm, followed by a peaceful ending in a major key.

Though the incidental music for *The Tempest* was intended to be associated with the theatre and so none of its numbers can be classed as short symphonic poems, the storm with which it opens is akin to that mighty upheavel in *Tapiola*, and is one of the most terrific storms in musical history. It is pure nature music, though in Shakespeare's play the tempest is made by Prospero by means of his magical powers and sailors figure in the scene.

Sibelius is, indeed, one of the great nature poets of music. But he also conveys the emotions and thoughts of humanity within the framework of masterly structures, whether partly traditional or of his own invention. He is not an extrovert like Chopin or Tchaikovsky, but rather an introvert, whose feelings, as contained in his music, run deep, though they are controlled by his strong character and are not always or immediately apparent on the surface. He wrote some eloquent songs. And his one great piece of chamber music is the string quartet, op. 56, dating from 1909, and significantly called *Voces intimae* (Intimate voices): its five movements are, again (like the symphonies), not just patterns in sound; they are intimate expressions of human moods, whether smiling, contemplative, or exciting.

Some of Sibelius's music *is* austere; but austerity, after all, is not only a phenomenon of nature, but one part of the human predicament.

I have, however, found no austerity in the music of Carl Nielsen. He was a man of wide and deep human sympathy, with a love for his fellowmen, as well as for nature. He came of humble origins, the son of a house-painter and local musician in a Danish village. Both his parents were musical, and young Carl adored music—the songs of the birds, the native folk-songs, and the music of Bach, Haydn, Mozart, and Beethoven when he had the opportunities to become acquainted with them. He was humorous, quick-witted, kindly, and generous. He became a great reader: Plato's *Republic* was his bedside companion. He recognised the greatness of Wagner, but did not really love his music dramas, which he regarded as undramatic. And he had no use for detailed programme music. In instrumental art, he was chiefly bent on expressing the fundamental, general characteristics of human nature. Even in his First Symphony (1892) he sought to convey humanity as he saw it in his early manhood—not with any romantic gaze, nor through any attempt at individual portraiture, but in its basic features of emotion and thought. The Second Symphony eloquently describes *The Four Temperaments*—choleric, phlegmatic, melancholic, and sanguine. In the Third Symphony, *Espansiva*, he shows the smiling countryside of Denmark and the generosity and hospitality of its people. The Fourth is *The Inextinguishable*—mankind's evolution and determined struggle for existence and survival. The Fifth Symphony—the climax of his work—conveys a mighty conflict between man's 'progressive, constructive instincts' (as Dr Robert Simpson[77] calls them), and the hostile forces which confront him but which are ultimately defeated. In all these great works—and in other instrumental compositions—Nielsen is more concerned with big, human issues and characteristics, than with pictorial or detailed description. In his utterly original, Danish way, he was a true artistic descendant of Beethoven and Brahms, and fundamentally in contrast with Wagner and Richard Strauss.

In an age when Strauss was developing the byways of psychopathic manifestations and depicting the external scene by means of ingenious devices, when Schoenberg, finding himself unable to go further than Wagner either in the diatonic or the chromatic idiom, was exploring the futilities of atonality and inventing a twelve-note technique to succeed the musical language which had gradually evolved through the ages, Nielsen, like his great contemporaries, Elgar, Sibelius, and Janáček, was demonstrating that tonality was certainly *not* exhausted, but that through the art of true genius and penetrating insight, it was still capable of revealing new, unsuspected depths and heights of human grandeur.

Nielsen ultimately achieved this tremendously important result

[77] *Carl Nielsen, Symphonist*, p. 86.

by his novel method of progressive tonality, which began in his First Symphony, with its truly astonishing changes of key, and reached its climax in the Fourth and Fifth Symphonies and the first movement of the Sixth. To end a work, or even a movement, in a different key from the one in which it started (after various tonal transformations in between), was Nielsen's great technical landmark; it is, however, not just a device of technique, but a natural reflection of the emotional and spiritual evolution of the music. Both the Fourth and Fifth Symphonies also evince a remarkable function assigned to the drums, which aggressively enter into a violent struggle with the other instruments and are gloriously defeated, as though evil is being overcome by good. With Nielsen, 'music is life'; there is no romantic origin in his art, as in the early works of Sibelius. It is, so to speak, bound up with real life at every turn. But in the Sixth Symphony his optimism deserted him, possibly because of his failing health due to *angina pectoris*: in its great, tragic, first movement, he is still at the height of his powers, but that is followed by a bitter, mocking *Humoresque*, and though the ensuing Adagio, for all its despair, does something to redeem the effect of this, there is an ambivalence about the final variations, as though Nielsen is trying to put on a brave front to his personal suffering.

Though his music was for a long time known in this country almost entirely by his symphonies, he was a very versatile composer. He wrote three concertos—for violin, flute, and clarinet. The two latter came after the Sixth Symphony; but the flute concerto (in two movements only, like the Fifth Symphony) shows no trace of bitterness; it opens with an Allegro moderato which has a profound charm throughout; the Allegretto is attractive and humorous, with a slow section in its midst; at the end, the flute is, as it were, debunked—one might almost say, *debagged*! by the bass trombone. Evidently Nielsen had recovered from the pessimism of his last symphony. Even the occasional perverse and quirkish passages in the solo part of the clarinet concerto are only reflections of the irascible qualities of the otherwise warm-hearted, generous friend portrayed in this work, which at other times is of melting beauty.

His piano music started in his youth and ended in his sixties. The theme with Variations (1916) is based on a beautiful, slow, thoughtful theme, which his rich imagination subjected to a very wide scope of transformation both technically and spiritually. The

Piano Music for Young and Old (1930) consists of twenty-five pieces ranging from simplicity to profundity, revealing an astonishing variety of moods and Nielsen's characteristic surprises in turns of phrase and intervals.

Nielsen composed a number of chamber music works. For instance, the Fourth String Quartet in F (1906) is a very beautiful, delicately written composition; the Wind Quintet (1922) is a work of great charm, skill, wit, and loveliness. And Nielsen's aversion from detailed programme music did not prevent him from composing for orchestra two exquisite, short tone-poems: *The Dream of Gunnar* (1908) is based on the Icelandic story of Gunnar's journey to exile in Norway and resting and dreaming on his way there; *Pan and Syrinx* follows a tale in Ovid's *Metamorphoses*, in which the nymph Syrinx, pursued and terrified by Pan, is pitied by the gods and changed into a reed.

This brings me to a brief mention of Nielsen's vocal and operatic work. *Hymnus Amoris* (for soloists, chorus, and orchestra), an early composition (1896), set to Latin words, beautifully portrays love, as experienced by children, adults, mature folk, and, finally, old people. The choral and orchestral *Sleep* (1904) is not so utterly peaceful as the name might suggest, for the middle section of the three is a nightmare. *Springtime in Fyn* (for soloists, chorus, and orchestra) is youthful in spirit, cheerful, simple, and fragrant—though it is a fully mature work in date (1921). I have not had a chance to see either of Nielsen's two operas and have only been able to hear the overture of *Maskarade* (1906)—a breezy, jolly little prelude to a comedy; *Saul and David* (1902), which I heard by radio, is fine, dramatic, deeply felt music, with a rich score; it is the product of a noble and distinguished mind.

Nielsen's three motets (1929) are lovely *a capella* works: *Afflictus sum* is based on Psalm 38 and is very moving and expressive; *Dominus regit me* (Psalm 23) is serene and soothing; *Benedictus Dominus* (Psalm 31) is quicker and is a joyous prayer. I hope one day to hear *Commotio*, which he composed for organ at the end of his life.

Nielsen was not a religious man, and those three choral works are human rather than supernatural in quality. But there is no doubt that he had a most exalted, as well as profound, musical mentality, which corresponded to his personal character.

CHAPTER THIRTY-FIVE

Back to France and England (Fauré; Vaughan Williams, Walton, Tippett and Britten)

I feel that I have a slight personal link with Gabriel Fauré. A certain Dr Lesieur was at one time medical adviser to my uncle Charles Mendl and his first wife (Elsie de Wolfe) in Paris, and this doctor and his charming Scotch wife, Janet, were friends of Gabriel and Madame Fauré. Janet herself was a trained nurse and masseuse, and after Elsie's death and during the rest of Charles's life and that of his second wife, Yvonne, she continued, as a widow, to care for the old man. As I mentioned earlier, Yvonne, though very much younger than Charles, had a long and fatal illness and pre-deceased him by fifteen months. Throughout this sad time, Janet bravely shouldered the burden not only of nursing Charles in his closing years and of helping to nurse Yvonne, but of running the flat at 10 Avenue d'Iena (whilst continuing to live in her own flat). In the course of my occasional visits to Paris to see Charles in his advanced old age, she told me of the friendship between herself and her late husband and Monsieur and Madame Fauré, and often said what a kindly and charming man Fauré was. It was no surprise to me that when I flew to Paris for Yvonne's funeral, I found that Fauré's beautiful and noble Requiem was sung at the church service. The funeral arrangements had been made by Janet. No more appropriate or moving music could have been selected. I have always loved the Fauré Requiem, with its message of utter serenity and its significant omission of the 'Dies Irae'. Though it was not given in the U.K. until 1936, I had heard it before World War II, including a notable performance at the Three Choirs Festival in Worcester Cathedral in 1938. But never have I been so affected by it as on this occasion in Paris.

246

Fauré's first engagement to a lady with whom he had fallen in love was broken off by her. Six years later he married Marie Frémiet: it was a union of quiet domesticity, marked more by mutual respect and understanding than by passionate ardour. Fauré dedicated his long life to his art. His last years, like those of Beethoven and Smetana, were overshadowed by deafness. He was a great composer, whose music is performed in England only fairly frequently, and not often enough to make lovers of the art as familiar with it as they are with the works of his eminent contemporaries of other nations. Apart from the Requiem, he was one of the greatest masters of song, solo pianoforte music and chamber music in the generation just after Brahms. He was, I think, the finest of all the French song writers since Berlioz. His songs and instrumental works are in marked contrast to those of Debussy or Ravel. For he was content to use the diatonic system of the 19th century, with certain modal influences from the ancient past; and yet, by reason of its sheer inspiration and true musicianship, his art is markedly individual and in no sense old fashioned. It is the product of an extremely refined mind, but its emotions run deep and are always under control. Just as he was 'reserved and undemonstrative' (as Norman Suckling observes[78]) in private life, so he never showed off in his art. His music is constantly genuine and human. It flows like a river. It is utterly natural, and, though frequently subtle, it is simple to understand, and sensuous, without being sensual. It does not seek to express bizarre or extravagant, or even passionate, feelings. And apart from incidental music for the theatre, of which the best-known is that for *Pélléas et Mélisande*, and his opera *Pénélope* (which, alas!, I have never heard), the great Requiem and some other liturgical pieces, and his wonderful songs, he was content for the most part to compose sonatas, nocturnes, barcarolles, quartets, and quintets which tell their own tale and need no verbal programme. He is a kind of modern French counterpart to Chopin or Brahms, in the world of pianoforte and chamber music and song, with the essential difference that his art is *not*, as theirs is, largely romantic in quality, but restrained, poised, and transparent. He is a master of skilful modulations and harmonies and of beautiful, flowing melody.

Excepting the Requiem, which I knew between the Wars, most of my experience of Fauré's art has been gained since World War II. Meanwhile, great things were happening in England. I have

[78] Norman Suckling: *Fauré*, p. 17 (The Master Musicians Series).

already written about Elgar, Holst, and the British-born, though rather cosmopolitan, Delius. The career of Ralph Vaughan Williams, who had some Welsh blood as well as English in his veins, overlapped the two periods. He produced major works, in an astonishing variety of fields, throughout my music-loving life almost until his death in 1958—whether in peace or war: music for orchestra, chamber music, choral works, songs, hymns and carols, operas, music for dancing on the stage, and film music. His art is essentially English, redolent of the English countryside and the character of England's people; and rooted in the English folk-song tradition and in so much that is finest in British literature.

Thus, the first large-scale work of this son of a maritime nation was *A Sea Symphony*—a great seascape, cast broadly in the structure of an orchestral symphony, but largely choral and thus partaking also of the nature of a cantata. His next symphony was inspired by the sights and sounds of London; and the third a *Pastoral Symphony*, utterly different from Beethoven's and reflecting four successive aspects of the countryside: it owed a debt to the landscape of France in war-time (!), but is, like Beethoven's, universal in its outlook. After that, he startled the world with his harsh, revolutionary, dissonant Fourth Symphony, and then, paradoxically enough, conveyed the atmosphere of *The Pilgrim's Progress* in his tranquil, noble Fifth Symphony, composed amid the agony of the Second World War; and he waited to express the turmoil in his soul until after that ghastly conflict was ended, in the Sixth of his symphonies, which, however, finishes with a last movement of quiet, unearthly mystery.

Among his earlier orchestral, shorter, works, I would select *The Lark Ascending*, that exquisite piece for violin and orchestra which he prefaced by some lines from George Meredith and which he dedicated to Marie Hall, and the sublime *Fantasia on a Theme by Thomas Tallis* for double string orchestra and string quartet.

The 20th century English poetry which Vaughan Williams set to music early in his career was that of A. E. Housman, in his eloquent and beautiful song-cycle *On Wenlock Edge*. He drew on the American poet Walt Whitman again and again—in the lovely little choral work *Toward the Unknown Region*, in *A Sea Symphony*, and in parts of *Dona Nobis Pacem*—and on Robert Louis Stevenson in his ever-fresh *Songs of Travel*.

But the Bible, Shakespeare, and Bunyan, were, I think, the greatest of his literary influences. *The Pilgrim's Progress* seems always to

248

have been in the background of his mind, at least it came to the surface in his early, one-act opera *The Shepherds of the Delectable Mountains*, in the Fifth Symphony, and in the full-scale opera on the subject, which included *The Shepherds* again as one of its scenes. The opera 'The Pilgrim's Progress' did not win as much favour with the public as, in my judgment, it deserved. I loved it and was greatly impressed by it—a unique masterpiece, one of the few examples of genuinely religious music on the stage.[79]

This brings me to the part which religion played in Vaughan Williams's creative activity. He edited the English Hymnal for use in the Church of England, and was part editor of *Songs of Praise* and *The Oxford Book of Carols*. The *Tallis* Fantasia is based on a tenor melody which Tallis wrote for Archbishop Parker's Psalter, 'Why fumeth in sight ye Gentiles spight?' The quiet, peaceful *Mass in G minor* is one of the most beautiful settings of the Mass since Bruckner. *Flos Campi*, for viola, small wordless chorus and orchestra, has quotations from *The Song of Solomon* for each of its six movements, and the music is mystical in character. *Benedicite*, *Dona Nobis Pacem*, and *Hodie* ('This Day') are full of noble, simple, religious feeling. *Sancta Civitas* is a deeply felt oratorio set to words from the Book of Revelation, with additions from Taverner's Bible and the Sanctus of the Communion Service. *Job*, a *Masque for Dancing*, is a marvellous orchestral evocation of the Biblical story and William Blake's superb drawings.

Yet Ursula Vaughan Williams, the composer's widow, in her charming biography,[80] tells us that though he had been confirmed at Charterhouse 'as a matter of course' and went on going to church 'so as not to upset the family', he was actually an atheist in his later years at the school and at Cambridge, afterwards a 'cheerful agnostic' and 'never a professing Christian', in spite of the church traditions in his family. He loved the Authorized Version of the Bible, and the religious music of Bach, which he conducted with such authority.

Ursula Vaughan Williams[81] also recounts that he said later in life that of all his choral works *Sancta Civitas* was the one he liked

---

[79] I have written more fully about this very beautiful musical morality in my book *The Divine Quest in Music*, pp. 230-1.

[80] Ursula Vaughan Williams: *R.V.W., A biography of Ralph Vaughan Williams*, p. 29. She married him in 1953; his first wife had died in 1951 after 53 years of a devoted marriage.

[81] ibid., pp. 162-4.

best, and that 'it epitomizes much of his thought, belief and imagination.... The images of the river and the tree' (here and in "the yet unwritten *Pilgrim's Progress*") 'come from many mythologies', not only from Christianity. Vaughan Williams's own copy of the score has a quotation from F. J. Church's translation of Plato's 'Phaedo': 'A man of sense will not insist that things are exactly as I have described them. But I think he will believe that something of the kind is true of the soul and her habitations, seeing that she is shown to be immortal, and that it is worthwhile to stake everything on this belief. The venture is a fair one and he must charm his doubts with spells like these'. Mrs Vaughan Williams quotes from the article which her husband wrote on *The Letter and the Spirit* (in *Music and Letters*, 1920—reprinted in *National Music*, O.U.P., 1963) while he was beginning *Sancta Civitas*, and in which 'he summed up what he believed, both then and for the rest of his life: "Before going any further, may we take it that the subject of all art is to obtain a partial revelation of that which is beyond human senses and human faculties—of that in fact which is spiritual? And that the means we employ to induce this revelation are those very senses and faculties themselves? The human, visible, audible and intelligible media which artists (of all kinds) use, are symbols not of other visible and audible things but of what lies beyond sense and knowledge".'

It is, therefore, fair to say that he was certainly no materialist. Though he was agnostic, he was sufficiently spiritual-minded to be able to compose and arrange and edit Christian texts; their essential character seized upon his imagination, and this resulted in artistic creation. He, so to speak, composed like a Christian, even though he could not believe in the doctrines of Christianity; and he certainly behaved like one, for throughout his life he was constantly helping his fellow human beings. He was warm-hearted, noble, and courageous. In World War I, already middle-aged, he served as an orderly in the R.A.M.C. and later as a subaltern in the Royal Garrison Artillery (the Heavies), both at home and overseas: 'he was a kind, firm, and considerate officer'.[82] He hated the war; but though he could have stayed in the U.K., he felt bound to carry out what he believed to be 'his responsibility as a man, his duty as a citizen'.[83] And he did everything that an elderly man

[82] Letter from A. J. Moore to Ursula Vaughan Williams, 1958—quoted by her. ibid., p. 130.
[83] ibid., p. 132.

250

could do even in World War II to support a righteous cause. He helped refugees from the Nazi terror, and was a stalwart opponent of injustice in individual cases. It is no wonder that he was universally loved and respected. 'The towering furies of which he was capable, his fire, pride, and strength'—which his widow tells us[84] were all revealed in his Fourth Symphony, fit quite convincingly into this picture.

The exuberant and humorous sides of his nature were shown not only in private life but in his early opera *Hugh the Drover*, in the *Five Tudor Portraits* and in *Sir John in Love*, that delightful musical embodiment of *The Merry Wives*. But his greatest Shakespearean work, I think, is the *Serenade to Music*, originally for sixteen solo voices and orchestra, that wondrously beautiful setting of the immortal lines praising the art of music from the last Act of *The Merchant of Venice*, when Lorenzo and Jessica are sitting together outdoors on a lovely star-lit night and he tells her about the music of the spheres, before the minstrels come to sing to them. He showed a great gift for serene music, as we have seen elsewhere; another instance is the lovely string quartet No. 2 in A minor, *For Jean on her birthday*.

This astonishing veteran followed his sixth symphony with three more! The *Antartica* (No. 7), suggested by his incidental music for the film *Scott of the Antarctic*, impressively illustrates what 'programme music' is, for it aptly recalls certain non-musical ideas or events, without imitating them. The movements of the whales and the penguins are only incidental to the broad conception of man confronted with nature in her most austere, bleak aspect, in a symphony of great beauty and strength. The 8th Symphony reflects varying human emotions, ending joyously: the scherzo is for wind only, the serene Cavatina for strings alone. The Ninth Symphony starts in spiritual conflict, goes on to a menacing second movement and a sinister one next, but the Finale is *tranquillo*, though it only reaches complete spiritual peace and gentleness as the work ends in E major.

He died a few months after finishing that work—a great Englishman, a great musician, and a benefactor of his countrymen and of the world.

With William Walton I come to the first composer born later than myself to be considered in this book. Ernest Newman told us

[84] Ursula Vaughan Williams: ibid., p. 190.

to keep our eyes on Walton many years ago, when the latter was very young. He had captivated everybody with his brilliantly witty and charming music (originally for six instruments), accompanying Edith Sitwell's *Facade* poems, which were recited rhythmically; there have been various arrangements of it including ballet versions and two orchestral suites.

Walton has created four works for solo instruments and orchestra. The *Sinfonia Concertante*, with its pianoforte part, was more successful in its revised, 1943, version than in its original (1927) form, and when I heard it again in 1968 I once more enjoyed the terse, energetic allegro, the meditative andante, and the lively Finale. In the highly original Concerto for viola and orchestra (1928-29), the opening andante begins in reverie, rises to ecstasy, and returns to tranquillity; the ensuing *vivo* is brilliantly clever, cunningly scored, and imbued with vigorous life, whilst the Finale combines counterpoint with the spirit of the dance, represented by the rhythm of the tarantella but interpreted as part of life in a deeper sense. Then in 1939 came the Violin Concerto, complicated in technique and thought, but deeply impressive, with an *andante tranquillo* which is sometimes sad, sometimes peaceful, a 'presto capriccioso alla napolitana' which races along at a breakneck speed until it is interrupted by a slow kind of waltz, and a long, melodious Finale, with reminiscences of earlier themes. In 1956 we had the Cello Concerto, with its romantic *moderato*, its quick, sardonic, second movement, and, lastly, its profoundly beautiful theme and variations.

Meanwhile, Walton gave us two symphonies. The First (1932-5) has been justly acclaimed as one of the greatest symphonies of the century. In December, 1934, we had only the first three movements —the grand, tragic *Allegro assai*, the *presto con malizia* in angry mood, and the melancholy *andante*: these left us all waiting eagerly for the Finale, which was completed almost a year later and brought relief, ending in triumph. Twenty-five years later, the composer produced his second symphony, whereupon several critics objected to Walton not having marched with the times, i.e. the *avant garde* who had come to the fore meanwhile. The truth, as I see it, is that Walton is far too sincere an artist to jump on the 12-note, or any other, bandwagon that happens to be fashionable for a time. The first movement is terse, bracing, and vigorous; the slow movement, of great beauty and tenderness and thoughtfulness; the *Passacaglia* has a powerful ground bass, ten masterly variations,

252

a decisive, resolute *fugato*, and a confident, even joyous coda. There is no falling-off in Walton's powers in this fine work. He pursued his own way, too, in the Partita for Orchestra (1958), with its energetic first and third movements, its meditative and charming middle one, its clear structure and brilliant orchestration throughout. High spirits have often been a feature of his art—witness the *Portsmouth Point* and *Scapino* overtures. The string quartet in A minor (1947) was written subsequently to many of Schoenberg's and Webern's dodecaphonic works; but Walton had too much sense and dedication to his true artistic inclinations, to follow their idiom, which would not have suited his purposes: it is modern, yet based on tonality—in four movements, with the profoundly beautiful third slow, movement as the climax of the whole. The sonata for violin and pianoforte (1949) is another example of modern romanticism.

No one, I think, has tried to find fault with the much earlier *Belshazzar's Feast*, that tremendous, though brief, Old Testament oratorio; it was too stunning in its impact, whilst the lovely chorus *By the waters of Babylon* sounded the contrasting note of those enduring the sorrow of exile. The *Coronation Te Deum* (1952) was written in Walton's characteristic idiom of forthright expression.

Some voices were raised to criticise the opera *Troilus and Cressida* for being romantic and therefore already out of date when it appeared (1954). How foolish are these diatribes! Romanticism, as I have said so often that I fear my readers may accuse me of repetitiveness, is a permanent, or recurring, quality of human nature, varying only in degree at different stages of history. One of the chief values of this great opera is that, instead of following Shakespeare's embittered version, it reverts to Chaucer and ennobles the story, turning Cressida into a romantic, tragic heroine; the music matches Christopher Hassall's libretto in its passion and its ultimate exaltation.

By remaining true to his natural artistic instincts, and refusing to compose in any style that would have been alien to his sincerely felt inspiration merely because it had become fashionable, Walton has retained the affection, admiration, and respect of music lovers.

Michael Tippett's art is more difficult to understand than Walton's, though the first compositions of his which came into prominence were comparatively simple and immediate in their impact. These were the Concerto for double string orchestra (1939) and

253

the oratorio *A Child of our Time* (1941)—a most moving, eloquent, and beautiful work in an idiom still diatonic or else chromatic, yet individual and modern. The Negro spirituals are convincingly woven into a score which expressed the composer's indignation at the terrible racial persecutions carried out by the Nazis and his compassion for the victims, but which ends in hope and tranquillity.

He was still writing simply, in his lovely unaccompanied motets *Plebs angelica* and *The Weeping Babe*. But when he reached his First Symphony (1945) he seemed more detached in his outlook: the craftsmanship of this music is consummate throughout; there is cool emotion in the slow movement and a delicate charm in the scherzo. By the time of the Second Symphony (1958) his orchestral art seemed at first more intellectual than emotional; yet on further hearings I found the opening allegro bracing and vigorous, the adagio like a beautiful lake, the Presto brilliant, quirkish, and fantastic, and the Finale still restless, then quieter in mood, but ending joyfully. The piano concerto (1956) is poetic and subtle, at times gentle and almost childlike in its purity, though it becomes more complex; it has an elusive and visionary slow movement, and a quick, playful Finale, in the midst of which the soloist has some almost Spanish rhythms to play.

The Vision of St Augustine, for baritone, chorus and orchestra, is a work of penetrating vision, imagination, and great mastery, in which Tippett does not hesitate to use acute dissonance at times.

I have deliberately left his two remarkable operas to the last. *The Midsummer Marriage* (1955) is a symbolic opera, with a *prim' uomo* (Mark) and a *prima donna* (Jennifer) who have spiritual illusions, contrasted with a second pair of lovers whose illusions are social. Jennifer at first rebuffs Mark, but the archetypes 'take charge' (as Tippett puts it), she rises to a 'heaven' and he goes down to a 'hell'—which are, really, purifying ordeals—and eventually the two are transfigured. The music is often complex or mystical, but it ends in blissful simplicity. *King Priam* is in marked contrast. It is a tragic music-drama of great power and imagination, with strong emotional impact, fired by unity of subject (Man's choice). The utterance is stark, terse, and intensive.

In short, Tippett's art is intellectual as well as spiritual, human and profound. Much of it is dissonant, but much is *per contra*, hauntingly beautiful; all that I have heard is significant and striking.

254

My own experiences of the music of Benjamin Britten began
with the production of 'Peter Grimes' in June, 1945. In my book
Adventure in Music[85] I wrote: 'the fact that the whole work is
dominated by ... so miserable a creature as Grimes.... prevents
me from including it among the great tragic music-dramas of all
time'. (Edward Sackville-West) in his essay on the musical and
dramatic structure of *Peter Grimes*,[86] said that it is not a music-
drama, but an opera, because the voices, not the orchestra, predominate. But I still do not think that there is any basic distinction
between opera and music-drama). However, though Grimes *is* a
miserable creature, there is more pathos in him, according to
Britten's music and Montagu Slater's libretto, than there is in
George Crabbe's poem, in addition to sadism. The work is a
tragedy, not a sordid melodrama, and when I reflect on the mastery
with which Britten has expressed the atmosphere of the Suffolk
fishing Borough, the moods of the sea and the storm, the human
characters—the tender-hearted Ellen, whom he hopes to marry
but who is maternal in her attitude to him, the kindly retired sea-
captain Balstrode, and the others—I feel now that it is a great
opera; it begins with the inquest on Peter's first apprentice, in the
presence of a crowd of villagers, and it ends, not with his suicide
at sea, but with 'the cold beginning of another day', as the life of
the Borough returns to normal.

Britten has a great gift for tragedy, largely because, in addition
to his musical imagination and talent, compassion is a vital part
of his nature, at any rate as evinced in his art (I do not know him
personally). Hence *The Rape of Lucretia*, a kind of chamber opera,
based on the old pagan tale of horror, but framed in a Christian
setting by the commentators in the Prologue and Epilogue. *Billy
Budd*, considering its all-male cast, has astonishing variety: we
have the atmosphere of the sea again, the songs of the sailors, the
tense drama of the terrible story, the long succession of common
chords while Captain Vere is off the stage to tell Budd the court's
verdict, the deep humanity of the music, the spirit of forgiveness,
repentance and comfort so eloquently conveyed. *Gloriana* received
so beautiful a production as the *Coronation* opera in 1953 at
Covent Garden that in spite of the excellence of the performance
its musical quality was, somehow, not then fully realised by critics
or audiences. I can claim to have enjoyed it tremendously then,

[85] R. W. S. Mendl: *Adventure in Music*, p. 99.
[86] *Peter Grimes*, Sadler's Wells Opera Books, p. 27.

and when it was revived at Sadler's Wells, I realised, as others did, that it is a great opera. There are many attractive features, for much of the music is melodious both in the songs and the dances for the Masque and at the Court ball. Yet this is not only English history, but tragedy—perhaps too tragic for Coronation time. It leads to the execution of Essex as a traitor, and to the grief of Queen Elizabeth, who reluctantly signs his death warrant. Once more, Britten has expressed deep compassion in his music.

The Turn of the Screw is a masterly opera, based on Henry James's novel. The scoring is deft and delicate, and some passages, such as the welcome and the earlier ones associated with the children, are charming. As befits the subject, however, the music is often chilly, grizzly, and eerie, and there is too much monotony of mood and feeling. In great tragedies there is excitement, and, in the greatest of them, colour. In this work there is neither. This was probably inevitable if an opera was to be based on this particular story at all, and no one could have set James's conception more appropriately than Britten has done. I have heard it several times, but alas! I have not really *enjoyed* the experience, though I am as capable of enjoying tragedy as comedy. There is a difference between enjoyment and admiration.

Meanwhile, Britten had been turning to comedy as well. *Albert Herring* is good fun in parts, but in spite of its many felicities is somewhat long-drawn-out for the tenuous subject, though this is partly due to the libretto. *Let's make an opera* is a light-hearted entertainment for children, who always seem to enjoy it—a kind of opera within an opera. Britten's comedy triumph is the opera for which he and Peter Pears wrote the libretto based on *A Midsummer Night's Dream*. I have heard it said that this work is not joyous enough, compared with Shakespeare's play; but the lovers' quarrel and the superb music for the rude mechanicals both in rehearsal and in the performance of *Pyramus and Thisbe* before Theseus and Hippolyta and the courtiers and the rest, are full of wit and humour which is both robust and subtle. The nocturnal magic of the wood and the fairy atmosphere are marvellously conveyed. This is a richly imaginative score.[87]

The Prince of the Pagodas, with choreography and scenario by John Cranko and music by Britten, is a lovely ballet, both to see and to hear. The composer again reveals his insight into fairyland.

[87] I have written more fully about this exquisite opera in *Adventure in Music*, pp. 114-5: (in the middle of p. 115, 'distant' is a misprint for 'distinct')

I found the final divertissement too long (in 1957), but otherwise the music is colourful, multifarious, and enchanting.

Britten is both versatile and prolific. He has also composed chamber music, song cycles for soloists both with pianoforte and with orchestra, purely orchestral symphonies and one for solo voice, chorus, and orchestra, concertos, choral works, and, more recently, 'church operas'. I can only be selective here.

The string quartet No. 2 in C (1945) struck me as being structurally the work of a very accomplished composer; but Britten is a man who needs the stimulus of words, or at least of extra-musical ideas, to fire his imagination. Thus the purely orchestral *Sinfonia de Requiem* (originally written in 1940 for the Japanese Government in commemoration of the 2,600th anniversary of the Imperial dynasty, but rejected by them, and dedicated 'in memory of my parents') has a profoundly sad *Lacrymosa*, a terrifying *Dies Irae*, and a comforting and utterly tranquil *Requiem aeternam*. The *Spring Symphony*, op. 44, (1948), for three soloists, chorus and orchestra, is in four contrasted parts, roughly corresponding to the traditional symphonic movements, but is set to English poetry from most varied sources and periods, all impregnated with spring feeling—16th century (anon.). Spenser, Nashe, Peele, Clare, Milton, Herrick, W. H. Auden, Barnefield, Blake, and Beaumont and Fletcher, with 'Sumer is y cumen in' interposed. It is a most vivid, fresh and joyous work.

The *Variations on a theme of Frank Bridge* (1937) are not entirely absolute music in the sense of being simply sound patterns; for not only are they linked with Britten's memory of his much loved and respected master, but they have associations with dance rhythms and with the thought of death. Even the *Variations on a theme of Purcell* are based on a splendid melody from Purcell's incidental music to Aphra Behn's play *Abdelazar, or the Moor's Revenge*, though they were originally intended to show to 'young persons' the different uses of the various instruments of the orchestra. The Cello Symphony (1964), in four movements, is something between a symphony and a concerto: intense and tragic at the outset; then, weird and even macabre; next, solemn and almost funereal' and finally, affirmative and majestic.

Les Illuminations (1937), for high voice and string orchestra, is a very imaginative setting of eight songs by Rimbaud, preceded by a *Fanfare*. The *Serenade* for tenor, horn, and strings (1943) is a cycle of lovely songs, voicing different conceptions of Night and set to six poems on the subject—*Pastoral* by Cotton, *Nocturne* by Tennyson, *Elegy* to words by Blake, the anonymous (15th century) *A Lyke-Wake Dirge*, Ben Jonson's *Hymn to Diana*, and Keats's Sonnet *To Sleep*. The 1958 *Nocturne* for tenor, obbligato instruments and string orchestra, set to poetry by Shelley, Tennyson, Coleridge, Middleton, Wordsworth, Wilfred Owen, Keats, and Shakespeare, is another beautiful cycle, a worthy follower to its predecessor.

Britten has written many lovely choral compositions, apart from the *Spring Symphony*. His *Hymn to St Cecilia*, unaccompanied and set to words by W. H. Auden, is a beautiful work, coming very appropriately from a composer born on November 22nd (St Cecilia's Day). *A Ceremony of Carols* is a somewhat unequal creation. But the *St Nicolas Cantata* (1948) grows upon me with each successive hearing: the finest sections, I feel, however, are No. 4 *He journeys to Palestine*, with the delicate accompaniment on two pianos, Britten's additions to the hymn melodies, especially *The Old Hundredth* (in No. 5), *Nicolas and the pickled boys* (No. 7), and the simple and attractive No. 8—*His Piety and Marvellous Works*; I love the waltz medium, but still find its gay dance rhythm (in No. 2, *The Birth of Nicolas*) somewhat incongruous in this work.

The *Cantata Academica* (1959), commissioned for the 500th anniversary of Basle University, is a cheerful, festive *pièce d'occasion*, but not Britten at his greatest. The *Cantata Misericordiam*, on the other hand, composed specially for the Red Cross celebrations at Geneva in 1963, is a most moving embodiment of the story of the Good Samaritan, for tenor, baritone, small chorus, and various instruments.

The *War Requiem* (1962), for three soloists, instrumental ensemble, full chorus, boys' choir, organ, and orchestra, marked the climax to which Britten's religious compositions had been moving throughout the years. The words of the Latin Mass for the Dead are marvellously interwoven with nine poems by Wilfred Owen, which help to make the work supremely relevant to the 20th century. Owen was killed at the age of twenty-four, on the Western Front, only a week before the armistice of November, 1918, and his words from a Preface to a book of poems which he was preparing are quoted at the head of Britten's score: 'My subject is War and the pity of War. The poetry is the pity. All a poet can do is to warn.' This is a most profound masterpiece, in some places dissonant and disturbing, in others supremely beautiful and

258

comforting. It ends in peace and harmony—both in the technically musical and the spiritual sense of the term—as an English and a German soldier whom he had killed in battle meet in a vision after death in 'some profound dull tunnel' and are reconciled, and the glorious music of the boys' choir, soprano solo, chorus, and orchestra, escorts them into Paradise.

Britten's church operas began with *Noye's Fludde* (1958), a setting of one of the Chester Miracle Plays to be performed mainly by children, with a few adults, complete with *Noah's Ark* and a delightfully naïve 'flood' and 'rainbow' when I saw it in St Pancras Church: Britten always composes simply, for performances by children, yet never lowers his artistic level. *Curlew River* (1964), 'a parable for church performance', with libretto by William Plomer, is a kind of Christianised version of the medieval Japanese *No* drama, *Sumidawaga*, by Jûrô Motomasa (1395-1431), transferred to an English setting of Curlew River and a church in the Fens. It starts (and ends) with a procession of monks and acolytes singing the plainsong hymn *Te lucis ante terminum* and then performing the parable of a demented mother seeking her lost child: there are six soloist-singers, a very small chorus, and seven instrumentalists. At the outset, both words and music are very mournful, but from the moment when the other characters start to express pity for the madwoman and to pray for her, until the dénouement when her dead son's voice is heard and his spirit actually appears, the work becomes consolatory and illumined with a Christian message of faith, hope, and love, which subdue the previous anguish. Apart from the plainchant, the music is not, strictly, melodious, but speaks in a 20th century kind of unending melody which sometimes uses dissonance (in the instruments) but is vocally more in the nature of an eloquent recitative and an ecclesiastical chant. It is a most moving creation. *The Burning Fiery Furnace* (1966) is also a church parable, equally beautiful, and conceived for a similar type of performance, but is based on the Biblical story of Shadrach, Meshach, and Abednego, in the Book of Daniel, chapter three.

Unfortunately, I have not yet been able either to hear or see the third 'Parable for Church Performance', *The Prodigal Son*.

This sounds as though I have broken off, rather than finished, this chapter. Well, of course! Britten, God bless him! is twenty-one years my junior.

CHAPTER THIRTY-SIX

Backwards and Forwards

What a lot of composers I have discussed! And yet how many who are either great or have been acclaimed as such have scarcely been mentioned by me! In my Prologue (chapter one) I said that 'this is essentially a book about my love of music and the composers who have meant most to me or have made appreciable contributions to my musical experience'. As it is a kind of musical autobiography, it seems to me relevant to refer, however briefly, to various other composers whose works I have either enjoyed or have at least recognised from my personal experience as being important in the musical scene.

Our own Golden Age of music in the Tudor and early Jacobean period has meant a great deal to me for a good many years. In addition to Byrd (discussed in chapter 23), Tallis, with his glorious forty-voiced motet *Spem in alium* and his other religious music, both Latin and English; the exquisite madrigals and other secular part-songs of Morley, Weelkes, and Wilbye; the church music and madrigals of Orlando Gibbons—all these have refreshed my spirit and enchanted my ear. What a relief it is to turn back to them after listening to some of the horrors which the 20th century has inflicted upon us!

It is only in comparatively recent times that I have extended my acquaintance of German music backwards in time to the period before Bach, by hearing, for example, the noble, more austere, but expressive and dramatic, religious music of Heinrich Schütz.

Vivaldi is also a post-World-War-II discovery for me. No wonder that Bach loved his music so much. What has struck me forcibly about it is that here is an early 18th century master with a distinctly *romantic* side to his artistic nature, in addition to his gift of portraying emotions and describing Nature in instrumental forms. I have chiefly got to know him as a delightful composer for string instruments, especially in violin concertos. His beautiful, vivid, and expressive setting of the Gloria of the Mass is the only example of his church music which I have been lucky enough to hear.

François Couperin is another partly romantic composer of the Vivaldi epoch. His enchanting pieces for clavecin are permeated by dance rhythms and mostly bear fanciful or romantic descriptive titles with which the music is entirely in keeping; and in addition to his chamber music, in which beautiful melodies and charming dances abound, he was a great composer for the church, creating in his youth two organ masses which consist of exquisite organ interludes between the various parts of the liturgy, a series of fine motets, and later in his life the three *Leçons de Ténèbres* for one or two voices with organ and viol continuo, which are full of religious feeling.

Switching back to Italy and to the 17th and very early 18th centuries, Corelli's works for strings, in some of which Kreisler used to excel as the soloist, and Domenico Scarlatti's delicate little sonatas for harpsichord, have consistently refreshed me: I have never been a great enthusiast for the tone of the harpsichord unaccompanied, and am not averse from hearing Scarlatti's works played on a modern piano, provided that the soloist is fine-fingered enough, but I must admit that, like Couperin's, they are better suited to the type of instrument for which they were written, whereas Bach's *klavier* compositions, if performed on a piano by such artists as Harold Samuel, James Ching, Myra Hess, Denis Matthews, or Rosalyn Tureck, are sufficiently universal in time and character to overlap the centuries to the modern instrument.

In recent years—thanks to visiting Italian players and the B.B.C. —I have been able to realise that Boccherini composed a lot of beautiful and delicate chamber music besides the famous and delicious Minuet in A which has been performed in an orchestral version in England ever since my boyhood.

Moving on in Italian musical history, I come to Rossini, Bellini, and Donizetti. I have never been a 100 per cent Rossini enthusiast, but have found the wit and fun of the *Barbiere di Siviglia* irresistible. Inevitably it invites comparison—not to its advantage—with Mozart's *Figaro*, because each is based on a (different) part of the same story. But Rossini's opera is pure farce—perhaps the finest farce in the operatic world—and the sparkle and pace of the music are so brilliant that one readily accepts the lack of emotion. *Le Comte d'Ory* is a charming opera; and so is *La Cenerentola*, but I miss the *magic* of the original Cinderella fairytale, which the librettist and composer deliberately excluded; and I am not an addict of *coloratura* (whether for soprano or, as here, for contralto), unless it be used, as Mozart employed it, to express some kind of emotion such as the furious or revengeful feelings of the *Queen of the Night* in *Die Zauberflöte* or the murderous determination of Vitellia in *La Clemenza di Tito*. Rossini's 'coloratura' is mere ornament, designed to show off the technical skill of the performer. And that, I am afraid, is partly what puts me off Bellini and Donizetti to some extent; but I have enjoyed the purity of line, the elegant legato of the melodies, and the composer's dramatic sense, in *Norma*. Donizetti's *Lucia di Lammermoor* did not interest me very much, but *Don Pasquale* is an enchanting and delightful comedy.

Rossini's gift is, for the most part, for music which is either happy or comic, rather than serious or tragic. This is in keeping with the character of this genial, courteous, witty and good-humoured man. Who would have guessed—without being told—that the stimulating overture to *Semiramide* (at which I was absolutely *electrified* once by Toscanini) is the prelude to a tragedy? Even his *Stabat Mater* is charming and theatrical in style, rather than intrinsically religious or liturgical. Yet he showed in *William Tell* that he could write fine serious music for a serious operatic subject, though the opera is far too long and is dull in parts. The overture, I am glad to say, is often with us in concert programmes, and is almost like a short symphony in four connected movements, each representing Rossini at his greatest: a slow introduction, beautifully describing a tranquil Alpine scene; one of the grandest storms in musical history; a beautiful *Ranz des Vaches*; and a rousing, victorious Finale, in quick tempo, which never fails to stir an audience to enthusiasm.

In the last part of his life, Rossini wrote some delightful pieces for pianoforte and other instruments, some of which Respighi most skilfully orchestrated for that joyous ballet, *La Boutique Fantasque*.

Liszt's music is a strange medley of authentic emotion, empty rhetoric and even bombast, charm, glitter, vivid description of Nature, and sincere religious feeling. You get glitter and real charm side by side in the First Piano Concerto in E flat, cheerfulness and vigour in the Hungarian rhapsodies, charm again and genuine emotion in *Les Années de Pélérinage*, romance and rhetoric in the Second Piano Concerto in A, and a curious combination of this rhetorical element with real grandeur of spirit in the B minor

Sonata for piano—a work which, I always feel, just misses being one of the great pianoforte sonatas of all time.

Liszt is enormously important from the standpoint of musical history, in having invented the symphonic poem as an art-form; admittedly, its origin can be traced back to the greatest of Beethoven's dramatic overtures—*Leonora No.* 2 and *No.* 3, *Coriolan,* and *Egmont*—and to his Pastoral Symphony (especially, perhaps, the three connected last movements of it—the Peasants' Festival, the Storm, and the Shepherd's Thanksgiving after the Storm); and I do not think that any of Liszt's symphonic poems are great masterpieces. Nevertheless, he was the pioneer of a form of music which his successors developed and which reached its zenith in Elgar's glorious *Symphonic Study: Falstaff.* Liszt's sacred choral art is not among the greatest devotional compositions of the world, but it does contain some beautiful, intrinsically religious music, for example in the *Requiem* and the oratorio *Christus.* In my humble view, his supreme masterpiece is the *Faust Symphony,* in which each of the three principal characters of Goethe's great work, Faust, Gretchen, and Mephistopheles, is portrayed respectively in the three movements in brilliant fashion, and the work ends with a short setting of Goethe's final *Chorus Mysticus.*

Liszt's music has been with me, on and off, all my life; he is not one of my favourites, but as a composer he has his great moments; he must have been one of the very finest pianists who ever lived; and as a man, side by side with his amatorial adventures, he was a marvel of self-sacrificing generosity and kindness to his fellow-musicians and others.[88]

I have hitherto discussed only two Russian composers, Tchaikovsky and Mussorgsky. Borodin and Rimsky-Korsakov have also played their part in my musical enjoyment—Borodin, chiefly because of the splendid Symphony No. 2 in B minor, the eloquent and moving Second String Quartet in D, and, above all, the colourful and melodious, though undramatic, *Prince Igor.* Nowadays we do not hear or see so much of this very fine, albeit rambling, opera, apart from the vivid and deservedly popular Polovtsian choral dances; I had the privilege of hearing it performed by Russian soloists, with the great Chaliapin in the part of Khan Khontchak. Borodin had a rich lyrical gift and a flair for beautiful instrumentation.

I greatly enjoyed three of Rimsky-Korsakov's operas, *The Snow*

[88] I have written more fully about Liszt in Chapter 12 of *The Divine Quest in Music.*

Maiden, Sadko, and *The Golden Cockerel*—which has been revived here more recently. There is a wealth of lovely melody, brilliant and masterly orchestration in Rimsky-Korsakov's scores, and
in *The Golden Cockerel* a fascinating blend of fairy tale with
satire. *Antor* is really an interesting kind of symphonic poem in
four movements, rather than a symphony. *Scheherazade* is a richly
coloured suite describing four tales from the Arabian Nights, with
a sort of orchestral recitative connecting them, as Scheherazade
passes from one story to another to keep the Sultan Shahriar entertained. (The ballet devised for some of this music is very striking
and tragic, but quite irrelevant to the stories which the composer
sought to depict—and, as such, unsatisfactory from a music lover's
standpoint).

Skriabin and Medtner are two other Russian composers who at
different times figured fairly prominently in my musical experience. Skriabin created a sensation in London in the years just
before World War I with his striking orchestral works: *The
Divine Poem*, which is something between a symphonic poem and
a symphony and presents a struggle between sensual desires and
the 'divine joy' of the spirit; *The Poem of Ecstasy*, which is indeed
ecstatic, but also hysterical, though masterly in its handling of its
material; and *Prometheus: the Poem of Fire*, in which magic is
portrayed with great fervour, though its keyboard of light somehow did not prove successful in practice. Skriabin came to London
and performed his earlier piano concerto in F sharp minor with
the Queen's Hall Orchestra under Sir Henry Wood; it proved to
be a readily accessible work, romantic and distinctly indebted to
Chopin, though in a more modern idiom. The same applies to some
extent to his more original compositions for pianoforte solo, which
continue to give pleasure on those occasions when they are performed nowadays. Though some reflect the influence of Chopin,
there is also a diabolic element in them, inherited from Liszt. The
career of this intriguing composer was cut short in 1915 by his
death at the age of forty-four.

I was something of a Medtner fan for a short time in the late
1920's. He was over here from his native Moscow and his subsequent visits to Germany, U.S.A. and Paris, in 1928, as pianist and
composer, and ultimately was to live in England from 1936 until
he died (aged seventy-one) in 1951. On his father's side he had
German blood in his veins, and this probably accounts for the
Central European, albeit individual, character of his music. He be-

longs essentially to the diatonic/chromatic tradition; but though he was conservative, his art expresses deeply felt emotions in generalised forms, without any attempt at detailed or picturesque description. He was, first and foremost, a composer for the piano, and though he wrote *Fairy Tales*, *Dithyrambs*, *Novels*, and *Forgotten Melodies*, as well as sonatas, he never went beyond such vague titles as those; even his songs were reflections of the general mood or atmosphere of the poem, rather than of its literary details; and the pianoforte part in them is as important as the voice. I have always found his sincere, imaginative, romantic, thoughtful, serious-minded music very attractive.

Humperdinck is a *petit maître*, but is not to be regarded as a kind of light-weight Wagner, just because he was obviously indebted to Wagner's orchestration; for otherwise his musical mentality was utterly different from that of his mighty predecessor and compatriot. *Hänsel und Gretel* is an enchanting fairy opera —a musical counterpart to the Grimm story. *Königskinder* is also enchanting, though its tragic ending has prevented its being the regularly popular children's opera that the other has been. I was present at its first Frankfurt performance in 1911, when the composer was present, looking physically like a modern Socrates! After that I heard it on two or three more occasions. He also wrote the attractive, though less remarkable, incidental music for *The Miracle*, of which Max Reinhardt gave the first production, in London at Olympia, but which my wife and I saw when it was revived at the Lyceum Theatre, transformed into the semblance of a church: we remember how lovely Lady Diana Duff Cooper looked, as the Madonna.

But this post-Wagnerian euphony in Germany and Austria did not really last beyond Mahler and Humperdinck. Already, Richard Strauss had started the falling-off in Teutonic greatness with his sadistic *Salome* and his blood-bath in *Elektra*, the strident din of battle in *Ein Heldenleben*, and its cacophonous 'enemies', and the crude imitation of the actual bleating of sheep which is the one blot on the otherwise masterly, splendid, and human music of *Don Quixote*. Schoenberg lowered the Wagnerian idiom into the overripe plums of *Gürrelieder* and the all too luscious, long drawn out strains of *Verklärte Nacht*, until he realised that he could go no further in that direction. A half-way house, as it were, to something new, was the First Chamber Symphony, in which his muse has a slimmer figure and still has a key (E major), but which could

265

scarcely be called great. Thence he passed into atonality and composed that miserable nightmare *Erwartung*, which is duly dissonant but left one listener, at least, quite unmoved. After that, he produced *Pierrot lunaire* (1912), in which the chamber instruments are made to go crazy, while the narrator utters low moanings or screams her head off fortissimo in an apparent endeavour to drown the nasty sounds of the players; and, by way of contrast, the Four Songs with orchestra (op. 22), which are merely monotonous. The time had come, he thought, for music to be not just atonal (keyless), but to have a new language altogether. So he scratched his head, and invented twelve-note technique, to replace (so far as he was concerned) the old major and minor system—serial music based on four, twelve-note, arbitrary tone-rows, twelve because there is that number of notes in the chromatic scale; transpose each of these rows to the twelve notes of that scale, and you have plenty of scope for a variety of invention. It looked ingenious on paper, but was liable to produce sounds that were very hard on the ear.[89] This new method was pursued in various works—chamber music, the violin concerto, and the opera *Moses and Aaron*, with a libretto by Schoenberg himself, based on the Book of Exodus; I have heard it several times, in addition to seeing the marvellous Covent Garden production in 1965. Before the first performance at our Royal Opera House, there was not a great demand for seats, but the moment that the reviews appeared in the Press and the public were told that the scene of the Golden Calf in Act II was being performed as an orgy of drunkenness and voluptuousness, not excluding rape, on the stage, the crowds flocked to see it. There is, of course, nothing to suggest this in the Old Testament text (Exodus XXXII), where the people worship the Calf with burnt offerings and peace offerings, eat and drink, play, dance and sing. The orgy of drunkenness and sexual excess is Schoenberg's invention. When the music was subsequently given a *concert* performance by the same singers and players at a Prom., the Albert Hall was less than half full. The idea behind the opera is superb. Schoenberg was a deep thinker, and was quite justified in adapting the Bible narrative and making Moses a great, but far from eloquent, prophet and leader and Aaron the eloquent mouthpiece (see Exodus IV, 10-16) and the man who sinned in giving the people the Golden Calf. The religious conception of the drama is wonderful, and it is

[89] I have written more fully about twelve-note technique in *Adventure in Music*, pp. 33-4.

unfortunate that Act II (beyond which Schoenberg did not compose any more music) ends with Moses falling to the ground in despair, as the people follow the pillar of fire and the pillar of cloud on their way towards the Promised Land without him (this, of course, is a departure from the Biblical story, in which the pillars of fire and of cloud appear before the crossing of the Red Sea, and all sorts of things happen after *Exodus* and ultimately, towards the end of *Deuteronomy*, Moses leads them as far as Mount Nebo, whence he can see the land, but is not allowed to enter it himself and dies on the mountain). *As it stands*, the performance ends in tragedy for Moses, whereas Schoenberg conceived the opera as ending with his spiritual triumph. Aaron's sudden death, in the synopsis for the uncompleted Act III, is also not in the Bible, where he dies on Mount Hor at as late a point in the great story as Numbers XX, 28. The music is uniformly dissonant and distressing to the ear. Schoenberg had become wedded to his twelve-note technique, and had acquired such mastery of it that he composed in it quite naturally; for the ordinary music-lover there is nothing to 'catch on to', as there is in the case of many composers later in time than him, such as Tippett or Britten. I do not believe that I would recognise the music of this opera again, even if I were to hear it twenty times! It makes its impact, but—whether loud or soft—what a painful one! Nor am I convinced by the *Sprechstimme* idea (which Schoenberg had previously used in *Pierrot lunaire*). Moses speaks throughout, he never sings, the intention being (according to Egon Wellesz's introductory note to the Covent Garden programme) that he should 'refuse to express his ideas in poetic language', because he could not put his thoughts into words; Aaron was to be his mouthpiece, and so Aaron sings. Yet Schoenberg called himself a disciple of Bach, Beethoven, and Brahms (among others) and therefore it is strange that he should have thought that music is not an appropriate means of expressing the most divine, religious thoughts and ideas. *They* did so by means of music. In denying music to the part of Moses, Schoenberg, so far from having 'a stroke of genius' (as Wellesz says), abrogated his function, in my view, and lost a great opportunity: here, if anywhere, was his chance of proving that he could write sublime music. At the end of Act II, Moses exclaims 'Oh, Word, Word, Word that I lack!' I felt almost inclined to cry out 'My dear fellow, you've been speaking *words* to us for most of the evening; it is music, music, music, that you lack!'

267

I am afraid that I have not fared much better with Webern, who adopted Schoenberg's twelve-note system. His works often do have the merit of brevity—so that one's agony is soon over!—and they are full of subtlety and refinement and masterly workmanship. Many of the orchestral and chamber music pieces are odd little whiffs of sound. Some people find this music beautiful: if they honestly enjoy it, God bless them! I regret that I cannot share their enthusiasm.

Personally, I can see rather more in the art of Alban Berg. Obviously, he was a highly gifted composer. *Wozzeck* is largely a painful score, expressing a sordid story, but Marie's prayer and the compassionate orchestral interlude before the last scene are beautiful by any reckoning. *Lulu* is wholly twelve-note and tells an even more sordid tale in music of unrelieved dissonance. But in the violin concerto, which Berg wrote shortly before he died and dedicated to the memory of the beautiful daughter of Mahler's widow by a second marriage after her tragic death at eighteen from poliomyelitis, his twelve-note medium yields ultimately to the diatonic idiom and ends in consolation on the basis of a lovely Bach chorale. Would that this might have proved to be an omen of the future development of music!

Ravel was a few months younger than Schoenberg. He, too, was regarded as a dangerous revolutionary—at the outset. This seems strange to us nowadays, for his music is firmly based on tonality throughout his career. But he was a very original composer and enlarged the harmonic vocabulary, even though he did not do this in so definite a way as Debussy did with his use of the whole tone scale. Carlotta de Feo once said to me that she was inclined to think that among French composers he was even greater than Debussy. I would not go so far as that; for I feel that he had not as *deeply* imaginative a poetic gift as Debussy: his music is, as it were, rather nearer the surface. None of his works has the depth of insight, the penetrating vision, that the other master revealed in the *Three Nocturnes* or *La Mer* or *Pelléas et Mélisande*, nor is his string quartet on a level with Debussy's. And one could not conceive Debussy creating a piece such as Ravel's popular *Bolero*, which undoubtedly makes its sensational impact, but is simply a long crescendo of increasingly elaborate orchestration based on insignificant thematic material. Nevertheless, Ravel was a great, attractive, and subtle composer. *L'Heure espagnole* is a delightful and witty little operatic comedy. *Daphnis et Chloé* is a

268

brilliant evocation of the Greek legend on an extended scale, richly and superbly orchestrated. *Ma Mère l'Oye* is a charming setting of Perrault's famous fairy tale. *La Valse*, which some critics do not rate highly in his *oeuvre*, always seems to me to be a wonderful transformation of the 19th century waltz medium into a 20th century French idiom. *Le Tombeau de Couperin* is both enchanting and moving. *Sheherazade* is a lovely song cycle—dreamy, sad, and exotic—and the *Trois Poèmes de Stéphane Mallarmé* are a subtle and beautiful composition for the unusual combination of voice, pianoforte, string quartet, two flutes, and two clarinets. Ravel had a genius for instrumentation, and presented some of his works in alternative versions either for pianoforte or for orchestra, so successfully that there is nothing to choose between them. His orchestral arrangement of Mussorgsky's *Pictures for an exhibition* is far more interesting than the pianoforte original! Yet it is nowhere unduly elaborate. Ravel was, for the most part, an exceptionally fastidious artist, and his compositions for solo piano, such as *Pavane pour une enfante défunte, Jeux d'eau, Gaspard de la nuit*, and *Valses nobles et sentimentales*, are the products of a poetical and very sensitive mind.

Unlike Mendelssohn, Mahler, Offenbach and Milhaud, all of whom were of Jewish blood, Ernest Bloch—who was born in Switzerland, lived also in Belgium, Germany, France, Italy, and eventually became a citizen of the U.S.A.—composed a good deal of which is intrinsically Jewish in character. He wrote that he tried to transcribe in his art 'the Jewish soul, the complex, glowing, agitated soul that I feel vibrating throughout the Bible ... the venerable emotion of the race that slumbers way down in my soul'. Though anger and a desire for revenge were foreign to his own nature, he could, as an artist, express them, as well as grief and despair, in his setting of Psalm 137 for soprano and orchestra, but not more eloquently than the poetical idea of sea, river and mountains participating in the worship of the Lord in Psalm 114. He voiced profound emotion and yearning in *Schelomo* (Solomon) for cello and orchestra, based on the Book of Ecclesiastes which was traditionally attributed to King Solomon. The *Israel* Symphony passes through intensity to serene entreaty at the end. Above all, in his *Sacred Service* for baritone solo, chorus and orchestra, he exalts the Jewish Sabbath morning service into Judaism's gift to all mankind in the worship of a loving God and the brotherhood of men.

This explains why so much of Bloch's music is not specifically

269

Jewish, but universal. In *Voice in the Wilderness*, for pianoforte and cello, he meditates in six sections, on man's life and ends in spiritual triumph. In the string quartets and the piano quintet he delves into deep human emotions. In the Symphony in E flat (1954-5), composed in his old age, the music is terse, impressive, but more restrained than in the works of his early or middle periods: it is thoughtful, rather than highly emotional. And human emotions and thoughts, whether Jewish or universal, were not the only inspiration of his music. In *Winter-Spring* (an early work) he had beautifully portrayed natural scenes, and in the 'symphonic fresco' *Helvetia* (completed in 1928), the mountains seem to be almost as important as the inhabitants of his native land.

Bloch did not use actual Hebrew musical elements to any great extent, and doubted whether the traditional ones attributed to such sources really came from them or from elsewhere. In any case, in his art he interpreted 'the Jewish soul' in the spirit rather than in the letter, and in its noblest form; and he was concerned with something wider than Judaism.

Bartók and Kodály were close friends, both Hungarians, and both deeply imbued with the spirit of Hungary's folk music, into which they made intense researches. Yet in other respects, as artists they were poles apart. Bartók started traditionally enough, and in his one-act opera 'Duke Bluebeard's Castle' (composed in 1911) he had not given up the diatonic/chromatic idiom, though it contains some elements of his later modernism: he tells the old tale in a symbolic form, by means of music which is evocative, suggestive, and at times beautiful even to conservative ears, and also profound. But as time went on, he gradually turned his back on tonality, and resorted neither to that nor to twelve-note technique (except to a small extent), but to almost any method which suited his highly individual and flexible purposes—whether ancient scales, oriental, modal or pentatonic, or the whole-tone scale or quarter-tones. His music is often difficult to understand, especially in the third of his six string quartets. But the effort is always immensely worth while, for Bártok was a profound composer and, indeed, one of the finest musical geniuses of the 20th century. I myself think that the view which has been expressed, that his string quartets are the greatest since Beethoven's, somewhat overstates the case—when one remembers the achievements of Brahms, Franck, Debussy, and Janáček for instance, in this field —but they become increasingly rewarding the more frequently one hears them. Bartók's rhythms are always striking, whether in his quartets, piano concertos, pieces for solo pianoforte, or in the *Music for strings, percussion, and celesta*; and in the last phase of his life his art became increasingly approachable, so that most music lovers, I fancy, would join me in calling the Concerto for Orchestra, the sixth string quartet, the violin concerto, and the third piano concerto, beautiful and enjoyable even at a first hearing.

By contrast, Kodály was not a revolutionary composer. His absorption in Magyar folk music found a counterpart in his natural gift for melody. His instrumentation is always artistic, his scores essentially melodic. Thus, the *Ballet Music* (1925) and the *Dances for Galanta* are evocative, melodious, and picturesquely orchestrated. The *Variations on a Hungarian folk-song* (The Peacock) have a 'rich, not gaudy' orchestration, and a superb variety of moods and colours, whilst the *Concerto for Orchestra* finely expresses emotion through counterpoint in a modern (1940) but approachable idiom. *The Spinning Room* (a scene from Transylvanian village life)— really a short, one-act opera—is full of simple, attractive, Hungarian folk-tunes embedded and absorbed into a beautiful, characteristically Kodály-ish score. Like most British music lovers, I have never heard the opera *Háry Janos* complete, and know only the delightful and imaginative music contained in the orchestral suite based upon it. The *Psalmus Ungaricus*, a setting of Psalm 55 for tenor solo, chorus and orchestra, is a masterpiece of strength, fire, and grandeur. In the Symphony (1961), Kodály continued to compose charming melodies firmly entrenched in the key system, with Magyar rhythms. He may not be so profound or intellectual a composer as Bartók, or historically so striking, but he is an important figure in 20th century music.

In 1927, Hindemith wrote: 'What is to be generally regretted today is the loose relation maintained by music between the producer and the consumer'. So he favoured *Gebrauchsmusik*—work-a-day music, utility music, as it has been called, music 'made as decently as I could' (according to his description): he called himself a workman, and wrote works that would be useful for the young, even for children at play, for amateurs, films, community singing, or mechanical instruments. But later on he declared that what he meant was that music serves ends beyond itself, is an instrument in the larger purposes of life. I confess that on my first acquaintance with his early, so-called *Gebrauchsmusik*, I felt that this marked a falling-off from the finest legacies of his great Teutonic predecessors. But as time went on, and I discovered these 'larger purposes of life' in his more mature and greater works, I came to admire and to enjoy them in ever-increasing measure. We may agree with Hindemith's theories to the extent that there should be a relation between composer and listener. But the term utility or work-a-day music is scarcely applicable to such creations as *Das Unaufhörliche, Mathis der Maler, Nobilissima Visione*, the Symphony in E flat, or *Die Harmonie der Welt*.

The oratorio *Das Unaufhörliche* (The Unceasing) is based on a poem by Gottfried Benn, which conceived the infinite, life-giving Power as beneficent, and Hindemith's music is deeply felt and often awe-inspiring. *Mathis der Maler* was Mathias Grünewald, the 15th century German painter, and Hindemith's libretto for his opera shows Mathis's spiritual conflict between his devotion to the development of his genius and his desire to share with his fellow-men in their struggle at the time of the Peasants' War in Germany: when their revolt is crushed, Mathis escapes with Regina, the daughter of their leader (who has been killed), and in the woods describes to her one of Grünewald's actual paintings, *The Concert of Angels*, to contrapuntal, celestial music; when she sleeps, there arises from the darkness a vision of his picture *The Temptation of St. Anthony*, with Mathis representing the saint, and wild music ending in a victorious Allelujah. *The Entombment* (eloquently evoking Grünewald's painting of that name) is played just after her death. The opera ends with Mathis leaving his employment with the Archbishop of Mainz, and going with his paintbrushes, pencils, and colours, alone out into the world. It is a most beautiful and impressive opera. Before it could be produced, Hindemith created a very fine symphony, similarly entitled, of which the first movement (*Concert of Angels*) is the overture to the opera, the second (*Sepulture*) is the entr'acte after Regina's death, and the Finale, *Temptation of St. Anthony*, is adapted from the corresponding scene of the opera.

Nobilissima Visione is music for a ballet with choreography by Massine, about St Francis of Assisi: his deep meditation, his mystical union with Mistress Poverty; a march of soldiers (almost light music); a serene *Pastorale;* and a Passacaglia, *Hymn to the Sun*, with an earnestness of purpose pervading all its variations, and finishing in triumph. The Symphony in E flat is in four movements —the first vigorous and optimistic, the second meditative, the third bustling and piquant, with a quiet, elusive trio, and the Finale determined and ending in glory. The *Symphonic Metamorphoses on Themes by Weber* (1943-5) are a sort of quasi-symphony, and rather fun, though marking something of a return to *Gebrauchsmusik*. The *Symphonia Serena* is not really very serene, but it is at various times pastoral in character, charming, witty, gay and carefree. The symphony *Die Harmonie der Welt* is associated with the 17th century religious, philosophical and scientific career of Johann Kepler, though with three titles taken from the 6th century Roman thinker Boethius: *Musica Instrumentalis*, dissonant, but striking, illustrates Kepler's struggles; *Musica Humana* is not only human and tender, but spiritual: *Musica Mundana*, concerned with Kepler's idea of the Music of the Spheres, strives to Heaven and ends in a joyous fortissimo.

Hindemith did not believe in twelve-note technique, but relied rather on the chromatic scale and the natural laws of acoustics. In his book *A Composer's World*, he grants that music for entertainment ought to be provided, but thinks that moral effort is the hall-mark of a work of art.

Though I may not be here to witness this, I should not be at all surprised if, in the passage of time, Hindemith comes to be regarded as the most significant composer to have sprung from Germany or Austria since Mahler. Nor if Busoni, whose *Doktor Faust*, especially, I have admired and enjoyed on three occasions, grows in the esteem of music lovers as time goes on.

Before I turn to Stravinsky, I feel bound to mention briefly three Russian composers who, though frankly they have not been great favourites of mine, have naturally made their impact on me, as prominent figures whose works have entered frequently into the experience of any regular listener to music. Rachmaninov's Second and Third Piano Concertos have long been very popular, and therefore there must be more in them and in his cantata *The Bells* than I have been able to discover; the fault probably lies in me! His large-scale works have always seemed to me to be, as it were, romantic continuations of Tchaikovsky, but not nearly up to his level. The C sharp minor prelude for pianoforte solo has been played so much as to become hackneyed; the other piano preludes include a freat deal of charming and accomplished music. But rightly or wrongly. I have regarded Rachmaninov as more distinguished as a pianist than as a composer: he was one of the finest pianists I have ever heard, and a very great interpreter of Beethoven.

273

Prokofiev and Shostakovich are obviously very gifted men; but though there is clearly a lot to be said in favour of a creative artist producing music which is readily understood by his contemporaries and—in these two instances—particularly by his compatriots, I feel that to be *obliged* to comply with the wishes of the Government of his country, as regards the very character of his creations, is not really conducive to the full development of his talent. Many of the great composers of the past had to rely on employers or patrons, if they were not to die of starvation; but they were usually free to follow the promptings of the spirit and imagination within themselves—or those of God—as determining the actual *quality* of their music. Freedom of the mind is essential to the complete blossoming of the creative gift. Nevertheless, Prokofiev was an extremely accomplished artist, capable of composing both witty and serious, deeply felt, instrumental music for the concert room. His *Romeo and Juliet* music has been much praised, but is not up to the level of the marvellous Bolshoi ballet for which it was created (and still further below the glories of Shakespeare's poetry in the play); and I confess that, listening to his music for the charming *Cinderella* ballet, I regretted that Tchaikovsky, that master of fairy ballets, had not left us a ballet score for this most lovable of fairy tales!

Shostakovich had shown such conspicuous promise in his First Symphony that we all, I think, hoped for great things to come. But he proved to be an uneven composer. His Fifth and Tenth Symphonies are emotionally moving and consummately put together. He had grown up in the political and cultural atmosphere of the Soviet system, and within the artistic limitations to which he was thus acclimatised, it is remarkable that he has achieved what he has done.

Stravinksy is a unique case in the history of music. A leopard cannot change its spots. But Stravinsky has shown that a composer can change not only his style, but the very character of his art, not once only but several times, especially if he is granted a long life. This is not a matter of the gradual *evolution* of a great artist, such as happened with Beethoven (who only lived to fifty-six) and his three successive periods, or Verdi, who became an octogenarian and took a long time to advance from the merely talented operas of his younger days to the masterpieces of his old age. One of Stravinsky's finest scores is *The Firebird* (dating from 1910), which showed the influence of Rimsky-Korsakov, but is a beautiful and imaginative embodiment of a fairy story; genuine fairy music is to be found, too, in the charming short opera *The Nightingale* (1914). *Petruchka* (1911) is a brilliant study in the grotesque: it is not beautiful, because the subject of the ballet did not demand this; and it is not, mostly, human, because three of the four main characters are puppets, though performed by human beings. In 1913 came *The Rite of Spring*, which startled everybody with its crudities and violent dissonances, combined with jug-jug-rhythms. I saw the first London production of it as a ballet, with Lydia Sokolova as the victim of this pagan cult, and have heard it many times since then in concert halls. Stravinsky had never written anything of a similar nature, and although it has been called epoch-making I have never been able to trace that it has influenced any other composer. It remains a masterly, but soul-less, *tour de force*. *The Soldier's Tale* (composed in Switzerland during World War I), in which a soldier sells his soul to the devil, is clever, odd, eccentric, and, again, masterly, but an inhuman work, in which there is as much speaking by a narrator as there is music, played by a few instruments. In *The Wedding*, on the other hand, there are four singers, chorus, four pianofortes, and percussion. When I first heard it, years ago, I thought it rather fun; now it seems to me just a box of tricks—all rhythm, not much harmony, no melody, and no soul.

After this, it is small wonder that Stravinsky felt that it was time for another change. He waved his magic wand, and hey presto! embarked on his neo-classic period! The music for the ballet *Pulcinella* was based on themes from manucripts then attributed to Pergolesi, and in any case dating from Italian 18th century trio-sonatas. *Oedipus Rex* is an 'opera oratorio', with the story taken from Sophocles's great tragedy. The composer apparently had the idea that the vernacular would be unsuitable for such an exalted subject, but somewhat oddly resorted to a *Latin* translation of Jean Cocteau's libretto; however, as most of the audience would not understand the Latin text any better than ancient Greek, a narrator—wearing a dinner jacket, in the Sadler's Wells' production that I saw—intervened periodically in order to explain what was happening—thereby breaking the illusion of the performance. The work is dignified and almost partakes of the nature of a holy ritual. Greek tragedy had, of course, ritualistic, religious origins. But the Sophocles play is tense and most exciting, as anyone must surely experience who has read it or seen it performed. Stravinsky's score, as usual, is masterly in craftsmanship, but it is too formal and dispassionate for the stirring drama on which it is based.

However, the composer's neo-classical sojourn in the world of ancient Greek legend bore happy fruit in the ballet *Apollo Musagetes* and the melodrama *Persephone*. *Apollo* is a cool, quiet, rather charming composition. *Persephone*, which is a blend of ballet, mixed chorus, solo tenor, and speaking voice, is in many parts beautiful musically and the choreography is Ashton at his best. The ballet *Orpheus* contains fine things, especially the moving passages which accompany the scenes between Orpheus and Eurydice; but the Furies are not furious enough—they are merely waspish, except for the brief, loud minute when tearing Orpheus to pieces. There is a short, serene apotheosis of Orpheus at the end. But the music is, on the whole, too detached in its outlook, too unemotional, and not human enough.

In *The Fairy's Kiss* Stravinsky again made use of a former composer's musical ideas—this time, one nearer to his own era and a Russian, Tchaikovsky—cunningly orchestrated and quirkily modernised. *The Rake's Progress* (1951) is a masterly operatic embodiment of the famous series of plates; I always feel that, much as I admire the art of Hogarth's pictures, which one can survey quite quickly if one wishes, I would not like to live with copies of them hanging on the walls of my abode, because the sight of a man's moral descent into insanity and the piteous ending would be an unhappy accompaniment to one's existence! And I am bound to say that when the story, with its dismal conclusion, comes to life, as it were, in Stravinsky's opera, *lasting a complete evening*, and is presented to our ears in musical terms, however clever and appropriate, I find the result singularly depressing.

The purely instrumental creations in several instances roughly synchronised with Stravinksy's vocal or stage works. The *Symphonies of Wind Instruments* date from about the same time as *Pulcinella* (1920): though in memory of Debussy, it is an austere, unemotional work, and so is the Octet (also for wind instruments) which came soon afterwards. The Capriccio for piano and orchestra (1929) is a clever composition, brilliant, charming in places on the surface, but even its slow movement lacks feeling. The *Dumbarton Oaks* Concerto (1938)—again for wind instruments —has a quiet charm, combined with piquancy, and Stravinsky's typically well-chiselled technique.

Meanwhile, he had started to write sacred choral music. The

Symphony of Psalms (1930) has a brief first movement in the nature of a chant; the second is a double fugue; the last movement is an impressive hymn of joy and praise, with a calm, spacious coda. Before Stravinsky came to compose his Mass in 1948, he had become a Roman Catholic; his setting of the liturgy is terse and rather austere.

There are two purely orchestral symphonies. The one in C (1940) is a light-weight symphony, piquant, charming, and delicately scored. The Symphony in Three Movements (1945) has a big pianoforte part; fierceness contrasts with gentleness in the first movement; in the second, the music for flute and pizzicato strings has a refined, slightly odd, charm; whilst the Finale combines both syncopation and monotonous energy.

In his old age, Stravinsky resumed composing religious works, and turned to the twelve-note technique—rather surprisingly in view of his aloofness from it till then. *Threni* is based on the Lamentations of Jeremiah: it is indisputably solemn, and no doubt he sincerely sought to express devout thoughts in it and intended the serial technique to be only a means to this end. It was left to Stravinsky—of all people!—to show that this medium can be dull! 'Cabin'd, cribb'd, confined' within its frustrating and depressing environment, he is actually driven in several places to repeating the same note over and over again, apparently for want of anything better to say. *The Flood* is a biblical allegory, with a text chosen from Genesis, the York and Chester Miracle Plays, and an anonymous poem, for narrator, speakers, two male solo singers, chorus, and orchestra. The words are much more striking than the music, which is either inexpressive or, frankly unattractive and incoherent. *For once*, I agree with Lucretius's sentiment contained in his famous line in the *De Rerum Natura* (concerning the nature of things)—

> *Tantum religio potuit suadere malorum*
> (So many ills has religion been able to produce).

Oh, for Benjamin Britten's refreshing embodiment of the same subject! *Abraham and Isaac* (1962) is less painful to the ear than twelve-note music usually is, but it does not *convey* the emotions, the spiritual struggle, and the ultimate relief, of the Old Testament story.

The ballet music *Agon* (1957) is partly in the twelve-note medium, and in proportion as it is not, it is the more readily appreciable—as in the Galliarde for flutes, mandoline, harp, piano, tympani,

277

and lower strings. It is all rather intriguing, the product of a cool, unemotional mind, more interested here in solving problems of strange sonorities and creating strange rhythms than in appealing to the feelings and hearts of listeners.

What an extraordinary career! I can think of no other composer who has presented such a variety of musical facets and styles. Of course, he has been granted a long life which has given him time to do so. But whereas most of the great masters in the past have evolved, sometimes from small beginnings, to their finest achievements later on, Stravinsky has never produced a finer score than *The Firebird* of 1910, with which he first fully captured the attention of the musical world. A masterly craftsman, a wonderful wizard, perhaps we might even call him a brilliant conjurer! By his astonishing technique and his almost bewildering changes, he has bewitched many music lovers away from being troubled by a certain remoteness or even hollowness within his musical soul, which—for all his mastery and his utter sincerity —to my mind, prevents him from being a really great composer.

Anyone who started his experience of the art of Olivier Messiaen by hearing such early works as the *Hymne* for orchestra (1932) or *L'Ascension* (1933) might have thought that he was in for a comparatively easy time: for they are not hard on the ear, especially compared to what music lovers have been expected to endure from various sources since then; and indeed *L'Ascension*, which comprises four *méditations symphoniques*, is still *based* on the diatonic system, and expresses its devoutly Christian conceptions in readily comprehensible music, first soft and slow, leading to a fortissimo climax, then pastoral in character, next imbued with a glad upsurging of the spirit, and finally mysterious and ecstatic. But Messiaen was a revolutionary at heart. In April 1954 at the Wigmore Hall I heard a complete concert of his piano music, marvellously performed by himself and Yvonne Loriod, and have listened to some of it since then on the radio. *Vingt regards sur l'Enfant Jésus* (1944) is an enormously long work for solo pianoforte: in spite of the dissonances and occasional perversities, there is real beauty in some of these pieces, and there is a genuine religious impulse behind it all, even though this is often obscured by cascades of notes which in the traditional sense do not harmonise with one another. He loves to play off rippling passages in the treble against a slow, possibly impressive, melody or chant in the bass. *Visions de l'Amen* for two pianofortes (1943) are seven

278

Amens in various manifestations, revealing similar contrasts of vision and similarly a strange blend of dissonance and harmony. Messiaen's art is either religious or picturesque, but it is never superficial. The *Turangalila Symphonie* (1948), written for an immense and elaborate orchestra, is elemental and even violent in its impact. But he sometimes springs welcome surprises upon us! *Et expecto resurrectionem mortuorum* (1964), for wind, bells, and percussion, in five movements, is strangely impressive and profound, and not at all dissonant; there are passages in unison and composed with a beautiful line.

His younger compatriot, Pierre Boulez, is, as it were, a musical research chemist. He revels in exploring extraordinary instrumental—and vocal—sonorities. I have listened patiently to the nine short movements of *Le Marteau sans Maître* for contralto, six solo instrumentalists and percussion, and to certain sections of *Livre pour quatuor* (string quartet)—Boulez believed in adding movements by degrees—and to the orchestral *Doubles*, and to the whole of *Pli selon Pli*, which takes one and a quarter hours for the orchestra to play. If you can honestly *enjoy* these experiments in sound, God bless you! I greatly admire Boulez as a conductor of Haydn and Debussy—and of Schoenberg and Webern, even though these two latter composers are not favourites of mine.

I had been unable to sense the expression of grief or compassion in Penderecki's *Threnody to the victims of Hiroshima* (1959-61), or any emotion or even intellectual thought in his *De Natura Sonoris* (1966), which seemed to me to be only a study in orchestral techniques. (His idiom is very advanced.) Both these works I found very hard on the ear. Perhaps the fault lay in me; but it was a pleasant surprise to find his *St. Luke's Passion* (1963-5) impressive, though I can hardly call it either enjoyable or beautiful. Some parts of it are definitely religious and solemn in character, and though there are very dissonant passages for chorus and orchestra, these are not entirely irrelevant to the fury of the crowd and the tragic story. It has links with Bach, and even with plainchant, and goes back to the Latin text.

My experience of Stockhausen's music not been a happy one (as W. S. Gilbert wrote about a policeman's lot!). *Zeitmasse*, for wind quintet, seemed to me to resemble the braying of an ass and to be far less attractive than the tuning-up of an orchestra. But Stockhausen is, of course, far from being asinine! He is a diligent experimenter in sonorities, as he showed also in the equally interesting, but equally painful, *Kontakte* for electronic sounds, pianoforte, and percussion. *Gruppen* (1955-7) employs three orchestras: with apologies to Tennyson, perhaps I may say of the audience in the Royal Festival Hall on February 21st, 1968—

> Orchestra to the right of them,
> Orchestra to the left of them,
> Orchestra in front of them!
> Into the sounds of hell
> Rode the three thousand!

Is it a masterpiece, as claimed? It is a masterpiece of experimentation in orchestral noises, but hardly, I suggest, a masterpiece of music! Some people could enjoy its technical adventures, no doubt. It seemed to me to have no emotional or spiritual content, and in any case to return a dusty answer to the music lover's quest for beauty.

And so, back to England. For I want to conclude this chapter by mentioning briefly a few works by certain composers who, in addition to those already discussed, have made their varying contributions in the 20th century to the great British musical renaissance which began with Parry and Stanford and Sullivan and reached its climax of glory in Elgar, and who have enriched my musical experience.

At the time at which I am writing this chapter, the art of Arnold Bax has been unduly neglected. He was a 20th century romantic composer through and through, an Englishman with a strong addiction to Celtic influences. He wrote four beautiful symphonic poems—*In the Faery Hills*, *The Garden of Fand*, *Tintagel*, and *November Woods*. In these he did not seek detailed description, but atmosphere and general character; and his symphonies are equally romantic, all seven of them in three movements, richly scored, expressing emotions and moods of great variety, in a modern idiom derived more from Wagner, Tchaikovsky, Rimsky-Korsakov, and Debussy than akin to the revolutionary languages of some of his contemporaries. His choral works, especially *Mater Ora Filium* and *This World's Joie*, are imbued with deep religious and mystical feeling. If there is no revival of the compositions of this gifted and imaginative artist, music lovers will be missing a great deal.

I have always enjoyed and admired the music of Arthur Bliss. I remember how exciting and even revolutionary *Rout*, for soprano and ten instruments, seemed in 1920, and his incidental music for

The Tempest the next year. It wouldn't seem so now! In 1922
(or 1923?) Beatrice Reid and I at a Queen's Hall concert found the
Colour Symphony, in four movements, very intriguing; an original
idea, embodying in music the various conceptions associated with
Purple, Blue, Red, and Green; and I was glad to find how fresh
it still sounded when it was revived in much more recent years.
Music for Strings (1935) is one of Bliss's finest works: the first
movement has vigour, yet also dignity; the slow movement is calm,
with a touch of melancholy; the Finale, quick and lively. The
Oboe Quintet (1927) is a work of great beauty. In the lovely
Pastoral, for chorus, mezzo-soprano, flute, drums and strings, he
drew on various poems for his texts, as he did in *Morning Heroes*
(1930), that moving tribute to his brother and all other comrades
killed in battle. (Bliss himself had a fine Army record in World
War I). This was a symphony for orator, chorus, and orchestra.
My experience of his stage works is confined to *Checkmate*, a
striking score for Ninette de Valois's fine, red and black, ballet
based on a game of chess, and *The Olympians*, an attractive opera
with music closely wedded to J. B. Priestley's interesting libretto,
which conceives the idea of the Greek gods visiting the earth
as strolling players and temporarily recovering their old power.

Edmund Rubbra is a fine symphonist. For instance, the Second
Symphony in D is a deeply felt, sincere work, cyclic in form,
and verging on tragedy until the final change to the major. In the
Sixth Symphony, the solemnity and mystery of the introduction
gives place to energy and determination in the Allegretto, the
slow movement is calm and stately, the *Vivace impetuoso* is a
scherzo in a kind of rondo form, and in the Finale, after an *andante*
introduction, the music progresses to a concluding blaze of glory.
Equally beautiful is the piano concerto in G, with its noble first
movement, its serene *Dialogue*, and its light-hearted *Danza alla
Rondo*. The *St. Dominic Mass* is simple, but striking, whilst the
Festival Te Deum, for soprano, chorus, and orchestra, is a majestic
setting of the liturgical song of praise.

Herbert Howells is an immediate contemporary of mine (born
1892). His *Elegy* for strings, written when he was twenty-five, has
a dreamy beauty. *Hymnus Paradisi* (1950), dedicated to the memory
of his only son, is one of the most moving religious works of
recent times, none the less so for being essentially simple, yet
individual in its idiom. The *Missa Sabrinensis* (Mass of the Severn)
(1954) is a richly coloured setting of the Mass, though the colours

281

are at times subdued or delicate; it is elaborately contrapuntal, but deeply felt, and consistently rises to the height of its great subject.

I turn now to an English composer of a much younger generation, Richard Rodney Bennett. His cantata *A London Pastoral* was written in his twenties—an attractive and charming work in three movements, based on Wordsworth's *Westminster Bridge* sonnet, the poem *London Lickpenny* in which the monk John Lydgate describes market scenes, and Laurence Binyon's *Soliloquy*. But one could not expect a man with so original a mind as Bennett's not to branch out into more advanced idioms as time went on. *The Mines of Sulphur* is a sombre, tragic opera. He rightly says that his First Symphony is more cheerful! Even this, however, has a somewhat fierce first movement, though with magical effects and a quieter second theme; some critics called the slow movement sad: I found it calm and serene! In this world of serial technique, even though tempered by traditional idioms, such different reactions are, perhaps, not surprising. The Finale is very dissonant and quirkish, with syncopated rhythms and a quiet, slow section, but a harsh ending. His three pianoforte pieces (from *A week of birthdays*), *Monday's Child*, *Tuesday's Child*, and *Wednesday's Child* (a slow fugue), are most fascinating. The trio for flute, clarinet, and oboe, is a clever series of patterns in sound. *A Penny for a Song* is a comedy opera with libretto by Colin Graham, based on John Whiting's play. It envisages a threat of a Napoleonic invasion of the Dorset coast. It is captivating, charming, witty, subtle, and even melodious at times, with masterly orchestration and a kind of Wagnerian unending melody in a later 20th century idiom employed in a spirit of comedy. The ending is serene and tranquil. The Piano Concerto starts with a quick, delicate movement —imaginative, almost to the verge of romanticism; the scherzo is fairy music, with a Puck-ish element; the slow movement, serious, thoughtful, and anxious, leads softly into the energetic Finale, which begins with abrupt knocks on the drum; but even here there are delicate moments. I found Bennett's Second Symphony (which has a pianoforte part, but no clarinets) arresting and enjoyable; its first movement is witty, dissonant, and brilliant; the slow movement, wistful, even sad at times; the Finale is *moderato* at first, then more emphatic, with quiet passages alternating with restless ones, and a sudden *fortissimo* finish. What an intriguing composer!

Some of this may seem at variance with what I have written about the twelve-note serial techniques as applied by Schoenberg, Webern and Berg. For Bennett also uses that technique; but he does not do so exclusively, and doubtless the value of method varies according to the way in which different composers employ it. On the whole, I have doubts about the merits or the future of the 'way' of Schoenberg and his followers, and have more faith in the ways pursued by Holst and Vaughan Williams, by Hindemith, Tippett and Britten.

CHAPTER THIRTY-SEVEN

Epilogue

In an interesting article in *The Times* (April 26, 1968), entitled 'The essential artificiality of opera', Stanley Sadie wrote: 'All the world may be a stage, and all the men and women merely players. But it is not an opera-house stage. People may act in their daily lives, but they do not sing. That is the basic artificiality of opera'—and he enlarged on this theme, giving many instances. This is, no doubt, largely true. But would he also say that the poetic drama is 'artificial'? The ancient Athenians did not speak iambics or chant anapaests in ordinary life, and the English Elizabethans did not talk in blank verse when they spoke to one another; yet Shakespeare makes Hamlet say that it is the function of the players 'to hold the mirror up to nature'. And I would suggest that opera, also, can, and often does, deal with basic emotions, thoughts, and aspirations of human nature, even though the means and devices which it employs are sometimes artificial. If opera is to be regarded as artificial simply because it involves singing, or indeed music, we should, if we are to be logical, have to describe many— perhaps most—artistic manifestations as artificial.

As Dr John W. Klein pointed out in *Musical Opinion* (June, 1964), Richard Strauss went to the opposite extreme, by declaring that opera represents 'the highest flowering of human civilisation'. This is perhaps understandable in a musician who had a special partiality for composing operas, though it is questionable whether his own achievements in this field are any finer or more important than his symphonic poems. But as a generalisation, it does not stand up to examination. Is opera, as such, 'higher' than religion or science or than any other form of artistic expression? Can it be said to be superior to the drama of Aeschylus or Sophocles, Shakespeare or Goethe; the sculpture of Pheidias or Michelangelo; the paintings of the great Italian, Dutch, Flemish, and Spanish masters; the epic poetry of Homer, Virgil, Dante, Tasso, Camoens, and Milton; the poems of Shakespeare, Goethe, Wordsworth, Keats, Shelley, and Browning; the Russian, English, French, and Spanish masterpieces of fiction; the great cathedrals of France, Italy, Germany and England? And so far as music is concerned, is opera a finer achievement than any other *type* of music?

Are any operas that have ever been composed hitherto greater than, if as great as, the liturgical masterpieces of Bach, the instrumental ones of Beethoven and his *Missa Solemnis*, or the finest oratorios of Handel? Do they surpass Schubert and Brahms and the non-operatic works of Haydn at their greatest?

There must be something wrong with a theory that ignores the fact that—in the sphere of music alone—even apart from Josquin des Prez, Lassus, Byrd, Palestrina, and Vittoria, all of whom flourished before opera began—Bach, Chopin, Brahms, and Elgar were not operatic composers; that Haydn and Schubert were at their finest outside the field of opera; and that Beethoven only created one (very great) work of the kind. Mozart's ideal was opera; but many Mozart-lovers feel that, wonderful as his operas are, they do not rise above his greatest symphonies, the summits of his chamber music, or his superb chain of piano concertos. Berlioz composed no greater masterpiece than *The Trojans*, and his other two operas were also wonderful in the genre; but it is not *because The Trojans* is an opera that we reckon it as fully equal to or even finer than his first two symphonies and his *Romeo and Juliet* or *The Damnation of Faust* or the Requiem and the Te Deum and *The Childhood of Christ*. Monteverdi, Gluck, Verdi, and Mussorgsky were mainly creators of operas; but that fact does not exalt them above the other greatest composers who were not! Strauss had, of course, an immense admiration for Wagner. *Tristan, Die Meistersinger, The Ring,* and *Parsifal* are tremendous masterpieces, even if they are not flawless, but the fact that they were written for performance in a theatre certainly does not place them above the highest, non-operatic achievements of Bach, Handel, Beethoven and Brahms.

The form of sonata or symphony—even apart from programme symphonies like those of Berlioz—is itself partly dramatic, with its contrast of mood and character between the themes even within a single movement, and its frequent resolution in climax; and certainly there is a great human, spiritual drama manifested in such works as the Fifth Symphonies of Beethoven and of Nielsen. There may be no individual persons present, but music, after all, deals in generalised emotions, and basically it is because we recognise that the musical embodiment of *generalised* emotions in the operas (or music dramas) of Wagner and Strauss are singularly appropriate to the particular characters on the stage or mentioned in the libretto that we can assign certain *leitmotives* to Wotan, Brünnhilde, Siegfried, Agamemnon, Elektra, and the rest; if they were merely artificially tacked on to the verbal presentations of those persons, the music would not be so dramatic: the association must be intrinsically suitable.

Wagner, essentially a man of the theatre, contended, as Ernest Newman put it,[90] that 'purely instrumental music had shot its last bolt with Beethoven, and that the choral ending of the Ninth Symphony is the unconscious, instinctive cry of the musician for the redemption of music by poetry'. This contention is hopelessly inconsistent with the facts. Beethoven himself is reported, indeed, to have said afterwards that the choral finale was a mistake; and though I and many others share Tovey's view that the great man was wrong in this afterthought and hold that the introduction of the voices in a sublime hymn of human brotherhood, with Schiller's words, was the supremely right conclusion to the work, his last string quartets, composed after the Ninth Symphony, would alone be sufficient evidence that there was indeed a future for purely instrumental art, for they are masterpieces unsurpassed in the whole world of music. Beethoven had, moreover, planned a completely instrumental Tenth Symphony, and his mighty achievements and those of Schubert (I am referring here to the non-vocal spheres of the art of Schubert, several of whose greatest instrumental compositions, indeed, were later in date than Beethoven's Ninth Symphony), were followed by the great instrumental works of Berlioz, Schumann, Chopin, Mendelssohn, Bruckner, Franck, Brahms, Tchaikovsky, Dvořák, Elgar, Debussy, Fauré, Sibelius, and Nielsen—to name no others! It would, indeed, be truer to say that, so far from purely instrumental music having ended with Beethoven, it reached its zenith in him, but that he stands fairly early in the history of the sonata, the symphony, the concerto, and the various forms of chamber music—in the light of all that has been accomplished in these directions by his successors.

Ernest Newman, though a tremendous admirer of Wagner as an artist, declared[91] that the logical outcome of Wagner's own theories was really the symphonic poem, rather than, or at least in addition to, the opera.

[90] *Wagner as man and artist* (1963 edition, Victor Gollancz, p. 259).

[91] *Musical studies*: essay on *Programme Music*. Cf. also Newman's 'Wagner as man and artist', 1963 edition, pp. 282 ff.

William Byrd, writing at a much earlier stage of musical history, before opera as an art-form had evolved and when the great masterpieces for instruments were all things of the future, maintained[92] that 'there is not any Musicke of instruments whatsoever comparable to that which is made of the Voyces of Man....'

There are many types of music, and it cannot truthfully be said that opera itself is a higher form than any other—or that hitherto even its finest manifestations have equalled in glory the very greatest achievements in the other branches of the art. Indeed, it would be possible to argue that purely instrumental music, just because (apart from symphonic poems) it is *not* for the most part associated with words, is, as a form, the consummate type of this most independent of all the arts. Actually, however, I believe (as I wrote in chapter four of *The Soul of Music*) that no one of the various *kinds* of music is either higher or lower than the others. Everything depends on the intrinsic quality of each individual composition.

However, Wagner thought otherwise, and I wish to return briefly to the subject of this mighty creator of opera, because, since I wrote my chapter twenty-four about him (except its relevant footnotes) Robert W. Gutman's interesting book, *Richard Wagner* —the man, his mind and his music—has been published.[93] As a biography, the book is extremely anti-Wagnerian, as any honest life of the *man* is bound to be nowadays. But Mr Gutman goes much further, for he links Wagner's personality indissolubly not only with the views expressed in his prose works, but with his dramatic librettos and his music. He ends by declaring 'He had dedicated one of the greatests talents of the century to ignoble ends'. This, I suggest, is going too far. What matters most to us today, after all, is the music, which Mr Gutman acknowledges to be incredibly beautiful. It is, however, undeniable that Wagner's crazy racialist ideas and violent anti-semitism were swallowed whole by Hitler and turned by him into the appalling mass-murder of millions of Jews which we have witnessed in the 20th century. Mr Gutman shows that even apart from the pamphlet *Judaism in music*, written in his younger days, Wagner in the essays and letters of his last years created a monstrous phantasma of fanatical, almost insane, anti-semitism, and that it was amid this nightmare

[92] William Byrd: preface to *Psalmes, Sonets, and songs of Sadnes and pietie* (1588).
[93] Published by Secker and Warburg, 1968.

that the ageing master created *Parsifal*. (Mr Gutman also maintains that *Parsifal* and even *Tristan* are imbued with homosexuality. This I find difficult to accept.) The actual libretto of *Parsifal* contains no racial elements, and it is only by reading the prose works (and/or Mr Gutman's book) that the association is apparent. It may well be that for a *fuller* understanding of *Parsifal* we ought to do this; but if or when we have done so, we still have to remember that *music* is incapable of expressing anti-semitism, *as such*—or, for that matter, Wagner's grotesque theory that Jesus was not of Jewish blood but had in his veins a kind of super-blood.[94] It can, and often does, convey cruelty or ruthlessness or sexual allurement, but nothing so specific as *racial* hatred, and much less, hatred directed against a particular race.

Nevertheless, in my old age, I myself would not wish, so to speak, 'to die in the arms of Wagner'! Ernest Newman, than whom no one in my experience has had more profound love and admiration for Wagner's *art*, once wrote to the effect that if he could be allowed to choose the piece of music which he would like to hear above all others before quitting this earthly life, he would name the sublime slow movement of Beethoven's last string quartet, op. 135. At such a moment, then, he would turn, not to Wagner, but to Beethoven. Newman also placed Wagner among the two or three greatest composers: I would never have suggested this, even in the period of my highest enthusiasm for Wagner—not in comparison with Bach or Handel or Beethoven. It is a remarkable fact that so many serious music lovers have an intense dislike of Wagner's music, not only of his libretti, though they have never read his prose-writings or even any books about him. I had this feeling myself in my younger days—before I knew anything about Wagner the man—and I know many people who have felt this aversion all their lives. A few have been members of the Jewish race who have turned against Wagner since the Nazi terror, but most of them have been of British blood who have no such personal grounds for their anti-Wagnerism. Brian Magee,[95] in the light of modern psychology, explains this by Wagner's unique expression in music of unconscious 'instinctual desires, especially erotic and aggressive ones', our normal repression of which produces an inner conflict in each one of us.

My conversion to Wagner in 1928 still holds to a considerable

[94] Robert W. Gutman, ibid., p. 425.
[95] *Aspects of Wagner*, chapter 3, pp. 54 ff.

extent; for it seems to me that the creation of music which is incredibly beautiful is *in itself* an achievement that cannot justly be described as an ignoble end. The problem is, I believe, more a matter of degree. I do *not* assert that 'Wahn! Wahn!' or the Prelude to Act III of *Die Meistersinger* or Wotan's *Farewell* to Brünnhilde in the third Act of *Die Walküre*, or King Mark's utterances in Act II of *Tristan* (even if a trifle lengthy) are not noble music, but only that even such examples as these are less profoundly noble than, for instance, the noblest passages in Bach or Handel or Beethoven or Brahms or Elgar. I do *not* contend that the sacred parts of *Tannhäuser* and *Lohengrin* and *Parsifal* are not religious at all, or that any of them are simply *sham* piety or *mock* Christianity or Black Masses, or even anti-Christian, as Mr Gutman maintains about *Parsifal*. Wagner was thoroughly immersed in the *Parsifal* legend (as he had been previously in the *Tannhäuser* and *Lohengrin* stories). I would put the matter, rather, in this way: that both the libretto and the music express the surface ritual, as it were, of Christianity, but do not strike at the reality underlying the roots of that ritual. Wagner was, indeed, incapable of doing so, for he was not Christian, either in character or in belief. It would have been quite beyond him to voice the simple faith that shines forth in the music of Palestrina, Byrd, or Haydn, the divine glory of Handel's *Messiah*, the penetrating Christian mysticism of Beethoven's *Missa Solemnis*, the profound conviction of Bach, the deeply religious, Biblical utterances of Brahm's Requiem, or the sublime journey of Gerontius's soul into Heaven as pictured by Elgar.

The love music in *Tristan* is deep and beautiful, in spite of the fact that the passion of the two lovers is *partly* due to an aphrodisiac; but it is, I feel, not, as it were, the last word—or the complete word—in portraying the love of man and woman; there is something missing in it which I find in the other instances of great love music mentioned in my twenty-fourth chapter. Wagner, I have suggested, did not *really* know what *true* love is; for him, it seems to be entirely self-centred and passionate; and as we listen to the music of Tristan and Isolde, so utterly absorbed in their mutual passion, we might remember that when Tannhäuser was expected, in the hall of song in the Wartburg, to sing of pure love in the presence of the Landgrave and Elisabeth and the nobles, he bursts out into a song in praise of Venus; that the love duet between Siegmund and Sieglinde has been described as 'surely

the most alluring love music' ever written; and that the one between Siegfried and Brünnhilde in Act III of *Siegfried* becomes
exultant rather than tender. 'Allurement': is that what Wagner
really felt about the love of man and woman? But it is also the
magic wielded by Venus, by the Rhinemaidens, by Kundry and the
Flower-maidens under the sway of Klingsor.

Wagner is, indeed, one of the supreme composers, but he is so
by reason of the width of his imagination, the range of emotions
in his music dramas, his vast architectural mastery, the infinite
variety of his portrayals of character and of nature. For greater
spiritual heights, for more idyllic and idealistic love music, for the
more profound and more exalted expression of religious feeling
and insight, we must turn to other composers. And because, for
me today, he lacks something in these ways as compared with
them, I am less enthusiastic about his art than I was for many years
from 1928 onwards. He has sometimes been described as 'the old
wizard': the phrase makes me shudder, for it is an apt description
of Klingsor! However, I have not completely renounced Wagner, as
Alberich renounced love for the sake of gold and world power;
but in my old age, I somehow do not need him, whereas I continue
to need the other composers about whom I have chiefly written in
this book.

Music, for me, can be simply entertainment: but in what are
its more important manifestations, it is a source of enjoyment; and
in its greatest aspects of all, it is, in my eyes, a spiritual enrichment
of life. And I think that I have sufficiently indicated in the fore-
going chapters which composers most fully respond to these needs.
I confess that, in spite of some honest doubts and intellectual and
spiritual struggles, religion is central to my existence. I mean religion in the widest sense: for me, it must, in the age in which we
live today, be allied to philosophy and science, though my own
knowledge of philosophy (beginning with 'Greats' at Oxford) is
modest, and I had no scientific training at all in my youth. Above
all, religion must be lived; of course it does not consist merely in
going to church and worshipping there, though this has been my
custom so far as health permits, or even in praying at home; church
worship and private prayer are each a means to an end—loving
our neighbours as ourselves, and loving them by our actions. By
so doing, we express our love of God. Now, these actions consist
in serving and benefiting our fellow human beings in any ways in
which our gifts or talents—whether humble or exalted—may en-

able us to do so, and certainly include the production of great works of art. Moreover, religion, in the broad sense, permeates every nook and cranny of life (though sometimes it does so in our subconscious selves), and it is only from that aspect that the view that art is entertainment ultimately makes sense. Though some art is only entertainment, the supreme manifestations of artistic genius are a great deal more than that, and the very greatest creative artists often do more than entertain us even when they did not consciously intend to do so. Bach's suites of dances, for instance, were presumably meant to be no more than the names imply, but the fragrance, the sweetness, the purity of spirit, and the fresh, manly vigour, of the various movements, are a gift from God and without any taint of the devil or of the evil in man. So, too, with the Brandenburg concertos and most of his other instrumental works: they were only intended to please, but they do, in fact, inspire us; whilst his organ music, in its majesty, its beauty, and also its charm, corresponds in the musical sphere to the loveliest sacred buildings in Christendom. Bach's liturgical, vocal art, in all its variety and devout feeling, is the richest, most comprehensive, and most moving embodiment of Christianity that the history of music has so far produced. It is, however, religious in the strict sense of the term, and it left open, as it were, the field for Beethoven—an even more myriad-minded creator, if that be possible—to show forth the glory of God in so-called secular instrumental music without the association of words and without even the historical link with the Church that is inevitably attached to Bach's organ works. That is Beethoven's *special* contribution to the art of music, and so to the betterment of mankind. His Mass in C is at least worthy to stand beside the great masses of Palestrina, Byrd, and Haydn (among his predecessors) and those parts of Mozart's Mass in C minor which were completed by the composer himself. The sublime Missa Solemnis in D is the only liturgical work which, in its very different way, is on a level with Bach's Mass in B Minor and the St. Matthew and St. John Passions. (Such glorious masterpieces as Handel's *Messiah*, Brahms's German Requiem, and Elgar's *The Dream of Gerontius* are—though religious in the strict sense—non-liturgical and therefore irrelevant for comparison in this context). *Fidelio*—that embodiment of heroism, loyalty, and tenderness—is one of the greatest operas in existence—perhaps *the* greatest. But speaking generally, Beethoven's unique gift to humanity was his instrumental music—in which let us, for the sake of simplicity, include the Ninth Symphony (the Mount Everest of all symphonies), as three of its four movements are entirely orchestral.

George Grove[96] wrote: 'Beethoven's symphonies will always remain at the head of music'. This statement requires qualification, for these works, though they (or at any rate the last seven of them) are, I agree, the greatest series ever composed, are not greater music than his piano sonatas or concertos or chamber music[97] or the finest of his overtures; nor would I be prepared to maintain that even the Ninth Symphony surpasses the Missa Solemnis or that any of them are *more* wonderful achievements than the very greatest of Bach's choral masterpieces.

Beethoven's instrumental art is imbued with a majesty of the spirit such as no other composer's purely instrumental, allegedly secular, music has equalled. This characteristic *begins* even in his youthful works, in the early sonatas, trios and quartets, in the first two piano concertos and the First and Second Symphonies. In his middle period, the varied emotions, thoughts and aspirations of mankind are expressed with a musical eloquence and profundity which always seem touched with nobility. Schubert (I am speaking here only of instrumental music) can be equally imaginative and tender; Chopin and Schumann and Berlioz, more romantic; Brahms was unsurpassed by any composer for human, emotional warmth, combined with graciousness and grandeur. Many of the symphonies and concertos of Haydn and Mozart, and concertos and other instrumental works of Bach are either adorable or gloriously beautiful (or both). But Beethoven's exaltation of spirit in terms of instrumental art (apart from the organ) surpasses them all. And in his last period he attained to heights of mystic vision into the eternal verities such as no other composer in any sphere of the art —except Bach—has reached. The Ninth Symphony towers over all symphonies, not at all because it was the first to have a choral element, but because it is more sublime in its beauty, shows more penetrating insight into the mystery of human existence, than any other. The last five sonatas are, simply, the most exalted music for the pianoforte ever composed. But perhaps the final quartets are the most remarkable achievement of all. Berlioz called for vast resources of chorus and orchestra and soloists in order to voice

---

[96] *Beethoven and his Nine Symphonies*—at the end of the book.
[97] I am, of course, speaking in general terms of these works as a series, in each case, without singling out individual ones.

293

his most tremendous imaginings; Wagner required a temple of the arts, and a union of all of them; even a far less complex musical personality such as Bach's found its most complete expression in stupendous works for double choir, orchestra, soloists, organ and harpsichord continuo, the Passions according to St. Matthew and St. John, and in the vocal and orchestral riches of the B minor Mass. But Beethoven needed only four string instruments—two violins, a viola, and a 'cello—in order to transport us into eternity. Admittedly, his approach is intellectual as well as spiritual. In these last outpourings of his genius he was gifted with far-seeing glimpses of Divinity; he became a musical seer; he dwelt on the heights in his art, in spite of all the heart-rending human circumstances of his final years, until death put an end to the struggle but proved only the gateway to the unutterably precious legacy which he left to mankind.

I have referred earlier to the decline of the Teutonic *leadership* in music (which formed a chapter of my book *The Soul of Music*). Since then, in the 20th century, we have witnessed, in my view, something more than that—a decline in the greatness of Teutonic music itself. Mahler, I have suggested,[98] was its last representative, though of course we cannot peer into the future nor foresee how posterity will view Hindemith. But it seems to me that since Brahms, or at any rate since Mahler, no music has come out of Germany or Austria really up to the level of that produced by their 18th and 19th century giants. Tovey wrote of *The Mainstream of Music*,[99] and evidently thought that in those two centuries it became almost entirely Teutonic though it had not been so before; in that essay he only mentioned Berlioz and Chopin once each, 'en passant', and Verdi, Franck, Dvořák, and the Russians not at all. However, it can hardly be denied that during those two hundred years, Germany and Austria gave us most of the mightiest composers.[100] But since Brahms, the mainstream has broken up into several rivers, rather than flowing into a Wagnerian sea, as Tovey suggested, and the greatest creators have come from Finland, Denmark, Czechoslovakia, and—England! What an irony, that the whirligig of time should have turned *Das Land ohne Musik* (the

[98] See Chapter 33.
[99] Included in his *Essays and Lectures on Music*, which were collected by Hubert Foss and published by the Oxford University Press in 1949.
[100] The fact that Bach and Handel were born in 1685 is, of course, irrelevant: their creative careers covered roughly the first half of the 18th century.

land without music), as the Germans used contemptuously to describe England, into the mother of a succession of musical geniuses, whilst Teutonic music sadly deteriorated! (I am, of course, referring only to composition: the Germans and Austrians love music as much as ever, and have continued to produce great performers).

Mr Gutman uses the word 'decadent' even of *Parsifal*; Wagner was, however, surely one of the giants. Nevertheless, I am not sure that the *seeds* of the future decline did not start with him. In recent years, I have come to think that the real *glory* of German/Austrian musical creation was maintained in the second half of the 19th century, not by Wagner, but by Brahms. Of course, one cannot, strictly speaking, compare two composers who shone in different fields: Wagner and Brahms were complementary to each other, and obviously there was room for both, in spite of Wagner's arrogant contempt for the art of Brahms, which he regarded as reactionary. But it is not only reasonable for a music lover to say that *personally* he prefers to be in the company of the one rather than the other, but also to hold, as a matter of opinion, that one is the greater figure in his sphere than the other in *his*. And on this footing, not merely do I enjoy listening to Brahms today far more than to Wagner, but I cannot avoid being conscious of the faults in Wagner's art which I have tried to explain—his unselfcritical long-windedness and excessive repetitions; the menacing clouds of *The Ring*, embodying in marvellous music, but at enormous length, a rather unpleasant tale of pagan mythology from the Nibelung saga; the sometimes overheated atmosphere of the beautiful *Tristan*; the doubtful form of Christianity in the mystical *Parsifal*; and above all, Wagner's failure to rise to the greatest heights. Brahms, on the other hand, was so critical of his own work that he destroyed quantities of music which he felt to be below his best level, and produced masterpieces which not only ascended to the peaks of humanity and embraced mankind with their immense emotional range, their warmth and grace, but were also free from the imperfections of his mighty contemporary. In the compositions which he left for us there is not a superfluous note; his craftsmanship, his musical sculpture and architecture, so to speak, were virtually flawless. Yes, for me, today, Brahms is the greatest figure in Teutonic music since Beethoven and Schubert, just as Handel and Bach, Haydn and Mozart, were the supreme composers who spoke German as their native tongue among Beethoven's predecessors.

And I am afraid that I must go further even than this! Wagner was a mighty man of the theatre—and almost exclusively that. But there is one music-drama which I have come to regard as the greatest opera since *Fidelio*, and it was not written either by Wagner or by Verdi, but by Berlioz. *The Trojans* is, for me, the highest summit of the operatic world in the second half of the 19th century, and certainly no subsequent opera has approached it in glory; there are musical echoes from earlier scenes, but only one recurring *leitmotive*, the inspiring Trojan March. The music is a continuous web of sound, but Berlioz showed in this work (and elsewhere) a greater *lyrical* gift than Wagner, just as Schubert in his *lieder* surpassed Wolf in this respect. It is a musical story of the relationships or conflicts between love and the duty of fulfilling a divinely directed destiny, embodying Virgil's great epic in 19th century musical terms—a far nobler tragedy than the Nibelung saga.

In this evening of my days, the composers whom I would choose as my musical companions are quite numerous: Tallis, Palestrina, Byrd, Gibbons, and any of their great contemporaries whose works come my way, Purcell, Vivaldi, Bach, Handel, Gluck, Haydn, Mozart, Beethoven, Schubert, Berlioz, Chopin, Mendelssohn, Schumann, Bruckner, Franck, Brahms, Bizet, Mussorgsky, Tchaikovsky, Dvořák, Sullivan, some of Delius and Bloch and Bartok, Fauré, Debussy, Janáček, Elgar, Falla, Nielsen, Sibelius, Messager, and—among 20th century English composers—Vaughan Williams, Holst, Walton, Tippett, Britten, and Bennett. I include Sullivan and Messager, because great light music is a necessity for me; and I must add Weinberger's *Schwanda the Bagpiper*, which is not only brilliantly witty and charming, but contains the most irresistible polka ever invented! This list may cause some surprises; it has obvious omissions, but it contains only those whose music I *most* want to hear.

And so, as I travel along the valley of old age, I bequeath to my fellow lovers of the art these thoughts about the composers whose creations, extending over 400 and 500 years, have so much enriched spiritually a long life in which the enjoyment of music has played so vital a part.

> 'Grow old along with me!
> The best is yet to be,
> The last of life, for which the first was made'.
> —Robert Browning: from *Rabbi ben Ezra*

Bibliography

I acknowledge my debt to the following books:

J. S. BACH
C. H. H. Parry: *Johann Sebastian Bach*
Albert Schweitzer: *J. S. Bach*, translated by Ernest Newman
C. Sanford Terry: *J. S. Bach: a biography*

BEETHOVEN
Emily Anderson: collected, translated and edited, *The Letters of Beethoven* (3 volumes)
Paul Bekker: *Beethoven*, translated and adapted from the German by M. M. Bozman
Martin Cooper: *Beethoven: the Last Decade 1817-1827*, with a medical appendix by Edward Larkin
George Grove: *Beethoven and his Nine Symphonies*
Burnett James: *Beethoven and human destiny*
Ernest Newman: *The Unconscious Beethoven*
Anton Felix Schindler: *Beethoven as I knew him*, edited by Donald W. MacArdle, translated by Constance S. Jolly.
Marion M. Scott: *Beethoven*
Edith and Richard Sterba: *Beethoven and his nephew*
J. W. N. Sullivan: *Beethoven*
A. W. Thayer: *The Life of Ludwig van Beethoven*, edited by H. E. Krehbiel, (3 volumes); revised and edited by Elliot Forbes, 2 volumes (1964).
Donald Tovey: *Beethoven* (unfinished)
Ernest Walker: *Beethoven*

BERLIOZ
Memoirs of Hector Berlioz, translated by Rachel (Scott Russell) Holmes and Eleanor Holmes, annotated, and the translation revised, by Ernest Newman
Hector Berlioz: *Evenings in the Orchestra*, translated by C. R. Fortescue
Hector Berlioz: A selection from his letters, selected, edited and translated by Humphrey Searle

Jacques Barzun: *Berlioz and the Romantic Century* (2 volumes)
Jacques Barzun: *Berlioz and his century* (paperback: biography only)
J. H. Elliot: *Berlioz*
Tom S. Wotton: *Hector Berlioz*

BIZET
Winton Dean: *Georges Bizet, his life and work*

BRAHMS
Karl Geiringer: *Brahms, his life and work*
Walter Niemann: *Brahms*, translated by Catherine Alison Phillips
Richard Specht: *Johannes Brahms*, translated by Eric Blom

BRUCKNER
Werner Wolff: *Anton Bruckner, rustic genius*

BYRD
Edmund H. Fellowes: *William Byrd*

CHOPIN
Arthur Hedley: *Chopin*
Selected Correspondence of Fryderyk Chopin, selected by Arthur Hedley
Basil Maine: *Chopin*
Guy de Pourtales: *Chopin, a man of solitude*, translated by Charles Bayly, Jnr.
Alan Walker (editor): *Frederic Chopin* (various authors)
Herbert Weinstock: *Chopin*

DEBUSSY
Edward Lockspeiser: *Claude Debussy* (The Master Musicians)
Edward Lockspeiser: *Debussy: his life and mind* (2 volumes)
Leon Vallas: *Claude Debussy*, translated by Maire and Grace O'Brien

DELIUS
Thomas Beecham: *Frederick Delius*
Eric Fenby: *Delius as I knew him*
Philip Heseltine: *Frederick Delius*
Arthur Hutchings: *Delius*

DVOŘÁK
Alec Robertson: *Dvořák*
Otakar Sourek: *Antonin Dvořák*

ELGAR
Michael Kennedy: *Portrait of Elgar*
Basil Maine: *Elgar: his life and works*
Diana McVeagh: *Elgar*
Mrs Richard Powell: *Edward Elgar: Memories of a Variation*
W. H. Reed: *Elgar as I knew him*
Percy M. Young: *Elgar, O.M.*
    (Editor): *Letters of Edward Elgar*
    (Editor): *Letters to Nimrod, from Edward Elgar*

FAURÉ
Norman Suckling: *Fauré*

FRANCK
Vincent d'Indy: *César Franck*, translated, with an introduction, by
  Rosa Newmarch
Leon Vallas: *César Franck*, translated by Hubert Foss

GLUCK
Alfred Einstein: *Gluck*
Ernest Newman: *Gluck and the opera*

HANDEL
Newman Flower: *George Friderick Handel*
W. S. Rockstro: *The Life of George Frederick Handel*

HAYDN
Karl Geiringer: *Haydn*

HOLST
Imogen Holst: *Gustav Holst, a biography*
    The music of Gustav Holst

JANÁČEK
Hans Hollander: *Leos Janáček*, translated by Paul Hamburger

MAHLER
Bruno Walter: *Gustav Mahler*

MENDELSSOHN
H. E. Jacob: *Felix Mendelssohn and his times*, translated by Richard and Clara Winston
Eric Werner: *Felix Mendelssohn*

MONTEVERDI
Denis Arnold: *Monteverdi*

MOZART
E. J. Dent: *Mozart's Operas*
Alfred Einstein: *Mozart*
Mozart's letters: selected and edited by Eric Blom from the letters of Mozart and his family, translated and edited by Emily Anderson

MUSSORGSKY
M. D. Calvocoressi: *Modest Moussorgsky*

NIELSEN
Robert Simpson: *Carl Nielsen, Symphonist*

PALESTRINA
Henry Coates: *Palestrina*

PURCELL
Franklin B. Zimmerman: *Henry Purcell, 1659-1695: his Life and Times*

SCHUBERT
Richard Capell: *Schubert's Songs*
Maurice J. E. Brown: *Schubert: a critical biography*

SCHUMANN
Joan Chissell: *Schumann*

SIBELIUS
Cecil Gray: *Sibelius*
     Sibelius: the Symphonies
Robert Layton: *Sibelius*

BIBLIOGRAPHY

RICHARD STRAUSS
Norman Del Mar: *Richard Strauss*

SULLIVAN
Thomas F. Dunhill: *Sullivan's Comic Operas*
Arthur Jacobs: *Gilbert and Sullivan*

TCHAIKOVSKY
Gerald Abraham: *Tchaikovsky, a short biography*
Edwin Evans: *Tchaikovsky*
Herbert Weinstock: *Tchaikovsky*

VAUGHAN WILLIAMS
Hubert Foss: *Ralph Vaughan Williams*
Ursula Vaughan Williams: *Ralph Vaughan Williams*

VERDI
F. Bonavia: *Verdi*
Francis Toye: *Giuseppe Verdi*

WAGNER
Robert Donington: *Wagner's 'Ring' and its Symbols*
Robert W. Gutman: *Richard Wagner, the Man, his Mind, and his Music*
Brian Magee: *Aspects of Wagner*
Ernest Newman: *Wagner as man and artist*
   Wagner Nights
   The Life of Richard Wagner (4 volumes)
George Bernard Shaw: *The Perfect Wagnerite*
Jessie L. Weston: *Legends of the Wagner Drama*

WOLF
Ernest Newman: *Hugo Wolf*
Frank Walker: *Hugo Wolf, a biography*

GENERAL
The Encyclopaedia Britannica (11th and subsequent editions)
Grove's Dictionary of Music and Musicians (3rd, 4th and 5th editions)
The Oxford History of Music

The New Oxford History of Music

Percy C. Buck: *The Scope of Music*

Ferrucio Busoni: *The Essence of Music*

Neville Cardus: *Ten Composers*

Deryck Cooke: *The Language of Music*

E. J. Dent: *Opera*

Alfred Einstein: *Greatness in Music*

Hubert J. Foss (editor): *The Heritage of Music*

Ralph Hill (editor): *Chamber Music*

Frank Howes: *Man, Mind, and Music*

Kobbe's Complete Opera Book, edited and revised by the Earl of Harewood

Constant Lambert: *Music, ho!*

Ernest Newman: *Musical Studies*
  A Musical Motley
  A Musical Critic's Holiday
  Opera Nights
  More Opera Nights
  From the World of Music
  Testament of Music

C. H. H. Parry: *Studies of Great Composers*

Robert Simpson (editor): *The Symphony* (2 volumes)

Alec Robertson (editor): *The Concerto*

Stravinsky: *Stravinsky in conversation with Robert Craft*

Oliver Strunk: *Source Readings in Music History*

Donald Tovey: *Essays in Musical Analysis* (6 volumes)
  Essays and lectures on Music
  A Musician Talks (2 volumes)
  Musical Articles from the Encyclopaedia Britannica

Index

303

INDEX

305

Beethoven - Ludwig Van Fur elise Minuet

Bach - J. S. J. Christ Ambrosius

Brahms. Johann

Chopin Frederi

Dvorak

Elgar

Haydn Joseph

Handel

Mendelssen Felix

Strauss

Tschaikoscy. Peter Piano No 1.

Verdi

Wagner

Mozart Wolfgang Amadeus.

Piano No 21. Night Music

Opera

Beethoven - Fidelio

Wagner Tristan The Ring

Elgar dream of Gerontius

Mozart. Magic Flute Cose for tutti

Elgar – English.
    sweet gentle charm.
    Dream of Gerontius.
    derl summs of leaves.

Bishop Score
state
Pos.
cons
dil
level.

Plasma oestriols.

Fetal Kick CSROs, 10 · 2hrs.
  Clin. sugg. Macriniff
Mod delay method of delivery.
4/5 genes.